Contents

Use in chapter on alternative solutions or other countries' experiences

Section III: Environmental Courts?

— Good.

`not very helpful._

Section IV: Conclusion

Public Interest

Perspectives i

LW

A Division of John Wiley & Sons
London · Chichester · New York · Brisbane · Toronto · Singapore

Published in the United Kingdom by Chancery Law Publishing Ltd
Baffins Lane, Chichester
West Sussex PO19 1UD, England

National Chichester 01243 779777
International (+44) 1243 779777

Published in North America by John Wiley & Sons, Inc
7222 Commerce Centre Drive
Colorado Springs CO 80919, USA

British Library Cataloguing in Publication Data

A copy of the CIP entry for this book is available from the British Library.

ISBN 0471 95173 0

Typeset in 10/12pt Garamond ITC by
York House Typographic Ltd, London

Printed and bound in Great Britain by
Biddles Ltd, Guildford and King's Lynn

Paper used is 100% recycled post-consumer waste.

Preface

Although the defence of the environment is of such immense importance, until recently the majority of English lawyers were abysmally ignorant as to the role which the law could play in its protection. The subject of environmental law did not exist for the majority of law schools and the ignorance of academic lawyers was shared by most practitioners and judges.

Despite this environmental law did exist. However, its existence was not easy to detect and its development had been ignored. The development had been, to borrow Professor de Smith's memorable description in relation to judicial review, "sporadic and peripheral" and, I would add, haphazard. Although the word environment would not appear in head notes of the law reports, increasingly over the last decade the courts have been tackling environmental issues of the greatest importance. Numerous applications for judicial review, which concerned local and central government decisions as to the environment, were treated as covering a distinct topic, such as planning. Nuisance actions were environmental law actions by another name. Many criminal cases involved the commission of environmental offences. Collectively, therefore, the courts have been protecting the environment. But their approach has been fragmented and not comprehensive.

The situation is changing rapidly. Large firms of solicitors have established or are about to establish environmental law departments. There has been a deluge of writing on the subject. There are now numerous authoritative textbooks to be found in any adequate law library. Encyclopedias on environmental law do now exist. There is an excellent Journal of Environmental Law and the Environmental Law Reports are in their second year. The literature already available gives an extensive coverage of the source material, including the increasingly important regulations and directives from Europe. Environmental law has become an extremely fashionable subject. Is this book just part of the trend, no more than one more manifestation of the new fashion of lawyers to be concerned with the environment? I think not. Its source is an important conference which took place at the Institute of Advanced Legal Studies in London in October 1993. The contributors to this book played a significant role at that conference and the contents reflect their contributions. They examine the public interest in environmental law issues from a range of different backgrounds, legal systems and directions. Their combined contributions provide a comparative picture which is, as far as I am aware, not available elsewhere. They cover between them the whole range of environmental law issues. They provide for the reader a wide comparative international perspective of environmental law.

I am certain that if environmental law is to develop as it should in this country, we have not only to modify our existing law and legal institutions, we have to consider adopting a much more radical approach. This is what has already happened in other parts of the world. A reader interested as to what could be the nature of the reform that is needed will find here an abundance of material to assist him. There is provided a clear picture of the existing approach in this country to environmental regulation, as well as examples of what can be achieved by the more comprehensive approach adopted in other jurisdictions.

There is also a wealth of sensible criticism of the present position in the United Kingdom. The decisions of the House of Lords do not escape critical comment. One of those decisions is the recent case of *Cambridge Water Company* v *Eastern Counties Leather PLC* [1994] 1 All ER 53. I was a party to that decision and I therefore read with particular interest the kindly but uncomplimentary comparison between the House of Lords approach to protection of the environment in that case with the approach of the Philippine judiciary in a recent case involving the protection of the environment in that jurisdiction (*Oposa* decision of the Philippine Supreme Court of 30 July 1993).[1] When we gave our decision we were not aware of the approach of the Philippine Supreme Court. I do not suggest that this affected our decision. However, in coming to our decision we were in fact seeking to find the proper balance between the various interests involved and we were not unaware of the possible impact of our decision on environmental protection by the law. The case involved clarifying the parameters of liability and we would have been interested to know that the judges of another supreme court regarded it as being part of their role "to *establish*, and not merely act upon society's values with regard to the environment" and to provide "legal cladding to environmental principles".

One of the subjects with which this book deals is an old hobby horse of mine. It is the role which an environmental court, with a unified jurisdiction to resolve different disputes and issues involving environmental law, could play. The relevant contribution is by Justice Paul Stein, who is a very experienced member of the Land and Environmental Court of New South Wales. I have for some time believed that this Court provides a model which could and should be reproduced in this country. Justice Stein provides a convincing support for this view. If an environmental court were to be established in this country, cases which have an impact on the environment would be more rapidly, more efficiently and more economically resolved than they are at present. The court would provide better access to justice than is now available for the citizen. It could also overcome the problems which exist at present due to the multiplicity of different types of legal proceedings, inquisitorial, criminal and

---

[1]See Chapter 16, section II (7).

civil, following an environmental disaster. It would provide the comprehensive approach which I believe is preferable to the present fragmented approach.

Readers will turn to this book for assistance for many different reasons. However, whatever is the reason, I will feel confident that the reader will find information in this book that will not be conveniently available elsewhere and that as a result of turning to this book he will be better informed than he was previously as to the public interest perspectives of environmental law.

The Right Hon The Lord Woolf

Introduction

The quality of the environment is of increasing public concern. The inter-related, global problems of development and population pressure, unequal enjoyment of the Earth's resources between rich and poor, loss of biodiversity and declining water, soil and atmospheric quality are so serious that 178 countries endorsed the Rio Declaration, 1992. The 27 principles of the Rio Declaration and the Agenda 21 action-plan for sustainable living indicate a high level of concern for improved environmental management. Neverthe-less, the squandering of resources and habitats has continued since 1992. Governments appear helpless or even careless in the face of consumerism's avaricious onslaught on an environment that at once belongs to nobody and everybody.

The reasons for this state of affairs are legion, ranging from the nature of modern political economy to simple absence of political will and imagination. Without citizen involvement, government environmental policies are doomed. As our leaders declared:[1]

> "Environmental issues are best handled with the participation of all concerned citizens, at the relevant level."

This view is shared by many of the contributors, who see the law as one means whereby citizens can bring their concerns to bear on the faltering steps of government. *Public Interest Perspectives in Environmental Law* explores ways in which the legal system can introduce into decision-making a greater awareness of community and environment. The contributors consider the state of public interest environmental law in various countries and suggest law reforms and avenues for advocacy in the UK.

The book has developed from papers presented at a conference on the question "Environmentalist Law: Myth or Reality?" held in London in October 1993, and jointly organised by the University of London's Institute of Advanced Legal Studies and School of Oriental and African Studies and the Law Centres Federation. We have largely retained the format of the conference: overseas experiences in the first part, British commentaries in the second, and the same comparative approach regarding one institution for environmental manage-ment, namely the specialist environmental tribunal, in the third part. We have jettisoned the "environmentalist law" title of the conference, however, in

---

[1]Rio Declaration on Environment and Development, 1992, principle 10.

favour of *Public Interest Perspectives in Environmental Law*. "Environmenta-list" proved too cryptic, even for some of our speakers. In any event, the concept of "public interest" law is better known, in the environmental field along with many others, and expresses our concern with active, prospective and strategic uses of environmental law.

There are numerous and often competing "public interest" perspectives on what the role and content of environmental law should be. In its broadest political sense, public interest is akin to the concept of good government: everyone has their own point-of-view. Hence the plural in the title to this book, and the inclusion of some views which activists might regard as distinctly "grey" and putting forward anything but a "public interest" perspective.

In the legal context, however, public interest perspectives may be distinguishable from others because they seek to vindicate causes other than the property or financial interests of their advocates. This is particularly true in the environmental sphere, where public interest claimants assert diffuse ecological and human interests.

In practice, over the last 30 years "public interest environmental law" has come to refer to the activities of an international movement of activists and lawyers who seek to use and develop the law as a means for conserving the environment directly, for example through civil and criminal cases against polluters, and indirectly through the defence of protesters' civil liberties. A notable response of the movement to the global nature of environmental problems has been the development of a computer communication network, Environmental Law Alliance Worldwide (E-LAW), through which information on cases, polluters, experts, processes and laws is shared.

Governments have a critical role in representing the public interest, but given the complexity and importance of the task, and the limitations of mere representative, "ballot box" democracy, in which specific, detailed environ-mental policies are rarely the subject of electoral platforms, the participation of interest groups and citizens can play a complementary role as well. The Attorney General and government agencies usually enjoy unfettered discre-tion to bring proceedings to safeguard the public interest, stop public nuisances or compel the performance of public duties. This government role as sole custodian of public interest reflects a top-down, representative model of government which some reformers have sought to change. Justice is seen to be too complex for a single person or entity to be its exclusive guardian. The public interest movement seeks to influence institutions, particularly through participatory processes, so that more just treatment of under-represented people and interests results.[2]

---

[2]Dhavan R "Whose Law? Whose Interest?" in Cooper J, Dhavan R ed *Public Interest Law*, Oxford, Blackwell, 1986 at 22–24.

The range of contributions in this book reflects the variety of environmental problems and laws around the world. Nevertheless, there are some common threads. These are identified in the final chapter. For those concerned about the role of law, the final chapter also proposes one way of weaving those threads to strengthen and conserve our environmental fabric.

Acknowledgments

We wish to thank environmental lawyer Peter Roderick, and Jeannie Choo, Juliet Fussell and Hilary Lewis Rutley of the Institute of Advanced Legal Studies, London for assistance in organising the conference from which this book evolved.

The conference was sponsored by the Law Centres Federation Environment Project with funding from the UK Department of the Environment.

The Law Foundation of New South Wales, an independent trust which supports projects related to legal research, law reform and legal education, provided the airfares for Justice Paul Stein to attend the conference.

Michael Anderson, François du Bois and Andrew Harding wish to acknowledge financial support provided by the Economic and Social Research Council for the project on "Access to Justice in Africa and Asia" based at the Law Department of the School of Oriental and African Studies, London, as their chapters draw on research connected to that project.

Lord Harry Woolf's preface is much appreciated, particularly as it follows on from his chairing of the final session of the conference.

We thank Stephen Harvey, Andrew Prideaux and David Wilson of Wiley Chancery publishers. When we began to wonder whether this chicken would ever hatch, Stephen Harvey's enthusiasm for and particular knowledge of the subject matter provided a welcome boost of morale.

David Robinson thanks Susie Jacobs for supporting and encouraging him throughout. David also thanks Tim Jewel, Director of the Ashurst Morris Crisp Centre for Environmental Law, University of Southampton for his guidance.

EarthRights: The Environmental Law and Resource Centre

EarthRights was incorporated as a non-profit association in London in 1993. EarthRights aims to provide public interest, environmental law advice to individuals and community groups, and to conduct education, research and support programmes on the use of law to protect the environment.

In an experimental venture in 1994–95, the Legal Aid Board is funding EarthRights to work with a west London community in its campaign against the environmental impact of development works and air pollution.

Michael Anderson, Matthias Berger, Paul Bowden, Martyn Day, François du Bois, John Dunkley, Edesio Fernandes, Martin Führ, Betty Gebers, Stephen Grosz, Andrew Harding, Thomas Ormond, David Robinson, Gerhard Roller,

Phil Shiner and Justice Paul Stein have donated their royalties from the sale of this book to the EarthRights Environmental Law and Resource Centre. Glen McLeod has donated his royalties to the United Kingdom Environmental Law Association.

List of Contributors

Michael R Anderson is a lecturer with the School of Oriental and African Studies, University of London with interests in environmental law and human rights law, particularly in India.

Matthias Berger practises law in Dusseldorf and is a founding member of Germany's "Environmental Legal Assistance Fund eV."

Paul Bowden is a litigation lawyer and head of the environment group in the London office of Freshfields solicitors.

Martyn Day is a partner of Leigh Day & Co, London and specialises in representation of plaintiffs in toxic tort and environmental pollution cases.

François du Bois is a South African advocate and a lecturer with the School of Oriental and African Studies, University of London, with interests in comparative tort and environmental law.

John Dunkley is a solicitor with the EarthRights Environmental Law and Resources Centre, London and co-ordinated the Environment Project of the Law Centres Federation.

Edesio Fernandes is a Brazilian lawyer and town planner. Having completed his Ph.D at Warwick University in 1994, he is currently teaching and researching environmental law at the University of London. He is also a research associate at the Institute of Commonwealth Studies, University of London.

Martin Führ was formerly a staff lawyer of the Oko-Institut (Institute for Applied Ecology), Freiburg and Darmstadt, Germany. He now lectures at the Fulda Technical College. **Betty Gebers** and **Gerhard Roller** are staff lawyers with the Oko-Institut. In 1992 the Oko-Institut, in collaboration with the Foundation for International Environmental Law and Development (FIELD), London, was commissioned to prepare a study on access to environmental justice for the Commission of the European Community. **Thomas Ormond** was a research associate at Frankfurt University before joining the regional administration in Darmstadt.

Stephen Grosz is a partner of Bindman & Partners, London. He specialises in public and administrative law and European Community law. He has acted for the Friends of the Earth, the Oxleas Nine and the World Development

Movement in its successful High Court challenge of UK foreign aid funding for the controversial Pergau Dam in Malaysia.

Andrew Harding is a Senior Lecturer with the School of Oriental and African Studies, University of London with interests in environmental law and comparative public law, particularly in South East Asian countries.

Glen McLeod is an environmental law partner of the London office of Denton Hall, solicitors. At the end of 1994 he is returning to his native Western Australia to practise planning and environmental law with Mallesons Stephen Jaques, solicitors.

Colin T Reid is a Senior Lecturer in the Department of Law at the University of Dundee. His book on *Nature Conservation Law* (UK) was published in 1994.

Deirdre H Robbins is an environmental lawyer in Marblehead, Massachusetts, USA. She was an Assistant Attorney General in the Environmental Protection Division of the Massachusetts Office of the Attorney General from 1987 to 1993, and from 1993–94 worked for the *Review of European Community and International Environmental Law* (*RECIEL*), published in London by FIELD. In August 1994, she opened an office in Marblehead, to concentrate on plaintiffs' environmental cases, including citizen suits.

David Robinson, formerly a solicitor of the Environmental Defender's Office, Sydney, currently teaches and researches environmental law with the University of Southampton and the Institute of Advanced Legal Studies, London. He returns to environmental law practice in New South Wales in March 1995.

Phil Shiner is a solicitor with the Birkenhead Resource Unit, England. He is a specialist planning lawyer particularly concerned with the effects of urban regeneration on local communities.

Justice Paul Stein, AM has been a judge of the Land and Environment Court of New South Wales for 10 years, and has an interest in human rights, discrimination and consumer law as well as environmental law. In 1994 he was awarded membership of the Order of Australia (AM) for services to environmental law and the community.

Tables

TABLE OF EC & INTERNATIONAL TREATIES AND CONVENTIONS

TABLE OF CASES

TABLE OF EC SECONDARY LEGISLATION

TABLE OF NATIONAL LEGISLATION

Section I
International Experiences

Contents of Chapter 1

Public Interest Environmental Litigation in the United States

Chapter 1

Public Interest Environmental Litigation in the United States

Deirdre H Robbins

I. **Introduction**[1]

The United States has made a substantial commitment of government resources to environmental protection, and has by legislation also created citizen enforcers. In addition to thousands of federal, state and local officials who act to enforce the large number of statutes designed to protect human health and the environment, the US has many environmental citizen organisations (ECOs) which use the judicial system to ensure a cleaner environment.[2] Sometimes, citizen litigation (or proposed litigation)[3] is directed at governmental environmental agencies which plaintiffs allege are not properly doing their job of protecting the environment (although, as discussed below, suits must be limited to certain "mandatory duties", which term as a rule does not include discretionary regulatory decisions in individual cases). Cases brought against private defendants generally may only

---

Deirdre H Robbins is an environmental lawyer in Marblehead, Massachusetts, USA. She was an Assistant Attorney General in the Environmental Protection Division of the Massachusetts Office of the Attorney General from 1987 to 1993, and in 1993–94 worked for the *Review of European Community and International Environmental Law* (*RECIEL*), published in London by the Foundation for International Environmental Law and Development (FIELD). In August, 1994, she opened an office in Marblehead, to concentrate on plaintiffs' environmental cases, including citizen suits.

[1] See Appendix for a note on US legal citation form.

[2] Some of the better-known groups are the Natural Resources Defense Council (NRDC), Sierra Club, Audubon Society, Defenders of Wildlife, and the Conservation Law Foundation (CLF). Often, citizen groups will be formed around one local issue; *e.g.* see *Save Our Cumberland Mountains* v *Lujan*, 963 F.2d 1541 (DC Cir 1992), cert. denied, 61 USLW 3581 (22 February 1993); *Friends of the Crystal River* v *US Environmental Protection Agency*, 837 F.2d 1007 (6th Cir 1992). See Chapter 2 for a description of the major law firm ECOs.

[3] Controversies in the US are almost always the subject of settlement negotiations before suit is filed. In fact, some courts now require that plaintiffs certify that they have made efforts to resolve the dispute before filing suit, and almost all courts are moving toward requiring litigants at least to try alternative dispute resolution (ADR) before taking the court's time with pretrial matters and trial.

be brought after the ECO notifies the governmental enforcement body responsible for ensuring compliance, and a pre-existing enforcement action by the government body may bar the citizen suit.

In addition to litigation by ECOs formed for the purpose of protecting the environment, any of the 50 states may act as "citizens" and bring suits seeking to compel federal authorities to carry out their statutory duties. The "toxic torts" branch of litigation, in which private plaintiffs bring common law tort or private statutory actions against both public and private polluters for personal injury, may also have the effect of bringing polluters into compliance. Private suits for property damage, injunctive relief, and clean-up costs, may also be brought under the common law and statutes such as CERCLA,[4] although these are aimed solely at protecting private interests.

This chapter surveys the current state of public interest environmental litigation (PIEL) in the United States, and some of the hurdles that must be overcome before bringing a public interest environmental lawsuit. It discusses primarily federal law, which is the most active area of PIEL and which often drives state law, and briefly discusses state court PIEL cases. It does not consider criminal environmental enforcement, because in the US citizens have no right to bring criminal cases, and it does not discuss the role of local (municipal) authorities in environmental enforcement. On the whole, it must be said that the US ECOs have achieved considerable success as governmental watchdogs and environmental protectors and have proved a valuable part of the enforcement scheme.

II. **The structure of US environmental enforcement**

A brief description of the division of labour between the federal and state judiciaries and enforcement bodies might be helpful to an understanding of what follows.

The US Constitution, in article III, created the federal court system, consisting generally of trial ("district") courts (in what are now 13 circuits), federal courts of appeal for each of the circuits, and the US Supreme Court, whose decisions are binding on all district courts and courts of appeal.

Although states have no "external sovereignty" (they could not, for example, execute treaties), states do have independent "internal sovereignty", and in general possess all of the powers not delegated in the Constitution to the federal government.[5] Some state courts existed before the signing of the Constitution, and were the fora in which English law cases were heard (*e.g.*

---

[4]CERCLA (the Comprehensive Environmental Response, Compensation and Liability Act), *e.g.* allows private citizens to sue each other for cleanup costs. 42 USC s 9607(a)(4)(B).
[5]81A CJS, States, ss 16, 21, at 296, 308 (1977).

common law tort cases and criminal cases). These areas of the law were generally left by the Constitution as the province of the states, unless there is a basis for the exercise of federal jurisdiction. Federal authorities must have a constitutional basis to exercise either legislative or judicial power; thus, for example, "federal question" jurisdiction is one basis for a litigant to proceed in federal court, and goods which move across state lines in "interstate commerce" may be the subject of federal regulation. Federal jurisdiction may not be limited, controlled, expanded or eliminated by state action.[6]

The Constitution resolves potential conflict between federal and state law in article VI, paragraph 2, the "Supremacy Clause", which provides that the Constitution and laws of the US are the supreme law of the land, binding on all states. This means that federal law may "pre-empt" state law, if, in situations where both federal and state authorities have a basis for exercising power, the federal government has shown an intention to occupy an entire field of regulation, or the state law undermines the federal law. Inconsistent state laws which thwart a federal scheme could be rendered null and void by application of the pre-emption doctrine.[7]

In the environmental area, the federal government almost always has jurisdiction, usually because natural resources cross state lines or affect resources in other states in some way. The chief federal environmental agency is the Environmental Protection Agency (EPA), which has a national head-quarters office and regional offices similar to the federal districts in which courts sit. The federal government also has agencies assigned to certain types of resources.[8] The US Congress created all of these agencies by specific statutes, and it is possible to ascertain the powers and duties of each by consulting both its enabling act and the statutes it is charged with enforcing.[9] Federal administrative agency lawyers do not represent the agencies in court; the US Department of Justice does so, both affirmatively and defensively.

States may exercise jurisdiction over resources within their borders, and, unless they face a successful federal pre-emption challenge, are free both to

---

[6]*Harrison* v *St Louis, etc. R. Co.*, 232 US 318, 34 S Ct 333 (1914); *Sherman* v *Ulmer*, 201 F Supp 660 (D. Pa. 1961).
[7]An example of the use of the pre-emption doctrine in the environmental field is *United States* v *Akzo Coatings of America Inc* 949 F.2d 1409, 1454-1458 (6th Cir 1991), which held that a state may not require liable parties to perform a site cleanup inconsistent with the remedy chosen by the federal Environmental Protection Agency. However, *Akzo Coatings* recognised generally that states may enforce stricter cleanup standards than federal ones, and that EPA has a duty under CERCLA either to implement these state standards (known as "ARARs") or validly to waive them when choosing a remedy. *Ibid* at 1458.
[8]*e.g.* there is a Department of the Interior (DOI), a Fish and Wildlife Services (FWS), a National Oceanographic and Atmospheric Administration (NOAA), a US Forest Service, a Department of Energy, and so forth.
[9]*e.g.* under the Federal Water Pollution Control Act (FWPCA), EPA has certain powers and duties regarding rulemaking and permitting. *e.g.* 33 USC s 1311(b), setting time limits for EPA to issue effluent limitations.

legislate and to exercise judicial power over the same resources as the federal government regulates within their borders. Consequently, there are almost always both a state and a federal statute in a given area, such as a clean air act,[10] a clean water,[11] and a "CERCLA" cost recovery statute.[12] In general, states are permitted to enforce tougher standards, as long as this does not thwart a federal programme. In some cases, this is codified in federal law.[13] States have enforcement agencies which are parallel to the federal agencies.[14] The state counterparts to the Department of Justice are the offices of the Attorney General of each state, which usually handle all litigation matters, although some states keep the litigating attorneys in their departments or agencies of environmental protection.

In practice, as matters of efficiency and comity, federal and state environmental authorities often work together to divide up enforcement cases; for example, air pollution officials at EPA Region I, which covers Massachusetts and other New England states, may (but are not required to) forestall from bringing cases against a particular offender because state officials are doing so. If EPA determines that the state action is not bringing about adequate compliance with federal statutes, it may "overfile" in federal court. If an ECO believes that either a state or a federal agency has failed to do its job or has done it inadequately, it may attempt to sue the agency to compel it to act (if there is an actionable "mandatory duty", discussed in Section III). Or, more frequently, it may attempt to stand in the shoes of the agency by suing a polluter directly. Rather than existing as a sort of "super-enforcer" that may act as a "private attorney general", however, the ECO must meet certain requirements before it can bring either type of suit. These requirements, many of which are jurisdictional in nature, are discussed in Section III below.

---

[10]*e.g.* 42 USC ss 7401 *et seq*, (federal Clean Air Act) and Mass. Gen. L. ch. 111, ss 142A-E (Massachusetts Clean Air Act).

[11]*e.g.* 33 USC ss 1251 *et seq*, (Federal Water Pollution Control Act) and Mass. Gen. L. ch. 21, ss 26–52 (Massachusetts Clean Waters Act).

[12]*e.g.* 42 USC ss 9601 *et seq.* (federal "CERCLA") and Mass. Gen. L. ch. 21E (Massachusetts analog to CERCLA, allowing recovery of remedial and response costs and natural resource damages).

[13]The federal Clean Air Act, *e.g.* expressly states that tougher state enforcement is encouraged in some circumstances: "Nothing in this subsection [prevention of accidental releases] shall preclude, deny or limit any right of a State or political subdivision thereof to adopt or enforce any regulation, requirement, limitation or standard (including any procedural requirement) that is more stringent than a regulation, requirement, limitation or standard in effect under this subsection or that applies to a substance not subject to this subsection." 42 USC s 7412(r)(11). Regulatory requirements (*e.g.* emission limitations) are often the same, as federal and state officials consult each other. It is not unheard of for a state to set lower (*i.e.* stricter) limits, however.

[14]*e.g.* Massachusetts has a Department of Environmental Protection, a Coastal Zone Management Agency, a Department of Environmental Management, a Department of Fisheries and Wildlife, and so forth. All are overseen by a state cabinet-level Executive Office of Environmental Affairs.

III. **Legal basis for citizen suits**

A. **Federal law**

1. *Direct actions*

In the Clean Air Act (CAA) 1970[15] and the Federal Water Pollution Control Act (FWPCA) 1972,[16] the US Congress created the models for citizen enforcement of environmental protection. Today, many environmental statutes include similar citizen suit provisions.[17] Most of these provisions allow citizens to obtain injunctive relief, requiring either a government agency to perform a mandatory duty[18] according to the statute, or requiring a private defendant (or governmental defendant, if acting as a polluter)[19] to comply with regulatory or permit limits, or an administrative order, and possibly, to remedy any harm

---

[15]42 USC s 7604, the CAA citizen suit section, provides:

" . . . [A]ny person may commence a civil action on his own behalf –

(1) against any person (including (i) the United States, and (ii) any other governmental instrumentality or agency . . .) who is alleged to be in violation of (A) an emission standard or limitation under this chapter or (B) an order issued by the Administrator [of the EPA] or a State with respect to such a standard or limitation,

(2) against the Administrator where there is alleged a failure of the Administrator to perform any act or duty under this chapter which is not discretionary with the Administrator, or

(3) against any person who proposes to construct or constructs any new or modified major emitting facility without a permit . . . or who is alleged to have violated (if there is evidence that the alleged violation has been repeated) or to be in violation of any condition of such permit."

[16]33 USC s 1365, the FWPCA provision, reads:

" . . . [A]ny citizen may commence a civil action on his own behalf –

(1) against any person (including the United States . . .) who is alleged to be in violation of (A) an effluent standard or limitation under this chapter or (B) an order issued by the Administrator [of the EPA] of a State with respect to such a standard or limitation, or

(2) against the Administrator where there is alleged a failure of the Administrator to perform any act or duty under this chapter which is not discretionary with the Administrator."

[17]Examples of other citizen suit provisions are found in the Toxic Substances Control Act (TSCA), 15 USC s 62619, the Comprehensive Environmental Response, Competition and Liability Act (CERCLA) 42 USC s 9659, the Safe Drinking Water Act (SDWA), 42 USC s 300j-8 and the Endangered Species Act (ESA), 16 USC s 1540 (g).

[18]An important principle of law that is recognised in all citizen suit provisions is that a governmental agency, when acting in its regulatory capacity (i.e. not as a polluter) may not be ordered to perform a discretionary duty. Thus, for example, courts in PIEL suits may enforce specific timetables for promulgating regulations, or may order a federal agency to perform an environmental impact assessment if the court finds it has a non-discretionary duty to do so, but a court would not order EPA to promulgate a specific rule, conduct an enforcement case in a certain way, or reach certain conclusions in the EIS. When judicial review is appropriate (after the agency has acted with finality and as provided by statute), the agency's actions will be reviewed under the appropriate Administrative Procedure Act (APA) or other statutory provisions (such as the "arbitrary and capricious" standard) discussed in Section III(A)(2) *infra*.

[19]Most US environmental statutes define "person" subject to the statute to include the United States, a state, and municipalities or political subdivisions of a state. For a recent example of a successful case against a municipality, see *Hawaii's Thousand Friends* v *City and County of Honolulu*, 821 F Supp 1368, 23 ELR 21380 (D. Hawaii 1993).

already caused to the environment. ECOs can also obtain declaratory relief[20] and, under some statutes, civil penalties from private polluters,[21] attorneys' fees, and expert witness fees and costs. The most common form of relief sought by an ECO is injunctive relief, because it can compel cessation of the offending acts. The remedy for violation of an injunction issued by a court may be contempt of court, which can result in fines and even jail sentences. Civil penalties for violations are often authorised by statute to a maximum of US $25,000 per day per violation, and these can therefore be a powerful enforcement tool.[22]

2. *Judicial review of administrative action*

In addition to express citizen suit provisions allowing citizens fully to litigate a case, ECOs may challenge agency action under the Federal Administrative Procedure Act (APA), 5 USC s702, which provides judicial review of agency actions to any "person suffering legal wrong because of agency action, or adversely affected or aggrieved by agency action within the meaning of a relevant statute . . . ." Subject to the conditions discussed in Section IV (principally, proof of standing), judicial review to the Circuit Courts of Appeal is available as a matter of right; leave of court is not necessary. Review by the US Supreme Court is, however, at the discretion of that Court (see Appendix—"Cert. denied").

APA review can include a particular final agency decision in the case of a specific individual; the agency's rulemaking (*e.g.* a final agency decision not to include certain pollutants in regulations setting emission limitations would be challengeable *per se*, if made at the time of promulgation of the regulation); or

---

[20]"Declaratory relief" means a declaration from the court, for example, that a defendant's action or planned action is in violation of the law. The "case or controversy" requirement (discussed in the text at 13) is especially important here, as courts do not act in an advisory capacity. Although its ruling was later reversed, the 1993 district court NAFTA decision (see n 23 *infra*) granted the plaintiffs a declaratory judgment that the US Office of Trade Representatives had to prepare a Legislative Environmental Impact Statement on NAFTA. 822 F Supp at 31.
[21]Courts have generally held that penalties may not be obtained against governmental bodies. *e.g. United States Dept. of Energy* v *Ohio*, 112 s Ct 1627 (1992). An example of a statute allowing civil penalties to citizen enforcers is the FWPCA, 33 USC s 1365(a) (s 505). For a description of an ECO civil penalty campaign, see Chapter 2, section I(J), "The FWPCA Enforcement Campaign".
[22]The US environmental programme is based on the philosophy that if substantial penalties are obtainable by governmental and citizen enforcers (which, as a general rule, must be paid into state or federal treasuries), enforcement actions are more likely to have a significant effect on business behaviour. Otherwise, businesses might find expensive pollution control equipment not economically advisable to install, and small penalties as no more than a cost of doing business. See Robbins, "Doing Business in the Sunshine: Public Access to Environmental Information in the United States", 3 *Rev Eur Comm'ty and Int'l Envt'l L (RECIEL)* No 1, 26 (1994) (hereafter, "Doing Business").

other final decisions involving policy matters.[23] APA review, however, is generally limited to a review of the administrative record, with a few exceptions,[24] and to overturn an agency action the challenger bears the burden of showing one of a number of things (depending on the type of case), such as that the agency acted "arbitrarily and capriciously".[25] Not surprisingly, such a challenge is difficult to win, because agency discretion is given a great deal of deference. Courts are not to substitute their judgment for that of the agency (which has particular expertise), but are primarily to assess whether the agency followed proper procedures and gave due consideration to relevant facts.[26]

Some agency action is subject to review under statutes other than the APA. In the important area of hazardous waste liability cases (popularly known as "Superfund litigation"), the statute, CERCLA, provides its own version of judicial review of EPA's choice of a remedy for the site.[27]

One important area of PIEL judicial review cases under the APA is related to the National Environmental Policy Act (NEPA), 42 USC ss 4321–4370. Although NEPA has no citizen suit provision, agency action under NEPA can be challenged under APA. NEPA's principal purpose is to require federal agencies planning a project (either directly, or by providing a permit or funding) to file an Environmental Impact Statement (EIS) disclosing all potential environmental impacts and considering the environmental impacts of various alternatives. The "twin" purposes of NEPA are to ensure that the agency has properly considered the environmental impacts of all viable alternatives and chosen rationally among them, and to make the information available to the public.[28] Thus, the failure to file an EIS, or a complete EIS, creates an "informational injury" to the people with a need to know.[29] Informational injury cases are discussed in Section VII below.

---

[23]The best-known recent cases concerning review of such decisions are the three decisions concerning the North American Free Trade Agreement (NAFTA), in which the result was that the decision of the President to refer the NAFTA to Congress for ratification was not held not to be a final agency decision, in that the President is not an "agency". See *Public Citizen* v *US Trade Representative*, 822 F Supp 21 (DDC 1993), rev'd, 5 F.3d 549 (DC Cir 1993), cert. denied, No 93-560, 62 USLW 3451 (1993). The cases are discussed further in Section VII(A) on informational injuries.
[24]"Record review" may be circumvented, and the challenging party may instead get *de novo* review or even an evidentiary hearing, if, for example, he can show that the agency acted in bad faith, or that the record is materially incomplete. 5 USC s 706; *Moore* v *Madigan*, 789 F Supp 1479 (WD Mo 1992).
[25]See *Central Ariz. Water Conserva. Dist.* v *US EPA*, 61 USLW 3001 (1993)(citizen group found to have standing to challenge EPA rule, but EPA found not to have acted arbitrarily or capriciously).
[26]An example of judicial review in a recent environmental case which illustrates these procedural principles is *Committee to Preserve Boomer Lake Park* v *US Department of Transportation*, 4 F.3d 1543, 24 ELR 20142 (10th Cir 1993).
[27]See 42 USC s 9613(j).
[28]*Committee to Preserve Boomer Lake Park*, *supra* n 26, 24 ELR at 20146.
[29]Citizen environmental litigation groups have expressed concern whether such "informational injury" is sufficient to provide standing after *Lujan* v *Defenders of Wildlife*, discussed *infra*. See, *e.g.* McElfish, JM Jr., "Drafting Standing Affidavits After *Defenders*: In the Court's Own Words", 23 ELR 10026, 10028 (1993)(hereafter, "Standing Affidavits").

As stated above, states may also bring PIEL cases under federal statutes,[30] and private plaintiffs suing under the common law of negligence, or under a statutory cause of action may bring "toxic tort" or other private environmental cases which may have an enforcement effect.[31]

B. State law

Many states have express citizen suit statutes. Massachusetts, for example, has a statute allowing any 10 citizens domiciled in Massachusetts to sue for declaratory relief, and temporary and permanent injunctive relief, if "the damage caused or about to be caused by such person constitutes a violation of a statute, ordinance, by-law or regulation the major purpose of which is to prevent or minimize damage to the environment".[32] Massachusetts has other, more resource-specific, citizen suit provisions, for example in its Wetlands Protection Act, its Clean Waters Act, and its Toxics Use Reduction Act.[33] There is also a Massachusetts Administrative Procedure Act, like the federal APA providing for judicial review of state agency action, and a Massachusetts Environmental Policy Act which, like NEPA, requires EISs to be filed with the state agency – although MEPA applies to solely private projects as well as state-sponsored ones.[34]

Most other states have environmental statutes similar to those of Massachusetts, as most of them are modelled after the analogous federal statutes. While not nearly as extensive as federal cases, there has been some recent state court PIEL litigation. A few examples are mentioned in Section VII(G) below.

IV. Jurisdictional requirements for federal PIEL cases

The area in which public interest environmental plaintiffs have faced their greatest challenges (apart from that of funding, perhaps) is in meeting the strict access requirements which have been judicially, and not legislatively,

---

[30]*e.g. South Carolina ex rel. Medlock* v *Riley*, 23 ELR 20101 (DDC 1992). (State of South Carolina sued EPA to compel it to withhold certain funds from the State of North Carolina because of the latter's noncompliance with a regional waste disposal plan; *held*: EPA has no duty to withhold the funds).

[31]*e.g. Landrigan* v *Celotex Corp.*, 605 A.2d 1079 (NJ 1992) (holding that epidemiological studies provide sufficient evidence in toxic tort case). The usual basis for federal court jurisdiction in common law suits is known as "diversity jurisdiction", which applies when plaintiff and defendant are residents of different states. Some federal statutes also allow private causes of action which essentially sound in tort.

[32]Mass. Gen Laws ch. 214, s 7A.

[33]See Shelley, P "Public Interest Environmental Litigation", in McGregor, G ed., *Massachusetts Environmental Law*, Boston: Mass. Continuing Legal Education Inc., revised edn, 1993 at 4-13 to 4-14.

[34]*Ibid* at 4-14 to 4-15.

imposed, through use of the "standing" doctrine.[35] Section A sets down the basic constitutional requirements for federal court standing in environmental cases, and Section B analyses these requirements.

A. **Constitutional limits to standing**

Standing is a constitutional requirement for a federal court to be able to exercise jurisdiction in all federal cases, not just environmental ones. In addition to the jurisdictional requirements imposed by the Constitution, as interpreted by the courts, many courts have imposed "prudential" limits on standing, which are discussed in Section V.

Article III of the US Constitution, which deals with the judiciary, provides that federal courts have jurisdiction only in actual "cases" and "controversies". According to the traditional law interpreting this clause, in order to demonstrate standing under article III, a plaintiff must prove, at a minimum, that:

(1)   he has *personally* suffered some "actual or threatened injury as a result of the putatively illegal conduct of the defendant";

(2)   the injury "fairly can be traced to the challenged action"; and

(3)   the injury "is likely to be redressed by a favorable decision".[36]

In environmental cases, US Supreme Court Justice Scalia stated in the 1992 plurality decision *Lujan* v *Defenders of Wildlife* (hereafter referred to as *Lujan II*), that the US Congress is not free to confer on ECOs "an abstract, self contained" right to ensure that agencies (and this might be extended also to polluters) comply with the law.[37] Rather, the Constitution requires that the groups show that they have some interest different from that of the general public which gives them a right to use the courts to enforce environmental laws. As will be seen in Section IV(B), the courts' attempts to fit environmental citizen suit provisions into the traditional kinds of injuries necessary to establish standing has led to some apparently unusual results, which seem to contravene the intent of Congress in enacting the provisions, but which have proven to be a fairly minor obstacle for plaintiffs in practice.

---

[35]These restrictions at least initially met with the ire of some commentators. See Sheldon, K "*Lujan* v *Defenders of Wildlife*: The Supreme Court's Slash and Burn Approach to Environmental Standing", 23 ELR 10031 (1993).

[36]*Valley Forge Christian College* v *Americans United for the Separation of Church & State*, 454 US 464, 475 (1982).

[37]112 S Ct at 2143, 22 ELR at 20918. The *Lujan I* case was decided in 1990 (*Lujan* v *National Wildlife Federation*, 497 US 871, 110 S Ct 3177).

1. *Injury in fact – whose injury?*

Injury in fact suffered by individuals may be redressed by litigation brought on their behalf by organisations representing them.[38] An organisation must specifically allege and prove, however, that its individual members have suffered the injury and would themselves satisfy the requirements of standing, and that the general purpose of the organisation is consistent with the interest the group is pursuing in the suit.[39] If the individuals are not participating as plaintiffs in the lawsuit, the organisation must also show that neither the claim asserted nor the relief requested requires their participation.[40]

2. *Injury in fact – what kind of injury?*

Environmental injury sufficient for standing in a PIEL case means a demonstration that individual members have suffered, or are imminently threatened with suffering, harm to their particular personal interests as distinct from the interests of the general public. Article III interests are not limited to economic or physical damage (which has traditionally been protected by the judicial system), but also encompass aesthetic, recreational, and other environmental interests.[41] The US Supreme Court, however, has rejected the concept that harm to the environment is an injury to the general population, or even to the population in the vicinity of the resource.

The Supreme Court has held, in a line of cases beginning with *Sierra Club* v *Morton* in 1972,[42] and culminating with *Lujan II* in 1992, in effect, that concern for the environment, or even for a specific resource that is being depleted or contaminated, is not a sufficient "injury" to confer standing. It is not enough, in the Court's view, that the plaintiffs simply wish to know that the resource will not be harmed, or that the resource will "be there" should they ever wish to visit or use it; they must allege and prove that they actually use, or plan to use soon, the resource.[43] In addition to demonstrating a "place" concreteness (*i.e.* that the plaintiff is geographically near the threatened resource), the plaintiff must demonstrate "time" concreteness or "imminence" in his planned use.[44]

---

[38]*Warth* v *Seldin*, 422 US 490, 95 S Ct 2197 (1975); *Sierra Club* v *Morton*, 405 US 727, 2 ELR 20192 (1972); *Heart of America* v *Westinghouse Hanford Co.*, 820 F Supp 1265, 23 ELR 21371 (ED Wash 1993) (representational standing found).

[39]*Cf. Hunt* v *Washington Apple Advertising Comm'n*, 432 US 333 (1977).

[40]*New York State Automobile Dealers Ass'n* v *New York State Dept. of Envt'l Conserva.*, 827 F Supp 895, 24 ELR 20128, 20130 (NDNY 1993).

[41]*Sierra Club* v *Morton*, 405 US 727, 2 ELR 20192 (1972).

[42]*Ibid.*

[43]*Lujan* v *Defenders of Wildlife*, 112 S Ct 2130, 22 ELR 20913, 20916 (1992).

[44]*Ibid*, 22 ELR at 20915. The Court did state that there could be exceptions; *e.g.* an abutter to a proposed federal dam could challenge the licensing authority's failure to prepare an Environmental Impact Statement (EIS) even if the dam was not to be built for years to come. *Ibid*, 22 ELR at 20918 n 7. The issue of EIS litigation is discussed in the text in Section VII(A)(1).

Plaintiffs must do more than merely allege injury in fact; they must present oral or written testimony (the latter known as "affidavits") presenting concrete facts showing that the witness or affiant is "directly affected".[45] Thus, for example, in a case challenging the federal and state natural resource restoration and clean-up measures chosen for New Bedford harbour, a PCB-contaminated harbour rich in shellfish, it was held to be insufficient that members of the National Wildlife Federation (NWF) "use and enjoy, through fishing and swimming, recreational and other uses, the environment and natural resources in the New Bedford [harbour area]", as alleged in their affidavit; it was held that NWF "has not particularized these conclusory averments in any way."[46] NWF should have identified its members, stated their addresses, and documented "the extent and frequency of any individual use of the affected resources . . . ."[47]

Similarly, it is not sufficient that the Wilderness Society and the Sierra Club incontrovertibly will have a smaller amount of federal wilderness land in Alaska to use and enjoy for recreational purposes, if they cannot prove that any of their members used the precise parcels of land which were the subject of a proposed action of the Department of the Interior.[48] By contrast, in *Animal Protection Inst.* v *Mosbacher*, a case decided after *Lujan II*, an ECO was found to have standing when it alleged that its members planned to view whales in a certain area "this summer" or "in the summer of 1993 and 1994", which was held to allege sufficiently "concrete plans" to meet the *Lujan II* requirements.[49]

3. *Causation*

A plaintiff must also show that the complained-of activity is substantially likely to result in the injury claimed. For example, in the *New Bedford Harbour* case discussed above, the court held that NWF should also have specifically alleged and proved "a distinct and palpable injury flowing from the possibility of an inadequate clean-up" by the governmental bodies conducting the harbour clean-up.[50] The plaintiff need not prove that the polluter's activities or the government agencies' actions or inactions are the sole cause of his injury, but merely a contributing factor.[51]

---

[45]*Lujan* v *Defenders of Wildlife, supra*, 112 S Ct at 2138, 22 ELR at 20916.
[46]*United States* v *AVX Corp.*, 962 F.2d 108 (1st Cir 1992).
[47]*Ibid* at 117, 119.
[48]*Wilderness Society* v *Griles*, 824 F.2d 4, 12-16 (DC Cir 1987).
[49]*Animal Protection Inst.* v *Mosbacher*, 799 F Supp 173, 176-77 (DDC 1992). The group lost its case on the merits, however, as discussed *infra* at n 25 and accompanying text.
[50]962 F.2d at 119.
[51]*Public Interest Research Group of N.J.* v *New Jersey Expressway Auth.*, 23 ELR 20420, 20422 (DNJ 1992); *Public Interest Research Group of N.J.* v *Magnesium Elektron, Inc.*, 22 ELR 20362, 20364 (DNJ 1992).

4. Redressability

Finally, to establish article III standing, a plaintiff must show that the remedy he seeks is substantially likely to redress the injury he claims. If the *Lujan II* plurality opinion were the only guideline, this element could be difficult to prove if the plaintiff must show that, had the agency in question followed its own procedures properly, a third party would have altered his behaviour accordingly.[52] In rulings issued after *Lujan II*, however, lower courts have not required such a strict showing. In *Swan View Coalition* v *Turner*, for example, the district court rejected the notion that the existence of a potential third party intervening cause negates redressability:

> "The asserted injury in this case is that 'environmental consequences might be overlooked . . . as a result of deficiencies' in the biological opinion [under the ESA]. The fact that the [US] Forest Service might not alter its course in any way following the completion of a new biological opinion does not negate this asserted injury."[53]

One district court recently reversed its earlier ruling that plaintiffs lacked standing because they had failed to prove the "fairly traceable" element (which is actually causation, but is closely related to redressability). In the revised opinion, it held that citizens may sue "feeder" dischargers to a public sewage treatment plant for violations of FWPCA pre-treatment standards, even though the treatment plant that subsequently treats the effluent is not in violation of *its* permit for the pollutants in question.[54]

An appellate court, by contrast, found a lack of causation in the allegations of a group called American Bald Eagle that a proposed deer hunt near a reservoir would violate the ESA by exposing the bald eagle to lead from the slugs used for ammunition. The deer hunt was for the purpose of reducing the deer population, since the deer were consuming seedlings and gradually eliminating the root system needed to filter the water. Although it did not phrase the issue as one of standing (but rather whether there was a violation of ESA), the court found the evidence too speculative to establish "actual harm" that would constitute a "taking" under the ESA.[55]

---

[52]The *Lujan II* plurality opinion had this to say about redressability: "The most obvious problem in the present case is redressability. Since the agencies funding the projects were not parties to the case, the District Court could accord relief only against the Secretary: He could be ordered to revise his regulation to require consultation for foreign projects. But this would not remedy respondents' alleged injury unless the funding agencies were bound by the Secretary's regulation, which is very much an open question."
22 ELR at 20917. See also McElfish "Standing Affidavits", *supra* n 29 at 10029. McElfish suggests that plaintiffs try to remove third parties from the chain of causation by alleging direct injuries to themselves flowing from the challenged action if possible. *Ibid*.
[53]824 F Supp 923, 24 ELR 20318, 20321 (D Mont 1992).
[54]*Atlantic States Legal Foundation* v *Colonial Tanning Corp.*, 827 F Supp 903, 24 ELR 20058 (NDNY 1993).
[55]*American Bald Eagle* v *Bhatti*, 24 ELR 20173 (1st Cir 1993).

B. **Analysis of federal constitutional law regarding standing in environmental cases**

1. *The law of summary judgment*

Summary judgment is judgment granted for a party, either on the whole of the case, or on one or more issues, based on written affidavits rather than oral testimony.[56] The material facts regarding standing usually are not disputed in citizen cases, and the only issue is their legal effect. Therefore, the issue of standing in most environmental cases is disposed of on summary judgment, rather than after a full trial. Under the procedural law of summary judgment, there is a need for specificity of proof in the written affidavits. Affidavits must not rely on conclusory allegations such as those in the *New Bedford Harbour* case; rather, the affiant must allege specific facts to back up his assertions, and the facts must be admissible in evidence. This means, for example, that they must be based on the affiant's own personal knowledge and experience and not on what someone else has told him. And, the affiant must be qualified to give the testimony in question – a non-expert affiant could not offer scientific opinion about the fate and transport of contaminants, for example. The procedural law of summary judgment provides one explanation for the courts' rulings requiring concreteness and specificity.

2. *What is an environmental injury?*

Although summary judgment procedural law influences the *type* of proof required to show standing in environmental cases, the above analysis in a sense begs the question, because there is a need for the same kind of specific, admissible proof in all cases – the real question, in PIEL cases, is proof of what? Notwithstanding the law of summary judgment, it cannot be denied that the Supreme Court's view of environmental harm appears to differ from that of Congress, and is in effect an attempt to place a relatively new type of injury (environmental degradation) into an old and well-known category, something akin to a traditional personal or economic loss. The *Lujan II* Court's view of standing in endangered species cases provides a good example of the apparent difference in conceptual framework between Congress and the Supreme Court.

The *Lujan II* case involved the Endangered Species Act of 1973 (ESA),[57] which provides in relevant part:

(1)   that the purpose of the Act is the conservation of plants and animals threatened with extinction by the activities of human beings;

---

[56]See *Anderson* v *Liberty Lobby, Inc.*, 477 US 242, 247-48, 106 S Ct 2505, 2510 (1986); Fed R Civ P 56.
[57]16 USC ss 1531-1543.

(2) that a federal agency intending to take action affecting an endangered species must "consult" with the Secretary of the Interior or the Secretary of Commerce before taking any action affecting a species on the Endangered Species List (prepared by the Secretary of the Interior as required by the Act); and

(3) that "any person" may sue to enjoin "any person", including the US, from violating any provision of the Act or regulation thereunder.

In 1978, the Secretary of the Interior promulgated a rule that the ESA applies to federal agency action to be taken overseas. More than half the species on the Endangered Species List have primary ranges outside the US. In 1986, the Secretary replaced this rule with one limiting the scope of ESA to actions taken in US territory or on the high seas. Plaintiffs challenged this action as a violation of ESA.

Affiants in the plaintiff group alleged, *inter alia*, that they had taken trips overseas to observe and study certain listed species, or that they had a professional vocational interest in such species.[58] The Court found their plans insufficiently "concrete" and said injury in fact would exist only if the affiants had, or were about to have, a chance to study the species, and had "concrete plans" to do so, but the species no longer existed at the location covered by the plans.[59] It also held that the reinstatement of a rule is too vague a remedy to establish the redressability element of standing; the plaintiffs had not alleged specific agency action that would threaten a specific endangered species which would in turn directly affect them, and thus they lacked standing.

The holdings of the US Supreme Court restricting standing of ECOs within strict time and place limitations, and requiring them to prove the likelihood that the relief sought will allow their proposed use of the resource, arguably show fundamental misunderstanding of the nature and purpose of environmental laws, and thwart the intention of the US Congress in enacting environmental citizen suit provisions. By requiring members of the plaintiff group to file affidavits stating, for example, that they plan to visit the resource "this summer" and have airline tickets in hand, and that the remedy they seek will preserve the resource for their trip; the Court is saying, in effect, that endangered species exist for the use and enjoyment of humans. One must plan to "view" them, or "study" them, or otherwise use them to one's personal

---

[58] 23 ELR at 20916. In one instance, a member of the Defenders of Wildlife had averred that she had travelled to Sri Lanka in 1981 and observed the habitat of "endangered species such as the Asian elephant and the leopard" at the site of a development project, although she was "unable to see" any of the endangered species. When asked in deposition whether she intended to return to Sri Lanka, she said she did, and hoped "to be more fortunate in spotting at least the endangered elephant and leopard". When asked for definite plans, however, she responded, "I don't know [when]. There is a civil war going on right now. I don't know. Not next year, I will say. In the future." The Supreme Court characterised this evidence in these words: "Such 'some day' intentions – without any description of concrete plans, or indeed even any specification of when the *some* day will be – do not support a finding of the 'actual or imminent' injury that our cases require." *Ibid.*

[59] *Ibid* at 2139-40, 22 ELR at 20917.

advantage, or, in the *Lujan II* Court's view, there is no injury. This is arguably the precise opposite of Congressional intent in enacting the ESA, for it is designed to protect such species from the effects of human activity.[60]

The reason that the Court's decisions on standing are somewhat troubling is that article III requirements, being constitutional in nature, may not be expanded by an act of Congress. Thus, the US Congress has enacted environmentalist laws with citizen suit provisions with an apparent purpose of adding ECOs to the overall enforcement scheme, only to see the Court attempt to restrict the citizen suit provisions. At least for the present time, the US Congress is not free to enact citizen suit provisions which enlist public interest groups to assist governmental environmental agencies in protecting a resource for the public generally, for future generations, and to fulfil its role in the ecosystem. Congress may seek only to provide citizens with the means to prevent or redress direct and imminent economic, physical, aesthetic, recreational, or professional injuries to themselves. ECOs with a dedicated environmentally protective purpose must have members with the direct sorts of current "use" interests the Court requires if they are to carry out their purposes through PIEL cases.

It is reasonable to argue that article III's case or controversy requirement does not compel the kinds of imminent personal "use" injuries required by the Supreme Court. A showing of actual or imminent *environmental* injury should provide a sufficiently justiciable case or controversy so that any plaintiff sufficiently concerned to invest time, effort and money in bringing a case with no guarantee of success would have standing. Indeed, an environmentalist would most likely agree that the destruction through human activity of a wetland, an old-growth forest, or a species, harms everyone, and certainly everyone nearby.

As a practical matter, however, it does not appear necessary to make this argument, since the recent cases, including those decided after *Lujan II*, suggest that ECOs have adapted quite resourcefully to these requirements, do not view *Lujan II* as in any material sense a departure from the existing law of standing, and are generally readily able to assert the kinds of interests and injuries required by the Supreme Court.[61]

Also as a practical matter, such an argument could be used in cases other than environmental injury cases (*e.g.* one might argue that a change in the tax code affects the economy in such a way as to harm everyone), and thus the Supreme Court might fear that carving out such an exception in environmental cases could have consequences for the entire body of traditional law concerning standing.

---

[60]See 22 ELR at 20923.
[61]See *e.g. Portland Audubon Soc'y* v *Babbitt*, 23 ELR 21142, 21143 (9th Cir 1993), in which the court rejected the governmental defendant's argument that *Lujan II* "imposed a new, stricter burden on plaintiffs to establish with specificity an injury-in-fact caused by a challenged government action." The court found that the plaintiff ECO had established standing in the *Babbitt* case, an ESA case involving the spotted owl.

Finally, it should be remembered that the *Lujan II* opinion was a four-justice plurality opinion. Two concurring justices agreed that the plaintiffs had failed to demonstrate that they are "among the injured", but observed:

> "As government programs and policies become more complex and far-reaching, we must be sensitive to the articulation of new rights of action that do not have clear analogs in our common-law tradition . . . In my view, Congress has the power to define injuries and articulate chains of causation that will give rise to a case or controversy where none existed before, *and I do not read the Court's opinion to suggest a contrary view*."[62]

One justice would have held that the plaintiffs did have standing, believing that "the 'imminence' of such an injury should be measured by the timing and likelihood of the threatened environmental harm" and not the imminence of the plaintiffs' planned visits.[63] The last two justices dissented, believing the plurality opinion had applied too rigid a standard for actual injury, and preferring to assume that the non-party federal agencies would "try to follow the law" (so that redressability would be established).[64]

The lower court cases discussed in Sections V and VII *infra* suggest that the two concurring justices in *Lujan II* are right, that courts are to focus principally on the nature of the actual or threatened injury in conducting the standing inquiry, although the plaintiff group still needs to comply with the personalised proof requirements in *Lujan II* and demonstrate a redressable injury caused by the defendant's behaviour.

V. Other defences in PIEL cases

A. Prudential limits to federal court standing

In addition to the article III requirements for standing, the Supreme Court has established limits on the class of persons who may invoke the federal courts to hear cases. These "prudential" concerns are aimed at ensuring that persons do not raise the rights of others, and that the interests they are pursuing are within the "zone of interests" protected by the statute authorising their suit.[65] In a recent NEPA case, for example, plaintiffs lost because it was held that homelessness was not an "environmental" consequence which must be considered; the purpose of NEPA is not:

---

[62]22 ELR at 20920 (Kennedy & Souter, JJ, concurring) (emphasis added).
[63]*Ibid* at 20921 (Stevens J, concurring). Justice Stevens concurred because he did not believe Congress intended the consultation requirement of ESA to apply to activities in foreign countries.
[64]22 ELR at 20924-25 (Blackmun & O'Connor, JJ, dissenting).
[65]*New York State Automobile Dealers Ass'n v New York State Dept. of Envt'l Conserva.*, 827 F Supp 895, 24 ELR 20128, 20130 (NDNY 1993).

"to provide a process for addressing social and economic shortcomings in [American] society, but to ensure that agencies consider the consequences of their actions on the land, air, water, and other natural resources upon which our society depends."[66]

Industry groups have on occasion tried to use citizen suit provisions to challenge agency action that is, in their view, unreasonably protective of the environment at their expense. One result of the prudential limitations is that persons with purely economic interests are usually not permitted to sue under the environmental citizen suit provisions. For example, one court denied standing to a group of ranchers who formed the "Nevada Land Action Association" to protest against a US Forest Service plan for a national forest because it would restrict their livestock from grazing.[67] The court said that the purpose of NEPA, under which the ranchers challenged the plan, "is to protect the environment, not the economic interests of those adversely affected by agency decisions".[68] For similar reasons, an automobile dealers' association alleging primarily their own economic harm was held to lack standing to challenge implementing regulations for the Clean Air Act.[69]

In *Region 8 Forest Service Timber Purchasers Council* v *Alcock*, timber companies were held to lack standing to challenge environmentally protective actions of the US Forest Service.[70]

Operators of a tour boat business which transported tourists into a bay for the purpose of feeding dolphins challenged a National Marine Fisheries Service regulation, which had been promulgated pursuant to the Marine Mammals Protection Act (MMPA), prohibiting such action as "harassment" of marine mammals. Although the tour operators won in the district court, the Court of Appeals vacated the injunction they had obtained against enforcement of the regulation, finding it "clearly reasonable to restrict or prohibit the feeding of dolphins as a potential hazard to them."[71] If a plaintiff with standing has already brought a citizen suit, however, one with a tangible economic interest (such as a permit or property right) will probably be allowed to intervene as a party in the case.[72]

---

[66]*Morris* v *Myers*, 24 ELR 20165, 20167 (D Or 1993).

[67]*Nevada Land Action Ass'n* v *US Forest Service*, 8 F.3d 713, 24 ELR 20100, 20101 (9th Cir 1993).

[68]*Ibid.*

[69]The dealers claimed harm because they would not be able to sell less expensive federally-certified vehicles in New York State which had, as authorised by s 177 of the federal Clean Air Act, promulgated stricter standards (see *supra* n 13). *New York State Automobile Dealers Ass'n* v *New York State Dept. of Envt'l Conserva.*, 827 F Supp 895, 24 ELR 20128, 20131-2 (NDNY 1993).

[70]993 F.2d 800 (11th Cir 1993), cert. denied, 62 USLW 3451 (1994).

[71]*Strong* v *United States*, 24 ELR 20141, 5 F.3d 905 (5th Cir 1993). The court did not treat the issue as one of standing, but reached the merits of the claim.

[72]See *e.g. Resources Ltd.* v *Robertson*, 24 ELR 20026 (9th Cir 1993) (Intermountain Forest Industry Association allowed to intervene to support US Forest Service plan to allow logging in a certain forest); *Sierra Club* v *United States Envt'l Protection Agency*, 23 ELR 20999, 21000 (9th Cir 1993) (city which owns wastewater treatment plant and permits may intervene as of right in citizen suit versus EPA seeking to compel EPA to promulgate water quality standards for waters in and near city).

B. **Standing in state court**

There is no counterpart to article III of the US Constitution in the Constitution of the Commonwealth of Massachusetts.[73] Thus standing in PIEL cases is based on the language of particular environmental statutes, and is an issue of judicial docket management.[74]

In *Holden* v *Division of Water Pollution Control* (DWPC), a town was held to have standing to challenge a DWPC advisory ruling that a developer did not need a permit for a sewer connection, and the town's challenge succeeded.[75] The City of Boston was held to have standing to seek to enjoin construction of a new passenger terminal and parking garage under the state air pollution statute.[76]

Although on its face the ten-citizen statute discussed in Section III(B) above does not appear to require the 10 plaintiffs to establish unique personal injuries, causation, or redressability, and there is no state constitutional reason to interpret the statute in that manner, the state supreme court has "severely restrict[ed] the value of this jurisdictional grant . . . " by refusing to apply it to Massachusetts Environmental Policy Act decisions and decisions on siting hazardous waste facilities. The court does not construe agency decision as "damage" to "natural resources".[77] The fact that the state legislature has conferred standing on a group of 10 citizens, and the fact that standing limitations are prudential rather than constitutional, suggest that if the challenged action were that of an individual polluter, a court could choose to recognise standing arising from a concern for the resource, however, rather than requiring the imminent personal injury pleading that federal cases have imposed.

There is little law under the various Massachusetts citizen suit provisions. It is likely that the reason is that ECOs are far more likely to sue in federal court, where there is a stronger right to recover fees and costs (see Section VI(B)).

C. **Failure to provide notice**

Most of the federal citizen suit provisions require the plaintiff to provide notice before filing suit (typically, 60 days); the Supreme Court has held that these notice provisions are "mandatory conditions precedent" to bringing a lawsuit.[78] Also, the notice provisions have been interpreted to give a private

---

[73]This chapter considers Massachusetts as an example because that is the jurisdiction familiar to the author; no attempt is made to survey other states.

[74]Shelley, P *supra* n 33 at 4-11.

[75]376 N.E.2d 1259 (Mass App 1978). See generally Annot., "Standing to Sue for Violation of State Environmental Regulatory Statutes", 66 ALR 4th 685 (1988).

[76]*Boston* v *Massachusetts Port Auth.*, 364 Mass 639, 308 NE2d 488 (1974).

[77]*Ibid* at 4-15 to 4-16.

[78]*Hallstrom* v *Tillamook County*, 493 US 20. 24-26, 110 S Ct 304, 308 (1989).

defendant time to comply, and to give federal and state officials the first opportunity to enforce the law.[79]

The notice provisions have been strictly construed; plaintiffs must, for example, specifically identify the persons intending to sue and the violations of law that are being challenged.[80]

D. **Cessation of illegal activity (mootness)**

The US Supreme Court held in *Gwaltney of Smithfield Ltd* v *Chesapeake Bay Foundation, Inc.*[81] that plaintiffs could not proceed under FWPCA's citizen suit provision solely for penalties for past violations because of mootness. The defendant bears the burden of proving mootness, and must demonstrate that it is "*absolutely clear*" that the allegedly wrongful behaviour could not reasonably be expected to recur".[82] If the violations existed at the time the suit was filed, lower federal courts have allowed the penalties portion of the case to proceed.[83]

E. **Parallel federal or state enforcement**

A private defendant that is being pursued by the government may claim this in defence to a citizen suit, but the enforcement action must be under active and diligent prosecution by the government in order to constitute a bar.[84] Some of the statutes allow the ECO to intervene in the enforcement action. The rule that government enforcement actions bar citizen suits generally does not apply to agency administrative enforcements, but only to court cases.[85] The

---

[79]*Ibid*; *Connecticut Fund for the Envir.* v *Job Plating Co.*, 623 F Supp 207 (D Conn 1985). Under most federal citizen suit provisions, citizen groups also must notify federal agencies before a court can approve a settlement by consent with a private party, and the agencies have an opportunity to object to the settlement. In practice, citizen groups generally notify the agency charged with enforcing the statute early in the litigation process, to enlist their cooperation to help fashion a remedy that the agency will approve. Shelley, P *supra* n 33, at 4–21.
[80]*Washington Trout* v *Scab Rock Feeders*, 823 F. Supp. 819, 24 ELR 20069 (ED Wash 1993); *Public Interest Research Group of New Jersey* v *Hercules, Inc.*, 830 F Supp 1549, 24 ELR 20282 (DNJ 1993).
[81]484 US 49 (1987).
[82]*Ibid* at 66 (emphasis in original).
[83]*e.g. Atlantic States Legal Founda.* v *Tyson Foods, Inc.*, 897 F.2d 1128 (11th Cir 1990).
[84]See *Coalition for a Liveable West Side, Inc.* v *New York City Dept. of Envt'l Protection*, 830 F Supp 194, 24 ELR 20160 (SDNY 1993) (settlement with state, which provided for gradual phase-in of pollution control equipment, does not bar citizen suit because it does not end violations); *Sierra Club* v *Chemical Handling Corp.*, 24 ELR 20176 (D. Colo. 1992) (state action previously settled is not being "diligently prosecuted" at time Sierra Club suit is filed and does not bar it). Courts interpret the bar provisions narrowly; for example, the terms of the FWPCA have been held to bar only actions for penalties if EPA is seeking them; an EPA compliance action would not bar a suit for injunctive relief. *Washington Public Interest Research Group* v *Pendleton Woollen Mills*, 24 ELR 20231 (9th Cir 1993).
[85]*e.g.* 33 USC s 1365(b)(1)(B) (FWPCA); 42 USC s 300j-8(b)(1)(B) (SDWA).

doctrine of primary jurisdiction, which provides that an agency considering an issue should be allowed to finish its deliberations before resort can be had to the courts, may be applied by a court in deference to the agency, however.

F. Miscellaneous defences

Defences such as statute of limitations (for penalties), primary jurisdiction (see above), and abstention, are occasionally raised in environmental cases.[86] Also, targeted polluters tried during the early days of citizen suits bringing so-called "SLAPP" suits (strategic lawsuits against public participation),[87] but were generally unsuccessful as courts saw the cases as attempts to limit the constitutional rights of free speech and judicial access of the citizen groups.

One of the earliest of these cases, *Sierra Club* v *Butz*,[88] recognised an absolute privilege (not defeated by malice) under the First Amendment to the US Constitution guarantee of a right to petition the government for redress of grievances. The *Sierra Club* court held that the only way a defendant who has suffered economic loss because an ECO had successfully stopped it from using a natural resource (in that case, by logging activities) can bring such a claim is to show that the plaintiff's claim is a "sham" the real purpose of which is to injure the defendant. The court went one step further, and observed that it did not believe that activity aimed at preserving a natural resource was "the type of conduct for which state civil law can constitutionally impose liability."[89] Applying the "sham" standard to the case at bar, the court dismissed the timber company's counterclaim.

It appears that these types of claims and counterclaims for economic damages were a reaction to the early days of the environmental movement in the US,[90] because the author's research does not reveal them to have been brought in recent years, at least in federal courts.[91]

---

[86]Shelley, *supra* n 33, at 4-24. For a case raising the abstention doctrine, see *Sierra Club* v *Chemical Handling Corp.*, *supra*, n 84.

[87]See Pring, "SLAPPs: Strategic Lawsuits Against Public Participation", 7 Pace Envt'l L. Rev. 3 (1989).

[88]349 F Supp 934 (ND Cal 1972).

[89]*Ibid* at 939.

[90]See generally Note, "Counterclaim and Countersuit Harassment of Private Environmental Plaintiffs: The Problem, Its Implications, and Proposed Solutions", 74 Mich L Rev 106 (1975).

[91]There are still a few isolated cases in state courts, but most states have adopted the same "sham" test as the federal court in *Sierra Club* v *Butz*. *e.g. Protect Our Mountain Environment, Inc.* v *District Ct.*, 677 P.2d 1361 (Colo 1984). One recent case which probably stands a good chance of being reversed if appealed or challenged in federal court, *Florida Fern Growers Ass'n Inc.* v *Concerned Citizens of Putnam Cty.*, 616 So. 2d 562 (Fla App 1993), rejected the "sham" test and allowed a suit to go forward. The claimant had alleged, however, that the sole intent of the Concerned Citizens was to put the claimant's members out of business and that the alleged environmental concerns were a "sham", so the claim might have qualified even under that test.

VI. **Practical considerations**

A. **How are cases chosen?**

ECOs generally review reports that are required by law to be filed by regulated companies, and which are available to the public under various freedom of information provisions.[92] They also review environmental impact statements which are required to be filed by both federal and state law, for notice of intended projects that may affect the environment. Often, they will examine reports filed by public sewage treatment plants, to determine which feeder companies are sending toxics to the plant, and then pursue pretreatment cases against the feeders. They also act on "tips" from nearby residents.

Many considerations go into the decision to pursue a case, however, since the time and money involved in numerous court hearings and appeals may be substantial. Thus, it is rare for an ECO to pursue a case which will not have a major impact on the environment.

B. **How are cases funded?**

There are three ways in which ECOs obtain funding to pursue litigation in the US. The first is through donations and member dues, the second is indirect, through project grants from benevolent foundations. The third and least significant financially is through statutory rights to attorneys' fees in certain circumstances.

There is no general fee-shifting rule in the US; the American rule is that litigants generally pay their own attorneys, win or lose.[93] Where a statute provides that plaintiffs may recover attorneys' fees from defendants, as they do in federal (and in some state) civil rights, environmental and consumer cases, this is an expression by the relevant legislature that such litigation is to be encouraged as it is in the public interest. Many of the requests for attorneys' fees in federal cases are made under the Equal Access to Justice Act (EAJA), which provides that a court shall award attorneys' fees to a "prevailing party" in a civil action brought against the United States "unless the court finds that the position of the United States was substantially justified or that special circumstances make the award unjust."[94]

There is always some risk of loss in these cases. Fortunately for ECOs, the statutory attorney fee provisions, and federal court interpretations of them, have not required a strict win for fee recovery; even a losing plaintiff may recover fees if the court concludes that the plaintiff substantially accomplished

---

[92]See generally "Doing Business", n 22 *supra* and, on case choice by the major ECOs, Chapter 2 *infra*.
[93]*United States* v *110-118 Riverside Tenants Corp.*, 5 F.3d 645 (2d Cir 1993).
[94]28 USC s 2412(d)(1)(A). See also Chapter 2 *infra* at section I(I) "Attorney Fees", and n 64 and accompanying text.

his or its purpose in the litigation.[95] Public interest plaintiffs also receive encouragement from the fact that courts have generally held that attorneys' fees should be granted at prevailing market rates, which are determined largely by private attorneys that bill at hourly rates (except under EAJA, which limits hourly rates to $75). Thus, the prevailing ECO may be compensated for attorney time at a rate higher than it actually pays its attorneys, which allows it to use the extra funds for its general purposes, including covering any losses.[96]

VII. **Recent PIEL cases**

A review of cases reported in 1992–93 demonstrates the importance of ECO litigation in the US. If one assumes that the general rule applies in these cases that most cases settle before court adjudication, the large number of reported decisions suggest a considerable iceberg. Despite the restrictions placed by the US Supreme Court on environmental standing, ECOs have met the standing requirements in many cases decided since *Lujan II*, although they have not always succeeded on the merits. A few examples follow.[97]

A. **Informational injury cases**

Several statutes provide not only that certain persons must provide informa-tion to the government, but also that the government must make such information available to the public.[98] After *Lujan II*, and in consideration of some of the cases that had been decided just before *Lujan II*,[99] some

---

[95]Shelley, P *supra* n 33. See *Wilderness Society* v *Babbitt*, 23 ELR 21542 (9th Cir 1993) (plaintiff environmental group held to be "prevailing party" under EAJA in lawsuit that was settled, where lawsuit was a material or catalytic factor in the agency's decision to prepare an EIS; the underlying claim had a basis in law; and lawsuit was not frivolous, unreasonable or groundless). Compare *Forest Conserva. Council* v *Devlin*, 23 ELR 20995 (9th Cir 1993) (group found not to be "prevailing party" because its prelitigation efforts, not the lawsuit, caused the agency to withdraw a challenged timber sale). The courts will generally apply the analysis set forth in EAJA, barring a fee award if the position taken by the government is substantially justified, even if the statute authorising fees does not so provide. See *e.g. Chesapeake Bay Founda.* v *U.S. Dept. of Agriculture*, 24 ELR 20228 (DC Cir 1993), in which the court reversed an attorney fee award of $44,373, on the basis that the agency involved had taken a reasonable position concerning the confidentiality of documents under the Freedom of Information Act (5 USC s 552). The reasonableness of the government's position is not dispositive; it is only one factor to be weighed in assessing entitlement to attorneys' fees. 24 ELR at 20231.

[96]As in all cases in which attorneys' fees may be awarded, courts will scrutinise submitted bills to be satisfied that the time spent on various matters was reasonable. See *Environmental Defense Fund* v *Reilly*, 23 ELR 21144 (DC Cir 1993) (court disallows portion of plaintiff's request in amount of $17,773.50 because it found 3.5 hours to file a notice of appearance and 73.45 hours preparing two letters to EPA to constitute "flagrant overbilling").

[97]It should be remembered that some of these cases may be on appeal, or may still be appealed, and are subject to modification or reversal. Subsequent history should be researched.

[98]See Robbins, "Doing Business", n 22 *supra*.

[99]See *e.g. Foundation on Economic Trends* v *Lyng*, 943 F.2d 79, 84 (DC Cir 1991) (informational injury alone cannot establish standing); *Public Citizen* v *Office of Trade Rep.*, 782 F Supp 139 (DDC 1992) (earlier NAFTA decision, dismissed for lack of standing – see n 23 *supra* and discussed in the paragraph after next).

commentators and a few courts expressed doubt about whether plaintiffs alleging "informational injuries" would be able to meet standing requirements.[1] These fears have proven unfounded.

1. *NEPA and ESA cases*

The primary purpose of the National Environmental Policy Act (NEPA) is to disseminate information about potential environmental impacts. This information is needed to assist in the permitting process, and it also informs the public. The Endangered Species Act (ESA) also has an informational function, although its primary purpose is to protect endangered species (see section IV(B)(2) *supra*). The informational provisions of these statutes have been interpreted to give rise to an injury when there has been a failure to file the required report or do the required study, upon a fairly minimal showing of connection with (or possible injury to) the resource(s) in question. For example, in *Swan View Coalition* v *Turner*, discussed in section IV(A)(4), the court characterised the asserted injury as the fact that environmental consequences might be overlooked as a result of deficiencies in the biological opinion prepared under ESA, and found the defendant's assertion that the Forest Service might not alter its course following completion of a new biological opinion not to "negate this asserted injury".[2]

a. NEPA

One of the better known recent decisions involving informational injury is the case challenging the lack of an EIS for the North American Free Trade Agreement (NAFTA) brought by ECOs including the Sierra Club and Friends of the Earth. In the later district court opinion ("NAFTA II"),[3] the court provided some guidance to plaintiffs seeking to prove informational injuries. Whereas the earlier (1992) decision in the case ("NAFTA I")[4] had been dismissed for lack of standing, the 1993 decision (which was undisturbed by the Court of Appeals[5] and the Supreme Court),[6] held that the ECOs did have standing. The principal difference is that the NAFTA I plaintiffs alleged solely an informational injury,[7] whereas the NAFTA II plaintiffs also alleged the likelihood of specific environmental injuries, and the need for information about these

---

[1]See n 29 *supra*.
[2]824 F Supp 923, 24 ELR 20318 (D Mont 1992).
[3]822 F Supp 21 (DC Cir 1993).
[4]782 F Supp 139 (DC Cir 1992).
[5]The Court of Appeals reversed on another ground. 970 F.2d 916 (DC Cir 1992).
[6]The Supreme Court denied certiorari review without an opinion. No 93-560, 62 USLW 3451 (1993).
[7]See 782 F Supp at 141.

potential injuries.[8] The NAFTA II court decided to apply the following principle of "clearly established" law:

"[t]he procedural and informational thrust of NEPA gives rise to cognisable injury from denial of its explanatory process, so long as there is a reasonable risk that environmental injury may occur."[9]

The plaintiffs in *Salmon River Concerned Citizens* v *Robertson*[10] were held to have standing to challenge a plan by the US Forest Service to use herbicides as part of a reforestation plan at the programme design phase. They did not have to wait for a site-specific EIS. They lost on the merits, however, as the court found the programme EIS sufficiently complete.

In *Wilderness Society* v *Robertson*, the defendant argued that the effect of the challenged action (the failure to prepare an Environmental Assessment or EIS in relation to an application for a mining permit) was "too remote", in that other actions must intervene (such as various federal and state permits obtained) before mining could take place. The court, like the *Swan View Coalition* court, rejected the argument, noting that harm could be "threatened rather than actual and contingent rather than certain".[11]

Sierra Club v *Watkins*[12] represents another victory on the merits; plaintiff obtained a court order that the US Department of Energy had not performed an adequate environmental assessment before deciding to ship spent nuclear fuel rods from Taiwan through a port in Virginia.

b. ESA

One of the most active and most controversial areas of US PIEL has involved cases brought under ESA. The "spotted owl" cases in the Pacific Northwest have caused controversy by allegedly putting loggers out of work. The Ninth Circuit, which covers the west coast (California, Oregon, Washington, Montana, Idaho and Nevada) and has been the forum for most of these cases, has taken a fairly enlightened view of standing, even after *Lujan II*. In three recent cases, it has found standing and rejected arguments that might have appealed to more conservative courts.

The most recent, *Resources Ltd.* v *Robertson*, expressly rejected the ideas that plaintiffs must await specific timber sales (as opposed to an overall forest

---

[8]822 F Supp at 27-28. The reason the ECOs were not barred by principles of *res judicata* from bringing the second challenge is that the deliberations on the NAFTA had concluded and it was to be submitted to Congress, so they were in effect bringing a different case. The NAFTA I case challenged both NAFTA and GATT negotiations while they were ongoing, arguing that the "fast track" procedure on which they had been placed would effectively preclude them from challenging the final results. See 782 F Supp at 141.
[9]822 F Supp at 27, quoting *City of Los Angeles* v *National Highway Traffic Safety Admin.*, 912 F.2d 478, 492 (DC Cir 1990).
[10]798 F Supp 1434 (ED Cal 1992), aff'd, 980 F.2d 738 (9th Cir 1992), cert. denied, 61 USLW 3771 (1993).
[11]824 F Supp 947, 24 ELR 20062, 20063 (D Mont 1993).
[12]808 F Supp 852 (DC Cir 1992).

management plan), or must identify the precise acreage of a national forest which its members use or plan to use, in order to have standing.[13]

The second, *Portland Audubon Society* v *Babbitt*, resulted in an injunction against the federal Bureau of Land Management (BLM) prohibiting logging operations on BLM land used as northern spotted owl habitat; the decision was affirmed on appeal.[14] The plaintiff was held to have standing on the basis of affidavits stating that its members had observed and studied the owls, and would no longer be able to do so. The BLM was found to have acted arbitrarily and capriciously, and ordered to perform a supplemental EIS under NEPA.

The third, *Seattle Audubon Society* v *Espy*, held that the plaintiff had standing to challenge the Forest Service's spotted owl management plan, and did not have to wait to challenge a specific project.[15]

One recent case suggests just how political the "spotted owl" situation became. The Portland, Oregon Audubon Society achieved a legally and politically significant procedural victory when the court ruled that the Society is entitled to a "vigorous and adversarial" evidentiary hearing before a specially-appointed administrative law judge regarding whether the administration of former President Bush exerted pressure through *ex parte* communications with the Endangered Species Committee. *Ex parte* communications between an agency and "an interested person outside the agency" concerning a matter before the agency are banned under the APA, and the court held that the President and his staff are "interested person[s] outside the agency". The evidentiary hearing was to consider the "nature, content, extent, source and effect of any *ex parte* communication" and the parties were to report to the court after the hearing.

In *Bays' Legal Fund* v *Browner*, the court found insufficient evidence that the discharge of municipal sewage into two bays would harm endangered species such as the humpback whale and Kemp's ridley turtle.[16] The *American Bald Eagle* v *Bhatti* case discussed in Section IV(A)(4) resulted in a similar finding concerning the effects of ammunition purportedly ingested by eagles.[17]

2. *EPCRA cases*

Unlike NEPA and especially ESA, the Emergency Planning and Community Right to Know Act (EPCRA) has primarily an informational function (and a contingency planning purpose for chemical emergencies). EPCRA also

---

[13]24 ELR 20026, 20027 (9th Cir 1993).
[14]23 ELR 21142 (9th Cir 1993). See also Chapter 2 *infra*, nn 61 and 62 and accompanying text.
[15]Nos. 92-36529, 92-36564, slip op (9th Cir 1993), discussed in *Resources Ltd.*, n 13 *supra*, 24 ELR at 20027.
[16]828 F Supp 102, 24 ELR 20081 (D Mass 1993). This case also did not treat the question as one of standing, but the result is the same.
[17]24 ELR 20173 (1st Cir 1993).

contains a citizen suit provision.[18] Recent cases construing it suggest that courts may be willing to find standing on the basis of informational injuries alone, without any showing of potential environmental injuries.

In *Atlantic States Legal Foundation, Inc.* v *Buffalo Envelope*, the plaintiff ECO showed careful reasoning and foresight by submitting affidavits alleging, in addition to the organisation's information-providing function to local residents, that one of its members was a local emergency planner who needed the toxic chemical information to do his job, and another was a professor of environmental politics who also needed the information to do his job.[19] The plaintiff in *Atlantic States* did not allege any potential environmental injury; it merely alleged injuries stemming from violation of the right to know combined with a particularised need for the information. The court held that this was sufficient.[20]

In *Delaware Valley Toxics Coalition* v *Kurz-Hastings, Inc.*,[21] the court also recognised an informational injury, together with a particularised need to know, as sufficient to establish standing under EPCRA, and did not require an alleged environmental injury. Plaintiffs in *Delaware Valley* were groups whose purpose was to provide chemical information to their members, who lived, worked, and travelled near defendant's manufacturing facility. Defendant had filed late reports under EPCRA. Plaintiffs alleged that they had spent time and money discovering defendant's violations, and as a result these commodities were taken away from their usual informational activities. The court generalised that the loss of information required under EPCRA:

> "may inhibit the conduct of research and data gathering or the ability to aid in the development of appropriate regulations, guidelines, and standards . . . Persons experiencing such a loss of information may be found to have suffered a concrete and personalised invasion of their legally-protected interests."

It held that such lack of information can be an injury if the information is "essential to the injured organization's activities, and where the lack of the information will render those activities infeasible."[22] Having found an injury, it reasoned that if the plaintiffs "were in fact injured by a failure of the defendant to comply with the EPCRA", logically the "fairly traceable" element is met. Although the defendant had by that time filed the reports, the court also found redressability because the plaintiffs might obtain a declaratory judgment, penalties for the late filing, costs, and an injunction against future violations. The court also found the prudential standards had been met, and that it had jurisdiction for wholly past violations.

---

[18]See Robbins, "Doing Business", n 22 *supra* at 27-29.
[19]823 F Supp 1065, 1069-70 (WDNY 1993).
[20]"The right that the statute was intended to protect is essentially a 'right to know'." 823 F Supp at 1068.
[21]813 F Supp 1132, 23 ELR 20915 (ED Pa 1993).
[22]*Ibid.* at 1140, quoting *Competitive Enterprises Institute* v *NHSTA*, 901 F.2d 107, 122 (DC Cir 1990).

Because EPCRA's contingency planning purpose is not the only reason EPCRA makes information available to the public (*e.g.* simply having to file the reports has encouraged many companies to reduce use of toxics), the *Delaware Valley* decision would seem a defensible one. It would not seem necessary to go as far as the *Atlantic States* ECO did, and include a contingency planner among the affiants, in order to establish standing under the citizen suit provisions of EPCRA. For the moment, however, until appellate courts and ideally the Supreme Court have spoken on the issue, ECOs should probably err on the side of prudence and include particularised informational injuries of the type suffered by the contingency planner and the professor of environmental politics if their individual members have experienced them. The two cases suggest that it is not necessary to allege a potential injury to the environment (of the type alleged in NAFTA II) to show standing under the citizen suit provision of EPCRA, but this cannot be said with certainty unless and until supported by a ruling of the Supreme Court.

B. **MMPA cases**

The Marine Mammal Protection Act (MMPA) is closely related to the ESA. It prohibits the "taking" of any endangered marine mammals except for certain purposes.[23] "Take" is defined by regulation to include the killing or "harassing" of a marine mammal, or "the doing of any other negligent or intentional act which results in disturbing or molesting a marine mammal".[24] *Animal Protection Institute* v *Mosbacher*,[25] an MMPA case discussed in section IV(A)(2), challenged the importation of whales from Japan and Canada to be displayed in an aquarium in the US. While the case was pending, *Lujan II* was decided, and the trial court found it necessary to consider whether the plaintiffs had standing. It held that averments that the plaintiff's members planned to view whales in the areas from which they were to be taken "this summer" and in the "summers of 1993 and 1994" alleged a sufficiently particularised and temporally close injury. Plaintiffs were also held to have met the causation and redressability tests because, the court observed, "an invalidation of the permits will prevent the importation of the whales, and whales that cannot be imported are unlikely to be captured, at least for

---

[23]USC s 1371. Marine mammals and marine mammal products may not be taken, or imported into the US, except with a permit, which can be granted only for "scientific research, public display, or enhancing the survival or recovery of a species or stock . . . " *Ibid*, s 1371(a)(1). Marine mammals designated by the Secretary of Commerce as "depleted" may not be the subject of permits and may not be imported. *Ibid*, s 1371(3)(B).
[24]50 CFR s 216.3.
[25]799 F Supp 173 (DDC 1992).

delivery to [the aquarium in question]."[26] The court did uphold the permits, however.

C. **Water pollution cases**

The Federal Water Pollution Control Act (FWPCA) is an active source of PIEL litigation, and an example of a statute under which standing must be based on a strong connection with the resource in question, especially if the purpose of the suit is to enforce discharge limits and not simply to compel filing of discharge monitoring reports required by FWPCA. The New Jersey Public Interest Research Group (PIRG) succeeded in establishing in the district court just before *Lujan II* was decided that it had standing in a water pollution case seeking to enforce permit limits against an industrial concern. Its members alleged that they used the affected waterways for recreation and avoided eating fish from them (which they would have done if the fish were edible), and that they used the adjacent land for hiking and nature study. The appellate court upheld this decision, and the US Supreme Court denied certiorari review, after *Lujan II* was decided. PIRG also obtained a ruling that an ongoing state enforcement action did not preclude its suit. Finally, having jumped those two hurdles, PIRG won on the merits: the district court granted an injunction against further violations of the permit granted to the industrial concern in question.[27]

New Jersey PIRG achieved another victory recently in *Public Interest Research Group of N.J.* v *New Jersey Expressway Authority*,[28] decided after *Lujan II*. The court held that PIRG had standing to enforce a water discharge permit granted by EPA, on the basis of affidavits similar to those in the above case. Standing was not defeated by the fact that the discharges went to wetlands adjacent to the lake plaintiffs used, as plaintiffs submitted uncontroverted evidence of a groundwater connection between the two.

An ECO also won a recent decision holding that the act of coming into compliance by a private defendant (i.e. stopping the polluting acts) did not render a PIEL suit moot, because the group still had a right to seek civil penalties for past violations under FWPCA.[29] The court reversed a district court dismissal.

Several other recent water pollution permit enforcement cases have resulted in victories for plaintiffs, both in securing injunctive relief and in

---

[26]*Ibid* at 177.
[27]*Public Interest Research Group of N.J.* v *Magnesium Elektron, Inc.*, 222 ELR 20362 (DNJ 1992), aff'd, 983 F.2d 1052 (3d Cir 1992), cert. denied, 61 USLW 3788 (1993).
[28]23 ELR 20420 (DNJ 1992).
[29]*Atlantic States Legal Founda.* v *Pan American Tanning Corp.*, 23 ELR 20865 (2d Cir 1993).

obtaining penalty awards.[30] A few recent cases have resulted in losses, mainly on previously untested procedural grounds.[31] The ECO water pollution cases are further discussed at Chapter 2, section I(J).

D. Injunctions against federal and state agencies

As discussed above, it is difficult to obtain injunctive relief against a governmental agency, because the plaintiff must demonstrate a non-discretionary or mandatory statutory duty. ECOs have succeeded in meeting that standard in some recent cases.

In *National Wildlife Federation* v *US Environmental Protection Agency*,[32] where standing was not challenged, the NWF obtained a ruling that EPA must initiate withdrawal proceedings under the Safe Drinking Water Act (SDWA) against a state when EPA determines that the state is not in compliance with the SDWA.

In *Natural Resources Defense Council* v *Reilly*,[33] also a case with no issue of standing, the court ruled that EPA must promulgate standards under the Clean Air Act requiring "light duty" vehicles to have on-board vapour recovery systems.

In *Coalition for Clean Air* v *Southern California Edison*,[34] the court ordered EPA to promulgate a Federal Implementation Plan for the State of California under the federal Clean Air Act when it disapproved California's State Implementation Plan revisions, again finding a mandatory duty to act.

---

[30]In *Hawaii's Thousand Friends* v *City and County of Honolulu*, 821 F Supp 1368, 20 ELR 20788 (D Haw 1993), the city of Honolulu was ordered to pay $718,000 in civil penalties and to allocate $1 million for studies of impacts of discharges from its sewage treatment plant on public health and the marine environment. The plaintiffs also were authorised to obtain attorneys' fees and costs. The case contains a good discussion of the method for calculating penalties. In *Public Interest Research Group of N.J.* v *Hercules*, 830 F Supp 1525, 24 ELR 20270 (DNJ 1993), the court disallowed claims for violations not alleged in the 60-day notice letter, but allowed the discharge violations alleged in the letter to proceed. It denied the defendant's motion to exclude evidence of violations at other facilities owned by it, reasoning that such evidence may be relevant to the amount of penalty to be assessed. It also denied plaintiff's motion for a permanent injunction, in that there had been insufficient evidence that the violations were likely to continue, or that any injury arising from them is irreparable. By contrast, the Natural Resources Defense Council (NRDC) did obtain an injunction, because the court believed it had demonstrated irreparable injury arising from the Texaco Refining and Marketing Company's decade-long history of substantial permit noncompliance, in *Natural Resources Defense Council* v *Texaco Refining & Marketing, Inc.*, 23 ELR 21328 (3d Cir 1993). The NRDC case contains a good discussion of the elements of standing. The plaintiff obtained summary judgment against the defendant city on liability for violations at two wastewater treatment plants in *Coalition for a Liveable West Side, Inc.* v *New York City Dept. of Envt'l Protection*, 830 F Supp 194, 24 ELR 20160 (SDNY 1993).
[31]It was held in *Northwest Envt'l Advocates* v *City of Portland*, 24 ELR 20238 (9th Cir 1993), that FWPCA does not authorise suit against the holder of a National Pollutant Discharge Elimination System permit for direct enforcement of state water quality standards, even if such standards are adopted as permit conditions; only end-of-the-pipe effluent limitations are enforceable. The Second Circuit reached a similar result in *Atlantic States Legal Founda.* v *Eastman Kodak Co.*, 24 ELR 20234 (1993).
[32]23 ELR 20440 (1992).
[33]23 ELR 20549 (DC Cir 1993).
[34]971 F.2d 219 (9th Cir), cert. denied sub nom. *Southern Cal. Ass'n of Governments* v *Coalition for Clean Air*, 61 USLW 3584 (1993).

In *Arkansas Peace Center* v *Arkansas Dept. of Pollution Control & Ecology*, the plaintiff appeared to have achieved a significant victory when the court enjoined the defendant state agency from allowing incineration of wastes at a dioxin-contaminated site. The case was reversed on appeal, however, based on the well-established principle that removal and remedial decisions under CERCLA may be challenged only according to the procedures established by CERCLA, and the courts lack jurisdiction to enjoin CERCLA clean-ups.[35]

E. Defeating the preclusion defence

In *NRDC* v *Fina Oil & Chemical Co.*[36] the court found no preclusion of the citizen suit resulting from an EPA enforcement order. In *NRDC* v *Vygen Corp.*,[37] a citizen suit was held not to be precluded by an ongoing state prosecution. The cases cited in note 84 also held that there was no preclusion by reason of government action.

F. Striking back

Targets of environmental citizen suits have occasionally sought to use the courts either to advance their own economic interests, or to deter ECOs from bringing citizen suits by alleging malicious prosecution or abuse of process. The first variant is generally prohibited by prudential limits on standing, discussed in Section V(A). The second, so-called "SLAPP" suits, are discussed in Section V(F). Occasionally, a winning defendant will try to seek attorneys' fees from an ECO as well.[38]

G. State cases

A few examples of recent state cases (which, as stated above, are much less common than federal cases), are: *Florida League of Cities* v *Department of Environmental Resources*,[39] a challenge to rulemaking in which standing was found but the plaintiffs lost on the merits; *Maryland Waste Associates, Inc.* v

---

[35]23 ELR 20807 (ED Ark 1993), rev'd, 999 F.2d 1212, 23 ELR 21280 (8th Cir 1993). Although the plaintiff had brought the case under a different statute, the Court of Appeals said it was in reality challenging a CERCLA removal action.

[36]806 F Supp 145 (ED Tex 1992).

[37]803 F Supp 97 (ND Ohio 1992).

[38]Although the citizen suit provisions usually authorise attorneys' fees only for prevailing or substantially prevailing plaintiffs, a litigant may in principle obtain attorneys' fees by showing that a case was brought in bad faith or for vexatious purposes or was completely without legal or factual foundation. See generally *Washington Trout* v *Scab Rock Feeders*, 823 F Supp 819, 24 ELR 20069 (ED Wash 1993). The author of this chapter is not aware of any case in which defendants have succeeded in obtaining fees from an ECO, however.

[39]603 So. 2d 1363 (Fla Ct App 1992).

Maryland Waste Coalition,[40] in which the plaintiffs were held to lack standing; and *Trustees for Alaska* v *Gorsuch*,[41] in which the plaintiffs obtained a ruling that the Alaska Department of Natural Resources wrongly granted a permit.

VIII. **Conclusion**

There were dozens of PIEL decisions reported by US federal courts in 1992–93, and it is likely that the reported decisions are fewer than the number of cases being settled prior to or during litigation. Manifestly, ECO access to the judicial process in the United States has significantly contributed to improved environmental protection. In the overall scheme of environmental protection, however, ECO litigation is a relatively small part when compared to the activities of numerous federal and state enforcement agencies which operate to bring about environmental compliance – usually through negotiation, with litigation lurking as the ultimate tool. Citizen suit provisions have not, as some feared, opened any "floodgate". Instead, they have provided concerned citizens with the means to exercise a credible tool to assist in the environmental compliance process.

Atlantic States, NAFTA II, and all other successful standing cases demonstrate that ECOs are able to meet the standing requirements if they allege concrete, specific injuries that are within the "zone of interests" protected by the statute. If the statute is primarily intended to protect a resource, as are the FWPCA or the MMPA, it is imperative that the plaintiff allege at least some potential or imminent injury to the resource and a consequent injury to individual members of the plaintiff group which sets them apart from the general public. If the statute has primarily an informational but also a resource-protection purpose, as does NEPA, it is necessary to allege actual or potential environmental injury as well as informational injury. Although the *Delaware Valley* and *Atlantic States* courts have recognised an informational injury alone as sufficient for standing under EPCRA, provided that the purpose of the plaintiff group, or of the plaintiff's job, is to provide or use this information, it could be a risk to assume at this time that all courts will agree and not require an environmental injury as well, even under EPCRA. The cases discussed in this chapter demonstrate the kinds of allegations that are necessary to prove standing.

PIEL is an active branch of environmental enforcement in the United States. ECOs have made good use of environmental statutes passed by the US Congress in the 1970s and 1980s with citizen suit provisions, and have

---

[40] 612 A.2d 241 (Md 1992).
[41] 23 ELR 20276 (Alas 1992).

remained relatively undaunted by US Supreme Court decisions restricting their access to the courts on the basis of the law on standing. Environmental citizen suits are a valuable part of the overall environmental enforcement scheme.

Appendix
US Legal Citation

A brief explanation of commonly-used forms of US legal citation may be helpful. Legal citation is explained in full detail in the "Harvard Bluebook" (*A Uniform System of Legal Citation*).

"F.2d" and "F.3d" refer to the second and third sets of the Federal Reporter, in which are published decisions of the federal Circuit Courts of Appeal (see explanation of US legal system in Section II). The Federal Reporter is published by West Publishing Company of St. Paul, Minnesota, and is available at the Institute for Advanced Legal Studies (IALS) library in London, or at any US law library.

"F. Supp" refers to the Federal Supplement, also published by West, which contains decisions of the US district courts (the trial-level courts – see Section II). It is also at the IALS library.

"Cert. denied" means that the US Supreme Court denied a writ of certiorari, exercising its discretionary right to refuse to hear a case, thereby leaving the decision of the applicable Circuit Court of Appeals (of which there are 13 – see Section II) as the law in the circuit in question. The law in the 13 circuits need not be in harmony, and the US Supreme Court will often "take" a case to resolve conflict in the circuits. (Supreme Court decisions are binding on all circuits.) The refusal by the US Supreme Court to grant a writ of certiorari is done without a statement of reasons, and it is not possible to infer any reason, including agreement or disagreement with the lower court decision.

"USC" is the United States Code, the official compilation of all US federal statutes (those enacted by the US Congress), published by West. Each statute, when enacted, has its own section numbers, which usually do not correspond with their eventual section numbers in the US Code. For example, CERCLA Section 101 refers to that section of the original CERCLA statute passed in 1980, which became Section 9601 of Title 42 of the US Code. The US Code is at the IALS library.

"CJS" is *Corpus Juris Secundum*, a compilation of US legal topics published by West and available at the IALS library.

"ALR" is the *American Law Reports*, published by Lawyers Cooperative Press, Rochester, New York. It consists of "Annotations" (abbreviated "Annot.") on various topical issues, which collect cases from across the country on the topics in question. Annual supplements update the cases. Available at IALS.

"ELR" refers to the *Environmental Law Reporter*, published by the Environmental Law Institute in Washington, DC.

Contents of Chapter 2

Public Interest Environmental Law Firms
in the United States

Chapter 2

Public Interest Environmental Law Firms in the United States

David Robinson[1]

This chapter seeks to identify the laws and culture which have enabled US environmental advocacy organisations to grow. It then describes those organisations and their campaigns, such as the citizen suits instigated to stop illegal water pollution. Three internal management issues are discussed. The chapter concludes with an evaluation of the effectiveness of the public interest environmental law firms.

I. US legislative activism and the participatory ethos

A. Sixties – seventies environmentalism

The most important factor contributing to the growth of non-profit, environmental advocacy organisations[2] in the United States was the 1970s ground swell environmental concern. The Clean Air Act 1970 and the Federal Water Pollution Control Act 1972 (FWPCA) gave legislative expression to the nation's sense of urgency about protecting the environment. Even President Nixon, hardly an environmental activist,[3] reflected the extent of public concern. As he

David Robinson, formerly a solicitor of the Environmental Defender's Office, Sydney, currently teaches and researches environmental law with the University of Southampton and the Institute of Advanced Legal Studies, London. He returns to environmental law practice in New South Wales in March 1995.

[1] I am grateful for the generous assistance of Professor John Bonine, University of Oregon, and Ms Deirdre H Robbins, author of Chapter 1, for extensive comments on a draft of this chapter, and for the additional comments of Professor Nicholas Robinson, Pace University, New York.

[2] Whereas some commentators have distinguished environmental advocacy organisations from law firms (*e.g.* Trubeck DM, "Environmental Defense I: Introduction to Interest Group Advocacy" in Weisbrod BA ed, *Public Interest Law: An Economic and Institutional Analysis*, Berkeley, University of California Press, 1978 at 151–194), I use the expressions interchangeably, since lawyers have increasingly used non-litigious methods of advocacy.

[3] For example, President Nixon tried to block the exacting amendments proposed by Congress to the Federal Water Pollution Control Act 1972 (FWPCA) in 1972. See Chapter 6 of Yaeger PC, *The Limits of Law: The Public Regulation of Private Pollution*, Cambridge University Press, 1991.

signed the National Environmental Policy Act 1970 (NEPA) into law on 1 January 1970,[4] Nixon declared:

> "The 1970s absolutely must be the years when America pays its debt to the past by reclaiming the purity of its air, its waters, and our living environment. It is virtually now or never . . . "

B. **National Environmental Policy Act 1970 (NEPA)**

NEPA made prior environmental impact assessment (EIA) a legal requirement for actions by federal government agencies (s 102), and established a Council on Environmental Quality (CEQ), whose Guidelines set out environmental impact statement (EIS) procedures. At the same time, the Clean Air Act 1970 (s 309) gave a specific role in commenting on EISs to the Environment Protection Agency (EPA), established in 1971. By 1990 the EPA was commenting on and "rating" several hundred EISs annually. The EISs became vehicles for public communication and participation and cornerstones for the achievement of extremely ambitious environmental goals.[5]

C. **Judicial activism**

The EIS process was moulded through public interest litigation "that took words from NEPA that could have been interpreted in an innocuous manner and gave them real teeth".[6] The leading case was *Calvert Cliffs' Coordinating Committee Inc* v *Atomic Energy Commission*.[7] Presented with NEPA, foremost amongst environmental protection statutes attesting the government's commitment to control "the destructive engine of material 'progress' ",[8] Justice Skelly Wright carved a strong role for the judiciary to make the promise of the legislation become a reality. In *Calvert Cliffs* the petitioners challenged a decision by the Commission to grant a construction permit to a nuclear power plant. While an EIS had been prepared, it had not been considered by the Commission, which argued that this should take place at subsequent operation licence proceedings. Justice Skelly Wright disagreed. While NEPA gave federal agencies broad discretion as to merits, the procedural EIA provisions in NEPA required a strict standard of compliance. Rather than reading down the requirement to make a detailed statement on environmental impacts of proposed actions (for example, on cost and convenience

---

[4]Wilson JJ, "EOA and NEPA: Challenges and Goals", *EPA Journal*, 1988 January/February 22.
[5]For example, statutory objectives were set to eliminate the pollution of navigable waters by 1985 and prohibit the discharge of toxic pollutants in toxic amounts (FWPCA - PL 92-500, s 101(a)(1) and (5)).
[6]Bonine J, personal communication, December 1993.
[7]449 F2d 1109 (DC Cir 1971). For an explanation of US legal citation see the Appendix to Chapter 1.
[8]*Ibid*.

grounds) Skelly Wright J said that the requirement to undertake EIA "to the fullest extent possible" did not provide "an escape-hatch for foot-dragging agencies. Congress did not intend the Act to be such a paper tiger". He continued:

> "Indeed, the requirement of environmental consideration 'to the fullest extent possible' sets a high standard for the agencies, a standard which must be rigorously enforced by the reviewing courts."

Another early case[9] reinforces the point that the judiciary in the United States has made an important contribution to making environmental assessment laws a serious matter, not a mere public relations exercise. The case does not involve NEPA, but in fact the opinion of Justice Douglas, writing for the Supreme Court majority of seven, highlighted two principles which NEPA subsequently adopted. First, multiple uses (in this case using a river for fisheries, ecosystem maintenance and recreational purposes), rather than single uses (power supply) were preferred. Secondly, the "no-action" alternative (allowing the river to run free) needed to be considered.

D. Implementation

Even more ambitious than the environmental legislation was the regulatory and enforcement programme required to implement it.

The EPA soon became the largest single administrative agency of the US Government outside the military.[10] Pursuant to FWPCA the EPA faced the difficult task of determining short-term "best practicable technology" pollution limits, medium-term "best available technology" limits and new pollutant source standards for 28 industrial categories, which the EPA analysed into 500 subcategories of industry.[11] In addition, stringent quantitative controls on toxic pollutant emissions were to be formulated.[12] The task was all the more formidable bearing in mind the open decision-making process prescribed under FWPCA and the Administrative Procedure Act. Broad consultation and eventual challenges to draft regulations were possible and, in many cases, inevitable. The EPA faced political issues as to the cost feasibility of control technologies. Even in questions of a narrower, technical nature, scientific difficulties about risk and safe exposure levels existed. Further, "agency forcing" litigation could be initiated if the standard-writing timetable set in FWPCA was not met.

---

[9]*Udall* v *Federal Power Commission* 387 US 428 (1967), as discussed in Parker (see n 16 *infra*).
[10]Yeager *op cit* at 115–120.
[11]Yeager *op cit* at Chapter 6 ("Controls and Constraints: From Law to Regulation").
[12]The EPA substantially failed to control toxics. See the Nature Resource Defence Council suits seeking to prompt action by the EPA (the "Flannery Decree") at n 51 *infra* and accompanying text.

E. **Participatory process**

The FWPCA experience highlights how substantive law is inseparable from procedural requirements in the United States. Public participation has long been conceived as an active right, not limited to accessing environmental information, but extending to a role in the decision-making and law-enforcement processes. Hence, since the late 1960s lawyers have been at the forefront of the US environmental movement. An alternative view is that, rather than constituting a positive manifestation of the participatory and open nature of US environmental law, the ascendancy of lawyers in environmental issues is a negative result of contradictory legislation, which is always ripe for litigation.[13] "In no other political and social movement has litigation played such an important and dominant role."[14]

The environmental advocacy organisations were born as a result of the US participatory ethos. As with other environmental law principles, such as environmental impact assessment and open access to information, now being adopted worldwide (at least in principle), public participation rights (including the right of environmentalists to go to court) evolved initially in the United States. This was a manifestation of a pluralist constitutional and cultural framework. The checks and balances in the US Constitution separate and decentralise power. For example, the availability of information and the accessability of courts create a citizens' check, through the judiciary, on executive interpretation and implementation of the law. Another check against the tyranny of one sector of society is achieved by encouraging competition with other sectors. In the environmental context, this has meant allowing conservation groups to fight alongside development interests in decision-making. The representative model of democratic government, conceived prior to the enormous growth of government agencies and departments this century, has been replaced by a participatory, pluralist model.

The US pluralist environmental law model stresses procedural considerations[15] such as delegation and decentralised decision-making. Broad rights of standing, discussed below, reflect a policy of delegating and decentralising the rule-making and enforcement functions of the EPA to private citizens. Acknowledging the practical importance of standards set by delegated

---

[13]Smith JT II, "Observations on the Experience of the United States with Environmental Litigation" in *Current EC Developments: EC Environment and Planning Law*, Butterworths, 1991 at 297–304.

[14]David Sive, quoted in the preface to Turner T and Clifton C, *Wild By Law: The Sierra Club Legal Defense Fund and the Places it has Saved*, Sierra Club Legal Defense Fund and Sierra Club Books, San Francisco, 1990.

[15]The US "hard look" doctrine, requiring administrators to grant more than formal obeisance to arguments presented by contending groups, functions in practice like the British *Wednesbury* unreasonableness ground of judicial review: Craig PP, *Public Law and Democracy in the UK and the USA*, Oxford, Clarendon Press, 1990 at 121). While important procedurally, the doctrine is not discussed here. Note the importance of compliance with procedural requirements indicated in Justice Skelly Wright's leading case pronouncement on NEPA in *Calvert Cliffs*, n 7 *supra* and accompanying text.

legislation, citizens have broad rights to comment on draft regulations and their implementation.

Three features of interest representation in the United States are without parallel in other common law countries: environmental laws are rule-oriented, rules are made through open procedures, and the law is enforceable by citizens through open access to courts. These features warrant detailed consideration.

F. **Rule-oriented environmental law**

The US's justiciable environmental laws are rule-oriented, relying less in their interpretation, implementation and enforcement upon administrative discretion than the environmental laws of many other countries. The Endangered Species Act (ESA), for example, is rule-oriented. The attractions of the ESA for public interest advocates are that its language "admits of little bureaucratic maneuvering".[16] Federal agencies are prohibited from "taking" a listed species without a permit; the exceptions are narrow; and the agencies are also required to protect designated "critical habitat" for listed species. Where non-discretionary duties are given to federal government agencies, the law enables citizens to undertake an intervention procedure against the Administrator. "Agency-forcing" can be of two types: criteria specification or deadline-forcing.

Examples of criteria specification are found in the Clean Air Act 1970 and FWPCA, which include "shall" and other provisions clearly specifying the criteria upon which admnistrative decisions are to be made. In one case petitioners successfully challenged an EPA approval of a list of factors to be considered in exercising powers and responsibilities relating to air quality. The reason was that the list undermined the specification in section 108 of the Clean Air Act 1970 that public health should always take precedence over considerations of economic impact or technical feasibility.[17]

The leading citizen suit on the control of toxic substances is an example of deadline-forcing.[18] Two other examples are where legislation specifies that a regulatory agency "shall prepare" an environmental management plan for a particular area by a certain date, or where states have to submit plans to the EPA on how to implement national ambient air quality standards by a certain date (Clean Air Act 1970 s 109). Citizens can petition to enforce the deadline if the agency fails to meet it. Several agency-forcing cases reported in 1992–93 are discussed in Chapter 1, section VIII(D).

---

[16]Parker V (Executive Director, Sierra Club Legal Defense Fund), "Natural Resources Management by Litigation" in Knight and Bates (ed), *A New Century for Natural Resources Management*, Island Press, Washington DC, 1995.
[17]*Natural Resources Defense Council* v *Environmental Protection Agency (Georgia Plan)* 489 F2d 390 (5th Cir 1974).
[18]*NRDC* v *Train* DDC 1976; 8 ERC 2120 (discussed at n 51 *infra* and accompanying text).

G. **Open rule-making process**

Second, participation rights have been extended to rule-making, not just to implementation and enforcement. Under the Administrative Procedure Act 1946, public notification and comment is required as an integral part of the process of making delegated legislation, and in some cases agencies must also conduct public hearings. The Administrative Procedure Act thus moulds the way in which administrative discretion is exercised. Rule-making is publicly scrutinised, and the resulting rules are more responsive to the concerns of the regulated community and public interest groups.

Full participation by public interest groups in administrative decision-making is encouraged by the need to exhaust administrative remedies first before resorting to the courts, and by broadened standing in administrative hearings, reflecting the position before the courts. For example, the Sierra Club Legal Defense Fund participated in administrative appeals concerning over 50 forest plans during the 1980s.[19]

Open rule-making procedures made agencies more akin to mini-legislatures, a departure from the previous mini-court model of agencies dealing with comment from citizens.[20] Interest-group bargaining results from the open procedures. In this light, the criticism of Congress' environmental legislation as buck-passing the difficult and essentially political choices relating to environmental and economic trade-offs to the executive and ultimately the judicial branches of government should be considered.[21] The criticism reflects the representative, rather than the more recent participatory, pluralist paradigm of democracy. Without denying the need for strong direction in environmental legislation, the criticism offers no indication as to how legislatures alone can possibly cope with the complexity, detail and volume of environmental protection provisions needed to tackle environmental problems. Through the participatory model in rule-making and enforcement, the EPA and the judiciary have been able to flesh out and complement the framework provided by Congress.

Finally, the court system is open to environmentalists, both regarding formal rights of standing to be heard, and with respect to legal costs arrangements.

H. **Standing**

Locus standi rules are very broad. With regard to enforcement, "citizen suit" provisions were included in virtually all environmental protection enactments

---

[19]*Annual Report 1991–92.*
[20]Bonine J, University of Oregon, commenting on an earlier draft of this chapter.
[21]Smith JT *op cit*. This issue is further considered in assessing the contribution of public interest environmental advocacy organisations (see "IV Evaluation" *infra*).

of the 1970s and 1980s. Legislative enshrinement of the open standing policy had followed from a Court of Appeals' acceptance in 1965 of "aesthetic, conservational and recreational" interests as sufficient to enable the plaintiff to seek an injunction to block a hydroelectric plant.[22] A strong dissenting opinion of Justice Douglas in a 1972 Supreme Court case over a proposal by the Disney Corporation to develop the "world's largest ski resort" in the Mineral King wilderness area adjoining Sequoia National Park, and the majority opinion in the same case, gave further strength to the view that aesthetic injury or recreational use was sufficient to grant standing.[23]

Citizen suit provisions typically enable "any person" to sue for non-compliance with statutory provisions or with standards and regulations issued under the statute.[24] The right can be based upon non-economic aspects of environmental degradation, as the litigant acts as a private attorney-general to enforce public rights. While a more recent Supreme Court case has stated that Congress is not free to confer on citizen groups "an abstract, self-contained" right to ensure that agencies comply with the law, it is likely that, through careful selection of plaintiffs public interest organisations will continue to be able to meet the standing requirements, such as injury in fact, or an interest different from that of the general public.[25]

Congress has expanded and reinforced citizen suit provisions since 1970. The Senate Committee on Environment and Public Works, in discussing 1985 amendments to FWPCA, which contains the most widely used citizen suit provision, said:[26]

> "Citizen suits are a proven enforcement tool. They operate as Congress intended
> – to both spur and supplement government enforcement actions. They have
> deterred violators and achieved significant compliance gains."

I. Attorney fees

Under the "American rule" the loser does not have to pay the winner's attorney fees. The rule was considered in an environmental case in the early 1970s. In *Alyeska Pipeline Service Co* v *Wilderness Society*[27] the respondent

---

[22]*Scenic Hudson Preservation Conference* v *Federal Power Commission* 354 F 2d 608 (2d Cir 1965); cert. denied, 384 US 941 (1966).
[23]*Sierra Club* v *Morton* 405 US 727 (1972).
[24]Greve MS, "The Private Enforcement of Environmental Law", (1990) 65 *Tulane Law Review* 339 at 340. Greve cites 11 Federal environmental protection statutes with, and one without, open standing provisions. See also Chapter 1 (ns 14–18).
[25]*Lujan* v *Defenders of Wildlife* (1992) 112 S Ct; (1992) 22 ELR 20918 (discussed in Chapter 1). Criticised in "*Lujan* v *Defenders of Wildlife*: The Supreme Court's Slash and Burn Approach to Environmental Standing" (1993) 23 ELR 10031.
[26]Cited in Greve *op cit*.
[27]421 US 240, 95 S Ct 1612, 44 L Ed 2d 141 (1975).

environmental group succeeded in its attempt to prevent the issuance of an oil pipeline construction permit. Regarding costs, the Court of Appeals held that the Wilderness Society was entitled to fees as it had acted to vindicate important statutory rights, and to ensure the proper functioning of the government system. The Supreme Court reversed this ruling, however, on the grounds that only Congress could create exceptions to the American rule. Hence Congress stepped in. It responded to *Alyeska Pipeline* by inserting "one-way" attorney fee rights benefiting citizens, when the suit is against the government (and, in some cases, against private parties), as part of the citizen suit provisions in over 100 environmental and other statutes. In some statutes,[28] a citizen can still recover costs, even if he or she loses on a technicality.[29] The Equal Access to Justice Act 1980[30] complemented specific cost provisions in particular statutes. It enables prevailing individuals, groups and small businesses to recover fees from government agencies except where the position of the agency is found to be substantially justified, or special circumstances would make an award unjust. The usual fee-limit for attorneys and expert witnesses is $75 per hour (s 504(b)(1)), with the result that smaller and non-profit firms, having lower overheads, are the main beneficiaries of the section. A further limitation on the scope of *Alyeska Pipeline* is that it is limited to federal courts. Some state courts have accepted the private attorney general costs theory rejected in *Alyeska Pipeline*.[31]

If public interest plaintiffs win in court or through out-of-court settlements, salaried lawyers in the non-profit advocacy organisations can often charge attorney's fees based on prevailing market rates.

Such is the constitutional and legislative climate in which a number of environmental advocacy organisations were born in the 1970s. Some of these organisations will be considered individually. Before doing so, however, the following section presents an example – regarding the enforcement of water pollution law – of the type of legal campaigns which such organisations have collectively initiated.

J. **The Federal Water Pollution Control Act (FWPCA) enforcement campaign**

In 1982, private pollution law enforcement actions increased significantly when a coalition of environmental advocacy organisations headed by the Natural Resources Defense Council (NRDC) initiated an enforcement campaign.

---

[28]See, for example, s 505 of FWPCA (*infra*).
[29]See Chapter 1, particularly n 94 and accompanying text.
[30]Section 504.
[31]For example, the California Supreme Court accepted the theory in *Serrano v Priest* 20 Cal 3d 25, 141 Cal Rptr 315, 569 P 2d 1303 (1977).

President Reagan had been elected in 1981. While the law remained the same, the new administration had a radically different attitude to environmental protection. A new focus was on deregulation, with regulatory impact analyses required before the EPA could complete its regulatory drafting duties mandated under FWPCA. Enforcement was low priority. The EPA abolished its Office of Enforcement and reorganised its enforcement attorneys three times, with resulting loss of concentration and continuity on enforcement actions. Compared to the year before the Reagan appointee to the EPA, Administrator Anne Burford, took office, enforcement cases initiated at the behest of the EPA through the Department of Justice declined 78% (from 175 cases to 38 cases).[32]

Believing the EPA's administration of the FWPCA had been wanting, the NRDC took action, using section 505 of FWPCA, which allows any person to commence civil proceedings against alleged violators of the Act.[33] Funded initially from a seed grant, the campaign was sustained by fees recovered in earlier cases to fund later ones. The NRDC coalition filed with the EPA 162 of 214 notices to sue under FWPCA between 1982 and April 1984. Sixty days' notice to the EPA, the polluter and the state government of intention to sue is required to encourage government enforcement action and settlement. As further illustration of the dimension of citizen suits, and of the organisations which bring them, some 806 notices of intent to sue were filed with the EPA between May 1984 and September 1988, over one half by only five specialist, public interest advocacy organisations.[34] The campaign was only possible because environmental monitoring results, documenting violations of standards and permits, are kept at regional EPA offices and are available for public inspection. The environmental organisations "piggy-backed" into court on the basis of the industry self-monitoring results kept by the EPA.

Most of the notices to sue resulted in prompt settlements, virtually all defences raised by polluters having been rejected by the courts in the early months of the campaign. In addition to a schedule for installing new mitigation equipment and fines to be paid in the event of non-achievement of abatement requirements, settlements have been dominated by payments to environmental organisations, rather than to the Treasury.[35] As discussed above, the non-profit advocacy organisations could recover above-cost attorney's fees. Further, civil fines payable under US law to the Treasury can be "converted" into "credit projects" involving payments to environmental groups (other than the petitioner) for research, education or land acquisition. During early-mid 1980s, total penalties paid as a result of environmental citizen suits grew to

---

[32]Yeager *op cit* at 318–319, citing Brown MA, "EPA Enforcement – Past, Present and Future" (1984) 3:1 *Environmental Forum* 12–22.
[33]See Greve *op cit* at 351–359.
[34]These were the Sierra Club and Sierra Club Legal Defense Fund, the Atlantic States Legal Foundation, the Natural Resources Defense Council, Friends of the Earth and Public Interest Research Groups. *Ibid*.
[35]Greve *op cit* at 358 and 359, citing five studies and analyses of citizen-suit settlements in the period 1983–86.

several million dollars annually.[36] In 1987 the Bethlehem Steel Corporation agreed to pay a $1.5 million penalty ($1 million to a third party environmental fund and the balance to Treasury) to settle an NRDC suit relating to the illegal discharge of thousands of tons of toxic waste into Chesapeake Bay.[37] The NRDC Citizen Enforcement Project has continued since 1987. For example, in 1992 $1.68 million was awarded against Texaco Refining and Marketing for hundreds of breaches of FWPCA involving illegal discharges into the Delaware River. This was the third largest penalty exacted by citizens in the FWPCA campaign to date.[38]

The development of some of the major advocacy organisations in the United States is outlined in the following section.

II. Organisations

A. Conservation Law Foundation (CLF)

The Conservation Law Foundation of New England Inc (CLF) was founded in 1966.[39] It is the oldest environmental law organisation in the United States. The catalyst for its formation was a plan to develop ski slopes in Berkshire County Park. Residents and the Massachusetts Forest and Park Association opposed the plan. Eventually, the residents hired private lawyers who succeeded in blocking the proposal, but the scramble to organise and raise funds prompted a director of the Park Association to establish a specialist advocacy group. An urban planner, an engineer and three lawyers joined him as volunteers, who undertook CLF work in the evenings and at weekends. Initially, CLF's primary function was to disseminate information on environmental planning and open spaces. Major issues were freeway developments, wetland conservation and informing citizens of the rights contained in NEPA and many new, state environmental laws. An early milestone was its friend-of-the-court brief in a Massachusetts Supreme Court case, in which the CLF sought to revive the public trust doctrine regarding a highway proposal involving in-filling a lake.[40]

The CLF relied on support from volunteers until 1972, when it employed a salaried, full-time executive director. Fund-raising efforts enabled the organisation to employ a second staff attorney within a year. The CLF wrote guides on

---

[36]*e.g.* 30 private enforcement actions against polluters in Connecticut alone were settled for payments in excess of $1.5 million between 1983 and 1986. Another 31 cases outside Connecticut in the same period resulted in payments of $5.1 million. See Greve *op cit* at 359.

[37]Yeager *op cit* at 321 citing *NRDC Newsline* April/May 1987. See also *Twenty Years Defending the Environment: NRDC 1970–1990*, NRDC, New York at 35–37.

[38]NRDC *Annual Report 1992* at 13. See also Chapter 1, section VII(C).

[39]Information about the CLF has been drawn from CLF publications *The First 25 Years*, Boston, 1991 and the *Annual Report 1992*.

[40]The "*Arlington Spy Pond*" case, 1967, discussed in CLF, *The First 25 Years*, Boston, 1991 at 5.

the new environmental laws, and concentrated its limited resources on the rule-making process. As discussed above, considerable scope exists in the US to help draft the regulations which provide the important detail to implement environmental statutes. Hence, the CLF lobbied other interest groups and administrators, using litigation more as a threat than a routine tool.

One occasion where litigation was resorted to related to protection of Atlantic Ocean fishing grounds. The US Interior Department announced plans to auction off oil drilling sites around the Georges Bank fishing area. In a series of cases before the District Court, Court of Appeals and Supreme Court, the CLF, suing in its own name rather than representing clients, succeeded in obtaining an injunction and delaying the sale for a number of years. By that time legislation had been passed by Congress protecting fishing grounds, and eventually, in 1990, President Bush declared a moratorium on oil drilling until the year 2000. The initial victories were achieved by taking a different approach to the EIS – not challenging its deficiencies so much as highlighting the greater economic importance of long-term fishing in comparison with the potential oil yield. As with so many environmental cases, the battle was fought ultimately at a political level, with the court proceedings serving to buy time and publicity for the issue.

In 1979 the CLF began to employ scientists in its bid to focus on constructive alternatives to bad development projects. Furthering this objective, in the 1980s the CLF gradually focussed on issues it believed to be of importance, rather than waiting until court cases arose or conservation groups sought its advice. For example, the CLF forced the state and federal governments to clean up Boston harbour, the dirtiest in the United States, by obtaining a court-ordered schedule in 1983 for infrastructure improvements, including a new sewerage treatment plant. The CLF initiated campaigns in such areas as energy and water conservation, transportation policy and fisheries management. Regarding energy policy, it has stressed the use of economic tools. For example, it successfully lobbied three states to give utilities a financial incentive to invest in energy conservation. It won a major hydro-electric case by showing that, by making its mills more efficient, the paper company consumer could save as much energy as the proposed dam would generate. Similarly, economic arguments relating to low return on investment for ratepayers were the basis of the CLF's lobbying of a number of power utilities, which eventually withdrew their support from a 1983 proposal to build a second nuclear reactor in the New England region. The CLF's regional focus was reinforced through the opening of branch offices in Vermont in 1987 and Maine in 1991.

By further developing its energy case successes in the early 1980s, towards the end of the decade the CLF was able to convince the Connecticut Department of Public Utility Control to require far greater investment in electrical efficiency. When private power companies sought approval for rate increases, the CLF highlighted the spiral of increasing energy wastage resulting in higher prices to pay for more energy production. Eventually, a

New England-wide energy conservation promotion company was funded by the power companies to become an on-going CLF subsidiary.

The CLF continues to focus upon New England energy, transportation, recycling, fishing and water pollution issues, and the protection of public values on both private and public land (for example in ski slope and beach-front property management and water licensing and supply management). Its campaigns, while often rooted in law (such as its lobbying for the enactment of the federal Residential Lead-Based Hazard Reduction Act 1992), have an increasingly scientific, lobbying or awareness-raising focus. For example, the CLF recently published a parent-education pamphlet "Renovating Your Home Without Lead Poisoning Your Children", and lobbied for loans and grants for low- and middle-income property owners to remove lead hazards in homes.

While the CLF held a specific "advocates fund" of $1.33 million in 1992, fee recovery amounted to only $5,000 of its $2.4 million budget. Most of its income ($1.83 million) came from 46 charitable foundations. Membership fees and donations provided an additional $0.51 million. Energy project initiatives, funded by power-generating utilities, provided $1.28 million income. Of its total expenditure of $2.3 million, $1.94 million related to projects, principally energy, transportation, marine resources and land protection. Approximately 9% of its expenditure ($0.21 million) related to securing members and funding ("development"). In 1992 the CLF had 34 board members, 36 members of staff (11 lawyers, 5 scientists, 14 management, administrative and support staff and 6 development staff) and had the assistance of 27 "intern" lawyers and approximately 60 volunteers.

The CLF had an active case-load in 1992 of 146 cases in five states, as well as a number of federal and international aid cases. The breakdown of case-subject areas was transportation 37 (26%), energy conservation 35 (24%), land 24 (17%), water resources 15 (10%), environmental health (mainly lead issues) 15 (9%), marine resources 12 (8%), clean air 4 (3%) and legal services (general advice) 4 (3%).

B. **Environmental Defense Fund (EDF)**

In 1967 the Environmental Defense Fund (EDF) was incorporated in New York by 10 scientists, lawyers and conservationists.[41] For the next five years the organisation's scientists gave evidence in cases fighting the use of DDT and dieldrin. Fuelled by the awareness created by Rachel Carson's publication *Silent Spring* (1962), the media interest in the cases was great, as was the publicity for EDF when DDT, dieldrin and other broad-based chlorinated hydrocarbon pesticides were finally banned nation-wide in 1972. The

---

[41]Information on the EDF has been taken from its *Twentieth Anniversary Report 1967–87* and *The Year in Review – 1993*.

President of the World Wildlife Fund (WWF) in the United States, Russell Train, proclaimed the EDF's work in bringing about the banning of DDT as one of the most important legal victories ever won for wildlife. Conservation groups in many states sought out the EDF for legal and scientific assistance in other issues, and the national advocacy organisation began to grow.

The EDF has emphasised alternatives, often with economic advantages, to the developments which it has opposed. For example, in order to pre-empt attempts to expand coal and nuclear power plants, the EDF developed a computer model to consider combined energy alternatives, such as conservation, cogeneration and load management which was eventually utilised by power-generating companies. It pioneered an irrigation water-conservation strategy based on allowing water saved through conservation to be traded.

Ongoing campaigns of the EDF concern wildlife and habitat preservation, marine pollution, acid rain and solid waste.

The international focus of EDF is perhaps greater than any other environmental law advocacy group in the United States. It has long-standing involvement in issues relating to marine pollution, ozone depletion and climate change, international bank financing of Third World development projects, and preservation of Antarctica.

The EDF had an income of $22.3 million in the year ending 30 September 1993.[42] As with the other major advocacy organisations, donations are tax-deductible. Contributions and bequests from more than 250,000 members accounted for $13.21 million, grants from foundations $6.12 million, government grants $0.79 million and bequests $0.51 million. Legal fees accounted for $0.65 million. Investment income comprised $0.35 million, and miscellaneous other revenues $0.67 million. On the expenditure side, in order of magnitude the EDF channelled its scientific and legal resources to toxic chemicals and solid waste, wildlife and water resources, energy and air quality, education and legislative action programmes. Fundraising comprised 14% of total outlays.

The EDF's board of trustees includes representatives of funding institutions, business, environmental and community organisations, as well as academics and private lawyers. At its six offices in 1993 it employed 23 lawyers, 41 scientists and economists, 7 media and newsletter staff, 14 development staff, 10 membership and public affairs staff, and 56 policy, support and finance staff.

C. **Sierra Club Legal Defense Fund (SCLDF)**

The Sierra Club was established as a conservation organisation in 1892. From its inception it had lobbied for protection of the forests of the Sierra Nevada in California. After years of private negotiations between the Forest Service, the Department of the Interior and the Disney Corporation, in 1968 it appeared

---

[42] I thank Pat Connaughton, Executive Assistant of the New York office for assistance with the EDF figures presented in this and the following paragraph.

that a proposal to create the world's largest ski resort in the remote Mineral King Valley would proceed, as access through the adjacent Sequoia National Park had been granted. The board of directors of the Sierra Club took the (then unusual) step of authorising the filing of a lawsuit to prevent the development.

The Club's Legal Committee obtained an opinion on the prospects of success from the single employee of the Conservation Law Society of America. On the strength of that assessment it briefed private lawyers to initiate proceedings in the District Court, which granted a preliminary injunction. The Forest Service successfully appealed on the interlocutory question of whether the Sierra Club had standing to bring the case. The Sierra Club took the question to the Supreme Court, which in 1971 granted leave for the question to be heard. In 1972 a majority of the Supreme Court affirmed the Court of Appeals' decision, and found that the Club had no right to sue.[43] However Justice Douglas' celebrated dissenting opinion, influenced by Professor Christopher Stone's paper "Do Trees Have Standing?",[44] advocated the conferral of standing on natural objects to sue for their own preservation. Justice Blackmun agreed, and highlighted a changing judicial attitude to the law of standing:[45]

> "The case poses – if only we choose to acknowledge and reach them – significant aspects of a wide, growing, and disturbing problem, that is, the Nation's and the world's deteriorating environment with its resulting ecological disturbances. Must our laws be so rigid and our procedural concepts so inflexible that we render ourselves helpless when the existing methods and the traditional concepts . . . do not prove to be entirely adequate for new issues?"

While the Sierra Club had lost the Supreme Court case, the decision suggested an alternative approach to the litigation, which was followed in 1972 by amending the original proceedings before the District Court. The revised complaint highlighted the interests of individual members of the Club in Mineral King and added, as co-plaintiffs, some property owners in and near the valley. Finally, it argued that the ski-resort proposal was in breach of NEPA, which had been enacted after the original proceedings were filed; no environmental impact statement had been prepared. The District Court reimposed the interim injunction, and the battle moved to the political arena, with debate raging over the resulting draft and final environmental impact assessments issued in 1975 and 1976. In 1977 the case was dismissed by the District Court for want of prosecution after the interim judgment. However, in 1988 Congress added Mineral King to Sequoia National Park. The litigation had bought time for the political process to work.

---

[43]*Sierra Club* v *Morton* 405 US 727, 92 S Ct 1361.
[44]*University of Southern California Law Review*, Spring 1972.
[45]Turner T, *Wild by Law: The Sierra Club Legal Defense Fund and the Places it Has Saved*, SCLDF, 1990 at 21.

During the course of the Mineral King litigation, the Sierra Club Legal Defense Fund (SCLDF) was incorporated as a separate entity from the Sierra Club, partly to enable donations to the legal arm to be tax-deductible, unlike those to the political arm. It was led by lawyer James Moorman, who, since 1967, had worked on environmental law issues with the Center for Law and Social Policy, one of the first "public interest law firms" (that is, funded mainly by benevolent foundations). In 1971 the Ford Foundation granted $98,000 to establish the SCLDF. It began with two lawyers in San Francisco in 1971.

The SCLDF has taken legal proceedings to protect the wilderness and fishing grounds of Admiralty Island, Alaska (1969–86), and with regard to coal and nuclear energy politics around the Colorado Plateau (since the early 1970s). Redwood National Park became the subject of litigation (1973–76) which resulted in a plea by a District Court for Congress to adequately fund the national park and the surrounding, logging-ravaged land. The EDF successfully campaigned for enlarging the park and funding to undertake a tree-planting and restoration programme.

The SCLDF has a continuing campaign to save endangered species. Illustrating the changing perception of environmental litigation, by 1978 when the SCLDF instigated proceedings pursuant to the Endangered Species Act 1973 to protect the Hawaiian palila honey-creeper and its habitat, the bird itself was named as a leading plaintiff in the case, and joined by an alliance of conservation groups. No opposition was raised as to the palila's standing. Similar cases concerning endangered woodpeckers and owls have been brought, as have proceedings regarding driftnet fishing.

As a result of the oil crisis of the early 1970s, the oil, coal and natural gas industries placed increasing pressure on the federal government to determine applications for mining or pumping leases in the northern Rocky Mountains. An area of contention related to Forest Service land. Initially the Forest Service refused to determine applications, presumably believing that it might provoke an un-winnable fight. Copying the example of the environmental non-profit law movement, industries set up their own public interest law foundations.[46] Donations were tax deductible, and cases were instituted to force lease applications to be determined and to challenge any rejections. In these cases SCLDF lawyers supported the government. They illustrate participatory democracy in the form of competing interest groups. The cases also serve as a reminder of the need to scrutinise public interest claimants. The underlying financial interests of mining and oil companies made hollow the public interest claim of these "off-the-shelf", non-profit legal foundations.

While in more recent years the SCLDF has campaigned for international recognition of a human right to the environment at Rio de Janeiro and Geneva, it regards Endangered Species Act cases, ancient forest and timber sale cases, and air and water pollution cases as its core concerns.

---

[46]Pacific Legal Foundation of Colorado and Mountain States Legal Foundation.

In addition to its San Francisco headquarters, the SCLDF has regional offices in eight states. As at 31 July 1992 its budget was $10 million, with approximately 30 full-time lawyers. The SCLDF has 150,000 financial supporters, of which about one-quarter live in California. Contributions from individuals account for over 60% of total income. One method of fund-raising from individuals is through Earth Share, a federation of environmental organisations co-operating in workplace payroll deduction campaigns. In 1991–92 each of more than 40 foundations made grants to the Sierra Club EDF of over $5,000. Of the $10 million budget in 1991–92, approximately $1 million came in the form of legal services provided by outside lawyers on a reduced-fee or no-fee basis. Court-awarded attorney fees income amounted to $659,625. Some 81% of expenditure went to support litigation, while 19% related to fund-raising and administration.[47]

D. Natural Resources Defense Council (NRDC)

In 1969 a group of third-year Yale law students and some New York lawyers independently approached the Ford Foundation for funding to establish a law firm for the environment. The Foundation made a grant of $158,000, on condition that the two groups combined forces. Operating from three rooms of New York's Bar Building rented at a discount, the Natural Resources Defense Council (NRDC) opened its doors for business in 1970.[48]

In 1976, the law changed to allow limited lobbying by tax-exempt organisations, resulting in increasing involvement of the NRDC in law-making and regulatory processes. In its early years the NRDC changed from a role of representing other environmental groups to becoming a membership organisation advising its own members.

Reflecting strong technical and scientific backup, research and publications on environmental issues are a feature of NRDC campaigns. Foremost amongst these is its quarterly journal, *Amicus*. Consistent with the interdisciplinary approach of the NRDC, and of its broad readership (comprising 70,000 subscribers in 1987), *Amicus* is a journal for the general public on environmental affairs, combining investigative journalism with commentary on national and international policy, book reviews and poetry.

NRDC staff produce both technical and consumer-oriented publications on a number of issues. Amongst its 19 publications in 1992, for example, were a guide to energy efficiency, an agenda for clean water, its fourth databook on nuclear weapons, and guides to recycling, pesticides and rainforest conservation.

---

[47]*Annual Report 1991–92*.
[48]The following discussion is based on information contained in the NRDC *Fifteen Years Report 1970–85: Twenty Years Defending the Environment*, *Annual Report 1988*, *Annual Report 1992* and *Amicus Journal* (1987) 9:4.

While other advocacy organisations provide information to citizens and environmental organisations, the NRDC has extended its education to self-help workshops. For example, it trained 1,200 citizen activists to participate in reviews of industrial discharge permits, and, subsequently, in how to oversee revisions to state water quality standards. The NRDC water law enforcement campaign, discussed in Section 1(j), was only possible because of volunteer help from law students and citizens.

The cross-section of NRDC campaigns and cases is as broad as any of the US advocacy organisations. It has six major programs: air and energy, international and nuclear, water, land, cities and health.

In 1978 its litigation forced the EPA to produce a standard for airborne lead emissions from automobiles and industries, and in 1984 standards to control particulate emissions from diesel engines. The NRDC obtained a court order striking down a "sweetheart" deal between the EPA and General Motors, under which the EPA had agreed to overlook defective pollution control devices on 700,000 cars in return for a promise to make cars cleaner in the future. Following a 1972 court victory, which stopped the EPA from allowing industry to disperse pollutants through taller stacks, rather than through control devices required under the Clean Air Act 1970, in 1977 Congress adopted legislation reinforcing the court judgment. In 1988, as a result of negotiations between the NRDC and industry, Congress enacted the National Appliance Energy Conservation Act 1988, aimed at reducing energy use by imposing national appliance energy standards. Acting on an NRDC proposal, in 1992 some 24 power generation companies collectively offered $30 million to the first manufacturer to mass produce low energy-consuming, non-CFC refrigerators.

The NRDC has campaigned on resource pricing and conservation. In a 1973 case it forced the Bureau of Land Management to undertake environmental impact assessment of its grazing policy over semi-arid land. The NRDC has promoted the idea of cross-compliance, according to which farmers need to follow environmentally sustainable practices in order to qualify for federal agricultural assistance. The organisation is now campaigning for more advanced provisions in the Farm Bill, scheduled for re-authorisation in 1995. Against the threat of an NRDC court case to protect a spotted owl species, in 1992 the US Forest Service adopted a more benign management plan for forests in California's Sierra Nevada. Clear-cutting is forbidden, as is removal of the largest, oldest trees, and employment-creating forest-restoration initiatives are included.

The NRDC played a leading role in the campaign resulting in the decision of Congress in 1983 to terminate development of a plutonium prototype breeder reactor. It successfully campaigned for the passage of the federal Facilities Compliance Act 1992, which subjects federal agencies to the same standards that apply to private nuclear weapons plants, as well as the decision of Congress to ban nuclear weapons testing.

The NRDC believes that its health programme has affirmed the public's right of access to health and safety data on all marketed pesticides, has provoked more open decision-making practices between the chemical industry and the EPA, and was instrumental in the passage in 1992 of lead poisoning prevention legislation.

The international activities of the NRDC have included the drafting of recommendations, ultimately backed up through legislation, for environmental reform by multilateral development banks and the US Agency for International Development, providing information to foreign environmental organisations and governments on pesticides and toxic substances, and between 1985 and 1988, exchanges with the (then) Soviet Academy of Sciences regarding nuclear testing verification. Since the breakup of the Soviet Union, it has, in conjunction with the Federation of American Scientists, held workshops for Russian and US Government officials on verified dismantlement of nuclear weapons and the disposition of fissile material.

Perhaps the NRDC's most famous and influential litigation related to toxic chemicals. Under FWPCA, toxic pollutants (those causing death, disease or genetic mutation) were to be stringently controlled.[49] The basis for regulation was health grounds and effects on food chains. Economic factors were to play a lesser role in regulating toxic substances in comparison with conventional pollutants. The size of the task of listing toxic substances was enormous, and made more difficult because of uncertainty and controversy as to safe levels of exposure. The risk-benefit and cost-benefit analysis process inevitably resulted in the EPA erring on the side of industry. In bargaining with producers "over what is to be the reality of regulation, law inescapably reflects the favored status of major producers".[50]

The FWPCA gave the EPA non-discretionary toxic substance listing duties. When the EPA failed to meet the deadlines, the NRDC initiated a number of agency forcing suits, resulting in a judicially set, new regulatory framework and timetable for compliance regarding 65 priority toxic substances (the "Flannery Decree").[51] Even then, the timetable was modified in court eight times between 1979 and 1987. Aspects of the Flannery Decree were eventually incorporated in the 1977 FWPCA amendments.[52] The Flannery Decree had the effect of orienting the EPA away from the absolutist toxic effects considerations and towards the "best available [existing] technology" standard. This was more desirable from industry's standpoint, and, resolving the previous uncertainty as to how it should proceed, gave the EPA a mandate to draft regulations according to existing technological and cost factors at a time when other

---

[49]See n 5 *supra*.

[50]Yeager *op cit* at 296.

[51]*NRDC v Train* DDC 1976; 8 ERC 2120.

[52]Congress adopted yet another toxics regulatory approach in FWPCA 1987. These are finally being implemented in the 1990s.

branches of the EPA were in crisis and suffering budget cuts and deregulatory pressures.[53]

The NRDC has the largest legal and technical staff of the US environmental organisations. By 1992 its original six-lawyer office in New York had become a 30-lawyer network with offices in New York, Washington DC, San Francisco, Los Angeles and Honolulu. Technical support included 40 staff scientists and policy resource specialists. As at 1988, over one-third of the senior attorneys and scientists had over 10 years' experience with the organisation. In 1992 its program staff were supported by 26 assistants, an administration and finance staff of 28, a communications staff of 12 and a development staff of 32.

NRDC policy is set by its board of trustees, whose members include a minority of representatives of major funding organisations. The trustees are advised by six advisory volunteer boards.

The 170,000 members of the NRDC contributed 59% of its income of $18 million in 1992. Major, regular donations from approximately 400 individuals account for over one-quarter of total membership income. Over 100 foundations provided 32% of NRDC's income. Of the balance of 9% ($1.7 million) other income, court-awarded fees amounted to only $0.23 million. NRDC expenses for 1992 totalled $16.5 million. Of this, 77% was channelled to its "programs" (mainly the environmental programs, then scientific support and public education). While the organisation states that the cost of providing membership services in 1992 amounted to 6% of total expenditure, "development" and "management and general" accounted for an additional 9% and 18% of total expenditure respectively.

E. **The Western Environmental Law Center, Oregon and the role of smaller public interest law firms**

A choice for advocacy organisations relates to optimal size. The peak US law firms considered above have not followed the "small is beautiful" advice of the 1960s. They have developed branch offices in response to the increasingly regional, national and international dimensions of environmental problems. An issue is whether increasing size, or dependence on funding from conservative benevolent foundations and other institutions, results in bureaucratic lethargy, or even "capture".[54]

Some groups have preferred to remain small, allowing greater informality in organisational structure, and stronger links with "grass-roots" planning and pollution issues of local importance. Despite the lack of administrative support, they maintain that small-scale operation does not exclude undertaking work of wide, or even national significance. Understandably, the smaller advocacy firms tend not to be membership organisations, as membership

---

[53]Yeagher *op cit* at 216–234.
[54]"Capture" is also referred to in Chapter 16 at n 66, p 308.

services and development demand specialist resources beyond those which a handful of staff can provide.

Thus a number of smaller firms[55] complement the work of the four larger public interest environmental organisations already considered. They typically employ between one and five attorneys.

Additionally, there are approximately 12 environmental law clinics attached to universities. Each has one or two lawyers and from 5 to 20 students, usually students in their final years of post-graduate study. One of the founding environmental law clinics developed in Oregon in 1966. Two of the environmental law professors and activists at Oregon University, John Bonine and Michael Axline are also co-directors of the Western Environmental Law Center (formerly Clinic). Environmental law students can undertake part of their training by researching and running public interest cases at the Center.

Law clinics are an important component of legal education in US universities. In contrast to the position in the United Kingdom and many common law countries, in the United States less emphasis is placed upon formal training of graduates within law firms (articles of clerkship) or specialist, postgraduate colleges for the development of practical legal skills. In America these skills are developed as part of the law faculty education.

Another environmental litigation clinic is attached to Pace University Law School, New York.[56] The clinic has a classroom component and a practical component, in which supervised students act as attorneys. The main client of the in-house clinic is the Hudson River Fishermen's Association. The efforts of the clinic's students and professors have resulted in precedents being set regarding the FWPCA and the Resource Conservation and Recovery Act. In 1990 the clinic's students successfully challenged the budget-induced decision of Westchester County to close eight parks. The clinic interns filed suit to block the closing of the parks on two grounds – failure to prepare an EIS, and breach of the public trust doctrine, contending that the government breached its duty as trustee in denying the public access to the Hudson River through the parks. There is also an extern clinic, in which students represent the New York Department of Environmental Conservation at its regional offices, for example in enforcement cases relating to hazardous waste and pesticide misuse.

Smaller public interest law firms, such as the one at Western Environmental Law Center, Oregon, can contribute more creatively and independently than some of the "institutionalised", membership advocacy groups. For example, in 1980, taking up Justice Douglas' suggestion that "public concern for protecting nature's ecological equilibrium should lead to the conferral of standing upon

---

[55]These include the Southern Utah Wilderness Alliance, Atlantic States Legal Foundation, Trustees for Alaska, Headwaters, Center for Law in the Public Interest (Los Angeles), New Mexico Environmental Law Center, Southern Environmental Law Center and the Legal Environmental Assistance Foundation. The National Wildlife Federation has a number of regional legal offices.

[56]Information in this paragraph is sourced from the environmental law prospectus of the Pace University School of Law, 1992.

environmental objects to sue for their own preservation",[56a] Axline filed an administrative appeal in the name of Stryx Occidentalis Carina (the northern spotted owl) and the Lane County Audubon Society.[56b]

What follows is a discussion of three internal issues for public interest law organisations, and an initial assessment of their contribution in the United States.

III. Management issues

A. Salaries and social change

A development in 1983 at the CLF touched upon a sensitive issue to non-profit organisations: staff salary levels. Until then, staff turnover had been too high as poorly paid lawyers burnt out, or left for jobs which could support a family. In 1983, the CLF executive director began to assemble a team of staff lawyers and scientists with salaries nearly double what CLF lawyers had been paid previously. The result was greater staff longevity, with seven of the staff members employed in 1991 having over seven years experience with the organisation. For example, Peter Shelley had been a law student assisting CLF in the Georges Bank case, and then worked for five years with the Pennsylvania Attorney General's Department. He rejoined CLF when the salaries were increased. "The paradigm wasn't going to be lean, hungry and frantic. It was going to be a more competent, professional and sustainable kind of staff that was prepared to seek long-term employment with CLF."[57]

The decision of a social change organisation to follow the "professional" rather than the "lean" path will be problematic for some. Commitment, it could be argued, is indicated by the staff members' willingness to accept below-market salaries. On the other hand, perhaps a middle ground can be found, with salaries sufficiently high to build a career in the public interest field, though below what private lawyers are paid.

The pay issue also illustrates a phenomenon in the evolution of some advocacy organisations. They begin as fringe groups of concerned people working in their spare time. Broader social change ideologies, such as democracy in the workplace, may be promoted together with the environmental objectives. As the organisations began to employ more staff, fund-raise on a professional basis and plan activities and priorities, rather than waiting for clients to bring cases to them, the "lean" look can be replaced by a far more bureaucratic one. Certainly, the largest US environmental advocacy organisations have nothing of the "Seventies look" about them. They are now multi-million dollar organisations which have established their credibility before

---

[56a]See n 43 *supra*.

[56b]The northern spotted owl litigation was subsequently pursued by SCLDF. See n 76 *infra*.

[57]CLF, *The First 25 Years*, Boston, 1991 at 13.

the courts and agencies, and which compete with each other for clients, members and foundation support.

The above observation is relevant to countries with more fledgling conservation advocacy groups, such as Canada, the United Kingdom, Malaysia, Sri Lanka, India, Peru, Ecuador, Colombia, Australia and others, where choices have yet to be made regarding which of the divergent ideologies to follow. Some may wish to follow the more conservative path of the well-oiled, third voice in debates between developers and regulators, and seeking financial support from major institutions and foundations. Others will prefer to remain lean, without having to compromise broader agendas for social and lifestyle change which they regard as necessary to achieve sustainable living.[58]

B. **Networking and the Environmental Law Alliance Worldwide (E-LAW)**

Advocacy organisations and their client conservation groups have common goals. Communication is thus important for co-ordination and efficiency. As noted with regard to the NRDC water pollution enforcement campaign, organisations often pool their resources as co-plaintiffs in litigation.

One networking measure developed by the EDF since 1985 has been an Environmental Information Exchange, which seeks to make available EDF's legal and scientific expertise and data to environmental groups across the country. In return, recipient groups provide information on state and regional developments.

Another networking initiative is the annual public interest environmental law conference at the University of Oregon. It is the key gathering in the field. Starting from an initial 75 attendees in 1982, the annual attendance has grown to over 2,000 in the 1990s. With over 200 speakers on 90 different discussion panels, the event had become a festival of public interest law and science. Now organised entirely by law students, the conference has been the launching pad into a public interest law career for its student organisers, who as lawyers have gone to work for the National Wildlife Federation, the Southern Utah Wilderness Alliance, the Trustees for Alaska, the Nature Conservancy, US Senate committees, and other organisations. This aspect of the Oregon conference is significant, as public interest environmental lawyers comprise only about 2% of all environmental lawyers in the United States.

---

[58]"Sustainable living" is, on one view, preferable to the expression "sustainable development", which critics regard as potentially self-contradictory. The latter has been defined as "Development that meets the needs of the present without compromising the ability of future generations to meet their own needs" (World Commission on Environment and Development (Brundtland Commission), *Our Common Future*, 1987. Its economic implications have been discussed in Pearce D, Markandya A and Barbier EB, *Blueprint for a Green Economy*, London, Earth Scan Publications, 1989 and Pearce D, *Blueprint for a Green Economy 3: Measuring Sustainable Development*, 1993. For one example of statutory entrenchment of the sustainability concept, see Chapter 16 at n 36.

A further Oregon-inspired network is the Environmental Law Alliance Worldwide (E-LAW) and its use of electronic mail. E-LAW is an international network of public interest environmental lawyers dedicated to working together and sharing information across borders. E-LAW began work in 1991 and has helped lawyers from 50 countries work together to obtain expert evidence and data, legal precedents and general information on current environmental law issues, using electronic mail as a primary communication medium. E-LAW has offices in 13 countries and the US office of E-LAW has six staff with expertise in science, law and languages. E-LAW is particularly attractive for its potential for grass roots' advocates, not just specialists employed in large organisations, to communicate and become involved in issues of broader and international scope. For example, problems being tackled by the E-LAW network in 1993 and 1994 included packaging laws in the United States, international trade in wildlife and plutonium, pulp mills in Indonesia, toxic release and pollutant inventories in the United States and Australia, the use of leaded petrol in India and nuclear energy liability issues in Russia.

The E-LAW offices provide litigation support, scientific and technical research, research on comparative US law, information about multinational companies, advice on litigation and legislative strategies and links with attorneys, scientists and citizen groups with expertise on environmental issues. By supporting environmental attorneys in their own countries, E-LAW seeks to build a lasting structure to make law an effective tool to protect the environment in every country. Whereas the international environmental programs of some of the larger advocacy organisations have relatively weak links with organisations in the countries in which they advocate change, E-LAW is quite the opposite. It fosters environmental protection cases around the world by helping local advocates on issues they select, rather than by attempting to create a campaign headquarters within the United States.[59]

C. **Lawyer–client relationships**

US public interest firms both initiate proceedings in their own names and act on behalf of clients. Regarding the former, well-defined priorities for litigation are desirable. Close links with environmental organisations can ensure that the law centres' priorities reflect those of the broader environmental movement. External advisory or management boards can also advise on policy questions. With regards to acting on behalf of clients, there is a need for clients to be aware of the law centre's right to cease acting where essentially private

---

[59]Requests for assistance from E-LAW or offers of assistance to E-LAW public environmental attorneys around the world may be communicated by contacting the US office of E-LAW at elaw.usoffice@conf.igc.apc.org. E-LAW administers an Econet conference entitled elaw.public.int. The postal address of the US office of E-LAW is 1877 Garden Avenue, Eugene, OR, 97403, USA.

interest questions emerge. In contrast to the traditional client–lawyer relationship, public interest lawyers have an ideological stake in the outcome of a case. Public interest lawyers will be more selective of the clients and instructions they are willing to accept. A clear understanding of objectives is desirable, as those of the client may vary from those of their public interest lawyers. For example, the client may, for campaigning purposes, wish the lawyer to fight at all costs, whereas the lawyers will not be willing to act unless there is an arguable legal case.[60] While advocates may face this problem in representing many causes, both private and public, it is likely to be more of a problem in public interest issues, in which political and other non-financial factors play a greater role in the decision to litigate. Similarly, where compensation is an issue, a particular client may wish to accept an offered sum in out-of-court settlement; however the lawyer may wish for a precedent to be set in court.

IV. Evaluation

While recognising that public interest environmental law firms comprise only a very small cog in the extensive legal and environmental decision-making machinery, since the 1970s the firms examined in this study have flourished, even in the face of declining financial support and membership of other environmental organisations in the United States.[61]

The organisations are funded principally by donations from members and grants from philanthropic foundations. The four largest organisations examined in this chapter spent, in the years stated, between 6 and 15% of their income on fund-raising, and received between 0.2% and 6.6% of their income from awards of attorneys' fees.[62]

Enforcement of environmental laws by public interest non-government organisations can augment and spur the efforts of government regulatory

---

[60]Most state civil procedure codes, and rule 11 of the federal civil procedure code, require lawyers to certify that they have investigated and found a basis for the case to be brought, both in fact and in law.

[61]The membership of Greenpeace USA declined from 2,500,000 in 1990 to 1,700,000 in 1993. Over the same period, the membership of National Audubon Society decreased from 578,000 to 542,000, membership of the Sierra Club decreased from 622,000 to 550,000 and membership of the Wilderness Society decreased from 404,000 to 300,000. Part of the reason is said to be the disappearance of the element of alarm, particularly present when "the frightening [Reagan-appointed] James Watt was Secretary of the Interior", the success of new "brown" lobbying groups, and the perception that some green groups have been "co-opted by big money" from charities, grants and investments (Horn B, "Environmental Groups: As Green Turns to Brown", 5 March 1994, *The Economist* 53).

The above criticisms do not appear to be applicable to the legal advocacy organisations studied, which rely to a greater extent on income from members, and which, as described, work in less visible and media-driven ways than some other organisations, such as Greenpeace. Over the same period the membership of EDF in fact grew from 200,000 to 250,000, and that of NRDC from 138,000 to 170,000 (*ibid*).

[62]Awarded attorneys' fees accounted for the following percentages of total income for the organisations examined: CLF: 0.2% in 1992; EDF: 2.9% in 1993; SCLDF: 6.6% in 1991–92; and NRDC: 1.3% in 1993.

agencies.[63] However, Greve has argued that "the real purpose and effect of citizen suits is not efficient law enforcement but the subsidization of political constituencies".[64] Greve objects to the diversion of settlement payments by pollution offenders away from the Treasury and to environmental organisations under "credit project" arrangements. Perhaps caution is needed regarding the destination of settlement funds to dissuade opportunistic, rather than public interest litigation.[65] However, if caution is needed to prevent opportunism, it is also needed to keep alive private enforcement actions, which have countered periods of government agency inactivity. The complaint that settlement proceeds do not finish in government coffers rings hollow for settlements achieved through non-government initiative after government inaction. In any event, the financial operations of the four largest advocacy organisations examined indicate that court-awarded fees are an extremely small source of funds. Finally, transfer payments from illegal polluters to environmental organisations for the purposes of education and land conservation would appear to be uncontroversial and benign.

An appraisal of the advocacy organisations must also consider the environmental laws which enable them to exist. The early public interest cases on NEPA succeeded because the legislation contained clear standards on substance and procedure. Public interest advocates preserved through the courts the legislative gains introduced by NEPA in the inevitable period of low-visibility politics following the passage of the law.[66] In contrast, subsequent water resource development challenges failed in their attempt to obtain substantive review of agency decision-making because the legislation was vague about the grounds of judicial review.

One criticism of US environmental law has already been discussed: it sets ambitious goals, but delegates the all-important task of balancing economic and environmental factors to the EPA. Faced with scientific uncertainty, an open and challengeable standard-setting process, and ultimately questions of a political rather than technical nature, the EPA cannot cope, and excessive litigation results as mandatory timetables to issue regulations are sought to be enforced, standards are challenged, and the EPA finds opposition both when it brings and fails to bring enforcement actions. Critics argue that the legislation is disingenuous about the true cost and practicability of environmental goals,

---

[63]Greve *op cit* at 340–341.

[64]Greve *op cit* at 392.

[65]As noted, penalties paid in citizen suits brought to stop illegal pollution do not go to the plaintiff organisations, but to the US Treasury or to environmentally beneficial projects. I have heard of only one instance of opportunistic litigation, relating to a lawyer in Oregon, unsupported by environmental groups, who is said to bring deadline-forcing actions against the Forestry Service with the intention of settling out of court upon payment of his legal fees (Professor Susan Smith, Willamette University College of Law, Salem, Oregon, personal communication 1992).

[66]Trubeck DM and Gillen WJ, "Environmental Defense II: Examining the Limits of Interest Group Advocacy" in *Public Interest Law: An Economic and Institutional Analysis*, Berkeley, University of California Press, 1978 at 216.

enabling citizen suits to interfere with the ability of public agencies to craft compromise solutions. Further, critics charge that citizen suits throw too broad a role onto the federal court judges. Economic cost and environmental benefit questions, it is argued, should be determined by the legislature, not the executive and, by default, the judiciary. Because the legislation is so ambitious, yet delegates all-important detail, it has become a litigious minefield.

As argued earlier,[67] the criticism places anachronistic reliance on the potential of legislation, and the separability of the three government functions. It appears to be rooted in a view of representative democracy which has long been rejected in favour of a more participatory and pluralist model. Congress cannot possibly handle the immense detail of environmental regulation. Rule-making is properly the concern of the executive, under the supervision of the judiciary and always open to public scrutiny. The "Flannery decree" illustrates the potential synergy of the arms of government. The EPA response to FWPCA regarding toxic substance control was inadequate, and the judicial decree helped it over an impasse by setting an achievable standard-setting agenda for toxic substances, and ultimately provided the basis for amendments to legislation. Another example of public interest litigation "focusing public attention on a problem and forcing Congress to address it",[68] is the debate in forestry management on clear-cutting. Congress had avoided the issue, deferring to state delegations from big timber-producing states.[69] However, public interest litigation created a precedent which escalated the controversy and placed the issue high on the priority list for Congress, which duly enacted the National Forest Management Act 1976.

With regard to the criticism that citizen suits can interfere with the ability of public agencies to craft compromise solutions, this reflects a view that agencies alone can reflect the public interest. As Bonine[70] points out, however, agencies can indeed be better equipped to implement laws if interests other than those of the regulated community are put forward:

> "The only way that the agency action can steer a middle course, with the constant onslaught of industry lawyers (who will always have the right to participate because of the economic interest of their clients) is to have a robust public interest bar and right of participation. Then the agency officials can occasionally do more than half-implement the law, compromising between the will of the people in passing it and the resistance of the industry being regulated. The 'compromise' can now take into account the environmentalist perspective as well."

---

[67]See the text accompanying n 21 *supra*.
[68]Parker *op cit*.
[69]*West Virginia Division of Izaak Walton League Inc* v *Butz*, 367 F Supp 422 (NDWV 1973), affirmed 522 F 2d 945 (4th Circ 1975), as discussed in Parker *op cit*.
[70]Bonine J, personal communication on an earlier draft of this chapter.

Assessment of the effects of US environmental activism in terms of case outcomes is bound to be misleading. While many of its cases have ended as courtroom defeats, the SCLDF argues for a broader assessment of the effectiveness of its litigation. Litigation is merely a means which "can prolong battles until the public at large becomes aware of the dispute and can work its will through its elected representatives".[71] The SCLDF argues that litigation puts power into the hands of the otherwise powerless. "It is the one means by which citizens can demand that their rights be respected, that their laws be enforced and obeyed".[72] The opposite also applies: bad environmental projects do proceed, despite initial, successful legal challenges relating to non-compliance with technical or formal requirements.

One argument against legal activism relates to the waste associated with adversarial litigation. Relationships between regulatory agencies, industry and the public may become guarded. The possibility of frank disclosure of an environmental problem is reduced where there is the threat of litigation. The massive proportion of the total costs of US Superfund litigation going to lawyers fighting over the liability of potentially responsible parties, rather than to actual remediation of contaminated sites, is cited as an example of the wastefulness of regulatory systems which rely on litigation.

In analysing the criticism that environmental litigation is wasteful, full cost accounting should be used. For example, in deciding whether to extract minerals from a natural area having spiritual significance to indigenous people, ecological importance and recreational value, cost-benefit analyses may understate the non-financial considerations. Yeager argues that cost-benefit analyses will inherently be biased, "reflecting the favoured status of major producers".[73] The benefits of litigation resulting in protection of basic but non-financial ecological values can also be easily neglected by those arguing against citizen suits. There are substantial financial costs in battles to protect the environment, but these must be seen in the light of the more fundamental cost posed by the threat of environmental degradation.

Further, respect for alternative viewpoints can develop where interested parties have recourse to the courts. Injunctions can allow agencies to find better ways of achieving their long-term objectives. For example, injunctions following the northern spotted owl case[74] and a windstorm provided impetus

---

[71]Turner *op cit* at xvii.
[72]*Ibid*.
[73]Yeager *op cit* at Chapter 8, "Ecology, Economy and the Evolution of Limits"; see also at 296.
[74]*Seattle Audubon Society* v *Moseley* (WD Wa., No. C92-479WD, 14 May, 1993). The northern spotted owl litigation has resulted in more than 15 federal trial and appellate court judgments addressing the responsibilities of three federal agencies under a half a dozen environmental laws (see also Chapter 1, section VII(A)(1)(b). The litigation has compelled the government to take major steps to protect old-growth forests and the species which inhabit them: True TD (SCLDF attorney, Seattle), "Litigation to Protect the Northern Spotted Owl and the Ancient Forest Ecosystem" unpublished paper presented at the Environmental Law Network International (ELNI) annual conference, 13–15 October 1994, Strasbourg. The Secretariat of ELNI is the Oko-Institut, whose address can be found at n 1 in Chapter 3.

for a change of management approach by the Forest Service in one part of Oregon. "Stewards" were appointed for long-term, multi-use management, not just timber production, and clear-cutting was banned. The District Ranger attributed "chaos, controversy, injunctions and blowdown" as the four factors which enabled a change of direction, and the opportunity to try a more holistic approach to forestry.[75]

It should also be remembered that litigation is only one tool of advocacy organisations – education, consciousness-raising, research and law reform are important aspects of their work. In fact, the profile of some of the largest organisations is now more non-litigious than litigious. The EDF, for example, described more than 20 non-litigious activities[76] as compared with only three court cases[77] as its achievements for 1993. The advocacy organisations are multi-faceted, working for change through policy process, media and Congress as well as the courts. By becoming constituent organisations, representing hundreds of thousands of members, they have also increased their lobbying strength beyond that of mere advisers. In the context of interdisciplinary approaches to environmental management – through scientific research, education, lobbying, partnerships with industry and litigation – it is apparent that to focus on the wastefulness associated with litigation is out of proportion to the role of court cases in the broader agenda of advocacy for change. If litigation is wasteful, then so too must be policy debate, media reporting and scientific research, because each involves exploration of environmental management options which may not ultimately be followed.

A final rejoinder to the "litigation is wasteful" criticism of environmental advocacy organisations is premised on the desirability of enlarging governmental and citizen responsibility for the environment. Broadened environmental responsibility has been long-recognised as a prerequisite for change.[78]

---

[75]Parker *op cit*.

[76]The variety and creativity of these activities warrants listing: obtaining the co-operation of major paper buyers to increase the demand for environmentally preferable paper; a river habitat protection - clean-energy generation project in conjunction with a power company; public service advertising to promote recycling and combat lead poisoning; devising and advocating a plan to improve air quality and reduce water pollution in cities bordering Mexico; use by an additional power company of the EDF computer program to improve energy efficiency; promotion of alternatives to single-occupant motor vehicles; participation in a "clean air credits" project to stimulate private investment in cleaner motor vehicles; undertaking pollution testing in the Arctic Circle; advocating re-authorisation of the Endangered Species Act; initiating a pilot project to pay land-owners who improve the suitability of their land for the endangered red-cockaded woodpecker; advising Vice-President Gore on environmentally sound options to reduce flooding; and lobbying the World Bank and the African Development Bank on environmentally destructive dam, mining and rainforest-felling projects. See Environmental Defense Fund, *The Year in Review – 1993*.

[77]One case established that NEPA applies to government activities outside US borders (such as the incineration of rubbish at a US research station in Antarctica). Another case, concerning the lead and cadmium content of ash from the incineration of solid waste, is to be heard by the Supreme Court. The third case helped defend California's green marketing law, which seeks to prohibit misleading advertising claims in advertising and labels. *Ibid*.

[78]Lutz RE, "The Laws of Environmental Management: A Comparative Study" (1976) *American Journal of Comparative Law* 447–520; Robinson D, "Public Participation in Environmental Decision-Making" (1993) 10 *Environmental Planning and Law Journal* 330.

The principle of public participation was endorsed by 178 countries present at the Earth Summit.[79] If a citizen or an interest group has a concern, but (for any number of reasons) cannot obtain action from government or industry, then advocacy organisations can help to bridge the gap. Litigation, just one "arrow in the quiver" available to advocacy organisations, can widen debate through the media and put pressure on government to deal with the problem. Advocacy organisations thus provide a credible avenue for concerned people to express their commitment.[80] For example, even the conservative *Wall Street Journal* has described the role of the NRDC as that of a "shadow EPA", drafting legislation, winning lawsuits, forcing agencies to rethink regulations, and conducting private enforcement of water pollution offences. Without citizen suits, sceptical attitudes about the inertia of governments and industry would result in genuinely concerned people dropping out of the environmental body politic. Environmental advocacy organisations thus allow ideological commitment to be filtered and expressed in a number of practical ways.[81]

On a comparative level, patriotism should play no part in assessing the US experience. Too often observers from other common law countries summarily dismiss US litigious culture, without considering the efficacy of discretionary or less participatory environmental management systems in their own countries. A hybrid of elements developed from the experience of various jurisdictions should be considered.

A comprehensive analysis of the effectiveness of the industrial water pollution control regime in the United States has concluded that only modest improvements have been made in the last two decades.[82] There is no doubt, however, that a pivotal role in achieving compliance has been played by advocacy organisations. For example, with only four members of staff and a budget amounting to only 2% of EPA's own water enforcement budget, in 1984 the NRDC brought more suits against violators than the agency.[83] The control of industrial pollution is essentially a bargaining process. A fact of present political economy is that a state's dependence upon production and profits

---

[79]Principle 10 of the Rio Declaration on Environment and Development, 1992.
[80]Cited in NRDC, *Twenty Years Defending the Environment 1970–1990.*
[81]Ayres R, in NRDC, *Twenty Years Defending the Environment 1970–1990* at 19.
[82]Yeager *op cit* generally and at 242–250 in particular. Yeager concludes that implementation of the FWPCA substantially reduced discharges of conventional pollutants, such as dissolved oxygen, faecal coliform bacteria, suspended solids, total dissolved solids and phosphorus, in some regions and "worst case" examples in the United States. However, water quality considered nationwide had not improved by 1982, some 10 years after the dramatic FWPCA amendments. Non-point source pollution and the near total failure of the FWPCA program regarding toxics were to blame. The nation had accomplished little more than an "unstable holding action" against the environmental deterioration associated with a real gross national product increase of over 40% in the period 1970–82. Economic impacts of the clean water law were tolerable during the period. In attempting to balance economic costs and environmental benefits, the law appeared to have favoured the former, particularly regarding the control of toxics. The law may have created a diseconomy of scale for smaller industrial concerns, however, who could not afford to negotiate with the EPA as effectively as large corporations.
[83]Yeager *op cit* at 321.

ultimately outweighs its mandate to protect the environment.[84] That being so, it is all the more important to enable citizens to oversee agency actions, to contribute, albeit with unequal resources, to standard-setting and rule-making, and to be able to call on the courts for help where, for capture, dependence, inertia, lack of resources or political pressure agencies fail to implement or enforce the law.

Further empirical analysis is needed. This survey suggests, however, that four benefits appear from the work of the environmental advocacy organisations in the United States. First, the credible threats posed by the activities of the organisations would appear to act as catalysts for preventive action by industry, and enforcement efforts by regulatory agencies. Secondly, they have created an additional level of accountability for regulatory agencies, who have been forced to explain when deadlines are not met, or pollution offences are overlooked. Thirdly, they have highlighted contentious environmental issues, often using the media. This has enabled greater public awareness and debate before final decision-making, and more considered political determination of the issues. Finally, in opening the doors of the legal system and by broadening the flow of information,[85] the environmental advocacy organisations have allowed administrators, legislators and judges to better assess the impact of their decisions in terms of all affected interests.

---

[84]Yeager *op cit* at Chapter 7.
[85]Justice Thurgood Marshall, "Financing Public Interest Law: The Role of the Organised Bar" (1975 address to American Bar Association). Cited in American Bar Association, *Legal Education and Professional Development – An Educational Continuum*, 1992 at 72.

Contents of Chapter 3

Access to Justice: Legal Standing for Environmental Associations in the European Union

Chapter 3

Access to Justice: Legal Standing for Environmental Associations in the European Union

Martin Führ, Betty Gebers, Thomas Ormond and Gerhard Roller

This chapter presents the results of an "Access to Justice" study undertaken by the Öko-Institut eV. (Institute for Applied Ecology), Germany in co-operation with the Foundation for International Environmental Law and Development (FIELD), United Kingdom, in 1992.[1] The objective of the study was to draft a proposal for a European Community (EC, now the EU)[2] Directive on Access to Justice which provides legal standing in environmental matters for environmental associations.

Although the EU Commission has removed the proposed Access to Justice Directive from its current work programme, we think it is worthwhile to present the proposal to a wider public. However, it must be kept in mind that the following proposal is not an official draft of the EU Commission but a proposal of two private research institutions.

The chapter commences with a background to the proposed Directive, continues with a survey of the legal standing of environmental associations in a number of countries, and outlines the legal basis for the proposal. The text of the proposed Directive follows. The concluding section comments on each of the articles of the proposed Directive.

---

*Martin Führ was formerly a staff lawyer of the Öko-Institut (Institute for Applied Ecology), Freiburg and Darmstadt, Germany. He now lectures at the Fulda Technical College. **Betty Gebers** and **Gerhard Roller** are staff lawyers with the Öko-Institut. In 1992 the Öko-Institut, in collaboration with the Foundation for International Environmental Law and Development (FIELD), London, was commissioned to prepare a study on access to environmental justice for the Commission of the European Community. **Thomas Ormond** was a research associate at Frankfurt University before joining the regional administration in Darmstadt.
[1] The full text of the "Access to Justice" study, including German and other non-English language bibliographic references, is to be published by the Öko-Institut eV, Bunsenstrasse 14, 64293 Darmstadt, Germany (forthcoming).
[2] Since the Maastricht Treaty on European Union, 1992 came into effect on 1 November 1993, the formal title of the European Community has become the European Union. For historic reasons, however, this chapter uses the new title only in the context of future prospects of the Union.

I. **Background**

A. **The Community policy context**

Article 130r of the EC Treaty,[3] as amended by the Single European Act 1986, specifies the objectives and principles of the Community's environmental policy. These objectives are to preserve, protect and improve the quality of the environment, to contribute towards protecting human health and to ensure a prudent and rational utilisation of natural resources. To achieve these objectives, the Community must base its action on the principles of taking preventive action, of giving priority to rectifying environmental damage at source, and of ensuring that the polluter pays.

These objectives and principles have been detailed in the various Community Action Programmes on the Environment since 1973. The Fourth Programme (1987–92)[4] emphasised the importance of implementation of Community environmental legislation, and the EC Commission's intention to promote implementation and enforcement. The Fifth Programme "Towards Sustainability", presented to the Council by the EC Commission on 27 March 1992,[5] acknowledges the positive impact that previous measures and programmes have had on certain environmental problems, but notes that these efforts do not appear to be sufficient to meet increased pressures on the environment. In view of the current and anticipated trends in economic and social activity within and outside the EU and considering, in particular, the additional strains that economic growth in the Internal Market will put on the environment, the Fifth Programme calls for a more progressive and better co-ordinated policy and strategy for the environment and sustainable development. In particular, the Fifth Programme advocates the involvement of all levels of society in a spirit of shared responsibility, requiring a deepening and broadening of the range of instruments used to complement legislation.

In the context of this policy, the Fifth Programme attaches equal importance to public authorities, public and private enterprises, and to the general public – notably including non-governmental organisations (NGOs). Each member of the general public has a number of crucial roles to play: apart from being necessarily a consumer of goods and services and a direct producer of pollution and waste, he or she is expected to care about the quality of the general environment, personal health, and the quality of life of future generations, and to act as a responsible citizen with the possibility of influencing policies and decisions. As regards NGOs, the Fifth Programme appreciates their role in the process of awareness-building, the representation

---

[3]The Rome European Economic Community Treaty 1957, renamed the EC Treaty by the Treaty on European Union 1992.
[4]OJ 1987 C70 at 1; made by Council Resolution of 19 October 1987.
[5]COM (92) 23 final. The Fifth Programme covers the period 1993–2000.

of public interest and concern, and motivating and engaging members of the general public themselves.

Within the legal and administrative framework of the Member States, involvement of the public means, first of all, that the public must be enabled to participate as fully as possible in decision-making processes. In addition, the Fifth Programme calls for an accessible and efficient complaints facility to be developed at local, regional and national levels, and for individuals and public interest groups to have practicable access to the courts.

As good knowledge and information is essential for the individual's ability to play his or her full potential role in practice, the Council has adopted a Directive on Freedom of Access to Information on the Environment (Dir 90/313/EEC). This Directive awards individuals the right of access to information. Where their requests for information are unreasonably refused, ignored, or inadequately answered by a public authority, they can seek judicial or administrative review of the decision in accordance with the relevant national legal system.

Promoting the involvement of the public in decision-making processes and thereby improving the standard of environmental protection is also one of the underlying objectives of the EC Directive on the Assessment of Environmental Effects of Certain Public and Private Projects (Dir 85/337/EEC).

B. **Basic objectives of this proposal**

The above EC laws and the implementing national legislation will contribute to better information and more participation of the public in environmental matters. They affect, however, only indirectly and marginally the problem of inadequate implementation of substantive environmental law within the EU. This problem has two dimensions. First, Directives on the environment are often transposed incompletely or belatedly into national legislation. The number of infringements, as detected by complaints to the EC Commission and by the Commission's own inquiries, has been increasing constantly since 1978; over the entire EC they amounted to more than 500 in 1990.[6] Secondly, rules of EC or national environmental law are often not fully and equally enforced by the administrative authorities. As a rule, the authorities in the Member States lack the personnel and equipment necessary to fulfil their legal obligations adequately. When the public interest in environmental protection conflicts with individual economic interests, the latter tend to prevail. A crucial reason for this is the legal imbalance of power between the representatives of the conflicting interests. Administrative decisions in environmental matters – for example the granting or refusal of an emission licence or a planning permission – can always be challenged by the private party who applied for the

---

[6]Krämer L, "The Implementation of Environmental Laws by the European Economic Communities" (1991) 34 *German Yearbook of International Law* 9 at 31.

licence. In contrast, persons or groups working in favour of environmental protection face great difficulties in some Member States when they want to represent this common interest in administrative or judicial proceedings. In certain types of cases, where an administrative decision with adverse effects on the environment does not affect the property or health of individual neighbours directly, no administrative or judicial review will take place at all. This unequal risk of review is likely to distort the authority's exercise of discretion to the disadvantage of the environment. In other cases, where the administrative authorities fail to take action against contraventions of environmental law which do not affect individual rights directly, a third party often has no legal remedy in the matter, and the illegal practices may continue for a considerable period of time.

The first aim of the proposed Directive, therefore, is to ensure that the legal imbalance of power between environmental and economic interests is redressed, so that prescribed environmental measures are effectively enforced and illegal practices stopped.

The EC Commission has made great efforts to monitor the implementation of environmental law by the Member States. When it is found that EC law has been transposed incompletely or incorrectly into national law or the law has been badly enforced by the national authorities, the Commission initiates proceedings under Article 169 of the EC Treaty and as a last resort may refer the matter to the European Court of Justice (ECJ).[7] The ECJ is then empowered formally to find an infringement of EC law, but the affected Member State alone decides what conclusions to draw from the judgment and how to comply with it.[8]

Despite increased monitoring by the Commission in recent years – 168 letters of formal notice to the Member States, 39 reasoned opinions and 14 references to the ECJ in 1990 – the effect seems to be limited. As confirmed by the 1990 Commission Report on the Implementation by Member States of EEC Environmental Law,[9] the quality of the environment within the EC continues to deteriorate steadily, and the EC legislation which should be protecting it is failing to produce satisfactory results.

The conclusion to be drawn from this could be to strengthen the powers of EU organs *vis-à-vis* the Member States and enlarge the Commission's staff and equipment. To some extent this seems desirable in order to remedy the obvious deficiencies of the EU's monitoring system. However, it is highly questionable whether a central authority like the Commission will ever be able to control effectively the implementation of environmental law over such

---

[7]The Commission formally requests the Member State to submit its observations on the obligation which the Commission alleges the Member State has failed to fulfil. If settlement cannot be reached, pursuant to Art 169 the Commission issues a "reasoned opinion".

[8]Section 171 provides that the Member State "shall be required to take the necessary measures to comply with the judgment of the ECJ".

[9]Commission document P-5 of 8.2.1990, quoted by Krämer *op cit* at 49.

a large territory as the EU. Apart from this practical reason, the principle of subsidiarity, as laid down in Article 3b of the EC Treaty, and not least the widespread (and understandable) public distrust of "big government" speak against any large-scale extension of administrative powers at a EU level. The preferable solution to the problem, therefore, is to promote decentralised implementation of environmental law. This is precisely what can be achieved by improving the access to national courts and complaints facilities for citizens and organisations who act in the interest of environmental protection.

In this context, litigation in the courts should, in practice, be seen as a last resort. The main effect of establishing a more open access to the courts will be preventive, since the mere possibility of a lawsuit will induce public authorities and business enterprises to examine more carefully the compatibility of their decisions and activities with environmental law. Besides, a functioning system of administrative review can prevent many disputes in the law courts. The more informal and less confrontationist mechanism of administrative complaint such as exists in Denmark, Ireland and the Netherlands, favours swift and pragmatic solutions and can well serve to create a basis of confidence between the general public, the competent authorities and industrial and business enterprises.

Rights of members of the general public or of public interest groups to the correct implementation of environmental law do exist in the legal systems of some Member States and partly already in EC law. Apart from procedural rights guaranteed by EC Directives, such as the right of the public to participate in proceedings for environmental impact assessment and freedom of access to information on the environment, the ECJ has confirmed in recent judgments that EC law also confers substantive rights in certain areas of environmental protection. In its judgments of 28 February 1991 ("ground water")[10] and 30 May 1991 ("sulphur dioxide – suspended particles"),[11] the ECJ has held that the obligation on Member States to prescribe certain limit values in the interest of "human health" – as contained in the respective EC Directives – creates rights for all affected individuals and that such rights must be able to be asserted, by invoking binding provisions of EC law, in the national courts. In addition, in the *Factortame* case,[12] the ECJ emphasised that national courts are under a duty to set aside any national legal provision which might prevent, even temporarily, EC rules from having full force and effect. The net effect of these cases, together with the Directives on lead and nitrogen dioxide emissions (Dirs 82/884/EEC and 85/203/EEC) and on waste disposal (Dirs 75/442/EEC and 78/319/EEC),[13] all of which are based upon the protection of

---

[10]Case 131/88, *Commission v Federal Republic of Germany* [1991] ECR 825.
[11]Case 361/88, *Commission v Federal Republic of Germany* 1991 *Informationsdienst Umweltrecht* (IUR) 152.
[12]Case 213/89, *R v Secretary of State for Transport, ex parte Factortame Ltd and others* [1990] ECR 2433.
[13]Rights in this case may be limited to neighbours of waste disposal facilities.

human health, amounts to the emergence of enforceable environmental rights for practically all members of the general public.

As the decisions of the ECJ look to the wording of individual Directives and their reasoning and do not acknowledge rights of citizens against other private persons or businesses, they can only provide a piecemeal guarantee of access to justice in environmental matters. The proposed Directive, therefore, intends to harmonise the situation in the different fields of environmental litigation.

The legal situation varies widely between the Member States of the EC. These disparities in access to justice tend to lead not only to different standards of environmental protection in the Member States but also to unequal conditions of economic competition. It is thus also in the interest of the establishment and functioning of the Internal Market that the legal provisions of the Member States concerning administrative and judicial review in environmental matters should be approximated.

II. Survey of the legal standing of environmental associations in various countries

This section overviews of the situation in many of the Member States of the EC as well as in some other countries, particularly in the United States and Switzerland.[14]

A. Situation outside the European Union

1. *United States*

"Citizen suits" are an important element of US environmental law and of its implementation in practice. The term generally means the possibility for any person or group of people to bring an action against a violator of a rule of environmental law or against a governmental agency which fails to perform a duty under that law. This right of action has been created on the one hand by the courts in interpretation of common law and section 702 of the Administrative Procedure Act, and on the other hand by express provisions in nearly all federal and state environmental statutes since the early 1970s. The court decisions under common law and most statutes require the plaintiff to

---

[14]The major source for the following overview is Führ M, Roller G (eds), *Participation and Litigation Rights of Environmental Associations in Europe*, 1991, 196pp (being revised papers of an international conference held in Frankfurt in 1990, published as Vol 1 of Studies of the Environmental Law Network International, Vol 1, ISBN 3-631 43648-3, copies of which can be ordered for DM 59 plus postage/packaging from Verlag Peter Lang, Frankfurt, facsimile 49 69 787893). The overview has been supplemented with recent information from experts in various countries.

show an interest which is or may be adversely affected. This formula, as a rule, has been interpreted very liberally.[15] It is sufficient to show an "injury in fact", such as a decrease in the aesthetic and recreational value of a natural landscape or an identifiable, even if indirect, degradation of the environment in the plaintiff's place of residence. Environmental groups have standing if any of their members passes the "injury in fact" test.[16]

Some states, beginning with Michigan in 1970, introduced so-called Environmental Rights Acts, allowing any person or group to bring an action merely on the basis of an alleged injury to the environment.[17]

Under most environmental statutes, the plaintiff may only seek an injunction ordering the other party to stop its infringement of the law, or the government agency to perform its duty. Four federal statutes – the Clean Water Act, the Resource Conservation and Recovery Act, the Comprehensive Environmental Response, Compensation, and Liability Act (CERCLA) ("Superfund" statute) and the Clean Air Act as amended in 1990 – additionally grant a right to sue for civil penalties against persons "alleged to be in violation" of the law. The US Supreme Court has interpreted this clause as meaning that the violation must be on-going at the time of filing the suit. In an action of this type, the federal trial courts may order the polluter to pay a sum up to a maximum of $25,000 per day and violation. These penalties are payable to the US Treasury.[18]

In order to stimulate government enforcement of the law and give the violator an opportunity to comply, the environmental statutes usually oblige the plaintiff to give 60 days' notice to the alleged violator, the relevant state administration and the Environmental Protection Agency (EPA), before initiating proceedings. Moreover, a citizen suit may not be filed if the state or EPA have commenced and are diligently prosecuting an enforcement action. The plaintiff is also under a duty to show that he has participated in possible administrative proceedings and exhausted the available extra-judicial remedies.[19]

Citizen suit provisions have broken with the general US rule that each litigant must pay its own costs and attorney's fees, by giving the court authority to award costs of litigation – including reasonable attorney's fees – to any prevailing or substantially prevailing party. This enables big environmental

---

[15]See Chapter 1.

[16]Leading cases: *Sierra Club* v *Morton* 405 US 727 (1972); *Association of Data Processing Service Organisations* v *Camp* 397 US 150 (1970); *United States* v *SCRAP* 412 US 669 (1973).

[17]In Michigan: s 2 (1) of the Environmental Protection Act 1970 (State of Michigan Enrolled House Bill No 3055), PL No 127, 1970; *cf.* Slone, "The Michigan Environmental Protection Act: Bringing Citizen-Initiated Environmental Suits into the 1980s" (1985) 12 *Environmental Law Quarterly* 271.

[18]Bulatao L., "Citizen Suits Under the United States' Clean Water Act", in: Führ/Roller *op cit* at 121 *et seq.*

[19]See, for example, s 505 of the Clean Water Act (US Code, Title 33 – 1365), s 310 of the CERCLA 1980 (42 USC – 9659), s 7002 of the Resource Conservation and Recovery Act (42 USC – 6972), s 304 of the Clean Air Act (42 USC s 7604), s 20 of the Toxic Substances Control Act (15 USC s 2619), s 1540 of the Endangered Species Act (USC T 16), s 300 j-8 of the Safe Drinking Water Act – all of the above also contained in the annual edition of "US Environmental Laws", prepared by the US Bureau of National Affairs (BNA).

associations, such as the Natural Resources Defence Council, to develop "enforcement programs" which are entirely self-sustaining.[20]

The practice of citizen suits in the 1970s and 1980s has not confirmed initial fears that the liberal standing rules would lead to a "dogging of the courts". Studies made in Michigan, a state with the widest possible right of action, demonstrate that the 120 or so citizen suits filed under the Environmental Rights Act of that state within five-and-a-half years of its coming into force constituted only 0.02% of the total number of cases.[21] Under the federal Clean Water Act, the citizen suit provisions of which are by far the ones most often used in the United States, about 400 such actions were brought between 1983/84 and 1990, as compared with 90,000 discharge permits which were in effect during the same seven years.[22]

According to the Michigan studies, most of the proceedings were initiated by local environmental associations and *ad hoc* citizens' groups. Their duration was relatively short, whereas the success quota (58%) was far above average. Under the federal Clean Water Act, the plaintiff's chances of winning are even higher, due to the statutory obligation on companies to monitor the discharges from their plants and file monthly reports with the EPA, which are then made available to the public. On the strength of this information, the outcome of most citizen suits is clear from the beginning so that companies are interested in reaching a settlement at an early stage of the proceedings. The vast majority of citizen suits end in this way, whereby the plaintiff associations frequently oblige the polluter to contribute funds to an environmental project.[23]

Citizen suits acquired great importance as a means of enforcing the law, especially in the years of the Reagan administration when the number of enforcement actions by EPA was drastically reduced.[24]

2. *Switzerland*

Switzerland was the first European country to establish a right of action for environmental associations. Article 12 of the Federal Nature and Heritage Conservation Act (*Bundesgesetz über den Natur- und Heimatschutz; Loi fédérale sur la protection de la nature et du paysage*) 1966 (NHCA 1966) enables nationwide associations which, according to their statutes, devote themselves to nature and heritage conservation or related, purely non-commercial objectives, as well as municipalities, to appeal against certain

---

[20]Bulatao, in: Führ/Roller *op cit* at 123 *et seq*. The NRDC enforcement programme regarding water pollution law is described in Chapter 2 at Section I(J).

[21]Haynes JK, "Michigan's Environmental Protection Act in its Sixth Year: Substantive Environmental Law from Citizen Suits" (1976) 53 *Journal of Urban Law* 589.

[22]Bulatao, in Führ/Roller *op cit* at 124.

[23]Bulatao, *ibid*; Bizer/Ormond/Riedel *op cit* at 53.

[24]See also Chapter 2 at n 32 and accompanying text.

administrative decisions. They may lodge an administrative appeal to the federal government or a judicial appeal to the Supreme Court (*Bundesgericht*) against orders and decrees in so far as these are subject to federal appeals, (*i.e.* if the decisions are taken in fulfilment of a duty under federal law). Over and above the public works projects of federal authorities, this applies notably to all forest-clearing permits.

In addition, article 55 of the Environmental Protection Act 1983 grants the same rights of appeal and remedies at the cantonal level to nationwide environmental associations founded at least 10 years before the initiation of proceedings and officially recognised by the federal government. While these rules of admission are more restrictive than those of the NHCA 1966, the sphere of application is in one respect wider: the associations may challenge all cantonal as well as federal planning and building approvals of those projects to construct permanent facilities for which environmental impact assessments must be undertaken. Again, the law awards *locus standi* also to municipalities (art 57 of the Act).

The third law to permit association lawsuits at the federal level is the Trails and Footpaths Act 1987, which has likewise opted for an accreditation procedure for national, specialist organisations administered by the Swiss Department of the Interior.

The appeals generally have the effect of suspending the execution of the contested administrative decisions. Annulment or alteration of decisions contravening environmental law is the main object of such lawsuits. At present there is no cause of action to recover environmental damages in Switzerland.

According to a study made in the late 1970s, the number of association appeals under the NHCA 1966 in the Supreme Court was 81 in the first 11 years of operation of that Act, representing a proportion of less than 2% of all judicial appeals [under that Act]. The associations won their cases far more often than the average plaintiff (in about 45% of administrative and judicial appeals, as compared to the average of 9.3 and 17.5% respectively). More recently, a total of approximately 40-50 actions per year have been brought by environmental associations at the federal and cantonal levels. While their percentage of the overall case-load of the courts is rather small, their success rate of about 50% is extraordinarily high.[25]

The studies on the subject have emphasised the positive effect of association lawsuits on environmental protection in Switzerland. It is, for instance, essentially put down to actions against clearing permission under the NHCA 1966 that many Swiss forests were preserved from the pressure of economic expansion in the early 1970s. Today, prevention is commonly regarded as the main effect of the associations' right of appeal. Its mere existence is often sufficient to induce a more cautious treatment of the environment by

---

[25]Leimbacher J, "The association lawsuit in wildlife and heritage conservation procedures and in environmental impact assessment procedures in Switzerland", in Führ/Roller *op cit* at n 14 *supra* at 27 therein.

developers and authorities, and to pave the way for reasonable compromises in the stage prior to litigation.

3. *Other countries*

The United States and Switzerland are the best-known but not the only countries outside the European Union which have made way for public-interest actions by environmental associations and/or concerned individuals.

In Norway, the requirement of "legal interest" under section 28 of the Administration Act (*Forvaltningsloven*) and section 54 of the (Civil) Procedure Act (*Tvistemalsloven*) does not exclude actions by groups such as the Norwegian Nature Conservancy Association claiming to represent the interests of its members, even though such actions seem to be rare.

In Poland, the legislation of the communist era gave certain officially licensed "social organisations", such as environmental associations, trades unions, and neighbourhood committees, the right to lodge administrative appeals and initiate proceedings in administrative, civil and criminal courts. However, before the establishment of democracy in 1989 the legislation was ineffective. The change of the political system and particularly the reform of the Administrative Procedure Code 1990 have improved this situation in practice.

In Canada, environmental groups and individuals are accepted as plaintiffs or "intervenors" in the administrative tribunals. In the course of the 1980s, especially since the enactment of the "Charter of Rights and Freedoms" and the *Finlay* case in 1986, courts liberalised their rules of standing to some extent as well. The Canadian Supreme Court now acknowledges a "genuine interest" of the plaintiff and accords "public interest standing" to concerned citizens or groups of persons, if there is no other reasonable and effective way to bring the matter before a court[26].

A similar relaxation of the standing test in environmental matters has taken place in New Zealand during the 1980s.[27]

In India, the courts have traditionally interpreted the Constitution (arts 32 and 226) as providing a basis for public interest litigation by citizens and organisations in a wide range of matters.[28]

In Brazil, the new Constitution of 1988 expressly provides for an *actio populars* against acts of public authorities which are harmful to national wealth, administrative morality or the environment, including the cultural

---

[26]See (also for other Commonwealth countries) Feldman D, "Public Interest Litigation and Constitutional Theory in Comparative Perspective" (1992) 55 *Modern Law Review* 44 at 52, 55 and 67.
[27]Feldman *op cit* at 52.
[28]Feldman *op cit* at 53.

heritage (art 5(LXXIII)). A statute of 1985 also allows environmental associations with legal personality to bring a "public civil action" in order to stop environmentally harmful activities or claim compensation.[29]

B. **Situation in the Member States**

1. *Belgium*

Before an administrative decision on the environment is challenged in court, the plaintiff must file a complaint with a superior administrative authority. Admission to this administrative review is granted to anyone who can show a legitimate "interest to appeal". This term is interpreted widely – as with the participation in public inquiries – so that public interest groups for the defence of the environment and, to an increasing extent, members of the general public are included.

Actions for annulment of an administrative decision may be brought before the Council of State. The standing requirements here are somewhat stricter than in the complaints procedure. According to a Flemish decree of 28 June 1985 concerning emission authorisations, the plaintiff must either be a natural or legal person likely to be directly disturbed by the contested project or operation, or a legal person whose assigned task it is to protect the part of the environment which will be affected in the given case. Generally, the Council of State admits environmental groups only if they have legal personality and pursue a collective interest distinct from the interests of their members. In addition, their standing in court depends on whether the effects of the contested project are local, regional, or national, and their own field of action, as defined by the articles of association, precisely corresponds to this impact. In some cases, applications for annulment of a decision have also been turned down because the plaintiff association has been deemed not "representative" enough on account of the fact that few members were living in the affected municipality.

The law on association standing in the civil courts is currently undergoing change.[29a] New legislation on the subject has recently been enacted. Until now the relevant provision has been Article 17 of the Judicial Code (*Code Judiciaire, Gerechtelijk Wetboek*) which strikes out any action where the plaintiff cannot show a personal interest (*qualité et interêt*). The supreme Belgian court, the *Cour de Cassation*, construes this clause narrowly, limiting the scope of relevant interests of a legal person narrowly to such matters as patrimonial assets and reputation. Although some courts of first and second instance have moved over the last 15 years towards the recognition of

---

[29]See Chapter 5.
[29a]Seu de Sadeleer, "La Loi du 12 janvier 1993 concernaut un droit d'action en matière de protection de l'environment" (1994) 1 *ELNI Newsletter* 54.

environmental rights, thus allowing individuals as well as associations to sue for the preservation of a healthy environment, the *Cour de Cassation* has until now adhered to its restrictive line.

Similarly the *Cour de Cassation* also excludes public interest groups from acting as a private prosecutor in criminal proceedings.[30]

Following an intense debate in the 1980s, during which no less than nine different bills on the subject were tabled in parliament, the parliament adopted a law on the right of action of environmental associations in 1993. The Act grants this right of action only to associations which have existed with legal personality for at least three years, whose non-profit-making character has been recognised, and whose articles of association embody the objective of environmental protection and determine the geographical scope of activity. In addition, the association must prove in court a link between its objectives, its activities, and the specific public interest affected in the given case. When admitted, the plaintiff may only apply for an injunctive relief (*action en cessation*) to stop activities of private persons which contravene provisions of environmental law. The Act does not contain any remedy as to damages or restoration of the environment.

Interim relief in Belgium used to be exclusively entrusted to the civil courts. The law of 16 June 1989 has now made it possible for the Conseil d'Etat to suspend the effect of an illegal administrative act, at least in principle. The scope of application of the law is, however, very heavily circumscribed, requiring the plaintiff to base his or her claim on a violation of articles 6 or 17 of the Belgian Constitution (equality before the law and freedom of education). This condition will rarely be fulfilled in environmental lawsuits. Since the regular proceedings before the Council of State usually take several years, whether an environmental association or a concerned citizen will get access to effective short-term remedies depends on the openness of the relevant civil court to public interest litigation.

2. Denmark

Denmark has a highly developed system of administrative review in environmental matters. By 1917 a two-tier system of nature conservation boards had been established where appeals could be lodged against administrative decisions relating to nature conservation. The right of appeal was given to the Danish Nature Conservation Society (*Danmarks Naturfredningsforening*), which is still by far the largest environmental NGO in the country.[31]

According to the Environmental Protection Act 1973, administrative decisions relating to the environment and taken by municipal and regional

---

[30]Judgment of 24 November 1982, 1983 *Revue de droit pénal* 390 (*"Ligue de Droits de l'Homme"*).
[31]Rehling D, "Legal standing for environmental groups within the administrative system – the Danish experience and the need for an international Charter on Environmental Rights", in Führ/Roller *op cit* at 151 *et seq.*

authorities may be challenged by complaint to the Environmental Protection Agency (*MiljŸstyrelsen*), which is attached to the Ministry of the Environment. The complainant may appeal against its decisions to the Environmental Appeals Board (*MiljŸankenævnet*), a quasi-judicial body composed of independent officials whose decisions are binding on the administration. Originally, access to the environmental complaint facilities was restricted to persons who could claim to have an "individual and significant interest" in the outcome of the case (*i.e.* who were directly affected by pollution at their home or place of work, or whose property rights were infringed in some way). In 1982 the rights of appeal were extended to the *Naturfredningsforening* concerning licences, mandatory orders or prohibitions in matters of air and water pollution, and to the Danish Angling Society (*Danmarks Sportsfiskerforbund*) concerning decisions about the discharge of effluents into inland waters, as well as to the Consumer Council and the Workers' Economic Council within their respective sphere of activity. The Environmental Protection Act 1991, which entered into force on 1 January 1992, enables Greenpeace and two fishing associations to challenge decisions affecting the maritime environment. The same Act also gives local environmental groups access to the complaint facilities in circumstances in which they have sought to participate in the preceding administrative procedure.

The *Naturfredningsforening* estimates that it brought altogether about one thousand cases before the various appeal boards since 1917 and won approximately 50% of them. According to official sources, 20 appeals were lodged by environmental associations in 1989 against discharge licences, amounting to contestation of approximately 10% of the licences issued in that year. The number and proportion of appeals, however, appear to be declining.

Administrative courts, in the strict sense, do not exist in Denmark. The ordinary courts of law have jurisdiction to review the decisions of the administrative authorities and the *MiljŸankenævnet*. The scope of this review is limited, however, to formal irregularities and obvious infringements of substantive law. The standing requirements are the same as before the administrative appeals boards, but the cost of litigation is quite high, whereas an application for administrative review is free of charge. Therefore, and in view of the swiftness of the administrative complaints procedure, legal actions in the courts for environmental reasons are relatively rare.

The proceedings for administrative review usually have a duration of four to eight months. Due to this, applications for interim relief – which may be granted by the local authorities – constitute at most 1% of all appeal cases.

3. *Germany*

The German Administrative Judiciary Statute (VwGO), section 68 *et seq* provides for an administrative complaints procedure and generally obliges a would-be plaintiff to go through it before seeking judicial review of administrative action or applying for administrative action to be taken in the administrative courts. The administrative review is omitted in cases where the administrative act concludes a formalised planning procedure.[32]

The judicial review standing requirements in the complaints procedure are the same as for an action in the administrative courts, which are discussed below.

The administrative courts have exclusive jurisdiction to review administrative decisions and also to grant interim relief in matters of public law. According to VwGO section 42(2), standing to sue generally requires plaintiffs to show that their rights are violated by the administrative act or its denial or omission. The provision is construed narrowly by the courts and means that plaintiffs must base their claims on a private right conferred on them by law (such as the right to property or good health) and that they must invoke a norm of law whose very purpose is to protect individual rights and which has been infringed in the given case ("protective norm doctrine"). This limits the access to court essentially to property-owners living near a construction project or an industrial plant. The extent of the protected neighbourhood differs greatly, however, according to the relevant statute. The range of protective norms has been evolved by the courts on a case-to-case basis and has slightly expanded in recent years. They still exclude, among others, the whole of (substantive) nature conservation law, most of the rules of water protection law and, generally, all limit values based on the precautionary principle.[33]

Environmental public interest groups have no rights of their own except where expressly granted by the Federal Nature Conservation Act (*BNatschG* hereafter "FNCA") or the nature conservation statutes of the states (*Länder*). FNCA, section 29 gives certain participation rights to associations which promote the aims of nature conservation and have undergone an official accreditation procedure. These rights apply in the preparation of certain regulations, programmes and plans, before an exemption from a nature reserve or national park ordinance is granted, and in formalised planning procedures for public works projects which affect the natural environment. According to recent case-law, administrative decisions which have been taken in violation of these participation rights may be challenged by the associations in court.

---

[32]Sections 70 and 74(1) of the Administrative Procedure Act 1976 (*Verwaltungsverfahrensgesetz, VwVfG*). The text of this federal law is for all practical purposes identical with the laws which the West German *Länder* enacted simultaneously for their sphere of jurisdiction. Partial English translations of the VwVfG and the Administrative Judiciary Act 1960 (*Verwaltungsgerichtsordnung*) are given, for example, by Singh MP, *German Administrative Law*, 1985, at 164 *et seq*.
[33]For details see Ormond T, "Environmental Group Actions in West Germany", in Führ/Roller *op cit* at 81 *et seq*; Greve MS, "The Non-Reformation of Administrative Law: Standing to Sue and Public Interest Litigation in West German Environmental Law", (1989) 22 *Cornell International Law Journal* 197. See also Chapter 4.

In addition to this, seven of the 16 German states (Bremen, Hessen, Hamburg, Berlin, Saarland, Sachsen-Anhalt and Brandenburg) have embodied a right of action for accredited associations (*Verbandsklage*) in their statutes. In four of the seven states this right is limited to nature reserve exemption cases and public works planning cases, while in Hamburg it is limited only to the former. The new legislation of the eastern state of Sachsen-Anhalt (like that of Berlin until 1990) contains a subsidiarity clause which prohibits *Verbandsklagen* whenever there exists a right of action under VwGO, section 42 for anyone else. This could render the provision largely inapplicable because, theoretically, the municipalities (as the main estate-owners in Eastern Germany) always have a right of action. Only the new laws of Brandenburg and the city-state of Berlin open access to justice for associations regarding infringement of nature conservation law generally and, in Berlin, certain provisions of water law. The governments of some other states are currently considering proposals for an introduction or (moderate) extension of association rights.

Generally speaking, the courts have given a very narrow interpretation to the *Verbandsklage* provisions. As a result, the right of action of associations has only gained marginal significance. Since 1979, when it was first introduced in Bremen, a total of about 70 actions (including interim and ancillary proceedings) have been brought in German administrative courts.

In the civil courts, standing to sue likewise depends on a plaintiff's individual claim of right. Exceptions exist in the field of consumer and competition law where associations aiming at consumer protection or fair trade may sue for discontinuance of unfair general trade conditions or competition practices. There is no similar statutory right in environmental matters which would enable public interest groups to bring prohibition actions directly, for example against the operator of a polluting facility or to claim compensation for damage to the environment.

The same is true for criminal proceedings: members of the general public or public interest groups may not act as private prosecutors or joint plaintiffs in environmental crime cases, except where they themselves have suffered injuries to health or property.

Those parties who pass the standing test benefit from a relatively effective system of remedies, offering interim relief in particular. Administrative complaints and legal actions against administrative acts normally have suspensive effect. This may be set aside by the public authority with a specific "order for immediate enforcement" on grounds of preponderant public interest, which, in turn, can be quashed by an application to the court to restore the suspensive effect. Accredited associations, in so far as they have a right of action, may also avail themselves of these remedies, including the interim injunctions and declarations.

The German law of costs operates on the basis of the "loser pays" principle, from which there are only minor exceptions relating to unnecessary expenses caused by the successful party.[34] The fees of the court, counsel and experts are regulated by scales as part of statute law and depend essentially on the sum in dispute. Lawyers and experts may charge higher fees on a contractual basis, although the losing party has to reimburse its opponent for such expenses only up to the amount indicated in the scales. This limits the cost risk to some extent. Nevertheless, any action to prevent a major building project may cost approximately 10,000 Deutschmarks, mainly due to the cost of obtaining the technical expert opinions which have become a decisive factor for the outcome of environmental lawsuits.

Legal aid from state funds is available only to persons with a low income for the defence of their individual rights.[35] The possibility of legal aid for environmental associations and others acting in the public interest does not exist.

4. *Ireland*

Under Irish statutory law, appeals against local authority decisions concerning the development of land, the discharge of effluents to waters and sewers, and the emission of air pollutants lie to the Planning Appeals Board (PAB, *An Bord Pleanala*). This is a quasi-judicial administrative tribunal independent of the government. Any person may lodge an appeal against decisions to grant or refuse a planning or pollution authorisation, except in cases concerning the discharge to a sewer where only the applicant for a licence is given access to the PAB. Similarly, special amenity orders and conservation orders by local authorities under the Local Government (Planning and Development) Act 1963 may be contested by any person in an appeal to the Minister of the Environment. There is no administrative review, however, of decisions under nature conservation or waste disposal law.[36]

Decisions of the PAB are final, but a further appeal lies to the High Court on a point of law.

Environmental associations frequently make use of the right of any person to appeal. Nevertheless, their share of the litigation is small. While the total number of appeals against decisions on planning permits, for instance, amounted to between 2,200 and 2,500 in the late 1980s, less than a quarter of these were lodged by third parties (persons other than the applicant for the permission), and of these the great majority came from neighbours of the prospective development.

---

[34]VwGO, s 154 *et seq*; further provisions are contained in the Court Fees Act (*Gerichtskostengesetz*), as revised in 1975.

[35]The rules on legal aid (*Prozesskostenhilfe*) embodied in s 114 *et seq*. Civil Procedure Code (*Zivilprozessordnung*) are also applicable before the administrative courts (VwGO, s 166).

[36]Scannell Y, "Legal Basis of Participation in Administrative Procedures in Ireland", in Führ/Roller *op cit* at 5 *et seq*.

As in Denmark, there are no special administrative courts in Ireland over and above the Planning Appeals Board. The High Court in Dublin, however, offers more important and more widely used judicial remedies for environmental purposes than the ordinary law courts in Denmark. Standing to sue is accorded very generously, partly because of citizen suit provisions in statutory law. Section 27 of the Local Government (Planning and Development) Act 1976, in particular, grants any person the right to apply for an order prohibiting the continuance of a development or the unauthorised use of land, whether or not that person has an interest in the land. The same right exists in water and air pollution law for the purpose of preventing any sort of pollution that was not authorised by a licence, or if the terms of the authorisation have not been complied with.[37]

Further, members of the general public and environmental associations may seek judicial review of administrative decisions which they consider to be *ultra vires*. This also applies to decisions under those statutes (such as the Wildlife Act or the National Monuments Act) which do not provide for an appeal to the Planning Appeals Board.

While it is possible in this way to set aside administrative decisions and stop illegal practices which threaten the environment, members of the public or environmental associations cannot obtain damages in these cases, because the courts hold the view that statutory duties of care are not owed to individuals or associations.

In Irish criminal law, any person has the right to prosecute for statutory criminal offences, unless it is specifically excluded. This right, however, usually enables only a summary prosecution in the lowest courts, attracting only a small penalty. As an exception, the Water Pollution Act 1977 allows every citizen to prosecute on indictment for certain major offences under that Act, a right which so far has never been used by individuals or environmental groups.

Administrative appeals or judicial remedies in Ireland do not have suspensive effect. However, interim injunctions granted by the High Court can be a quick and efficient relief by which damage to the environment can be prevented or stopped at an early stage.

The fees payable in Planning Appeals Board procedures are reduced for appeals by the National Trust (*An Taisce*) and other environmentally concerned organisations.

The courts are given a wide discretion on awarding costs. The general rule is that they follow the event, that is they depend on the outcome of the case. Costs are subject to taxation by the court unless they are agreed between the parties. Normally, costs are assessed on a basis which does not provide for full recovery.

---

[37]Local Government (Water Pollution) Act 1977, s 11; Air Pollution Act 1987, s 28; *cf*. Scannell *op cit* at 12.

5. *Italy*

Apart from in town and country planning cases, few opportunities presently exist for citizens to participate in administrative proceedings or to seek administrative review of environmentally relevant decisions in Italy. A bill introduced to Parliament in 1991 would, if enacted and implemented, change the current situation.[38]

More important is the judicial relief which can be obtained in the administrative courts. Originally, as in most other countries, standing to sue depended on the plaintiff being able to show a violation of his "own rights and lawful interests" (art 24 of the 1947 Constitution). After an intense political and legal debate, in which a majority of scholars advocated an extension in favour of environmental interests, several court opinions in the 1970s and early 1980s widened the access to justice to associations pursuing aims of environmental protection. Parliament followed in 1986 by embodying a right of action in Law No 349 concerning the establishment of a Ministry of the Environment and rules on the matter of environmental damage. According to Articles 13(1) and 18(5) of that Law, environmental associations which fulfil certain conditions as to programme, strength and internal structure, and have been recognised by ministerial decree, may appeal to the administrative courts for annulment of illegal administrative decisions relating to the environment. A subsequent decree of 20 February 1987 gave official recognition to 13 environmental associations. In 1990, about 40 principal proceedings were initiated in the administrative courts under the new law. Bureaucrats have acknowledged the preventive effect, both in terms of environmental damage and the eruption of social conflicts, of the right of action.

Law No 349/1986 also enables the accredited associations to intervene in criminal proceedings and claim (for the benefit of the Treasury) compensation for environmental damage. They are not allowed, however, to initiate the prosecution. Nor do they have standing in civil proceedings, so they may not sue any other person or business to stop illegal practices directly or claim damages under private law.

Actions for annulment in the Italian administrative courts do not have suspensive effect, but the courts are empowered to grant interim relief on application.

Pursuant to the Code of Civil Procedure (art 92) rules on cost apportionment, which are also applicable to administrative litigation, the unsuccessful party generally has to bear the costs of the proceedings. The judge may, however, split the court fees and make the parties pay their own costs, not only if the action has been partly successful but also for reasons of equity or fairness. The administrative courts often make use of this provision.

---

[38]Carrubba C, *Participation Experience in Italy*, in Führ/Roller *op cit* n 14 *supra* at 127 *et seq*.

6. *Luxembourg*

Following the French example, the Luxembourg Nature Conservation Act 1982 has set up a system whereby certain associations recognised by the responsible minister enjoy more rights in administrative and judicial proceedings. The special status is given to associations of national importance, whose articles of association have been published in the Government *Gazette* and which have exercised their statutory activities in the field of nature conservation and environmental protection for at least three years.

The recognised associations may challenge decisions under nature conservation law in the administrative courts. This right of action has been extended in 1982 by a judgment of the Conseil d'Etat to administrative decisions concerning dangerous or polluting installations.[39]

According to Article 43 of the 1982 Act, recognised associations may act as a "civil party" in criminal proceedings concerning infringements of nature conservation law.

7. *The Netherlands*

For most decisions in environmental matters, the rules as to procedures of participation and appeal are contained in the General Environmental Provisions Act 1979 (WABM 1979), as replaced on 1 March 1993 by the *Wet Milieubeheer*. Any member of the general public who submitted objections during the administrative proceedings or who can demonstrate that it was reasonably not possible to do so, is also entitled to appeal against the final decision. This appeal used to be a form of administrative review by the Crown, that is the Minister of the Environment on advice of the Administrative Disputes Division of the Council of State. The decisions of the Minister – which nearly always followed the opinions of the Council of State – were not subject to a further judicial review. After the European Court of Human Rights held in 1985 in the *Benthem* case that this institutional arrangement did not fulfil the conditions of Article 6 of the European Convention as to an "independent tribunal", temporary legislation on Crown disputes, in force until 1993, gave the Council of State jurisdiction to decide on the appeals instead of merely advising the Minister. Therefore, in more recent times it has been more appropriate to speak of judicial review by an administrative court. No change has been made concerning the standing requirements, so that any person, and thus also environmental associations, have the right to apply for annulment or for the issuance of an administrative decision if they have participated in the previous administrative proceedings.[40]

---

[39]Judgment of 8 December 1982 (information provided by the *Mouvement Ecologique*).
[40]Robesin M, "Participation of environmental organisations in legal procedures in the Netherlands", in Führ/ Roller *op cit* at 108 *et seq.*

The old procedure of appeal to the Crown still applies to local structure plans under the Physical Planning Act. Again, any person who made use of his or her participation rights may lodge the appeal which then is decided on by the Minister, advised by the Administrative Disputes Division of the Council of State.

All decisions for which no special procedure of participation and appeal has been regulated by law – for instance, building licences in exemption from a local structure plan or the refusal by an authority to enforce binding legislation – may be challenged by appeal to the Judicial Division of the Council of State. Under the Official Decisions Administrative Jurisdiction Act (Wet AROB), this kind of appeal presupposes a violation of the plaintiff's own "interests". The court has interpreted this term liberally and granted a right of action to legally constituted associations founded for environmental purposes, as against decisions which adversely affect these purposes. This interpretation has been embodied in Article 79 of WABM 1979, according to which the environmental aims of non-governmental organisations shall be regarded as "their own interests".

Since a decision of the Supreme Court (*Hoge Raad*) in 1986, concerning the dumping of contaminated sludge in the "Nieuwe Meer", environmental associations also have access to the civil courts. They are able, in this way, to sue a polluter directly, petition for a restraining injunction and, possibly, also claim compensation for clean-up and restoration costs. Civil actions are, however, still relatively rare due to the considerable cost-risk.

Article 12 of the Code of Criminal Procedure gives persons and organisations who have an interest in the prosecution of an offence the right to complain to the criminal court about non-prosecution. This instrument may be used by environmental associations to enforce the prosecution of environmental crimes under the Penal Code.

Appeals to the Council of State do not have suspensive effect but the appellant may, within one month after the administrative decision was taken, ask the Chairperson of the Administrative Disputes Division to suspend the decision or make temporary provisions until the judgment in the principal proceedings is rendered. The request will be granted if the execution of the decision in the meantime involves such high costs or changes circumstances in such a way as to anticipate the outcome of the case. In the civil courts, the injunction provides an effective interim remedy restraining the defendant from continuing with environmentally harmful activities.[41]

The cost of civil litigation is much higher than that in an administrative appeal. Whereas the plaintiff in a civil lawsuit faces a cost-risk of 10,000 guilders or more, the administrative review procedure currently costs him or her only a fee of 225 guilders. This explains why smaller environmental

---

[41]Article 80 of Wet AROB.

organisations, as a rule, cannot afford to avail themselves of the remedies under civil law.

8. *Portugal*

While Article 52 (1) of the Portuguese Constitution 1976 guarantees to any citizen the right to petition the administration for the performance or review of a decision, there does not exist, at present, a formalised procedure of administrative review.

Article 52 of the Constitution also stipulates that all citizens may initiate legal proceedings for the defence of their own rights as well as of the laws of the Constitution and the public interest. This provision, combined with the constitutional right of every citizen to a humane, healthy and ecologically balanced environment (art 66) have established the *actio popularis* for environmental purposes in Portuguese law. Actions of this type generally have to be brought before the ordinary courts of law, not the administrative courts.[42] In addition, a 1987 law has given special status to certain environmental associations. Those which have legal personality, whose exclusive aim is in the area of environmental protection (including the defence of the cultural heritage), and whose number of members exceeds a certain minimum, graded in accordance to their national, regional or local field of activity, may challenge all administrative acts violating the legal provisions protecting the environment and the quality of life.[43]

According to Articles 52 and 66 of the Constitution and to the Framework Law on the Environment (arts 40–42), citizens and associations also have the right to bring an action directly against a polluter with the objective to stop illegal activities or to claim damages.[44]

Furthermore, under Article 7 of the Law on Environmental Associations, the associations may assist the prosecution in proceedings relating to environmental crimes.

Under Portuguese law, a legal action is not in itself sufficient to suspend the effect of administrative decisions or to stop environmentally harmful activities immediately. The plaintiff must apply for an injunction in court.

Environmental associations are exempted from court fees in the proceedings where they take part as plaintiff or assist the prosecution.[45] Nevertheless, shortage of funds and staff explain why only four to five actions have been brought by those associations since 1987.

---

[42]Article 45 Framework Law on the Environment (*Lei de Bases do Ambiente*) of 7 April 1987.
[43]Article 7 of Law No 10/1987.
[44]*Cf.* Lemos P, "Participation Experience in Portugal", in Führ/Roller *op cit* n 14 *supra* at 30.
[45]Article 13 of Law No 10/1987.

9. Spain

A system of administrative review exists under the Administrative Procedure Act 1958. Appeals may be brought by individuals and also by associations. The administration is obliged to answer those appeals within three months. If the appeal is unsuccessful or the administration does not reply in time, the way is open to judicial review.

Standing to sue depends, as a rule, on the violation of personal rights.[46] Some environmental laws, however, contain exceptions to this rule and allow the *actio popularis* against infringements of the law.[47] Citizens and associations may thus, in principle, contest many administrative decisions in the courts and also initiate criminal proceedings.[48] In practice, however, such actions seem to be quite difficult and ineffective. This is mainly due to the excessive length of the proceedings (on average 6–10 years) and the lack of interim relief.

In recent times the number of criminal prosecutions has increased – due to co-operation between environmental organisations and the newly created environmental prosecutors. In 1991 more than 50 investigations took place and 19 cases where brought in the penal courts.

Environmental associations have only a very limited access to civil courts because the standing is based mainly on individual property rights. In so far as the rights of private neighbours are concerned, very recently a wider interpretation of the neighbourhood relationship has lowered the burden on the plaintiff. Nevertheless, the restrictions are evident and, therefore, actions against private enterprises which affect the environment adversely are, in practice, not possible.

Appeals against administrative decisions do not have suspensive effect. Exception to this rule is only possible to prevent irreversible damage. In practice, the interpretation of the exception is very limited and in most cases the administrative decision is not suspended. Further, the most important interim measure (so-called "*interdictes*") can be interposed only by the owner of an interest in land and not by an environmental organisation.

The administrative procedure is relatively cheap because an attorney is not required. In civil and criminal procedures the burden of cost is quite high. As a rule, the loser pays the costs of the winner in the civil court. In criminal proceedings, the usual expense is around 100,000 pesetas; a civil law suit may

---

[46]Administrative Court Act 1956. Following a decision of the Constitutional Court (60/1982) the plaintiff must prove a "legitimate interest". The jurisprudence has provided an interpretation in which the environmental aims of organisations under private law shall be regarded as "legitimate interest".

[47]*Ley de Suelo* No 1346/1976 (Land Act), art 235; Water Act, as amended in 1985; Fisheries Act, art 58; Decree implementing the Air Pollution Act, art 16; Decree on Environmental Impact Assessments, arts 3 and 4; Ordinance on Polluting Activities, art 30.2.a.; Law on the Preservation of Spaces and Species 1989. See also Alvarez Baquarizo C, "Civic Participation in the Implementation of Environmental Legislation in Spain", in Führ/ Roller *op cit* n 14 *supra* at 36.

[48]Article 270 of the Penal Code.

be much more expensive. Legal aid is available only to natural persons and only if their income is less then twice the minimum wage benchmark.

10. *United Kingdom (England and Wales)*

A third party has no statutory right to administrative review of an environmental decision as discussed in Chapters 8–12. The decision may by challenged by way of judicial review in the High Court. To have the necessary standing the applicant must have a "sufficient interest in the matter to which the application relates" (Supreme Court Act 1981, s 31(3)). In the 1982 *Inland Revenue Commissioners* case [1982] AC 617, the House of Lords provided a liberal, if complex, interpretation of section 31(3). The judgments indicate that an applicant with a good case is likely to be deemed to have standing and that pressure groups should not be precluded from access to the courts by "outdated technical rules". However, recent judicial authority suggests that a restrictive construction of "sufficient interest" is employed in relation to environmental law enforcement. Environmental associations and pressure groups may have standing but this is not always the case. Courts appear to be more ready to attribute sufficient interest to those groups or organisations which have a proximate and enduring concern either with the subject matter of the litigation or with those persons who would have standing (*R* v *Poole Borough Corporation ex parte Beebee* [1991] COD 264, [1991] JPL 643). A group of objectors who as individuals have no cognisable interest cannot establish one by simply organising together (*R* v *Secretary of State for the Environment ex parte Rose Theatre Trust* [1990] 2 WLR 186). Individuals, in order to have standing, must show a greater interest in the decision than other members of the general public.

In an ordinary private law action a plaintiff must have some private legal right or proprietary interest recognised by law which has been violated by the defendant. Where the right enjoyed is a public right, the plaintiff will only have standing, in the absence of other statutory provisions, if he or she has suffered particular damage different from and greater than that suffered by the general public. It is a principle of English law that only the Attorney General can assert public rights in an ordinary civil action. If the Attorney general consents, a private person may pursue a relator action to prevent the commission of a criminal offence, restrain interference with a public right, compel performance of a statutory duty or abate a public nuisance.

Exceptionally, a private law action may be brought against a person for breach of statutory duty. Where a right to bring such an action is not expressly conferred by statute, the plaintiff must show that Parliament intended breach of the relevant statutory duty to be actionable by a person harmed by the breach.

By contrast, prosecution of those in breach of environmental provisions by private persons is not subject to any rules on standing. Consequently, in those, increasingly prevalent, areas where a criminal sanction is provided for the breach of environmental legislation, private prosecutions are becoming popular. In a recent prosecution by Greenpeace (Burton) of Albright & Wilson, the chemical company were fined £2,000 and ordered to pay £20,000 costs for unauthorised discharges into the Irish sea contrary to the Water Act 1989.

None of these actions has a suspensive effect on the original administrative decision. However, in civil actions and judicial review, effective relief is available by way of an interim injunction.

In civil cases, the courts retain an unfettered discretion to apportion costs as they see fit, although the basic rule is that "costs follow the event" so that the successful party will be awarded their costs. Costs are subject to taxation by the courts, and normally will not be recovered in full. Legal aid is not available for public interest litigation.

In criminal cases brought by way of private prosecution, there is no general rule that the costs of such a prosecution should be reimbursed. However, the court may order reimbursement from central funds if to do so would be just and reasonable. If the prosecution was successful in obtaining a conviction, costs may be awarded against the person convicted, as in the case of *Burton* v *Albright and Wilson* MCA 1375; [1992] 4 LMELR (now ELM) 56 (*supra*).

II. Legal basis of the proposal and general comments

Free access to justice for individuals and public interest groups in environmental matters serves to improve the implementation of environmental law and, therefore, to achieve the objectives of the EU environmental policy as set out in Article 130r of the EC Treaty. The proposed Directive is thus proposed as an initiative of the EU to achieve those objectives within the meaning of Article 130s of the EC Treaty.

In so far as administrative and legal proceedings concern the construction and operation of industrial facilities, it also affects indirectly the establishment and functioning of the Internal Market and could, therefore, come into the ambit of Article 100a of the EC Treaty. In the *Titanium Dioxide* case,[49] the ECJ held that where a Directive, from its objective and content, constitutes an environmental measure under Article 130s as well as a measure for the approximation of Member States' laws intended to serve the establishment and functioning of the Internal Market under Article 100a, the latter provision takes priority over the former. However, the *Titanium Dioxide* case concerned a Directive which directly regulated the details of an industrial production process, and whose main focus was clearly economic as well as

---

[49]Case 300/89, *Commission* v *Council* [1992] JEL 109.

ecological. The proposed Directive on Access to Justice, on the other hand, is entirely concerned with procedural rights in the field of environmental protection, in a similar way as the Directives on environmental impact assessment and access to information on the environment, the latter of which was based on Article 130s of the EC Treaty. The legal remedies which the draft Directive proposes to grant to environmental associations would mainly affect non-commercial projects and measures of public authorities and environmentally harmful activities of private persons outside the scope of economic competition. The indirect influence of the Directive on the conditions of industrial and agricultural production is the same which any Directive with an environmental purpose is bound to have – even the Directive on the Conservation of Wild Birds, which regulates the protection of bird habitats and thus the use of potentially cultivable land. To allocate this EU legislation entirely to Article 100a would hardly leave a reasonable field of application for Article 130s.

In order to find a practicable distinction between Articles 100a and 130r, one should look to the predominant object and content of a Directive and to its more or less direct effect on economic activities. In the given case, there can be no doubt that environmental issues have predominance over economic ones and that the effect on market conditions is only indirect and marginal. The proposed Directive is thus based on Article 130s of the EC Treaty.

The above study of the situation in the EU Member States has shown that there exists a variety of mixtures of administrative and judicial review in relation to environmentally relevant acts of administrative authorities. All Member States nowadays – at least since the statutory changes in the Netherlands following the *Benthem* case – have a system of judicial review, and most of them some kind of administrative review of decisions, although the form and the importance of each may be quite different. This means, in principle, that no Member State will be forced to remodel its institutions on account of this proposed Directive. Changes will have to be made concerning the access of common interest groups to institutions for the purposes of environmental protection and also, in some States, concerning the effectiveness of existing procedures and remedies and the rules of cost apportionment.

The proposed Directive does not regulate public participation in the process of administrative decision-making. Due to the variety of acts affecting the environment and the resulting differences in feasibility, time and extent of participation, this issue is too complex to be dealt with incidentally in the context of "access to justice". In line with previous EC legislation, especially the environmental impact assessment Directive (Dir 85/337/EEC), the matter could be regulated separately as part of other environmental protection Directives or in a specific "participation" Directive.

Provision of a right of action against administrative authorities exclusively would, however, be insufficient in view of the fact that the environment is often adversely affected, not so much by the positive acts of an authority, but rather by its failure to act against infringements of the law. Therefore, the draft

Directive would enable citizens to bring an action directly against polluters and other persons who cause harm to the environment, as well as administrative authorities. In order to avoid the confusing effect of parallel proceedings against administrations and polluters, and to respect national priority rules as far as possible, this direct way of action should, however, be limited to cases where the administration has refused or failed to act or where its intervention is clearly insufficient to remedy the situation and thus falls far short of its duties under environmental law.

III. Draft Proposal for a Council Directive Concerning Access to Justice in Environmental Matters

Preamble

The Council of the European Communities,

Having regard to the Treaty establishing the European Economic Community, and in particular Article 130s thereof,
Having regard to the proposal from the Commission,
Having regard to the opinion of the European Parliament,
Having regard to the opinion of the Economic and Social Committee,
Whereas the Community's environment policy, as set out in the Treaty and detailed in the European Communities" Action Programmes on the Environment,[50] aims at a high level of protection;
Whereas the Council declared, in its resolution of February 1993 concerning the Fifth Action Programme "Towards Sustainability",[51] that involvement of all levels of society in a spirit of shared responsibility will require a deepening and broadening of the range of instruments to complement normative legislation;
Whereas the Fifth Action Programme stresses the crucial role of the general public and of non-governmental organisations in environmental protection; whereas it particularly calls for an accessible and efficient complaints facility to be developed at local, regional and national level, as well as practicable access to the courts for individuals and public interest groups;
Whereas the Council adopted, on 7 June 1990,[52] a Directive on the freedom of access to information on the environment;
Whereas an accessible and efficient complaints facility in environmental matters will improve confidence between the general public, the competent authorities and industrial and business undertakings;

---

[50]OJ 1973 C112 at 1; OJ 1977 C139 at 1; OJ 1983 C46 at 1; OJ 1987 C70 at 1; OJ 1993 C138 at 1.
[51]OJ 1993 C138 at 1.
[52]OJ 1990 L158 at 56.

Whereas practicable access to the courts for citizens and public interest groups will ensure that their legitimate interests are protected and that prescribed environmental measures are effectively enforced and illegal practices stopped;

Whereas, in view of the principle of subsidiarity laid down in Article 130r (4) of the Treaty, it is desirable that the control of the implementation of Community environmental law should be decentralised as far as possible, the proceedings in national courts and administrative complaints facilities being an effective control mechanism of this kind;

Whereas the disparities between the laws in force in the Member States concerning administrative and judicial review in environmental matters can create inequality within the Community as regards the standard of environmental protection and the conditions of economic competition;

Whereas a specific guarantee of the access to justice for environmental public interest groups corresponds best to the legal traditions of the Member States and takes into account the prominent role of these associations in the practice of environmental protection;

Whereas it is necessary to grant to environmental associations practicable access to the courts and administrative complaints facilities, whenever administrative acts violate a rule of environmental law or a public authority refuses or fails to act against environmentally harmful activities, and does so in breach of its duties;

Whereas the successful defence of environmental interests in court requires an effective system of interim relief;

Whereas the overriding public interest in the correct implementation of environmental law justifies a considerable reduction of the plaintiff's cost-risk and a partial bearing of the costs by public funds in such environmental lawsuits;

Whereas the positive experience made in some Member States with citizen suit provisions in environmental law demands that the choice of such a legal concept should not be impeded in any way;

Whereas the operation of this Directive should be subject to a review in the light of the experience gained;

HAS ADOPTED THIS DIRECTIVE:

Article 1 – Objective

The object of this Directive is to ensure practicable access to the courts and to administrative complaints facilities for public interest groups in environmental matters.

Article 2 – Definitions

For the purposes of this Directive:
(a)   "environmental association" shall mean any non-governmental organisation which
  (i)   has as its primary objective the protection of the environment, of human health or of the cultural heritage, or the prudent and rational utilisation of natural resources, and
  (ii)   allows any person to join who supports the objectives of the association;
(b)   "environmental law" shall mean the law of the Community and the Member States relating to the protection of the environment, human health or the cultural heritage, or to the utilisation of land or natural resources;
(c)   "administrative act" shall mean any positive action of other than legislative or judicial character, taken by a public authority with external effect, including the authority's refusal to act;
(d)   "sub-statutory rule" shall mean any decree, ordinance, order, bye-law or other binding norm of environmental law below the level of legislation enacted by a national or regional parliament, including, *inter alia*, land-use plans, limit values for emissions, and quality standards;
(e)   "court" shall mean any institution exercising jurisdiction by force of law, composed of independent judges, and empowered to settle disputes by binding and enforceable judgments;
(f)   "environmentally harmful" or "harmful to the environment" shall mean causing actual or potential damage to the health of man or any other living organism, reducing the quality of air, water, or soil, interfering with ecological systems, or impairing the aesthetic appearance of the landscape or of natural or cultural monuments.

Article 3 – Administrative review

Any environmental association is entitled to make use of existing extra-judicial complaints procedures against an administrative act that it considers to be in breach of a rule of environmental law, without having to show an impairment of its own interests.

Article 4 – Judicial review of administrative acts and omissions

(1) An environmental association which considers an administrative act to be in breach of a rule of environmental law may bring an action in the courts for the annulment or alteration of that act without having to show an impairment of its own interests.

(2) Member States may make the legal standing of the plaintiff dependent on prior participation in administrative proceedings only if that participation could reasonably be expected.

(3) If the competent authority, in breach of a duty under environmental law, has refused or failed to act, the association may bring an action in the courts for the enforcement of the law. The courts shall have the power to compel the authority to fulfil its duty.

(4) In the case that the authority has failed to act as requested by an environmental association, Member States may prescribe a waiting period of up to 60 days after the request has been made before the plaintiff may commence the action.

Article 5 – Judicial review of sub-statutory rules

(1) An environmental association which considers a sub-statutory rule to be in breach of higher-ranking environmental law may bring an action in the courts for the annulment or alteration of that rule without having to show an impairment of its own interests.

(2) If a public authority is under a duty to draft a sub-statutory rule of environmental law and has failed to do so, an environmental association may, under the same conditions, bring an action in the courts for the enforcement of that duty. Member States may prescribe a waiting period of up to one year after the request before the plaintiff may commence the action.

Article 6 – Judicial remedies against environmentally harmful activities

(1) An environmental association may bring an action in the courts against any person whom it considers to carry out an environmentally harmful activity in breach of environmental law, without having to show an impairment of its own interests, if the competent public authority has refused or failed to act or if the action taken is obviously insufficient. The plaintiff association shall be entitled to all remedies that will effectively stop the harmful activity and enforce the measures required by environmental law. Besides those remedies, subject to the provisions of Community law on environmental liability it may claim damages or restoration of the environment.

(2) Member States may prescribe a waiting period of up to 60 days after notice of the alleged infringement has been given to the public authority and the prospective defendant, before the plaintiff may commence the action.

Article 7 – Interim relief

(1) Member States shall take the necessary steps to ensure that the access to court under Articles 4, 5 and 6 includes effective interim relief in urgent cases

and for the time pending judgment. The time-limits mentioned in Articles 4(4) and 6(2) shall not apply.

(2) In cases where a person or an authority act obviously in breach of a rule of environmental law, the plaintiff is entitled to demand the immediate suspension of this activity.

Article 8 – Costs

(1) Member States shall take the necessary steps to ensure that the cost of administrative and judicial proceedings under Articles 3 to 7, including lawyers' and experts' fees and possible security deposits, shall not cause a barrier to the commencement or continuation of such proceedings. In particular they shall ensure that a prevailing plaintiff obtains recovery of all costs reasonably incurred, either from the defendant or from state funds. If the action is unsuccessful but has been brought on the basis of an arguable case and in good faith, the plaintiff shall not be required to pay court fees or the costs of other parties, and these costs shall be borne by state funds. Exceptions may be made for unnecessary expenses caused by the conduct of the plaintiff.

(2) The court shall decide at an early stage of the proceedings on whether the association brought the action in good faith and has an arguable case. If the answer is positive, the plaintiff shall not be required to deposit securities for the indemnification of other parties.

Article 9 – Option for "citizen suit" provisions

Nothing in this Directive shall prevent Member States from retaining or introducing legislation that gives any person the right to institute administrative or legal proceedings in environmental matters.

Article 10 – Report

Four years after the date referred to in Article 11 (1), the Member States shall report to the Commission on the experience gained, in the light of which the Commission shall make a report to the European Parliament and the Council together with any proposal for revision which it may consider appropriate.

Article 11 – Entry into force

(1) The Member States shall bring into force the laws and regulations necessary to comply with this Directive by [18 months after the decision of the Council].

(2) The Member States shall inform the Commission immediately of all laws and regulations adopted in implementation of this Directive.

Article 12 – Addressee

This Directive is addressed to the Member States.

Done at . . . date
For the Council
The President

IV. **Comments on individual Articles**

Article 1 (Objective)

Article 1 defines the objective of the proposed Directive in its strict sense. The further-reaching objectives which the Directive seeks to achieve indirectly through the instrument of "access to justice", especially a stricter implementation of environmental law and thus a better quality of environmental protection in the Community, are not repeated here, as they are already expressed in the preamble of the Directive.

"Practicable" access to complaints facilities and the courts is supposed to mean not merely an access in theory and on paper but one which effectively works in practice.

Article 2 (Definitions)

Article 2 defines the basic terms used in the Directive, in so far as they are used in a specific sense.

"Environmental association" is to be understood in a broad sense, including not only organisations with legal personality but also citizen groups with a less formal structure, which nevertheless must be able to formulate a common objective. The requirement that the protection of environment, health, and heritage, or the prudent and rational utilisation of natural resources, must be the "primary" objective of the association, is necessary in order to emphasise the element of commitment to the public interest. It implies that commercial enterprises and organisations for whom environmental protection is only one aim among many should not benefit from the rights created by this Directive. The requirement of open access to membership for anyone who supports the association's objectives is designed to ensure a minimum of internal democracy and prevent the misuse of power by small coteries pursuing particular interests of their own. A system of accreditation or licensing of

102

environmental associations by the government, as it exists in some Member States, is not considered as desirable here because it creates unnecessary bureaucratic barriers to public interest litigation and opens, at least potentially, the way for undue political influence. Instead, the Commission prefers a statutory formulation of objective requirements whose fulfilment should be ascertained by the court or administrative review body in the concrete case.

The definition of "environmental law" follows the formula explaining the Community's environmental policy in Article 130r of the EC Treaty, while including all legal provisions of the Member States as well as those of the Community. The text has been amended to include "cultural heritage" as an object of legal protection since it is also covered by the environmental legislation of several Member States and has been expressly mentioned as part of the environment in Article 3 of the Directive on Environmental Impact Assessments. "Land" has been added to the elements taken from Article 130r, in order to preclude disputes about whether this (*i.e.* the mere surface of the earth), is contained in the term "natural resources".

"Administrative act" should not be equated with the French *acte administratif* or the German *Verwaltungsakt*, since it is meant to encompass any non-legislative or non-judicial activity of public authorities without regard to a regulatory function or formal requirements. The only exception is to be made for activities whose effects are limited to the administration itself. Negative decisions of the authority shall be included, but not mere omissions which are covered by Article 4(3) and (4).

"Sub-statutory rules" do not fall into the category of "administrative acts" since they may be seen as part of legislation. Rules of this kind are of great importance in environmental law as they regulate the numerous technical details which go beyond the capacity of parliamentary statutes. They often contain the crucial decisions on emission limits, environmental quality standards or the use of land in a certain area which influence the state of the environment more profoundly than other instruments of law. Judicial review is of particular importance here and should extend to the whole body of norms below the constitutional or statute law enacted by parliaments of the Member States or their regions and below the law of the European Union.

"Court" is defined according to its function. Emphasised are the ideas of independence from the government – which excludes ministries or any other part of the administration – and the binding nature of its decisions – which excludes, for example, any informal arbitration board whose jurisdiction is based on voluntary agreement only. Beyond that, it does not matter whether the institution is an "ordinary" court or belongs to a separate order of jurisdiction ("administrative court").

The definition of "environmentally harmful" states various criteria which do not exclude each other and will regularly be fulfilled side by side. The meaning of "harm" in this context is not a purely scientific one; it is not limited to effects on the health of living organisms, the functioning of ecological systems or the quality of the various media, but also takes into account aesthetic standards in so far as they apply to the natural environment and cultural heritage.

Article 3 (Administrative review)

This article gives environmental associations the right of access to administrative review, in so far as it is provided by the national legal system, if they claim that the contested act of the administration violates a rule of environmental law. To correct actual breaches of the law is, as such, in the public interest, so that an impairment of the association's own rights and interests is not necessary.

Article 4 (Judicial review of administrative acts and omissions)

Article 4 grants the same right of access in relation to judicial review by the national courts. Two different situations are envisaged:

(i)   The public authority has taken a decision which the plaintiff-to-be regards as violating a rule of environmental law. Paragraph (1) opens the access to judicial review of this decision. As some Member States, quite legitimately, require the plaintiff to participate in the relevant administrative proceedings before he or she may challenge the conclusive decision, para (2) allows this on the condition that participation could reasonably be expected of the plaintiff. This means that the administrative proceedings must indeed have taken place, and the plaintiff must have been given the legal and actual opportunity to take part without high expense or other hardship.

(ii) The authority has been asked to make a decision which the plaintiff-to-be claims is its duty to make under environmental law (for instance to stop illegal pollution), but has refused to decide or has simply failed to do anything. In this case, para (3) opens the way to judicial review of the authority's omission. Since the administration must be granted a reasonable period of time to investigate the matter, para (4) allows the right of action to be suspended for 60 days after the authority has been informed. This period of time follows the "citizen suit" provisions in US environmental statutes.

Article 5 (Judicial review of sub-statutory rules)

Article 5 extends the possibility of judicial review to rules ranking below a parliamentary statute and also covers, like similar provisions in the United States, the case of a failure to draft a rule which is required by higher-ranking environmental law.

Article 6 (Judicial remedies against environmentally harmful activities)

Article 6 grants, under certain conditions, a direct right of action against persons (natural and legal ones) who are considered to carry out an environmentally harmful activity. However, as it is primarily the duty of the authorities to intervene against violations of the law, the association lawsuit is meant to be subsidiary. It is limited to the cases where the competent authority has refused or failed to act – as envisaged in Article 4(3) – or where the action taken by the authority is obviously insufficient to redress the situation and enforce the law. In these cases the plaintiff should be able to choose the remedy – an action against the administration or the polluter or both – according to which proceedings are most likely to achieve positive results for the environment.

The latter part of Article 6(1) gives more details as to the remedies which should be available in the court of the direct action. Apart from the restraining and mandatory injunctions envisaged here, environmental associations should also be able to claim restoration of the environment or damages. The details of this are to be regulated by the Community Directive(s) on environmental liability.

Article 6(2), similarly to Article 4(4), permits Member States to prescribe a waiting period of 60 days in order to avoid unfair "surprise actions".

Article 7 (Interim relief)

Effective interim relief is often crucial to the successful defence of environmental interests in court. Therefore, Member States' legislation should ensure that a plaintiff in these cases can attain quickly and without great difficulty a court ruling which suspends the effect of environmentally relevant administrative decisions or an injunction which effectively stops environmentally harmful activities.

Article 7(2) stipulates more precisely a right of the plaintiff to the immediate suspension of illegal activities in the obvious and most serious cases.

Article 8 (Costs)

The costs issue is fundamental in environmental protection actions. The proposed Article 8 states first the principle that costs should not provide a barrier for the commencement or continuation of such proceedings. The second clause puts this in concrete terms by obliging Member States to ensure that the plaintiff, if he or she succeeds, will recover all costs reasonably incurred, thereby removing any discretion that the complaints authority or the court may have under national law, and providing for the case where the losing party is unable to pay.

This Article will constitute the most conspicuous break with the procedural law of many Member States, in so far as it exempts the plaintiff from court fees and other parties' costs as long as the action was brought in good faith and on the basis of an arguable case. This reduction of the plaintiff's cost-risk is warranted by the consideration that there is an overriding public interest in the correct implementation of environmental law. Therefore, any initiative which aims in this direction should be encouraged and public funds should not be spared in limiting the financial risk for environmental associations that may be excessive, for example in cases where a company as a party to the proceedings makes full use of the available legal and technical expertise.

In some Member States a particularly serious obstacle for the plaintiff is posed by the high securities to be deposited for the indemnification of the defendant or other parties. Whereas Article 8(1) guarantees that in the end – when judgment is rendered – there will be no financial burden for an environmental association acting in good faith and with an arguable case, the barrier remains as long as these qualities of the plaintiff's action are not established. The purpose of para (2), therefore, is to ensure that the plaintiff's cost-risk is calculable at an early stage of the proceedings, to preclude lengthy, expensive, and fruitless litigation.

Article 9 (Option for "citizen suit" provisions)

The draft Directive proposes to open the access to justice for "environmental associations", that is common interest groups working in the field of environmental protection. This limitation has been preferred to the alternative of according the right of action to any member of the general public ("citizen suit") for a number of reasons:

(i)   the legal traditions of many Member States disapprove of the *actio popul"* as a means of defending the public interest in court, whereas most of them nowadays have granted specific rights of action to associations working in the field of environmental protection;

(ii) among the general public it is these associations in particular which today play a prominent role in the practice of environmental protection and also in the litigation for this purpose. They are the most likely to have the funds, the human resources, and the expertise to monitor the implementation of environmental law and organise activities in order to improve the current state of affairs;

(iii) a limitation of the right of action to common interest groups will have the effect of concentrating the legal and social conflicts, thereby facilitating a solution, and of providing a "filter" which prevents any frivolous and querulous litigation by individuals.

The last reason, in fact, does not carry as much weight as the former ones, since the practice in countries with liberal standing rules, like the United States and Ireland, offers no evidence for the claim that querulous actions are of great importance in reality.

The draft, therefore, contains an option clause (Article 9) designed to clarify that the Directive does not affect existing or future legislation of the "citizen suit" type within the Member States.

Article 10 (Report)

In order to review the effect of the Directive, the Member States are obliged to report to the Commission four years after the Directive's entry into force. The reports should contain a quantitative and qualitative survey of the experience gained from the extended access to justice in environmental matters.

Contents of Chapter 4

The Right of Environmental Organisations in Germany to Bring Suits and the Environmental Legal Assistance Fund eV

Chapter 4

The Right of Environmental Organisations in Germany to Bring Suits and the Environmental Legal Assistance Fund eV

Matthias Berger[1]

I. *Locus standi* in environmental matters in Germany

A. **Overview**

"*Wo kein Klaeger, da kein Richter.*"
"Where there is no plaintiff, there can be no judge."

The consequences of the situation described by this famous saying are well known in German environmental law. To ensure that courts overcome deficiencies in enforcing environmental law, the right of citizens to bring suits must be anchored in legislation. Generally, the German legal system only enables plaintiffs to sue when their own, subjective legal rights have been infringed.[1a] As a result, they can only bring proceedings if their own health or personal property is impaired. However, if the environment is damaged through private or public projects without thereby injuring private rights, neither individual citizens nor environmental organisations have standing to sue.

In specific, narrowly defined areas, environmental organisations in Germany have been granted participation rights and rights to bring legal

Matthias Berger practises law in Dusseldorf and is a founding member of Germany's "Environmental Legal Assistance Fund eV" (*Umwelt-Rechtshilfe Fonds e.V.*)
[1] I acknowledge the assistance of David Robinson with regard to the English version of this chapter and for his help in updating it.
[1a] See also Chapter 3, section II (B)(3) for a description of *locus standi* law and related topics in Germany.

proceedings. These rights are not dependent upon injury to health or property.

The extent of the rights of an environmental organisation is dependent upon whether the environmentally damaging behaviour complained of is that of a federal or a state government agency. This arises out of Germany's federal structure.

The federal government can control its own agencies by granting rights of action to environmental organisations. Similarly, the state parliaments can regulate the manner in which state and local administrations exercise their supervisory powers in environmental matters. State and federal parliaments have utilised these powers in varying degrees, resulting in the development of two types of legal proceedings for environmental organisations.

The Federal Nature Conservation Act (FNCA) grants environmental agencies a right to a hearing for projects which are deemed environmentally harmful. Concretely, this means that accredited nature conservation organisations are sent the underlying documents and are given an opportunity to voice their opinion concerning the project. The nature conservation organisations are, in effect, limited to exercising participatory rights by means of a submission prior to decisions being made on whether to exclude projects, including public works projects, from natural environment and national park protective provisions. For example, in North Rhine-Westphalia, there are approximately 12 accredited environmental organisations with a common office in Essen, to which notification of project proposals is made. Any organisation can request a copy of the environmental assessment of the proponent agency. Recent administrative decisions, for example a decision in the State of Hessen in 1993 declaring a road project consent void due to non-compliance with the obligation to advise the accredited environmental organisations, have affirmed the legal status of this right to comment on proposals. As challenges cannot be made on merits or substantive grounds, however, in practice the right to comment under FNCA is only a dull sword for environmental organisations.

At the state level, however, a more effective right of action has been introduced – the so-called altruistic organisation plaint. This form of action offers environmental organisations the opportunity to challenge specific administrative actions in the courts, based on a breach of substantive regulations of environmental law. Given that these regulations seek to protect the general public rather than private individuals or corporations, some of the states have relaxed normal rules of standing.

To a limited extent, plaints by altruistic organisations act as a control and have a preventive effect.

B. **Shortcomings**

The legal position of the environmental organisations described above has been significantly undermined as a result of four factors.

First, the organisations cannot participate in all licensing hearings of the federal and state agencies. The right of participation exists in only some projects regarded as particularly environmentally harmful. For several years, the range of these projects in which participation is possible has been steadily narrowed by legislative amendment.

The second limitation is that certain agencies, particularly at the federal level, are exempt from substantive control through court proceedings brought by altruistic organisations. Thus, environmental organisations cannot prevent the activities of the federal waterways, post office or rail agencies by way of court proceedings, even though the activities of these agencies are occasionally environmentally harmful. In principle, there is no means of controlling the potentially harmful activities of German and foreign armed forces on German soil.

Only 10 of the 16 states have adopted the legislation to allow altruistic organisations to bring suits. This is the third limitation. Neither North Rhine-Westphalia, the state with the highest population density and most industry, nor Bavaria, another significant state, have granted environmental organisations rights to participate in decision-making by state and local agencies. This appears to have little to do with the political leanings of the state as North Rhine-Westphalia is governed by the Social Democrats whereas the conservative Christian Social Union has the parliamentary majority in Bavaria.

Even in those states which have provided the environmental organisations with the possibility of bringing an altruistic plaint, the right of action is limited – and this is the fourth limitation – to violations of FNCA and regulations. German environmental law is codified in a number of other statutes which are not subject to altruistic organisation proceedings. These include the Water Act, the Waste Disposal Act, the Nuclear Act, the Genetic Technology Act and the Emission Protection Act (under which industrial pollution licenses are granted). The provisions of these acts can only be enforced by way of complaint from personally affected individuals and not by environmental organisations.

In summary, the position of environmental organisations in the courts is rather weak and, according to widely held opinion, should be strengthened. However, there is little likelihood that the situation will change in the near future. The Federal Government, controlled by the conservative Christian Democratic Union, has kept all significant amendment of environmental law on the back-burner.

II. **The Environmental Legal Assistance Fund eV**

A. **Background**

The legal effectiveness of environmental organisations in Germany is limited by a host of practical problems in addition to the restrictions mentioned above.

Under German procedural law, the loser pays in civil proceedings. This means paying one's own legal costs as well as those of the prevailing party. Environmental organisations are not granted any leniency with respect to court fees and expenses. Although by international standards neither court costs nor attorney fees are prohibitive in Germany, these expenses often explain why court proceedings in appropriate cases are rarely initiated. The cost of obtaining expert opinion also plays a role. Experts' fees can outweigh all other litigation expenses in complicated environmental proceedings.

The environmental organisations in Germany presently concentrate their efforts on nature conservation and have just begun, in the last few years, to develop political activities in other environmental fields.

Moreover, the members of most of Germany's large environmental groups do not see much potential for litigation to provide effective environmental protection. None of the environmental organisations employ full-time lawyers, and there are no equivalents to the US public interest firms such as the Nature Resources Defense Council, the Environmental Defense Fund or Sierra Club Legal Defense Fund.

A group of active lawyers and scientists saw the absence of environmental groups before the courts as a shortcoming. In August 1992 they established an association named the Environmental Legal Assistance Fund eV (*Umwelt-Rechtshilfe Fonds e.V.*), based on the above US models.

The aim of the association is to enable or encourage the bringing of environmental test cases. The association sets strict standards in its memorandum and articles of association for the selection of these cases. The legal questions involved must be of central and general importance for environmental protection. The decisions and reasons of the board of directors concerning the selection of proceedings are made public.

At present, the association has about 40 members and is financed solely though contributions from its members.

An important form of support offered by the association is that of publicising public interest court proceedings. The association publishes the facts and status of proceedings supported by it in a letter to members and the press. In addition, the Environmental Legal Assistance Fund eV sends copies of all briefs and other documents prepared for proceedings to third parties requesting them. Only reimbursement of copying and mail costs is requested. Because third parties are not entitled to inspect the court file, the publication of documents filed in court increases the accountability of the association and acts as a form of self-help for other affected parties.

Financial support for plaintiffs is also available. The association is non-profit-making and thus contributions to it are tax deductible. At present, however, the fund is too small (about DM 20,000) to allow payment of legal fees, and the litigation described below has been taken by members acting in a *pro-bono* capacity, with only limited reimbursement of some expenses in some cases. If the client can pay legal fees, these are set at modest, scale rates rather than calculated on an hourly rate (as is the case with commercial clients).

When funds permit, the Environmental Legal Assistance Fund eV plans to hire its own attorneys and scientists to bring proceedings.

As at November 1994, the association was supporting, in the manner described above, five test-case proceedings.

B. **Five current cases**

Case 1: Suit demanding traffic reduction in the city of Dusseldorf to reduce high level emissions

The concentration of harmful substances in the air has reached a point in Dusseldorf (capital of the state of North Rhine-Westphalia), as in many other cities, which can only be described as harmful to the long-term health of its inhabitants. More than 70% of such substances are emitted by automobiles. Consequently, it is crucial that the city, through its planning and other responsible agencies, attempts to reduce traffic congestion and thereby the level of harmful emissions.

The German Constitution guarantees the protection of citizens against harmful substances. Further, Article 3 of EC Directive 85/203/EEC sets maximum acceptable nitrogen dioxide concentrations for the air.

First, the plaintiffs seek the application of appropriate measures by the court to reduce the amount of harmful substances in the traffic-congested city. Secondly, they seek to have air quality measured where the pollution is greatest – in street "canyons" and at major intersections.

The case raises the issue of the enforceability of both the constitutional right of protection against harmful substances, as well as whether a citizen can sue for compliance with the EC Directive.[2] It asks the court to rule, in the absence of guidance from the German legislature, on the difficult questions of what level of air pollution constitutes a threat to health, and which party bears the onus of proof.

Filed in 1991, the proceedings had yet to be allocated a hearing date as at November 1994, apparently having been relegated to the "too hard" basket of the court.

Case 2: Right of access to environmental information

Germany has failed to incorporate the EC Directive on Freedom of Access to Environmental Information (Dir 90/313/EEC) into German law.

---

[2]A Directive can have "direct effect" against the Member State or an "emanation of the State" (*Foster v British Gas plc* [1990] 3 All ER 897) if it is clear and precise, unconditional and does not require further definition by the Member State. Ball S and Bell S, *Environmental Law*, London, Blackstone Press, 2nd ed. 1994, 48–50.

A group of citizens in Recklinghausen, North Rhine – Westphalia, have sought access to an expert opinion concerning weapons-related land contamination. The Directive is being interpreted by the defendant administrative agency so as to deny access in on-going administrative proceedings.[3] This interpretation contradicts the spirit and letter of the Directive. As almost all significant environmental data is in use in administrative proceedings of some sort or another, the interpretation negates the rights of citizens to information conferred by the Directive.

A further issue raised in the case concerns the reasonableness of fees charged by German agencies for providing information. For example, in one case a prohibitively high fee of DM 7,000 was charged.

Progress in this case was delayed in anticipation of legislative resolution of the questions raised while the Federal Government eventually made a law in July 1994 to apply the Directive on Freedom of Access to Information in Germany, the law does not address the two problems outlined above, namely the inaccessability of information the subject of administrative proceedings, and excessive costs.

Case 3: Destruction of a nature conservation area through the expansion of brown coal mining

The brown coal strip-mining near Cottbus, in the state of Brandenburg, is to be expanded in the near future in the direction of Lakoma, an adjacent village. A significant part of the Hammergraben, a medieval irrigation system having historic preservation status, lies close to Lakoma.

At present there are no permits for the expansion of the mining activities. Mine-licensing proceedings normally require an environmental impact assessment (UVP). The unification treaty between the Federal Republic of Germany and the former German Democratic Republic (GDR), however, appears to allow for a shortcut procedure without UVP and public participation.

In issue in this case is the high quality of the nature reserve over which mining activities are to be extended, and the desirability of considering alternatives to brown coal mining in the region.

Case 4: Sewage disposal charges – citizens subsidising industry

A citizen of Cologne, in North Rhine-Westphalia, is defending himself against an unfair sewage charge in which he must pay the same amount for each cubic metre of sewage as industries which discharge significantly greater amounts of harmful, trade-waste substances into the sewer.

---

[3]Article 3 of the Directive enables Member States to refuse a request for information on a number of grounds, including where it affects "The confidentiality of the proceedings of public authorities, international relations and national defence".

Trade-waste discharges corrode the sewage system and increase the cost of operating sewage works. The local government could demand a so-called "heavy polluter surcharge" and thereby distribute costs more fairly. Furthermore, the local government oversees only approximately 500 of the 5,000 companies which introduce significant amounts of polluted water into the public sewage system. This shows a deficiency in enforcement which results in private households having to pay too large a share of the cost of public sewage treatment.

Final determination of this case was delayed by a North-Rhine Westphalia appellate court decision late in 1994, a similar case concerning the fee levels set for the disposal of domestic waste, relative to the fees charged to dispose of more toxic, industrial waste. That case cast doubt on the validity of the broader system of sewage disposal charges. As a result, local governments are now reviewing their cost-recovery regimes.

Case 5: Resumption of land for high voltage electricity powerlines
A power company is currently constructing a new high voltage electricity route in Thuringia. The company obtained the necessary licence from the State Government according to the environmental planning provisions in force in the German Democratic Republic, prior to unification. Of course "property owners" in the GDR had no right to participate in the decision to grant the licence.

A property owner has refused to allow the use of her agricultural land for powerlines. As her land is enclosed by forest, her action could block the route.

The case considers the antiquated Energy Industry Act 1935. While resumption procedure has been considered by the courts, the legality of licensing procedures under this Act has not. The particular issue is whether it is legal to licence a private company to build powerlines where these are to the detriment of a third party who is not invited to participate in the licence proceedings. At first instance, in 1994 a district court ruled against the third party agricultural landowner. Leave to appeal was refused, thereby enabling final determination of the issue by the Constitutional Court, where proceedings are pending at November 1994.

Contents of Chapter 5

Collective Interests in Brazilian Environmental Law

Chapter 5

Collective Interests in Brazilian Environmental Law

Edesio Fernandes[1]

I. Introduction

This chapter discusses the main legal instruments available in Brazil for the defence of collective interests in environmental matters, especially the civil public action created by federal Law No 7.347/1985.

Brazilian environmental legislation has been progressively enacted since the 1930s, and special emphasis should be placed on federal Law No 6.938/ 1981, which determines the basic legal framework for environmental action, conservation and preservation. The federal Constitution 1988 dedicated a whole chapter to the matter of environmental protection. Dozens of environmental laws have been enacted subsequently by the federated states and municipalities, given that under the Constitution protection of the environment is a matter of concurrent competence of all levels of government.[2]

Despite legislative improvement, however, serious degradation of the country's urban, industrial and rural environments, including the Amazon region, continues. It has become evident that the environmental question in Brazil has a very clear politico-economic nature. Regardless of the interesting experiences of ecological administration in some municipalities – such as that of the internationally known Curitiba – the truth is that state action in environmental matters remains marginal, if not merely rhetorical. Indeed, by direct or indirect action, or by failing to act, the Brazilian state continues to be

*Edesio Fernandes** is a Brazilian lawyer and town planner. Having completed his Ph.D at Warwick University in 1994, he is currently teaching and researching environmental law at the University of London. He is also a research associate at the Institute of Commonwealth Studies, University of London.

[1] I am grateful to David Robinson for extensive structural and linguistic assistance and for comment upon several drafts of this chapter. I would also like to thank Tim Murphy, Robert Annibale and Anne Larrabure for their support and comments on an earlier version.

[2] Fernandes E, "Law, Politics and Environmental Protection in Brazil" (1992) 4 *Journal of Environmental Law*.

one of main agents responsible for the patterns of environmental degradation in the country.[3]

In this context, the use of law to protect collective environmental interests and rights has become increasingly significant in Brazil, both as a means of achieving concrete results and to promote a wider social awareness of environmental problems.

II. **The defence of diffuse environmental interests**

The improvement of environmental legislation has prompted the gradual enactment of specific legislation to enable the defence of collective environmental values, interests and rights. The first of such laws naturally expressed the concepts and principles of the liberal legal system long prevailing in the country, particularly those of individual and private rights, in the definition of *locus standi*.

The limitations of the liberal legal system in dealing with both the nature of environmental problems and the new forms of social conflict brought about by the country's intense urbanisation and industrialisation soon became apparent. As a result, new legislation has made possible the defence, in courts, of several forms of "diffuse" interests, including those concerning environmental protection.

Together with the recognition of the *collective right* to the environment, the new legislation accepts that some of the activities which produce significant environmental impact reach and affect an indeterminate number of people in different ways. Despite the lack of a clear and immediate association amongst them, all such people, as well as each of them, have a legitimate interest to take legal action, since the object of the legal protection – the environment – is juridically indivisible. In a significant reform of legal liberalism, although still within the broader framework determined by it, the more progressive legislation enacted since the mid-1980s in Brazil has modified, and widened *locus standi*.

There are three major legal instruments which enable, to differing extents and in different ways, the state and others to take legal action to defend the collective values inherent in the environment, namely, the traditional *acao popular* (popular action), the *mandado de seguranca coletivo* (collective writ of mandamus) and, above all, the *acao civil publica* (civil public action) created by federal Law No 7.347/1985.

---

[3]Fernandes E, "Constitutional Environment Rights in Brazil: distinguishing rhetoric from reality" (1993), paper presented at the conference "Human Rights Approaches to Environmental Protection in the Commonwealth and Beyond", promoted by the Commonwealth Institute and the School of Oriental and African Studies of the University of London, London.

A. **From the "popular action" to the "civil public action"**

Until the enactment of federal Law No 7.347/1985, the right of access to courts was mainly available to individuals claiming individual rights in their own names. The scope of such limited actions was made even more restrictive by conservative, and dominant, judicial attitudes in favour of economic exploitation of private property rights.

There was very little scope for the defence of collective interests, and the vast majority of the existing applicable instruments, legal and administrative, could only be used by public authorities.[4] As was typical of liberal legal systems, the state – conceived as a neutral agent in politico-economic-social life – was considered as the main guardian of collective interests and rights, and, therefore, was the main party given access to courts, while citizens were excluded.

Apart from those instruments available to the public authorities, the only legal instrument which could be used by citizens to defend collective environmental interests and rights was the popular action created by federal Law No 4.717/1965 and still in force. The popular action can be brought by any person enjoying political rights (not by associations) only against acts of the public authorities – and not private agents – which have caused damage to the "public patrimony".

The scope of the popular action is, therefore, very limited. Given the absence of alternatives before 1985, however, many popular actions were initiated by environmental organisations to preserve and defend the environment. The constraints were manifold.

First, since they could not bring the popular action in their own name, the existing environmental organisations had instead to "hide" behind the signatures of individuals, limiting the political dimension of the litigation. Secondly, they had to fight against the dominant, and very narrow, judicial interpretation according to which "public patrimony" was not considered to be the patrimony of the community, but only public property and public money. Thirdly, in most cases those people who tried to make use of the popular action to defend environmental values were also expected to prove and quantify economic cost in financial terms, which, naturally, was not an easy task.

In this context, litigation brought under federal Law No 4.717/1965 had very little impact. Only with the promulgation of the federal Constitution in 1988[5] was the scope of the popular action widened:

---

[4]There are many legal instruments which enable the state to promote environmental protection. These can be used in conjunction with the state's own enforcement mechanisms relating to public control of land, development and expropriation (Fernandes (1992) at n 2 *supra*).
[5]Article 5, LXXIII.

"Any citizen may bring a popular action which aims at annulling an act harmful to the public patrimony or that of an entity in which the state participates; to administrative morality; to the environment; to historical and cultural patrimony; except in the case of bad faith, the claimant will be exempt of costs and of the *onus da sucumbencia* (burden of defeat)."

The potential to defend the environment through law was also widened by the enactment of federal Law No 7.347/1985, creating the civil public action, which operates in addition to the popular action, as broadened by the Constitution. The main provisions of federal Law No 7.347/1985 will be discussed in more detail below. At this juncture, it is important to stress that its distinctive characteristic is the possibility of its use by non-governmental organisations against the state, corporations and individuals.

If non-government organisations (NGOs) were pressure groups until the enactment of federal Law No 7.347/1985, the new legislation recognised their legitimacy to promote the defence of collective interests as forms of interest aggregation. The struggle of NGOs could now take place within the domain of law as well.

B. **The Federal Constitution 1988 and the collective writ of mandamus**

The popular action and the civil public action were reinforced by the socially-oriented, less individualistic treatment given to collective rights and diffuse interests by the 1988 Constitution. The Constitution opened a new stage in the evolution of Brazilian environmental law.[6]

In fact, the provisions of federal Law No 7.347/1985 were pioneering instruments which paved the way for the Constitution, which, in its first article, recognised that the traditional forms of representative democracy – that Siamese twin of legal liberalism – are not sufficient to express Brazil's lively, and highly contradictory, political scene:[7]

"All the power emanates from the people, who exert it through elected representatives *or directly*, in the terms of this Constitution."

---

[6]I have described and analysed this evolution elsewhere (see Fernandes E, "Aspectos da Gestao Ambiental no Brasil" (1985) 8 *Revista de Saneamento Basico*; "Protecao Juridica do Meio Ambiente" (1987) 72 *Revista de Direito Publico*; and (1992) (at n 2 *supra*). The 1988 Constitution recognised the collective right to a balanced environment, giving both the state and the community the responsibility for its preservation as well as for its defence. On the whole, despite the need for the improvement of some of the existing laws – such as those governing the pollution of waters and the exploitation of mineral resources – environmental legislation in Brazil (as distinct from its implementation) is satisfactory, since concepts, powers, and instruments are well defined. Environmental laws have also to be viewed with the land use control law, the scope of which was widened by the treatment given to property rights by the Constitution (Fernandes E, "Urban Law and Urban Change: an analysis of the Brazilian case" (1991), paper presented at the Eighth Urban Change and Conflict Conference, promoted by the International Sociological Association, Lancaster.)
[7]Article 1; emphasis added.

Indeed, there is in the Constitution an initial movement to integrate participatory and representative democracy – namely, there is a slightly broader scope for the action of NGOs in the decision-making process, especially at the local level.

Article 5 of the Constitution recognised that associations "when explicitly authorised, have legitimacy to represent their affiliates, judicially or extrajudicially" (art 5, XXI). This principle was supported by the collective writ of mandamus (art 5, LXX, "b"), and the reinforcement of the civil public action (art 129, III).

The collective writ of mandamus created by the Constitution can be brought by associations legally constituted for at least a year in order to protect clear, personal (*líquido e certo*) rights of their members when explicitly authorised by them, which rights are not covered by *habeas corpus* or *habeas data*, whenever the agent responsible "for the illegality or abuse of power is a public authority" or an agent of public law "in the exercise of responsibilities of public authorities" (art 5, LXIX, LXX, "b"). The scope for the use of such an instrument is again restricted to suing public authorities, and the requirement that the plaintiff have a certain and personal interest in the subject matter prevents the use of the collective writ of mandamus in most cases of environmental damage. In fact, no such action has been brought to date.

III The civil public action

The civil public action created by federal Law No 7.347/1985, as amended by federal Law No 8.078/1990, is undoubtedly the most interesting and progressive legal instrument available to both citizen and state to defend and enforce collective environmental interests and rights. Although the law also covers other forms of diffuse interests – such as those of consumers – I shall analyse its contents exclusively from the viewpoint of "diffuse interests in environmental protection".

An English translation of the Civil Public Action Law is appendixed to this Chapter.

A. Nature and objectives

Although the legislation itself mentions a "civil public action", in fact federal Law No 7.347/1985 governs a number of actions of different natures – *declaratória* (declaratory), *constitutiva* (constitutive) and *condenatória* (condemnatory) – which can be brought, in isolation or in combination, for the defence of the environmental values, interests and rights protected by the Constitution and ordinary legislation. It deals with legal responsibility for environmentally damaging activities and liability for environmental restoration.

Some of the legal definitions are technically imprecise or even wrong. For example, although the preamble mentions a "civil action of responsibility", on the whole the legislation covers many more aspects than that of liability. Moreover, many of the concepts dealt with by the legislation are somewhat vague, and therefore they have to be defined by legal doctrine and jurisprudence. To some extent, this means that the reach of such provisions can be further widened through judicial interpretation, which would enable the legislation to follow, and to work as a significant instrument of changing attitudes to the environment. However, by the same token, the progressive intention of the legislation may be distorted by a reactionary utilisation of its vagueness and loopholes by conservative, and usually more powerful, groups, who will also be more in tune with the conservative nature of the Brazilian judiciary.[8]

In the absence of specific definition, it has been accepted that federal Law No 7.347/1985 adopted the same broad definition of the "environment" as federal Law No 6.938/1981.[9] Moreover, the 1985 legislation covers damage caused to goods which belong both to the "public", "social" and "cultural" patrimony, be they listed or not (art 1). Its provisions have to be combined with those established by the Constitution and other laws, and therefore the object of legal protection is extremely broad.

B. **Standing**

The most innovative aspect of the legislation is its treatment of *locus standi* (art 5). Civil public actions to defend the environment can be brought by the federal Union, federated-states, municipalities, and, to the extent of their powers and duties, their respective public companies, foundations and para-statal *autarquias* and "mixed-economy societies"; by the *Ministerio Publico*[10] of the Union and federated-states; or by those NGOs which have been legally

---

[8]For example, a member of the *Ministerio Publico* in the State of Rio de Janeiro has used federal Law No 7.347/195 against workers on strike, to defend "consumer's rights" (Antunes P de B, *Curso de Direito Ambiental* (1992), Rio de Janeiro, Renovar at 23).
[9]For an analysis of the legal concept of the "environment, see Fernandes (1992) at n 2 *supra*.
[10]Although relatively autonomous, the *Ministerio Publico* is an executive organ, and it exists at both the federal level – the Union's *Ministerio Publico* – and at the federated-state level – each of the 27 states in Brazil has its own *Ministerio Publico*. It corresponds to the historical institution of *parquet*; in the Brazilian version, it is a hybrid between the Attorney General's and the Public Prosecutor's offices, with civil as well as criminal prosecutorial roles. Article 127 of the 1988 Constitution defined the *Ministerio Publico* as a "permanent institution, essential to the state's juridicial function", its main attributions being "the defence of the legal order, of the democratic regime and of inalienable social and individual interests". As such, the *Ministerio Publico* must take part in, amongst many other cases, all actions involving minors, family law, etc, besides those actions in which the state itself is a party.

constituted to promote the protection of the environment. Any such entity can join, as *litisconsorte*, proceedings initiated by another.[11]

Article 5 is an exception to the general rule determined by article 6 of the Civil Procedures Code, according to which "nobody can claim, in his or her own name, the right of someone else, except when authorised by law". It is an example of "procedural substitution", since all the parties mentioned in the legislation act in their own name rather than as representatives.

Civil public actions can be brought against individuals, state-owned and private companies and the state. The *Ministerio Publico*, when not a party in the action, has to follow the procedure as an observer – *custos legis* – and replace the association if it discontinues a case it has initiated.

Any person can, and civil servants must, provoke the initiative of the *Ministerio Publico*, by providing it with information about facts which may come to constitute the object of a civil public action (art 6). Such representations must be supported by a description of facts – to avoid mobilising the judicial apparatus by mere hearsay – but the *Ministerio Publico* is free to make the decision as to whether or not to initiate the action. While the action by individuals is a discretionary, as well as a concrete means for the exercise of their citizenship rights, those civil servants who fail to inform the *Ministerio Publico* may incur the crime of *prevaricacao* (violation of duty) established by Article 319 of the Criminal Code.

Judges and courts who come across information which may justify the initiation of proceedings also have to refer it to the *Ministerio Publico* (art 7). They cannot initiate the actions by themselves and, again, the *Ministerio Publico* is free to decide on the matter – although some jurists[12] believe that it is obliged to undertake a civil inquiry (see below).

The most significant innovation brought about by federal Law No 7.347/1985 was the recognition of NGOs, called "associations" by the law, as legitimate parties, provided they have been regularly constituted for more than a year. The proviso is not definitive, however, since it can be dispensed with by the judge in order to accept actions brought by associations constituted for less than a year. This provision is an expression of the constitutional principle (art 225) according to which the community has the duty, as well as the right, to preserve and to defend the environment.

The *Ministerio Publico* has standing to take part in civil actions as claimant, co-claimant, substitute party and observer. It can also initiate a civil inquiry. This provision has given an environmental dimension to the action of the state

---

[11]For a discussion of article 2, involving the question of jurisdiction and competence, see Antunes at n 8 *supra*; Campos RC, *Acao Civil Publica* (1989), Rio de Janeiro, Aide; Mazzilli HN, *A defesa dos interesses difusos* (1988), Sao Paulo, Revista dos Tribunais; Mancuso R de C, *Acao Civil Publica* (1989), Sao Paulo, Revista dos Tribunais; Machado PAL, *Direito Ambiental Brasileiro* (1983), Sao Paulo, Revista dos Tribunais; Machado PAL, *Acao Civil Publica e Tombamento* (1987), Sao Paulo, Revista dos Tribunais; and Meirelles HL, "Protecao Ambiental e Acao Civil Publica" (1986) 165 *Revista de Direito Administrativo*.
[12]Antunes *op cit* at n 8 *supra*.

through the *Ministerio Publico*, whose role had previously been confined to criminal prosecutions.

Article 129 of the 1988 Constitution, repeating federal Law No 7.347/1985, listed amongst the institutional functions of the *Ministerio Publico* "the promotion of the civil inquiry and the civil public action for the protection of the public and social patrimony, of the environment, and of other diffuse and collective interests" (art 129, III). The broadened role of the independent *Ministerio Publico*, acting *ex officio*, is certainly one of the most important initiatives promoting the enforcement of social and environmental rights. It does not, however, replace the need for increasing public participation.

C. **Procedural factors**

The two main forms of civil public action – together with *acoes cautelares* (interlocutory injunctive proceedings) (art 4) and those Civil Procedures Code suits which are compatible with federal Law No 7.347/1985 (art 19) – are a *condenacao em dinheiro* (civil fine)[13] or an *obrigacao de fazer ou nao-fazer* (obligation to act or cease from acting) or both.

Since the legislation failed to establish a specific procedure for the course of such actions, doctrine affirms that the ordinary procedure established by the Civil Procedures Code is applicable, apart from the case of condemnatory actions, which can follow the *sumarissimo* (summary) proceedings.[14]

Article 4 authorised the utilisation of interlocutory injunctions. Such injunctions can take all the forms defined by the Civil Procedures Code – "preventive", "incidental", "restraining orders", etc. However, the bureaucracy of the judicial system in Brazil is such that, in many cases, the instrumental *acoes cautelares* often become true ordinary actions, losing their *raison d'être* – the immediate protection of a legal object – at some point on the way.

Article 12 established the possibility for the concession of *mandado liminar* (temporary restraining order) to put an immediate stop to harming activities, or in the case of a *acao cautelar*, to prevent them from starting. The *liminar* order can also impose a fine (art 12, para 2).

Other significant procedural aspects relate to the forms of evidence required. An interested party can obtain discovery of all documents and information necessary for supporting the initiating proceedings and, subject to claims of legal privilege, whoever possesses them must submit them within 15 days (art 8). The *Ministerio Publico* can, naturally, do the same, as well as requiring examinations and expert testimonies (art 8, para 1). The refusal, delay or omission of such documents and data constitutes a serious crime (art 10).

---

[13]Article 13 and Decree No 92.302/1986 and Decree No 96.617/1988 set out the conditions for the management of the money by a fund.
[14]Antunes at n 8 *supra*; Mazzilli at n 11 *supra*.

Since the legislation adopted the modern concept of civil responsibility, that is, of objective responsibility, it is sufficient to prove the existence of a causal connection between the action and the damage done. In the case of subjective responsibility, that is, responsibility with guilt, the sentence must be fully supported by a thorough investigation.

The *Ministerio Publico* can conduct civil inquiries before initiating cases (art 8, para 1). However, the legislation totally failed to establish a procedure for such administrative inquiries, and not surprisingly the only inquiries to date have been incomplete, flawed and unnecessarily bureaucratic. On the other hand, the legislation established a worthy review procedure where the *Ministerio Publico* is minded not to initiate a civil public action (art 9).

D. **Problems**

Federal Law No 7.347/1985 has very broad provisions, and its reach will depend fundamentally on the formation and consolidation of jurisprudence. Since dozens of actions have been taken since the law was enacted, many of which have already reached a final decision at the higher courts, it is possible to make a preliminary evaluation of its efficiency and impact, as well as its many shortcomings.

1. *Legal costs*

In a significant change in relation to the traditional legal system, art 18 of federal Law No 7.347/1985 established that no advance deposit or payment, comprising all sorts of expenses such as legal costs, emoluments and fees, is due when civil public actions are brought. Moreover, apart from *mala fides* cases, those associations which initiate the cases cannot be required to pay legal costs, procedural emoluments and expenses, as well as lawyers' fees. Article 17 established that, in cases of bad faith, both the association and its directors should be liable jointly for lawyers' fees as well as a fine equivalent to ten times the due legal costs, and should also be liable to pay compensation.

Such mechanisms are interesting, but not sufficient. In the Brazilian legal system, all those who initiate legal cases must be represented by lawyers (Constitution 1988, art 133), and the general Civil Procedures Code rule (art 20) is that the loser pays the amount being determined by the judge (usually corresponding to a percentage of the total value of the matter in dispute). This provision was conceived as a measure of equity between both contending parties and a liberal assumption that litigation takes place between equal parties.

Quite apart from the problem of quantifying environmental damage, which may be of a non-financial nature, the fees charged by lawyers are agreed in advance with clients, often at higher levels than those suggested by their professional associations. Most lawyers demand some form of advance payment. Lawyers are usually very expensive and, therefore, access to courts is restricted to those who can afford high fees.

Legal aid in Brazil is negligible, can only be provided by lawyers employed by official organisations, and is presently unavailable to fund collective interest cases.

In this context, it is laudable that, when defeated, environmental associations do not have to pay the fees of the other party's lawyers. Indeed, the costs rule in the Civil Procedures Code can never be applied to civil public actions, in which non-profit associations usually have to contend with powerful and affluent adversaries. However, federal Law No 7.347/1985 failed to provide that, when they win, the legal costs of associations should be awarded.

In practice, most environmental associations lack sufficient financial resources to pay their own lawyers, rendering the immunity against liability for the other side's legal costs of little value. The environmentally committed lawyers who represent associations generally do so for little, if any, payment; naturally, the level of their involvement is affected by this constraint.

The participation of lawyers in NGOs, as well as the creation of groups of lawyers committed to bringing legal actions on environmental and social matters, are nascent phenomena in Brazil. They are the result of the recent, though still incipient, re-democratisation of the country. Such initiatives would benefit enormously from a change in federal Law No 7.347/1985 to enable the winning party to recover its legal costs. Legal aid should be widened, so that it could be granted to autonomous lawyers and for collective claims. This should be part of a broader movement to extend access to justice in Brazil, which, in itself, should be regarded as a most important "diffuse interest".[15]

As a result of the cost problems indicated above, instead of initiating the action by themselves directly, most associations have had to rely on the initiative of the *Ministerio Publico*.

2. *Enforcement and judicial power*

One of the main weaknesses of the 1985 legislation is its failure to establish procedures for the execution of judgments. The procedures for both the action itself and for execution of judgment are governed by the Civil Procedures Code, which is limited to conflicts between individuals over individual interests and rights. The provisions of the Civil Procedures Code do not suit the collective nature of civil public actions, nor do they provide instruments capable of preventing or repairing environmental damage from many complex activities.

----
[15]Antunes at n 8 *supra*.

Even more seriously, environmental cases are hamstrung by the poor organisation and functioning of the Brazilian judiciary. The 1988 Constitution has not altered the workings of the judiciary which, having long been inadequate, were even more distorted under military rule (1964–1988). Judicial independence was eroded during military rule, both financially and politically, through the concentration of power and financial resources with the Federal Government. Even since the first steps towards re-democratisation, access to the courts remains limited by cost and delay. Corruption is common. In short, the Brazilian judicial system remains deeply elitist and obsolete.

Some jurists have proposed the creation of a specialised environmental court for environmental cases. This court would operate similarly to the other specialised courts already existing in Brazil: the Labour Court, the Electoral Court, the Military Court and the Federal Court. However, as general awareness of environmental matters in Brazil is still very limited, and the environmental movement is still nascent, a specialist environmental court seems far off. In my view, for the time being a much more important task would be the promotion of comprehensive environmental education for judges and members of the *Ministerio Publico*, as well as to law students.

E. Evaluation

Whilst the civil public action law has been in force for eight years, civil servants, judges and NGOs have made very little use of the action. As noted above, NGOs have had to rely, to a large extent, on the initiative of the *Ministerio Publico* because of a lack of funds to obtain on-going advice.

Actions have been brought by several representatives of the *Ministerio Publico* across the country, covering environmental issues such as the building of rubbish recycling plants, tree preservation, mining activities, logging operations, the protection of historico-cultural heritage, the protection of areas inhabited by indigenous people, building of nuclear reactors, etc.[16] Generally speaking, when it has not been legally required, the initiative of the *Ministerio Publico* has usually been a response to popular outcry. With rare exceptions, the members of the *Ministerio Publico*, as well as the vast majority of judges, are (cons)trained in a strong tradition of liberal legal scholarship, and their awareness of environmental processes is very limited.

In any event, it can be said that the history of the defence of collective environmental interests and rights through federal Law No 7.347/1985 has

---

[16]For more information on the main judicial decisions in civil public actions, see Antunes at n 8 *supra*. Amongst recent cases is the decision against the forestry company Aracruz, which, despite its award-winning environmental technology and standards, planted trees in conservation areas (in the coastal "Mata Atlantica") and on land belonging to indigenous tribes. The action was brought by the Union's *Ministerio Publico* after a public inquiry was set up to investigate accusations by environmental groups, including Greenpeace ("Brazilian court halts 'green' firm's forestry", *The Guardian*, 26 November 1993).

reflected the same conditions, distortions and limitations of the environmental movement in Brazil. The enactment of the legislation was a significant victory and, whatever its problems and imperfections, the scope opened by the law is considerable. However, as with all progressive laws, it should not be expected to change the environmental reality by itself; it should, instead, be regarded as one more instrument, and a powerful one, in the broader social struggle for the recognition, preservation and defence of environmental values.

IV **Conclusion**

Regardless of the merits of the environmental legislation as a whole, and despite some interesting local experiences of ecological administration, the environmental situation in Brazil has not generally improved after the promulgation of the 1988 Constitution. The explanation for this is to be found more in the country's political and legal system than in shortcomings of the specific legislation.

Despite the improvements which the Constitution has made to Brazil's politico-legal order, it has kept much of the "excluding", if not authoritarian, political system consolidated during the military dictatorship, as well as the obsolete, elitist and disorganised conditions of the justice system. As a result, environmental and other social values remain marginal in political and judicial decision-making.

However important the improvement of the existing laws may be, the *enforcement* of collective environmental interests and rights in Brazil will only be effective when, together with a broad reorganisation of judicial power, the country's democratic order is further widened to incorporate the participation of the population into the decision-making process.

To some extent, the improvement of the environmental situation in Brazil depends on international relations, particularly with regard to the problems created by Brazil's gigantic external debt. However, it will depend fundamentally on the permanent political mobilisation of Brazilian society, within and without the state apparatus, in its struggle to overcome the existing unfair socio-economic order and to ensure adequate conditions for broad popular representation and direct participation in the decision-making process.

Recent legislative and constitutional initiatives to defend environmental interests and rights in Brazil are part of the wider political process aimed to re-democratise the country through social mobilisation.

Appendix
Civil Public Action No 7 347/ 1985 (Brazil)

Law No 7.347, of 24 July 1985 – Governs the civil public action of responsibility for damage done to the environment; consumers; goods and rights of artistic, aesthetic, historical, touristic and scenic value; and takes other measures, with new wording introduced by Law No 8.078, of 11 September 1990.

Article 1 (Relevant diffuse interests)

Not excluding the popular action, the provisions of this Law govern the proceedings for damage done:
(i)   to the environment;
(ii)   to consumers;
(iii) to goods and rights of artistic, aesthetic, historical, touristic and scenic value; and
(iv) to any other diffuse or collective interest.

Article 2 (Jurisdiction)

The actions stipulated in this Law will be initiated in the jurisdiction of the place where the damage occurred, the judge of which will have functional competence to proceed and decide the case.

Article 3 (Remedies: fines and mandamus)

Under this Law, the civil action can seek a fine or the performance of an obligation to act/cease acting.

Article 4 (Remedies: injunctions)

For the purposes of this Law, interlocutory injunctions can be brought to prevent damage to the environment, consumers, goods and rights of artistic, aesthetic, historical, touristic and scenic value.

Article 5 *(Locus standi)*

The principal action and the interlocutory injunction can be initiated by the *Ministerio Publico*; the Union; the Federated States and the Municipalities. They can also be initiated by an *autarquia*, public company, foundation, "mixed-economy society" or eligible association, namely one which:
(i)   has been constituted for at least a year, in the terms of the civil legislation;
(ii) includes, amongst its institutional purposes, the protection of the environment; consumers; artistic, aesthetic, historical, touristic and scenic patrimonies.
Para 1 – If it does not participate in the case as a party, the *Ministerio Publico* will act as an obligatory observer of the law.
Para 2 – The public authorities and other associations legitimated under the terms of this article may join any proceedings.
Para 3 – In the event that an eligible association fails to proceed with or discontinues the action, the *Ministerio Publico* will take over its role as claimant.
Para 4 – The requirement of pre-constitution can be dispensed with by the judge, when there is a manifest social interest evidenced by the dimension or characteristic of the damage, or by the significance of the juridical value to be protected.

Article 6 *(Ministerio Publico* to be provided with information)

Any person can, and civil servant must, advise the *Ministerio Publico* of facts and relevant information which may come to constitute the object of civil public action.

Article 7 (Judiciary to provide information to *Ministerio Publico)*

If, in the exercise of their functions, judges and courts become aware of facts which may justify the initiation of a civil action, they must send the *Ministerio Publico* such information so that it can take due measures.

Article 8 (Access to information)

In order to support the initiating proceedings, the interested party can require from the competent authorities all the certificates and information considered necessary, which should be provided within 15 days.
Para 1 – The *Ministerio Publico* can open, under its presidency, a civil inquiry, or require certificates, information, examinations and expert testimonies from any public organisation, within the time it establishes, which cannot be less than 10 working days.

Para 2 – Only in cases in which the law determines secrecy can certificates or information be denied, in which case the action can be brought unaccompanied by those documents, their production being at the judge's discretion.

Article 9 (Review of the decision not to act)

After all measures have been taken, if the representative of the *Ministerio Publico* is convinced of the lack of basis for the initiation of the civil action, he or she will send the files of the civil inquiry to the archives, with explicit reasons.

Para 1 – Before they are sent to the archives, such files of the civil inquiry or other related pieces of information will be sent to the Higher Council of the *Ministerio Publico* within three days, on pain of grave fault being committed.

Para 2 – Until the decision on sending the files to the archives is ratified or rejected in a session of the Higher Council of the *Ministerio Publico*, the eligible associations can present written arguments or documents, which will be enclosed in the files of the inquiry or annexed to the related pieces of information.

Para 3 – The decision on sending the files and information to the archives will be subject to examination and deliberation by the Higher Council of the *Ministerio Publico*, according to its statutes.

Para 4 – If the Higher Council decides not to ratify the decision to send the files to the archives, it will promptly designate another representative of the *Ministerio Publico* to initiate the action.

Article 10 (Criminal sanctions for failure to provide information)

Refusal or delay in providing, or omission of technical data indispensable to the initiation of a civil action, when required by the *Ministerio Publico*, constitutes a crime, punishable by penalty of prison between one and three years, plus a fine ranging from 10 to 1,000 Readjustable Obligations of the National Treasure (RONT).

Article 11 (Specific execution and penalties)

If the object of the action is the performance of an obligation to act or not to act, the judge will rule on the initiation of the due activity or the cessation of the harmful activity, on pain of specific execution, or the imposition of a daily fine, if this is sufficient or compatible, regardless of whether the claimant has specifically sought such a ruling.

Article 12 (Temporary restraining orders)

The judge can authorise a temporary restraining order, with or without previous justification, in a decision subject to appeal.

Para 1 – By requirement of a public law entity which is an interested party, and in order to prevent grave damage to public order, health, security and the economy, the President of the Tribunal entitled to judge the appeal can suspend the execution of the temporary restraining order in a decision containing reasons, against which an appeal will be assigned to one of the panels of high court judges within five days of the publication of the act.

Para 2 – The fine imposed in a temporary restraining order will only be required to be paid when the defendant has exhausted all appeals pursuant to the adverse judgment, but will be calculated from the day on which the damage occurred.

Article 13 (Fines to be deposited into Environmental Restoration Fund)

If there is a civil fine, the compensation for the damage done will revert to a fund administered by a federal council or by state councils in the administration of which the *Ministerio Publico* and representatives of the community will necessarily participate, and the resources of which will be used towards the reconstitution of the damaged goods.

Only paragraph – While the fund has not been further regulated, the money will be deposited in an official financial institution, in an account with monetary correction.[17]

Article 14 (Effective date of judgments)

The judge can suspend the effect of appeals to prevent irreparable harm to a party.

Article 15 (Execution of judgment)

After 60 days of execution of the final condemnatory decision, if the association-claimant fails to promote the judgment, the *Ministerio Publico* will do so, while other parties are allowed equally to take such initiative.

Article 16 (Res judicata)

The final civil sentence will produce *erga omnes* effects, except when the action is dismissed on the grounds of insufficient evidence, in which case any

---

[17]"Monetary correction" is a mechanism used in Brazil to combat the country's chronic inflation.

party can initiate another action on an identical basis, making use of other evidence.

Article 17 (Proceedings in bad faith)

In the case of litigation conducted in bad faith, the association-claimant and the directors responsible for the initiation of the action will be jointly condemned to pay lawyers' fees and ten times the due costs, without affecting their liability to pay compensation.

Article 18 (Costs)

In cases governed by this Law, there will be no advance payment of costs, emoluments, honoraria for expert testimony or other expenses, nor liability of an association claimant for any other party's legal fees, costs and procedural expenses, except in the case of proven bad faith.

Article 19 (Procedure)

Except where inconsistent with this Law, the Civil Procedures Code, approved by Law No 5.869, of 11 January 1973, is applicable to the civil public action established by this Law.

Article 20

The Fund mentioned in Article 13 of this Law will be regulated by executive power within 90 days.

Article 21

Whenever compatible, the precepts of Title III of the Law which established the Code for the Defence of Consumers will be applicable to the defence of collective and individual rights and interests.

Article 22

This Law will be in force from the date of its publication [25 July 1985].

Article 23

This law prevails over the provisions of any inconsistent, existing law.

(Translated by author, with the assistance of David Robinson. Article headings have been added.)

Contents of Chapter 6

"Well-being" and "the Common Man": A Critical Look at Public Interest Environmental Law in South Africa and India

Chapter 6

"Well-being" and "the Common Man": A Critical Look at Public Interest Environmental Law in South Africa and India

François du Bois[1]

I. Introduction

There must have been very few countries where environmental rights and duties were not already adjudicated upon when Principle 1 of the Stockholm Declaration 1972 proclaimed that everyone "has the fundamental right to . . . an environment of a quality that permits a life of dignity and well-being, and . . . bears a solemn responsibility to protect and improve the environment for present and future generations".[2] Disputes arising from competing claims to benefit from natural resources, and from interference with someone's use and enjoyment of the environment, have long had some degree of access to justice in divergent social and legal contexts.

In disputes of this kind, the environment features as an instrument for the satisfaction of human wants; and rights and duties relating to the environment are intended to allocate the instrumental value of the environment equitably. The assertion of environmental rights and duties in the Stockholm Declaration, however, intimated a new approach – one which would recognise the environment as intrinsically worthy of protection. It envisaged placing environmental concerns which transcended rival claims to the instrumental value of the environment on an equal footing with those interests which had traditionally enjoyed recognition.

François du Bois is a South African advocate and a lecturer with the School of Oriental and African Studies, University of London, with interests in comparative tort and environmental law.
[1]The author is grateful to Jan Glazewski, Theunis Roux, Martin Lau and Michael Anderson for supplying some of the South African and Indian material referred to.
[2]UN Doc A/Conf48/14/Rev1, reprinted in (1972) 11 ILM 1416.

This new approach, therefore, held out the prospect of access to justice for the vindication of the public interest in environmental protection. By acknowledging the legitimacy of the environmental concerns of all, it also recognised the need for enabling participation in this process by those hitherto excluded.

A wide range of countries has sought to implement this new approach. In the United States the Clean Water Act[3] and the Clean Air Act[4] enable citizens to act as "private attorneys general",[5] a model followed in citizen suit provisions in subsequent environmental statutes;[6] in Australia, the New South Wales Environmental Planning and Assessment Act 1979 has opened the doors to any person to bring proceedings to remedy or restrain a breach of the Act;[7] in India the constitution has been amended so as to include environmental protection among the directive principles of state policy and fundamental duties of citizens;[8] and in countries as diverse as Norway and Burkina Faso substantive environmental rights have been incorporated in the constitution.[9]

The latter approach has also been adopted in South Africa's new interim constitution, and this chapter will explore the intricacies of establishing a framework for public interest environmental law through an exploration of that document. It will analyse substantive and procedural innovations contained in South Africa's constitution and, placing these in the context of Indian experience with public interest litigation, seek to determine the preconditions for a viable system of public interest environmental law.

II. Access to environmental justice in the South African Constitution

The contrast in the outcome of two planning cases had long been emblematic of the scope afforded by South African law for environmental public interest litigation. Whereas a property developer was able in *Administrator, Cape* v *Associated Buildings Ltd*[10] to use judicial review proceedings successfully to overturn the imposition of a planning condition designed to safeguard public

---

[3]33 USC 2151-1376.

[4]42 USC 7601-7642.

[5]Feller, "Private Enforcement of Federal Anti-Pollution Laws Through Citizen Suits: A Model" (1983) *Denver Law Journal* 553; Austin, "The Rise of Citizen Suit Enforcement in Environmental Law: Reconciling Private and Public Attorneys General" (1987) *Northwestern University Law Review* 220.

[6]Feller *op cit* at 555.

[7]Street CJ in *Hannan* v *Elcom (No 3)* (1985) 66 LRGA 306.

[8]Articles 48A and 51A(g) of the Constitution of India, introduced by the Constitution (Forty-Second) Amendment Act 1976.

[9]See n 34 *infra* and accompanying text. For other countries, see UN Doc E/CN4/Sub2/1992/7 *Human Rights and the Environment* – Progress Report Prepared by Mrs Fatma Zohra Ksentini, Special Rapporteur.

[10]1957 (2) SA 317 (A).

access to the slopes of Table Mountain, a public-spirited individual was refused standing in *Von Moltke* v *Costa Aerosa (Pty) Ltd*[11] to seek relief to protect the natural environment. Thus, although it was possible to seek protection against the state[12] as well as private defendants[13] for the personal interests served by a salubrious environment, a plaintiff who could not assert an interest in utilising the environment lacked the legally recognised interest necessary to obtain *locus standi*,[14] unless he could point to a clear breach of the law.[15] The intrinsic value of the environment received no legal recognition.

South African lawyers recognised this as a curtailment of access to environmental justice, and called for the insertion of an "ecological norm"[16] or a "conservation ethic"[17] into the law. When the enactment of a Bill of Rights loomed on the horizon, these calls came to be expressed in the language of constitutional rights.[18] Although a note of caution was sounded by one prominent environmental lawyer,[19] the two most influential participants in the negotiations which led to the adoption of the new Constitution – the South African government[20] and the African National Congress[21] – both published proposals for a Charter/Bill of Rights which endorsed the inclusion of an environmental right.

The Technical Committee on Fundamental Rights during the Transition, a body of lawyers charged with assisting the Negotiating Council by recommending specific formulations of the rights to be included in the new constitution, was therefore able to identify an environmental right as "one of the areas of agreement on minimal or essential fundamental rights and freedoms which can simply not be excluded in the transitional period."[22]

----

[11]1975 (1) SA 255 (C).

[12]*Dell* v *Town Council of Cape Town* 1879 (9) Buch 2; and, more recently, *Diepsloot Residents and Landowners Association and Others* v *Administrator, Transvaal and Others* 1993 (1) SA 577 (T); and *Eskom* v *Rini Town Council* 1992 (4) SA 96 (E).

[13]See, generally, Milton, "The Law of Neighbours in South Africa" (1969) *Acta Juridica* 149.

[14]See Rabie, "Towards Assuring the Administrative Furtherance of the Public Interest in Environmental Conservation" (1990) *Stellenbosch Law Review* 219 at 235.

[15]*Corium (Pty) Ltd and Others* v *Myburgh Park Langebaan (Pty) Ltd and Others* 1993 (1) SA 853 (C); *Bamford* v *Minister of Community Development and State Auxiliary Services* 1981 (3) SA 1054 (C).

[16]Van Niekerk, "The Ecological Norm in Law" (1975) *South African Law Journal* 78.

[17]Glavovic, "The Need for Legislative Adoption of a Conservation Ethic" (1984) *Comparative and International Law Journal of South Africa* 148.

[18]See Glavovic, "Human Rights and Environmental Law: the Case a for a Conservation Bill of Rights" (1988) *Comparative and International Law Journal of South Africa* 52; Glazewski, "The Environment, Human Rights and a New South African Constitution" (1991) *South African Journal on Human Rights* 167.

[19]Cowen, "Toward Distinctive Principles of South African Environmental Law: some Jurisprudential Perspectives and a Role for Legislation" (1989) *Tydskrif vir Heedendaagse Romeins-Hollandse Reg* (Journal for Contemporary Roman-Dutch Law) 3 at 23–25.

[20]Republic of South Africa: *Government's Proposals on a Charter of Fundamental Rights*, 2 February 1993.

[21]Constitutional Committee of the African National Congress: ANC Draft Bill of Rights, Preliminary Revised Version, Bellville, Centre for Development Studies, February 1993.

[22]Technical Committee on Fundamental Rights During the Transition: *First Progress Report – 14 May 1993* at 2–4.

Accordingly, article 29 of the Constitution of the Republic of South Africa[23] provides that:

"Every person shall have the right to an environment which is not detrimental to his or her health or well-being."

However, access to environmental justice was also inhibited by another feature of the approach to *locus standi* hitherto followed by South African courts. As a rule, standing was only accorded to an applicant seeking to vindicate a personal interest.[24] Indeed, this requirement has been restrictively interpreted so as to preclude an organisation from coming to court as representative of the interests of its members, as distinct from its own interests.[25]

In a country marked by inequality in litigation endowments, this hampered the effective utilisation by all potential beneficiaries of the opportunities available for recourse to law. It is no accident that the most prominent, recent environmental cases were brought by a private corporation,[26] a suburban residents' association[27] and a utility corporation.[28] The vital role played in India by individual activists and associations in vindicating the interests of rural and disadvantaged communities by acting as their representatives and surrogates, attests to the inhibiting effect of requiring a personal interest as foundation for *locus standi*.[29]

Article 7(4)(b) of the Constitution has ensured that this limitation will not affect litigation based on article 29. It allows relief in respect of an infringement or threatened infringement of a constitutional right to be sought by:

(i)   a person acting in his or her own interest;
(ii) an association acting in the interest of its members;
(iii) a person acting on behalf of another person who is not in a position to seek such relief in his or her own name;
(iv) a person acting as a member of or in the interest of a group or class of persons; or

---

[23]Act 200 of 1993.
[24]*Bamford v Minister of Community Development and State Auxiliary Services op cit; Milani v South African Medical and Dental Council* 1990 (1) SA 899 (T). An exception was recognised only where the life or liberty of another was in danger – see *Parents Committee of Namibia v Nujoma* 1990 (1) SA 873 (A); and Loots "*Locus standi* to Claim Relief in the Public Interest in Matters involving the Enforcement of Legislation" (1987) *South African Law Journal* 131.
[25]*Ahmadiyya Anjuman Ihaati-Islam Lahore (South Africa) v Muslim Judicial Council (Cape)* 1983 (4) SA 855 (C); *South African Optometric Association v Frame Distributors (Pty) Ltd* 1985 (3) SA 100 (O); *Natal Fresh Produce Growers Association v Agroserve (Pty) Ltd* 1990 (4) SA 749 (N).
[26]*Corium (Pty) Ltd and Others v Myburgh Park Langebaan (Pty) Ltd and Others* 1993 (1) SA 853 (C).
[27]*Diepsloot Residents and Landowners Association and Others v Administrator, Transvaal and Others* 1993 (1) SA 577 (T).
[28]*Eskom v Rini Town Council* 1992 (4) SA 96 (E).
[29]See Section IV "The procedural dimension" *infra*.

(v)   a person acting in the public interest.

The wording of para (v) in particular is vital. By robustly granting the right to enforce constitutional rights to anyone acting in the public interest, it relieves South African courts of the need to follow their Canadian counterparts in seeking to devise a concept of personal interest better attuned to the nature of constitutional litigation than the traditional approach to *locus standi*.[30] Cases like *Canadian Abortion Rights Action League*,[31] which denied standing to the League to challenge abortion legislation on the ground that it lacked a "genuine interest" in the matter, suggest that the notion of a sufficient interest lacks a meaning precise enough, once it is liberated from its common law restrictions, to serve as a clear guideline.

At the same time, the requirement that someone not seeking to vindicate his or her own right, or that of another person or group of persons, must act in the public interest, provides the courts with a measure of control over the misuse of court proceedings – something even the approachable Indian courts have felt a need for.[32] Australian experience indicates that the concept of public interest can be endowed with a meaningful content which combines flexibility with a fair measure of certainty.[33]

South Africa's new Constitution, therefore, contains provisions aimed both at broadening the array of environmental issues which can be brought before courts and extending the range of people with effective access to environmental justice. Both features are pre-requisites for the realisation of the new approach heralded by the Stockholm Declaration. However, closer scrutiny of these provisions suggests that public interest environmental law cannot simply be grafted onto a system previously geared to litigation revolving around the instrumental value of the environment. It necessitates a reconstruction rather than a mere expansion of existing legal categories. In the following sections of this chapter, that theme will be developed through an examination of the formulation adopted in article 29, and an exploration of changes in legal

---

[30]See *Thorson* v *Attorney-General of Canada* [1975] 1 SCR 138, 43 DLR (3d) 1; *Minister of Justice* v *Borowski* [1981] 2 SCR 575, 130 DLR (3d) 588, especially Martland J at 606.

[31]*Canadian Abortion Rights Action League Inc* v *Attorney General of Nova Scotia* (1989) 63 DLR (4th) 680.

[32]See *e.g. Chhetriya Pardushan Mukti Gangarsh* v *State of Uttar Pradesh* AIR 1990 SC 2060 where the petitioners were denied the opportunity by the Indian Supreme Court to use public interest litigation to further a "long history of enmity and animosity" on the ground that the advantages of this procedure should be confined to a "person interested genuinely in the protection of the society on behalf of the . . . community". See also *Subash Kumar* v *Union of India* AIR 1991 SC 420; reports of similar cases in *The Times of India*, 29 August 1990 and 6 September 1992; and Sorabjee, "Obliging Government to Control Itself: Recent Developments in Indian Administrative Law" (1994) *Public Law* 39 at 49–50.

[33]See especially the judgment of Stein J in *Oshlack* v *Richmond River Council and Iron Gates Developments Pty Ltd* (Land and Environment Court of New South Wales, (1994) 82 LGERA 236) on departure from the ordinary cost rule. The seriousness of the applicant's case, the significance of its leading to the interpretation of new statutory provisions, the public notoriety and controversy surrounding the site to which the application related, the applicant's altruistic motives, the impact of the case on the ambit and future administration of development consent and on the public and public bodies, were held to characterise the litigation as public interest litigation.

procedure instituted by the Indian judiciary to accommodate public interest plaintiffs.

III. **The substantive dimension**

In comparison with similar provisions in some other constitutions, article 29 is formulated in narrow terms. The new article 110b inserted into Norway's Constitution in 1992, for example, grants every citizen the right to an environment which does not endanger health, and to a nature where diversity and ecology are preserved.[34] Likewise, article 31 of the 1991 Constitution of Burkina Faso, provides that:

> "Every citizen shall have the right to initiate an action or to join a collective action under the form of a petition against these acts:
> – harming the public heritage;
> – harming the interests of social communities;
> – harming the environment or the cultural or artistic heritage."

The restriction of the ambit of article 29 to environmentally harmful acts which affect human health or well-being was deliberate. Various proposals had been made for the inclusion of a more wide-ranging provision expressing a positive entitlement. The South African Law Commission[35] and the government[36] had both endorsed the inclusion of a right to "the conservation and protection" of the environment, whilst the African National Congress[37] had proposed a right to "a healthy and ecologically balanced environment". Nevertheless, it was the substance of a recommendation from the Habitat Council[38] which was eventually adopted.

The reports of the Technical Committee on Fundamental Rights indicate the reasons for this decision. In its second progress report the Committee expressed the view that the inclusion of an environmental right "will at this stage only be warranted if it is formulated negatively and therefore restrictively".[39] The reason for this view lies in the Committee's conception of its task as being only to formulate rights germane to the transitional nature of the

---

[34]Quoted in Bugge, *Human Rights and Resource Management – an Overview* (paper delivered at a conference on Environment and Development in Developing Countries: National and International Law, Oslo, October 1993) at 15.

[35]South African Law Commission *Project 58, Group and Human Rights: Interim Report*, Pretoria, August 1991 at 696.

[36]See n 20 *supra*.

[37]See n 21 *supra*.

[38]Quoted in Glazewski, "Environmental Law and a New South African Constitutional Dispensation" (1994) *Environmental Liability* 16 at 17.

[39]Technical Committee on Fundamental Rights During the Transition: *Second Progress Report – 21 May 1993* at 8.

present interim constitution,[40] and to leave the formulation of further rights appropriate to "conditions of political and socio-economic reconstruction" to the constitution-making body created by that constitution.[41] More positively and extensively formulated environmental rights fell, in its view, in the latter category (*i.e.* "within the preserve of the elected constitution-making body").[42]

However, the Technical Committee pointed out "conservation of the environment is catered for under the concept of 'well-being'".[43] If South Africa's new Constitutional Court were to adopt this interpretation, article 29 would lead undoubtedly to an expansion of the category of environmental interests gaining access to the courts. It is certainly possible that the court will adopt this view, but it must be noted that influential environmental philosophers like John Passmore[44] and Richard and Val Routley[45] have raised doubts about the feasibility of grounding the case for wilderness preservation in a concern for human welfare.

Moreover, by presenting the advocacy of environmental protection as a claim to "well-being", the anthropocentric phrasing of article 29 forces environmental public interest litigation into the mould of instrumental concerns with the environment. In essence, it treats such litigation as a public law equivalent of nuisance, with the role of a proprietary interest being played by a more expansive constitutional right to well-being.

This is important, because environmental degradation has a disparate impact on human welfare. The well-being of property developers and their employees may be enhanced by projects which diminish the enjoyment others derive from the environment, through curtailing access to public amenities or degrading the environment aesthetically. Where poverty and lack of housing are rife, environmentally harmful acts may, indeed, enhance the overall well-being of many by providing them with shelter, food or fuel.

Deciding whether to prohibit an environmentally harmful act, therefore, inevitably involves determining whose welfare is to be sacrificed in another's favour. Since the very question at issue is the importance which is to be attached to a diminution in well-being, appeals to "well-being" cannot fully determine decisions about environmental protection. A standard is needed for

---

[40]See n 39 *supra*; and see especially Technical Committee on Fundamental Rights During the Transition: *Third Progress Report – 28 May 1993* at 1–8.

[41]The purpose of the present Constitution being, according to the Preamble, to provide for "the restructuring and continued governance of South Africa while an elected Constitutional Assembly draws up a final Constitution". Chapter 5 of the Constitution provides for the adoption of a permanent constitution within the next two years.

[42]See n 39 at 7; and Technical Committee on Fundamental Rights during the Transition: *Fifth Progress Report – 11 June 1993* at 13.

[43]Technical Committee on Fundamental Rights During the Transition: *Fifth Progress Report – 11 June 1993* at 13.

[44]*Man's Responsibility for Nature*, London, Duckworth, 1974 at Chapter 4.

[45]"Human Chauvinism and Environmental Ethics" in Mannison *et al* (eds) *Environmental Philosophy*, Canberra, ANU, 1980.

evaluating the importance which is to be attached to a particular reduction in welfare.

This difficulty is, of course, no different from that faced in nuisance cases. There the courts must also decide whose use and enjoyment of the environment is to be sacrificed. They do so in that context by applying a criterion of reasonableness, measuring the rival claims against each other by evaluating the interests they respectively serve. That, naturally, presupposes the possibility of distinguishing the interests each claim is intended to serve. It is possible to do so in nuisance litigation, because the interests surveyed are defined with reference to separate parcels of land. For example, in a nuisance action focusing on air pollution caused by the defendant, it is possible to distinguish the plaintiff's interest in being free therefrom from the defendant's interests, despite the fact that the latter may also suffer from the air pollution, because the court's attention is fixed on the parties' interest in the use and enjoyment of their respective parcels of land.[46]

However, once the accent falls on the all-encompassing notion of well-being, it is no longer possible to distinguish the parties' interests because the disparate social impact of environmental degradation is reproduced in respect of every individual. From a welfare perspective, the interests of both parties in the example given above will tug in different directions. The defendant's well-being will also be diminished by air pollution, and the plaintiff's enhanced by the defendant's contribution to economic growth. Thus, a prohibition of environmentally harmful acts may reduce and enhance the well-being of every individual simultaneously, and an authorisation thereof may similarly enhance and reduce the well-being of every individual.

Since everyone's well-being is reduced and enhanced simultaneously by either decision, it is not possible to distinguish separate interests in polluting economic activity and in environmental conservation that can be weighed up against each other *à la* nuisance. All that can be done, is to decide *a priori* which of the various welfare consequences of, for example, sacrificing an endangered species for the construction of housing is to be accorded the most weight. Hence, the formulation adopted in article 29 of the South African Constitution cannot assist a court in fulfilling its task to determine whether an environmentally harmful act was properly authorised. It will have no choice but to fall back on its own determination of the relative priority of environmental protection and environmentally harmful development.

The building of a viable basis for public interest environmental law, therefore, requires a more fundamental change than the adoption of a concept seeking to effect a compromise between conservation and development. Such an approach would recognise that environmental protection affects existing

---

[46]That is also why it is possible to distinguish the defendants's financial interest in the operations causing the pollution from increases in the plaintiff's welfare that might be brought about by the increase in social wealth flowing from the defendant's activities.

social practices and relationships profoundly, and that the challenge posed by the apparent conflict between conservation and development arises from the need to manage such social change equitably. It would, accordingly, seek to advance both of these values through supplementing a right to environmental protection with a right to the equitable distribution of the social costs thereof.

The danger remains, of course, that such a provision would be used primarily by those best placed – due to financial, educational and similar advantages – to pursue litigation. That may lead to only a partial realisation of the public interest in environmental protection. Indian experience in environmental public interest litigation has highlighted the consequent need for supplementing conceptual change with institutional change. It is to this that I now turn.

IV. **The procedural dimension**

The Indian Supreme Court has opened up access to the courts at least as widely as article 7 of the South African Constitution has done. There, too, the principle has been adopted that:

> " . . . where a legal wrong or legal injury is caused to a person or to a determinate class of persons by reason of violation of any constitutional or legal right or any burden is imposed in contravention of any constitutional or legal provisions or without authority of law or any such legal wrong or legal injury or legal burden is threatened, and such person is by reason of poverty, helplessness or socially or economically disadvantaged position unable to approach the Court for relief, any member of the public can maintain an action for an appropriate direction, order or writ . . . "[47]

Born, as it was, out of a concern with widening access to the courts, this amelioration of the strict requirements of the conventional approach to *locus standi* was accompanied by other procedural innovations. The Supreme Court and state High Courts, using the wide power granted to them respectively by articles 32 and 226 of the Constitution to issue orders and writs, have assisted public interest litigants in the expensive task of gathering evidence and have fashioned new remedies. "Public interest litigation", or "social action litigation" as some prefer to call it,[48] has developed into a distinct category of litigation.[49]

---

[47]*SP Gupta* v *Union of India* AIR 1982 SC 149 at 188.

[48]*e.g.* Baxi, "Taking Suffering Seriously: Social Action Litigation in the Supreme Court of India" in Tiruchelvan N, and Coomaraswany R, *The Role of the Judiciary in Plural Societies*, London, 1987.

[49]Rosencranz, Divan and Noble, *Environmental Law and Policy in India*, Bombay, Tripathi, 1991 at 25 point out that the enlarged notion of *locus standi* encompasses the analytically distinct concepts of "representative standing" and "citizen standing". The Indian courts themselves do not appear to make this distinction, and it plays no role in the characterisation of cases as involving public interest litigation.

The classic justification of the Indian approach to public interest litigation is to be found in *Gupta* v *Union of India*,[50] where Bhagwati J expressed the view that:

"If public duties are to be enforced and social collective 'diffused' rights and interests are to be protected, we have to utilise the initiative and zeal of public-minded persons and organisations by allowing them to move the Court and act for a general or group interest, even though they may not be directly injured in their own rights."

The notion of public interest litigation as specific "broadened forms of legal proceedings . . . in keeping with the current accent on justice to the common man and a necessary disincentive to those who wish to bypass the real issues on the merits by suspect reliance on peripheral, procedural shortcomings . . ."[51] has also brought about a situation where a court would not shrink from saying that, "Where . . . the Court is moved for this purpose by a member of a public by addressing a letter drawing the attention of the Court to such legal injury or legal wrong . . . the Court would cast aside all technical rules of procedure and entertain the letter as a writ petition on the judicial side and take action upon it".[52] Indeed, the abandonment of the usual formalities applying to the commencement of proceedings has become one of the hallmarks of Indian public interest litigation.[53] Moreover, Indian judges have been prepared to convert articles and letters published in newspapers into writ petitions, thus intervening *suo motu*.[54]

The evolution of public interest litigation has widened access to justice significantly, not least in respect of environmental degradation. It has enabled organisations and individuals to bring applications before the Indian Supreme Court and State High Courts[55] ranging from a bid to prevent the sale of part of the Calcutta Zoo for the construction of an hotel,[56] to an attempt to stop the construction of the large Tehri dam.[57] Indeed, one particular activist lawyer, Mr MC Mehta, has brought applications before the Supreme Court in respect of the pollution of the river Ganges,[58] air pollution caused by a Delhi chlorine plant[59] and by motor vehicles,[60] as well as the dissemination of environmental

---

[50]See n 47 *supra*.

[51]Krishna Iyer J in *Mumbai Kamgar Sabhha* v *Abdulbhai* AIR 1976 SC 1465.

[52]Bhagwati J in *People's Union for Democratic Rights* v *Union of India* AIR 1982 SC 1473 at 1483.

[53]Baxi, n 48 *supra*.

[54]Baxi, n 48 *supra*; and Agrawala, *Public Interest Litigation in India: A Critique*, Bombay, Tripathi, 1985 at 21. See also *Ram Pyari* v *Union of India* AIR 1988 Raj 124 where judges intervened after reading the "woeful story" in a local newspaper of a war veteran's widow left without a pension.

[55]For a recent overview, see Nelivigi, Poojitha and Rosencranz, "The Judiciary and the Environment: Recent Trends and Developments" (1993) *Environmental Policy and Law* 102.

[56]*Sachidanand Pandey* v *The State of West Bengal* AIR 1987 SC 1109.

[57]*Tehri Badh Virodhi Sangrash Samiti* v *State of Uttar Pradesh* JT 1990 (4) SC 519.

[58]*MC Mehta* v *Union of India* AIR 1988 SC 1037; and *MC Mehta* v *Union of India* AIR 1988 SC 1115.

[59]*MC Mehta* v *Union of India* AIR 1987 SC 965, AIR 1987 SC 1086.

[60]*MC Mehta* v *Union of India* AIR 1991 SC 1332.

information and education.[61] Of equal significance is the fact that it was by this avenue that cases reached the High Courts and the Supreme Court which enabled them to reinterpret the fundamental right to life guaranteed by article 21 to encompass environmental protection,[62] and to introduce the principle of absolute liability.[63] The evolution of public interest litigation in India as a specific procedure designed to cater for the "common man", has both extended the range of people whose interests are represented in court, and the variety of issues adjudicated upon.

The polycentric nature of the issues so brought before the courts, coupled with the ambition to provide effective access, has also altered the judicial role significantly. It has been observed, for example, that in *Rural Litigation and Entitlement Kendra, Dehradun* v *State of Uttar Pradesh*,[64] a case initiated by a letter concerning environmental degradation caused by limestone quarrying operations in the Mussoorie-Dehradun region:

> "the Supreme Court considered, balanced and resolved competing policies – including the need for development, environmental conservation, preserving jobs, and protecting substantial business investments – in deciding to close a number of limestone quarries . . . and to allow others to continue operating under detailed conditions. In rendering this judgement the court reviewed the highly technical reports of various geological experts and gave varying weight to the expert opinions."[65]

The commitment to making public interest litigation effective in such cases has led to the virtual abandonment of the traditional role of the higher Indian judiciary as presiding over adversarial proceedings concluding with an order to the parties. The courts have, first, become participants in the management and presentation of cases. The impossibility of dealing with each of the vast number of letters received[66] has necessitated the selection of only a small proportion for decision. This, combined with *suo motu* intervention, has

---

[61]*MC Mehta* v *Union of India* JT 1991 (4) SC 531.

[62]*LK Koolwal* v *State of Rajasthan* AIR 1988 Raj 2; *Madhavi* v *Tilakan* 1988 (2) Ker LT 730; *Kinkri Devi* v *State of Himachal Pradesh* AIR 1988 HP 4; and *T Damodar Rao* v *The Special Officer, Municipal Corporation of Hyderabad* 1987 AIR AP 171. As pointed out in the latter judgment (at 181) the Supreme Court had implicitly adopted the same view in *Rural Litigation and Entitlement Kendra, Dehradun* v *State of Uttar Pradesh* AIR 1985 SC 652. In *Subhash Kumar* v *State of Bihar* JT 1991 (1) SC 531, the Supreme Court finally adopted this view expressly.

[63]*MC Mehta* v *Union of India* AIR 1987 SC 1086. This decision also stimulated the amendment of the Factories Act 1948, the enactment of the Public Liability Act 1991 and the introduction of the National Environment Tribunal Bill in 1992 (*The Times of India* 6 September 1992).

[64]AIR 1985 SC 652, AIR 1985 SC 1259, AIR 1987 SC 359, AIR 1987 SC 2426, AIR 1988 SC 2187.

[65]Cunningham, "Public Interest Litigation in the Indian Supreme Court: A Study in the Light of American Experience" (1987) JILI 494 at 511–512. *Cf.* Singh J in *MC Mehta* v *Union of India* AIR 1988 SC 1037 at 1048: "We are conscious that closure of tanneries may bring unemployment, loss of revenue, but life, health and ecology have greater importance to people".

[66]Agrawala, n 54 *supra*, quotes reports of Acting Chief Justice Bhaskaran of the Kerala High Court saying in 1984 that an average of 30 to 40 such letters were received daily, with less than 10% of these being accepted as writ petitions.

made it possible for judges freely to determine the issues they would adjudicate on. Although members of the Supreme Court sought to counteract this by disapproving of the practice of addressing letters to a particular judge,[67] and creating a "Public Interest Litigation Cell"[68] the real problem is that the sheer volume of letters provides the judiciary with a wide discretion and engenders an opaque selection process.

The need to relieve public interest applicants of the cost and burden of gathering and presenting evidence has also led to close judicial involvement with the presentation of the applicant's case. For example, in *Rural Litigation and Entitlement Kendra, Debradun*,[69] the Supreme Court instructed an expert committee to inspect all limestone quarrying operations in the Mussoorie-Dehradun region, to investigate whether the Mining Acts were being observed and to report on the hazards they posed to people, cattle and their ecological impact. Again, in *LK Koolwal* v *State of Rajasthan*[70] a commissioner was appointed to report on the existence of insanitary conditions in Jaipur.[71]

When an applicant has gone no further in identifying the issues than is practical in a letter, postcard or telegram, and not even an affidavit is required,[72] the judicial determination of the questions to be investigated is virtually impossible to distinguish from framing the case on his behalf.

As Pathak J has observed, in public interest litigation the court "assumes a more positive attitude in determining the facts",[73] a position underlined by the court's willingness to treat such reports as *prima facie* evidence.[74]

Secondly, because cases of this nature arise from the failure of state bodies to prevent or curtail environmental destruction wrought by others, they invariably have a direct bearing on the activities of private individuals and corporations. In *Rural Litigation and Entitlement Kendra, Debradun*,[75] for example, the court's decision affected most directly the operators of limestone

---

[67]Pathak and Sen JJ in *Bandhua Mukti Morcha* v *Union of India* AIR 1984 802 at 848. See, however, the remarks by Bhagwati CJ in *MC Mehta* v *Union of India* AIR 1987 SC 1086 at 1090.
[68]". . . to which all letters addressed to the Court or the individual justices are forwarded and the staff attached to this Cell examines the letters and it is only after scrutiny by the staff members . . . that the letters are placed before the Chief Justice and under his direction, they are listed before the Court" (*per* Bhagwati CJ in *MC Mehta* v *Union of India ibid*).
[69]See n 64 *supra*.
[70]See n 62 *supra*.
[71]Baxi, n 48 *supra* at 44 identifies the use of publicly financed commissions, consisting of social activists, academics or court officials and judges of lower courts, to gather evidence as one of the characteristic features of public interest litigation. Sometimes the cost is ordered to be borne by the polluting factory, even though it is not formally a party to the proceedings (see *MC Mehta* v *Union of India* 1987 SC 965 at 979).
[72]"If the Court were to insist on an affidavit as a condition of entertaining the letters the entire object and purpose of epistolary jurisdiction would be frustrated . . . the Court has so far been entertaining letters without an affidavit . . . " (*per* Bhagwati CJ in *MC Mehta* v *Union of India op cit*).
[73]*Bandhua Mukti Morcha* v *Union of India op cit* n 67 *supra* at 839–841.
[74]See *e.g.* Bhagwati J in *Bandhua Mukti Morcha* v *Union of India op cit*.
[75]See n 64 *supra*.

quarrying operations, although the Government of Uttar Pradesh and the Collector of Dehradun were cited as respondents. This has produced a specific constitutional difficulty in India, where article 12 of the Constitution limits the application of fundamental rights – and hence of article 32 under which the Supreme Court has fashioned new fact-finding procedures and remedies[76] – to governmental bodies and authorities "under the control of the Government of India".[77] In the instant case the court nevertheless ordered the closing down of a number of private quarries, an approach endorsed in the *MC Mehta* case,[78] where its order specified in considerable detail the manner in which Shriram Foods and Fertilizer Industries had to conduct its operations in future after the occurrence of a gas leak. The twin facts that the Delhi Administration and the Inspector of Factories had promptly ordered the closure of Shriram after the event which provoked the hearing, and that the authorities had already launched an investigation into the adequacy of existing safety measures and the need for additional precautions, highlights the artificiality of viewing such cases as attempts to enforce public rights and duties against the state. Indeed, the peripheral role of the "formal" respondent was underlined by the court's willingness to entertain applications in the same proceedings that Shriram be ordered to pay compensation to the victims of the gas leak[79] and to order the payment of the petitioner's costs by Shriram.[80]

This "third party impact" of public interest litigation has repercussions which extend beyond the specifically Indian predicament of squaring it with the letter and spirit of the Constitution. It all too easily jeopardises procedural justice when the activities of large numbers of private polluters are in question, even where, as in the *MC Mehta* case,[81] they had been in clear breach of a statutory prohibition. In this instance the Supreme Court ordered that tanneries discharging untreated effluent into the River Ganges in breach of the Water (Prevention and Control of Pollution) Act 1974 be closed after they had failed to enter an appearance; those tanneries which had been represented in the proceedings were granted a reprieve of six months for the construction of appropriate treatment plants. However, in keeping with the informal procedure applied in public interest litigation, the only notice given to the tanneries

---

[76]Article 32 provides that " . . . (2) The Supreme Court shall have power to issue directions or orders or writs, *including* writs in the nature of *habeas corpus, mandamus*, prohibition *quo warranto* and *certiorari* . . . for the enforcement of any of the rights conferred by this Part" (emphasis added).
[77]This difficulty does not arise in the case of State High Courts which are granted equally broadly defined powers in article 226 in respect of "the enforcement of any of the rights conferred by Part III *and for any further purpose*" (emphasis added). Part III contains the fundamental rights provisions.
[78]*MC Mehta* v *Union of India* AIR 1987 SC 965.
[79]AIR 1987 SC 1086. Despite a lengthy discussion of the question whether private corporations were subject to the fundamental rights chapter in the Constitution, the court declined to decide the issue. Instead, it directed that actions against Shriram be instituted in the appropriate High Court (at 1098 and 1100).
[80]AIR 1987 SC 965 at 982.
[81]*MC Mehta* v *Union of India* AIR 1988 SC 1037.

was by way of "publishing the gist of the petition in the newspapers in circulation in northern India".

The desire to make the enforcement of public duties and the protection of diffuse interests effective has, thirdly, extended the courts' involvement beyond the resolution of disputes into the realm of administrative implementation. Because disputes over environmental degradation are situated in a complex web of intersecting patterns of social relations, they often necessitate the taking of positive steps which can only be implemented over time. When the subject-matter of litigation arises from long-standing administrative failures, the very factors which prompt a relaxation of procedural formalities also call for continuing judicial supervision of the implementation of court orders. Thus, in *Rural Litigation and Entitlement Kendra, Dehradun*,[82] the court found it necessary to set up a committee to monitor reforestation measures in the region and to oversee the running of three limestone mines which had been allowed to continue operations. A "rehabilitation" committee was also created to ensure that mine owners whose quarries had been closed were given alternative sites elsewhere. This can lead to judicial involvement with a case for several years. In this instance the letter initiating the litigation had been sent in 1983 and the principal orders made in 1985; in 1991 the Supreme Court was still issuing directions aimed at ensuring compliance with its orders.[83]

None of these developments is surprising; indeed, they mark out the success of public interest litigation in opening up the courts to a new range of people and interests. They flow inexorably from the Indian judiciary's striving to develop practices appropriate to the transformation of the judge's role into that of a "social auditor".[84] They have, nevertheless, elicited critical reactions which, taken together, point to the limits of grafting public interest litigation onto the conventional court structure.

The lack of transparency surrounding the selection of cases for determination has inevitably elicited accusations of bias.[85] So too have the procedures for assisting public interest applicants in the gathering of evidence. One eminent Indian academic lawyer has gone so far as to state that: "A judge who appoints commissioners would be inclined to appoint those whom or about whom he knows personally . . . Such commissioners are likely to be at least as biased as the judges who have been enthusiastic about PIL litigation".[86] Finally, the nature of the orders made and the exercise of jurisdiction over their implementation has led to accusations that the "Court is factually (not merely

---

[82]AIR 1985 SC 652 at 655–7 and AIR 1988 SC 2187 at 2209– 2211.
[83]See JT 1991 (5) SC 232. For a brief chronology of this series of cases, see Rosencranz, Divan and Noble (n 49 *supra*) at 57.
[84]Krishna Iyer J in *Fertilizer Corporation Kamgar Union* v *Union of India* AIR 1981 SC 344 at 354.
[85]Agrawala (n 54 *supra*) at 17 quotes a journalist writing that "some judges were choosing their litigants".
[86]Agrawala *ibid* at 26.

virtually) taking over the administrative function" and violating the doctrine of separation of powers.[87]

At the heart of these criticisms lies disquiet with the departure by the Indian courts from the traditional norms of procedural propriety in the promotion of public interest litigation. This departure is not surprising because the practices and procedures which were elaborated to give effect to these norms evolved in the context of a less ambitious institution, catering for a very different range of persons and interests. Now, however, the Supreme Court's "specific political role lies in its functioning as a parallel legislature and quite often as a parallel constituent body".[88] As public interest litigation is designed to serve interests whose realisation necessitates positive steps by the state to change the status quo, it was, perhaps, inevitable that it should overwhelm an institution traditionally geared to the vindication of the interests of those whose stake in the status quo has always provided them with access to justice.

These matters ought, nevertheless, to be taken very seriously indeed. The advocacy of public interest litigation flows as much from a conviction that the courts can deliver justice as it does from the belief that justice often requires affirmative steps by the state.[89] Indeed, judicial support for public interest litigation has been explicitly grounded on the conviction that: "the rule of law must wean people away from the lawless street and win them for the court of law".[90]

Since "bias even for a good cause, is bias all the same",[91] there is a danger that Indian public interest litigants might receive second-class justice. Moreover, in the context of "Court action extending into the future" shaping "the lives of large sections of the people, some of whom have had no voice in the decision . . . it is as well to remember that public approval and public consent assume material importance".[92]

Some Indian lawyers have, consequently, argued for the reform of judicial practices and procedures, with a view to finding appropriate ways of maintaining traditional procedural norms of impartiality in the face of a changed judicial role. In particular, more formalised methods of selecting letters for conversion to writ petitions, the creation of a dedicated court-based

[87]Agrawala *ibid* and Peiris, "Public Interest Litigation in the Indian Subcontinent" (1991) ICLQ 40 at 89. Concern with avoiding enmity with the other branches of government has led to refusals to order the introduction of legislation (*State of Himachal Pradesh* v *A Parent of a Student of Medical College, Shivula* AIR 1985 SC 911) and to interfere where the availability of resources and spending priorities have been at issue (*P Nalla Thampy* v *Union of India* AIR 198 SC 74). However, the latter position has been departed from (*e.g.* in *Municipal Council, Ratlam* v *Vardhichand* AIR 1980 SC 162 and *LK Koolwal* v *State of Rajasthan* AIR 1988 Raj 2). Nelivigi, Poojitha and Rosencranz (n 55 *supra*) at 107 take the view that the "only inference one can draw is that the Court defers to the political branches when large economic interests are at stake".
[88]Baxi, *The Indian Supreme Court and Politics*, Lucknow, Eastern Book Co, 1980, Introduction.
[89]Craig and Deshpande, "Rights, Autonomy and Process: Public Interest Litigation in India" (1989) *Oxford Journal of Legal Studies* 356 articulate the latter position cogently.
[90]Bhagwati J *SP Gupta* v *Union of India* (n 47 *supra*).
[91]Agrawala (n 54 *supra*) at 26.
[92]Pathak J in *Bandhua Mukti Morcha* v *Union of India* AIR 1984 SC 802.

fact-finding machinery, and greater involvement by respondents in the appointments of fact-finding commissioners and committees have been called for.[93]

Such reforms will, however, be of only limited utility. To the extent that they re-introduce discarded formalities, reforms of this kind will undo the success of public interest litigation in widening access to the courts. Judicial involvement in administration will also remain untouched. Moreover, they will not address the fundamental dilemma of which these matters are symptoms: the need created for an activist approach by the very issues and persons Indian public interest litigation seeks to cater for.

Hence, an effective system of public interest law cannot simply be grafted onto existing structures of adjudication. More fundamental institutional reform is called for than the liberalisation of legal practices and procedures. A reform of this kind would move beyond the identification of law with litigation, to establish a body capable of committing resources to the investigation of informally submitted complaints, conducting widespread consultation with affected parties and undertaking long-term supervisory functions. Courts would then no longer be seen as the first port of call for relief, and litigation would lend support rather than dominate public interest environmental law.

v. **Conclusion**

The anxieties evoked by these procedural innovations in India find resonance in reservations which have been expressed about substantive legal change through the enactment of an environmental right. Lawyers in South Africa, for example, have been concerned that such a right would involve judges in deciding matters falling properly within the sphere of an elected legislature.[94]

The two preceding sections have argued that these apprehensions retain their force when public interest law is grafted onto existing legal concepts. The "well-being" approach adopted in South Africa's new Constitution fails to rid courts of the dilemma of having to choose between development and environmental protection. The Indian approach to public interest litigation maintains the tension between procedural and substantive justice which it was designed to overcome.

These problems can only be resolved, and an effective system of environmental public interest law be created, if full recognition is given to the fact that environmental protection transcends conflicts between individual interests.

---

[93]See Agrawala (n 54 *supra*) at 16–20, 24 and 26. In *MC Mehta* v *Union of India* AIR 1987 SC 965 Bhagwati CJ called (at 981–2) for the creation of an independent centre of experts to assist the court in environmental cases.
[94]See Corder, Kahanovitz, Murphy *et al*, *A Charter for Social Justice: A Contribution to the South African Bill of Rights Debate*, Cape Town, Dept of Public Law UCT, 1992 at 52; and see Cowen (n 19 *supra*).

That calls for a substantive law which provides in equal measure for environmental protection and the just distribution of the social costs thereof, and an
institutional structure specifically designed to harness collective resources to
that end.

Contents of Chapter 7

Public Interest Perspectives on the Bhopal Case: Tort, Crime or Violation of Human Rights?

Chapter 7

Public Interest Perspectives on the Bhopal Case: Tort, Crime or Violation of Human Rights?

Michael R Anderson[1]

I. Introduction

Public interest litigation, whether environmental or otherwise, persistently faces the criticism that it is not conducted in the genuine interest of a broad public.[2] Detractors delight in pointing to a hidden private interest masquerading under the public guise. While it seems that such criticisms are only occasionally well-founded, they do raise the difficult question of the relationship between the activist lawyer and those whose interests are putatively represented. In law, the problem is usually reduced to the rather vexed issue of *locus standi*, depending upon whether the party has sufficient interest in the case. However, legal constructions of standing over-simplify important ethical issues. First, does counsel represent the views and interests of affected parties accurately in the timing and content of legal argument? Secondly, when lawyers frame social and environmental conflicts in a vocabulary acceptable to the courts, are the original complaints distorted or marginalised? Finally, when such conflicts may be resolved through either legal or political means, are there hidden costs involved in pressing for specifically legal resolutions?

At an ethical level, the central question is one of best professional practice and whether lawyers involved in public interest litigation represent the views of client groups in an accurate and responsible manner. This is particularly difficult where litigation is conducted under the banner of "empowerment".

---

*Michael R Anderson** is a lecturer with the School of Oriental and African Studies, University of London with interests in environmental law and human rights law, particularly in India.
[1]Lecturer in Law, SOAS, Thornhaugh St, London WC1H OXG, UK. The author is grateful to Emma Favata for research assistance and to David Robinson for useful comments upon an earlier draft.
[2]This is an updated and substantially revised version of a paper which first appeared as "Litigation and Activism: The Bhopal Case" *Third World Legal Studies*.

The disadvantaged or injured parties may be active participants in the legal process, or they may remain alienated, disempowered "victims" at the mercy of an ambivalent altruism. The very notion of empowerment houses a deep and pervasive ambiguity arising from its inherent paternalism. Is power the kind of thing that can simply be bestowed, or must it be seized actively? Who is empowered to empower, and what is their interest in doing so? On whose terms and for what ends? There is also a deeper problem: is the traditional client–lawyer relationship adequate to represent the broader interests which are the real subject-matter of public interest litigation? These questions may arise wherever public interest litigation occurs, but for the purposes of this chapter, they will be explored in the context of the litigation following the 1984 gas leak in Bhopal, India. The case is a reminder that legal categories and procedures place serious constraints upon the possibilities for popular participation in environmental public interest litigation, and yet it usefully demonstrates that political activism may be used to question and even breach those constraints.

II. Legal marginalisation

A graffito on the wall of the Union Carbide pesticide plant in Bhopal declares: "Killer Carbide must be Punished". It is emblematic of the frustration experienced by many people in Bhopal following years of litigation.[3] To local understandings, the injustice seems obvious. The leak of methyl isocyanate (MIC) gas from the Union Carbide[4] pesticide factory on 3 December 1984 resulted in at least 3,828 immediate and subsequent deaths,[5] an undetermined number of injuries and disabilities reflected in over 639,000 individual claims for compensation, and widespread loss of livelihood. Although it is known to

---

[3] The history of the litigation is recounted in a variety of sources. For the essential legal documentation with commentary, see Baxi U and Paul T, eds, *Mass Disasters and Multinational Liability: The Bhopal Case*, Bombay, Tripathi, 1985; Baxi U, ed, *Inconvenient Forum and Convenient Catastrophe: The Bhopal Case*, Bombay, Tripathi, 1986; and Baxi U and Dhanda A, eds, *Valiant Victims and Lethal Litigation: The Bhopal Case*, Bombay, Tripathi, 1990. See also Muchlinski PT, "The Bhopal Case: Controlling Ultrahazardous Industrial Activities Undertaken by Foreign Investors" (1987) 50 *Modern Law Review* 545; Anderson MR, "State Obligations in a Transnational Dispute: The Bhopal Case" in WE Butler, ed, *Control Over Compliance with International Law*, London, Martinus Nijhoff, 1991; Abraham CM and Abraham S, "The Bhopal Case and the Development of Environmental Law in India" (1991) 40 ICLQ 334; and Cassels J, *The Uncertain Promise of Law*, Toronto, University of Toronto Press, 1993.

[4] The factory was owned and operated by Union Carbide India Limited (UCIL), a subsidiary of the US parent company, Union Carbide Corporation (UCC), which owned 50.9% of UCIL stock through its wholly owned Hong Kong subsidiary, Union Carbide Eastern.

[5] This was the government figure as of 8 April 1993 (quoted in charge sheet, Sessions Trial No 257/92, Bhopal Court of Sessions, 8 April 1993), but many observers contend that the actual number is higher, with many gas-related deaths having gone uncounted both in the mass cremations following the gas leak and in subsequent years. As with much relating to the Bhopal litigation, reliable figures are not available due to a lack of comprehensive epidemiological data.

be carcinogenic and mutagenic, like many toxic substances, MIC has long-term health effects which are poorly understood, idiosyncratic, and still unpredictable, so that the 521,262 residents who are estimated to have been exposed[6] to the gas live in uncertainty regarding potential future effects. Where identified health effects include chronic fatigue, muscular pains, higher abortion rates, progressive pulmonary disability, and immune system deficiencies, it is not surprising that present symptoms and uncertain prognosis contribute to anxiety neuroses and neurotic depression.[7] While this host of hardships descended upon residents through no fault of their own, the simple fact that the leak occurred suggests that the plant's safety features were inadequate, while ample evidence indicates that the leak was directly attributable to faulty plant design and management errors. However, after over nine years of litigation, the patent injustice of the situation has failed to produce either a determination of liability or very much in the way of effective compensation for the survivors.

Moreover, right from the outset, people in Bhopal were largely excluded from the litigation process. Their distance from the putative mechanisms of accountability may be traced in three aspects of the litigation. First, the survivors of the leak are predominantly Hindi-speaking, many are illiterate, and most have little previous experience with litigation in India – much less with US lawyers who arrived to sign up claimants on contingency fee arrangements in the first week following the disaster. Many of the worst-affected areas were effectively slums whose inhabitants possessed neither the institutional skills nor the financial resources required to proceed against the corporation. These factors were compounded by the widespread occurrence of debilitating injuries following exposure to the gas. Until early 1987, court hearings on the question of appropriate forum took place in US courts – well beyond the participation or even observation of groups in Bhopal. When the hearings on forum were finally concluded in Union Carbide's favour, thus shifting proceedings from US to Indian courts on the grounds of *forum non conveniens*, neither individuals nor the many non-governmental organisations (NGOs) in Bhopal were consulted on the matter, even though the

---

[6]Dwivedi MP, *et al*, *Long-Term Epidemiological Study on the Health Effects of Toxic Gas Exposure*, Bhopal, Indian Council of Medical Research, 1991.

[7]An introduction to the literature on the health effects of MIC in Bhopal can be found in the following: Andersson N, *et al*, "Exposure and Response to Methyl Isocyanate – Results of a Community Based Survey of Bhopal" (1988) 45 *British Journal of Industrial Medicine* 469; Andersson N, "Long-Term Effects of Methyl Isocyanate" *The Lancet*, 3 June 1989 at 1259; and Lochan R, "Health Damage Due to Bhopal Gas Disaster – Review of Medical Research" (1991) 26 *Economic and Political Weekly* 1322.

opinion of the District Court relied heavily upon arguments regarding the aims and concerns of Indian citizens in the case.[8]

The second exclusion arrived in the form of the Bhopal Gas Disaster (Processing of Claims) Act 1985[9] by which the Central Government of India assumed a *parens patriae* role, arrogating to itself the exclusive right to represent and act in place of every claimant in the Bhopal litigation. Although section 4 of the Act permits the claimant to retain a legal practitioner at his or her own expense, it has left little room for the participation of independent counsel. The formulation of the plaints, the assessment of damages, and the decision to place a higher priority upon civil rather than criminal proceedings all originated in government offices without consultation of claimants in Bhopal.

Thirdly, section 3(2)(b) of the Act also accorded to the Central Government the power to enter into a compromise with Union Carbide. Between early 1985 and February 1989, the government intermittently conducted negotiations with Carbide in the matter of an out of court settlement. Again, representatives of Bhopal groups were neither present at the negotiations nor consulted as to their content. The full effects of this policy were felt on 14 February 1989 when Chief Justice Pathak announced,[10] in the form of a Supreme Court Order, the results of a settlement that had clearly been reached in negotiations between Carbide and the Government. The Union Carbide Corporation agreed to pay $470 million to settle all past, present, and future claims arising in relation to the Bhopal case.[11] The agreed order was announced in the midst of arguments before the court regarding interim compensation, in circumstances where the merits of the case had not yet been addressed, even in the Bhopal District Court. There were strong indications that the Government's motives in reaching the settlement were complicated

---

[8]*In re Union Carbide Corp Gas Plant Disaster at Bhopal, India in December 1984*, 634 F Supp 842 (SDNY, 1986), reproduced in (1986) 25 ILM 771; 809 F 2nd 195 (2nd Cir, 1987), reproduced in 27 (1987) ILM 62; *cert denied* 108 S Ct 199 (1987). For commentary, see Nanda VP, "For Whom the Bell Tolls in The Aftermath of the Bhopal Tragedy: Reflections on *Forum Non Conveniens* and Alternative Methods of Resolving the Bhopal Dispute" (1987) 15 *Denver Journal of International Law and Policy* 235; Darmody SJ, "An Economic Approach to *Forum Non Conveniens* Dismissals requested by US Multinational Corporations – The Bhopal Case" (1988) 22 *George Washington Journal of International Law and Economics* 215; and Yakpo EKM, "Application of *Forum Non Conveniens* in the United States – Bhopal and its Lessons for Developing Countries" (1989) 1 *African JICL* 139.
[9](1986) 25 ILM 884.
[10]Article 142(1) of the Constitution enables the Supreme Court to "pass any such decree or make such order as is necessary for doing complete justice in any cause or matter pending before it".
[11]*UCC* v *Union of India* (1989) 1 SCC 674. The settlement was announced as a judicial order, but there is little doubt that it was arrived at in negotiations between Carbide and the central government of India. This was affirmed by the Union Carbide India Limited spokesperson, S. Mitra: "Lawyers for both sides were there, and decided on $470 million. . . . This amount was agreed by the lawyers and the Government of India. Then it was announced in Court. If you look at the settlement you can tell this from the wording". (Personal Interview, 27 November 1989.)

by short-term political considerations,[12] particularly since none of the Bhopal groups were consulted as to the timing or content of the settlement.

III. **The dialectic of litigation and activism**

The marginalisation of activists and NGOs before the courts stands in sharp contrast to the centrality of their work within Bhopal itself. Immediately following the gas leak, a number of survivors combined, frequently with support from activists outside Bhopal, to form NGOs to co-ordinate local relief work. In the absence of adequate medical care and economic relief, the self-help organisations in Bhopal have been the most effective vehicles for coping with the medical, social and economic effects of the gas leak. They assumed a variety of forms, with diverse purposes and approaches. As concerns and tactics changed, some groups declined while fresh initiatives grew. In the first three to four years following the leak, five types[13] of activist groups were prevalent: apolitical relief and rehabilitation groups; groups which collected and disseminated technical, legal, medical, and political information; trade union organisations which mobilised support around workers' issues; international solidarity and support groups; and, finally, the explicitly political groups which have co-ordinated local relief, organised political demonst-rations, and actively participated in the litigation. It is the last category, of political groups, which endured and became the most important to the trajectory of litigation. One group in particular, the Bhopal Gas Peedit Mahila Udyog Sangathan (BGPMUS) – the Organization of Bhopal Women Worker Victims – has played a key role in challenging court decisions and demanding adequate compensation.[14]

Although largely peripheral to the actual process of litigation, peoples' organisations in Bhopal have followed the litigation closely and responded with forms of social and political action. It is difficult to overstate the influence of legal proceedings upon local political action. Particularly prior to 1989, when the prospect of an extended tort case seemed inevitable, the main issues of "relief, medical aid and rehabilitation grew to be viewed through the litigatory lens".[15] Just as technical legal terms have been incorporated into the vernacular, so too the timing of public demonstrations and the content of demands made upon the central and state governments have been influenced

[12]See, further, Jaising I , "Bhopal: Settlement or Sellout?" *The Lawyers* (March 1989), and Anderson MR, "Bhopal" (1989) 8 *Commonwealth Judicial Journal* 62.
[13]This typology draws upon Ravi Rajan S, "Rehabilitation and Voluntarism in Bhopal" 6 *Lokayan Bulletin* 3 (Jan-April 1988).
[14]The BGPMUS was founded in 1986 to protest the closure of a government-supported work scheme, but due to the commitment and discipline of its members it quickly became the most effective focus for political and legal agitation. It is supported by the Bhopal Group for Information and Action, and the Delhi-based Bhopal Gas Peedit Sangharsh Sahyog Samiti.
[15]Kumar R, *The History of Doing*, London, Verso, 1993 at 188.

by proceedings in court. The most important activist groups in Bhopal, including the BGPMUS, found that the agendas and idioms of their activism were increasingly influenced by legal forms.

In turn, political activism affected litigation. The best example of this may be seen in the events following the settlement of 14 February 1989. Immediately following the announcement of the settlement, groups in Bhopal exhibited several reactions. Some accepted it, others rejected it outright, and still others kept counsel in uncertainty. By March, a large number of demonstrations and letters to the press codified the emerging consensus that the settlement was unacceptable on several counts: first, the quantum of relief was too low either to provide adequate compensation or punish Union Carbide and its subsidiary for gross negligence; secondly, the groups in Bhopal were given no opportunity to participate in the decision-making process regarding the nature of the settlement or its impending distribution; thirdly, there was insufficient medical evidence to assess the scale of injury, thus precluding any final judgment; and, finally, Union Carbide had escaped the judicial process without ever facing the question of its legal liability for the gas leak. A number of groups filed both review[16] and writ[17] petitions seeking a reconsideration of the judicially announced settlement. While $465 million collected interest in a government bank account, the Supreme Court failed to act on the petitions.

Meanwhile, political action denouncing the settlement continued in Bhopal and New Delhi. The BGPMUS in particular opposed the settlement with consistent and tireless campaigning. Immediately following the announcement of the settlement, over 1,000 women from Bhopal travelled to New Delhi where they sat in protest on the steps of the Supreme Court. National and international media attention was widespread, with statements of solidarity arriving from Dublin, Amsterdam, London and New York. As the protest gathered pace, others registered their disapproval of the court's action, including leading academics and scientists,[18] as well as the former Chief Justice of the Supreme Court, PN Bhagwati, who condemned the settlement in an article prominently featured in the influential magazine *India Today*.[19]

Meanwhile, the BGPMUS and its allies continued to rally in opposition to the settlement – pointing to its shortcomings, but also using it as an emblem of their more quotidian struggle to cope with the continuing effects of methyl isocyanate. Meeting every Saturday in a Bhopal public park for several years, as many as 1,200 women gathered to discuss the practical and political matters involved in seeking medical relief, coping with accelerating illness, securing work, and supporting the legal campaign against the settlement. Their demonstrations kept the issue of the settlement in the news while statements

[16]Article 137 of the Constitution provides the apex court with the power to review its own orders or judgments.
[17]Under article 32 of the Constitution, relating to the enforcement of fundamental rights.
[18]See, *e.g.* the letters which appeared in the *Illustrated Weekly of India* (9 April 1989) at 34–35.
[19]*India Today* (15 March 1989) at 45.

of solidarity from groups in India and abroad put pressure on both the court and the Government to take some form of action.

Following the general elections of November 1989, activists sensed a new window of opportunity. The Rajiv Gandhi government had been replaced by a coalition of parties less eager to woo foreign investment and more inclined to sympathise with populist measures. A process of quiet lobbying began in Delhi. The effort was to persuade the new government to provide immediate relief to people in Bhopal and renounce the settlement of February 1989. In a letter sent to the new Prime Minister, VP Singh, two of the groups demanded: (i) an immediate hearing of the review petitions; (ii) the withdrawal of the criminal immunities granted in the February settlement; (iii) an announcement by the new government that the settlement was "morally wrong"; (iv) full public disclosure of information relating the Bhopal gas disaster and lifting of application of the Official Secrets Act; and (v) that Union Carbide be banned in all operations in India.[20] Subsequently, on 22 December 1989, the Supreme Court handed down a decision on three consolidated writ petitions regarding the validity of the 1985 Act granting *parens patriae* power.[21] The court upheld the Act, but found that the government had a legal duty to provide interim relief to the affected people of Bhopal until such time as the litigation reached a conclusion. The quantity and nature of the interim relief were left to executive discretion. The court also noted that the people of Bhopal would have an opportunity to make representations to the court in the hearings on the three review petitions.

The lobbying efforts, supported by the Supreme Court decision, paid rich dividends on 12 January 1990. The new government announced that: (i) the quantum of settlement was insufficient to the needs of people in Bhopal; (ii) the affected people of Bhopal were entitled to interim relief and that the amount and modality of relief would be decided in consultation with the representatives of the victims groups; (iii) the claimants possessed inalienable rights to legal remedy which brought into question the conferment of criminal immunities; and (iv) that the government would support the contentions of the activist groups in the review petitions.

Following a meeting with the most prominent activists in Bhopal, the government decided to grant interim relief of Rs 200 per month to all residents of the 36 municipal wards most directly exposed to the gas. Despite the small sums involved, this represented an important victory for the Bhopal groups, particularly the BGPMUS, which had argued for a universal entitlement to interim relief instead of relief based upon the merit of individual claims. This position was based on both pragmatic and principled grounds. The BGPMUS argued that the process of evaluating individual claims would be time-consuming, subject to corruption, and inevitably biased in favour of

---

[20]Cited in Baxi, *Valiant Victims, op cit* at n 3 lxii–lxiv.
[21]*Charan Lal Sahu* v *Union of India* AIR 1990 SC 1480.

literate and document-collecting individuals. Perhaps more importantly, the group advocated a reversal of the classical onus of proof, so that for purposes of dispensing interim relief (a political rather than legal measure), a person living in the gas-affected wards should be presumed to be injured unless proven to the contrary. Even with such a straightforward disbursement scheme, the difficulties of administering individual payments meant that only 42,000 residents received payment in the first month, and only 66.1% of residents surveyed in November 1991 were receiving payments.[22] Nevertheless, the victory marked a real improvement in the fortunes of Bhopal survivors, not least because the government had agreed to throw its support behind the review petitions seeking to overturn the 1989 settlement. Long suspicious of government actions, the activist groups in Bhopal had been able to turn the *parens patriae* power to their advantage, using political pressure to realign the arguments before the court on the pending review petitions. In short, sustained activism operating outside of the formal mechanisms of the law had made a decisive impact upon the course of litigation. What the events of 1989 and 1990 demonstrate is that where the mechanisms of tort law failed to deliver effective forms of accountability for ultrahazardous activity, the activist groups were able to mobilise political support, both informally and through parliamentary channels, to change the shape of litigation.

The political successes of activists had enduring effect, most notably in the continued payment of interim relief,[23] but when the government of VP Singh was voted out of power later in that year, the political advantage was lost. However, Singh's tenure had been long enough to allow his Attorney General, Soli Sorabjee, to argue that the settlement should be set aside. Thus, it was all the more disappointing when in October 1991 the Supreme Court finally upheld[24] the civil law provisions of the February 1989 Order. By this ruling, the possibility of a definitive determination of liability was closed forever.[25] However, the Bhopal groups scored a victory in the court's decision that the criminal proceedings quashed under the 1989 settlement should be restored. Also, the court finally directed the central government to set up at least 40 Claims Courts by February 1992 to begin processing individual claims under

---

[22]Bhopal Group for Information and Action, *Compensation Disbursement Problems and Possibilities: A Report of a Survey Conducted in Three Gas Affected Bastis of Bhopal*, Delhi, Centre for Education and Communication, 1992 at 7.

[23]The interim relief scheme was due to operate for three years from 1 April 1990, but in March 1993 the BGPMUS successfully argued that the scheme was still required since only 1,800 of the 639,000 claims had been processed. In May 1993, the interim relief payments were extended for an additional three years, although the value of Rs 200 monthly payments had declined to roughly £4.50.

[24]*Union Carbide Corporation* v *Union of India* AIR 1992 SC 248. For commentary upon the decision, see Jaising I, "Bhopal: The Lost Opportunity for the Victims" *The Lawyers* (November 1991) at 4; and Sen J, "Can Defects of Natural Justice be Cured by Appeal? *Union Carbide* v *Union*" (1993) 42 ICLQ 369.

[25]A later attempt to challenge the settlement in US courts failed at lower levels, and was finally denied *certiorari* by the US Supreme Court (*The Guardian*, 5 October 1993).

the authority of the 1985 Act.[26] For activist groups in Bhopal, it became evident that only two types of legal action were now possible: first, to lend support to the government in bringing criminal prosecutions against UCC and UCIL managers and, secondly, to use writ petitions to challenge any improper findings or orders in the Claims Courts.

IV. **Litigating strategies and the public interest**

In a context where the aggrieved individuals were largely marginalised by prevailing legal structures, a small number of lawyers were decisive in determining litigating strategies and framing the issues. An early instance of this could be seen in the enormous influence of US personal injury lawyers whose arrival in Bhopal immediately focused attention upon the prospects of a remedy in tort against UCC in US courts. However sound this strategy may have been, it did cause a two-year delay while Carbide deployed the *forum non conveniens* defence; it also distracted attention from the other forms of legal redress which might be available.

Broadly speaking, lawyers for the Bhopal groups identified three main avenues of legal approach. The first, and perhaps most intuitively obvious, especially to North American lawyers, was through the law of tort or civil liability, in which the principal issues remained questions of causation, strict or fault liability, parent company control, and methods of appropriate compensation. A second approach was available under the substantive and procedural protections of fundamental rights provided in Part III of the Indian Constitution 1950. Pursuing this line of argument, the deaths and injuries which occurred in Bhopal could be treated as a violation of the right to life under article 21, thus opening the doors to a variety of legal remedies, including a range of prerogative writs and monetary compensation. The third avenue for legal redress could be found in the criminal law, with the possibility of government prosecution of Union Carbide or its managers under the Indian Penal Code provisions for culpable homicide. Faced with this range of legal options, it is legitimate to ask what factors determined the litigating strategies of the lawyers representing the individuals and NGOs in Bhopal.

While a private interest lawyer would answer that the case is a straightforward matter of civil liability, few of the people in Bhopal saw it that way, as we shall see. Moreover, once the action before the US courts was dismissed, and new litigation strategies had to be formulated in India, there were compelling factors which favoured an approach based upon criminal law or constitutional rights. To anticipate somewhat, it matters a great deal whether a

---

[26]The court also directed UCC to provide funds for the construction of an additional hospital in Bhopal. At the time of writing (January 1994), Union Carbide has not complied with this order.

case like Bhopal is approached as a crime, a tort, or a violation of fundamental rights. At stake are not just different procedures and remedies, but also distinct vocabularies and ways of characterising the relationship between a polluter and society. If lawyers act essentially as strategists, choosing procedures and tactics most likely to succeed in court, then their legal strategies are also influenced by the prevailing legal culture and current fashion. Looking in turn to each of the three main legal principles – tort, constitutional right, and crime – it is instructive to seek what litigational incentives and disincentives were associated with each approach, as well as how it was viewed by activists in Bhopal.

A. **Tort approaches**

Leaving aside the complicating factors of parent company liability and the enforcement of foreign orders,[27] it was obvious from the first few days after the leak that the Bhopal case would be addressed in the United States principally through the law of torts, which is heavily favoured for personal injury cases. Even after the suit was dismissed by the US courts, the legal basis for all subsequent actions was a civil suit for $3.3 billion, lodged in the Bhopal District Court in September 1986. For lawyers fashioning a strategy for the post-US phase of litigation, the Indian law of torts, based largely upon the English law, offered a number of obvious attractions: it has ready-made categories for injury, standards for establishing liability, methods for construing causation and protocols for assessing the quantum of damages. On the negative side, however, tort actions in India are notoriously slow, involving a highly technical set of procedures which enable defendants frequently to drag out proceedings for years and even decades.[28] It was partially in anticipation of delay that Justice Deo of the Bhopal District Court acted *suo moto* in asking the parties to present arguments in respect of interim relief. Since the question of interim relief occupied both plaintiff and defendant in appeal until the judicial settlement was announced in February 1989, the merits of the case in civil liability were never argued before any Indian court.

Nevertheless, the vocabulary and presumptions of civil liability which were implicit in the legal proceedings provided ample opportunity for the activist groups in Bhopal to evolve criticisms. Some activist leaders operated from positions informed by Marxian theory, others drew upon populist anti-state and anti-industrial discourses, but most of the people involved in activist groups simply drew conclusions from their own experiences, built upon more demotic concepts of justice. A full description of these views, articulated

---

[27]These matters are ably discussed in Muchlinski, *op cit* n 3.
[28]The now classic statement of this point is made in "Affidavit of Marc S Galanter, 5 December 1985" reprinted in Baxi and Paul, *op cit* n 3.

over many years, is not possible here. Nevertheless, it is possible to highlight several illustrative ways in which the law of torts came in for criticism.

Some of the groups in Bhopal criticised the legal preoccupation with monetary compensation. They pointed out that monetary compensation was simply a way for Union Carbide to place a precise value on life and injury, so as to incorporate that value into its account books just as any other cost of production. It is not surprising that from 1985, Union Carbide pressed for an out of court settlement extinguishing all civil and criminal proceedings in return for a lump sum in line with its insurance cover. In contrast, members of the BGPMUS emphasised, particularly during 1989 and 1990, that monetary compensation was relatively low on their list of demands, especially if it assumed the form of a one-off payment. Experience showed that an influx of cash into the community would prompt merchants simply to raise the local price of goods, while creating fresh opportunities for lawyers, doctors, and disaster entrepreneurs to profit from the compensation. Moreover, payment of damages would place a full stop at the end of the litigational narrative, fostering the illusion that with the payment of compensation, the legal system had restored an equilibrium, accounting for all future pecuniary and non-pecuniary loss. In fact, the women point out, the physical and social effects of the gas are likely to continue for decades, particularly where progressive disorders may give rise to unforseen symptoms. In such circumstances, neither future pain and suffering nor loss of amenities of life could be predicted, much less evaluated, in a satisfactory manner. What the BGPMUS demanded in place of compensation was a four-part package: (i) full legal determination of civil and especially criminal liability; (ii) accessible, appropriate, and comprehensive medical care provided on a community-wide basis; (iii) provision of employment schemes and entrepreneurial opportunities to encourage local self-sufficiency; and (iv) long-term monitoring of continuing health effects.[29] Thus, the concepts of tort law were not rejected entirely, since appropriate compensation remained important to the BGPMUS and allied groups. However, they were not prepared to accept a lump-sum payment without recognition of their long-term needs for medical care and financial support. Moreover, it was stressed repeatedly that since monetary damages could never make good non-pecuniary loss, there was a need to supplement actions in tort with those based upon constitutional rights and criminal law.

B. Fundamental rights approaches

The ready relevance of constitutional rights to the Bhopal case stems from two factors. The first is that when the Central Government assumed the role of

---

[29]This summary is derived primarily from interviews conducted in November 1989.

parens patriae, it extinguished the rights of individuals to seek remedy in the law of tort, and created new rights against the state within the scheme of administrative compensation. Henceforth, grievances regarding findings of fact and law, including matters of compensation, could only be addressed within the framework of public law. For lawyers, this required that issues of liability, compensation and even complex matters of epidemiological evidence, be recast in a public law terminology.

The second factor which drew the Bhopal case within the ambit of constitutional law was the already vigorous jurisprudence on constitutional rights which informed the strategies of most activist lawyers. Since the early 1980s, certain judges in the Supreme Court and, more latterly, in the High Courts have placed liberal interpretations upon substantive rights, while activist lawyers have taken advantage of relaxed rules of standing and other procedural innovations to build a dynamic public interest litigation movement.[30] Because public interest writ petitions can go directly before the Supreme Court, and tend to receive priority treatment in a docket otherwise clogged with arrears, they offer an attractive alternative to the notoriously slow actions in civil liability. Since the drafting of writ petitions is a straightforward matter, unencumbered by the procedural requirements which apply under the Code of Civil Procedure 1908, advocates are understandably attracted to them as a vehicle for speedy relief.

In these circumstances, it was not surprising that activist lawyers pursued a strategy of "constitutionalising" the tort issues in the case.[31] While a full account of the constitutional issues in the Bhopal case lies beyond the scope of this chapter, the essential innovation was simple: it lay in treating personal injury claims as alleged violations of the right to life. The Supreme Court has for some time recognised that the right to life under article 21 extends beyond the right to a mere animal existence, and includes an entitlement to "the finer graces of human civilization which make life worth living".[32] Additionally, it has been willing to provide monetary compensation for unconstitutional

---

[30]Apart from relaxed *locus standi* rules, the courts have also treated letters as writ petitions, adopted non-adversarial proceedings, acted *suo moto* on the basis of newspaper accounts, and retained a supervisory jurisdiction for purposes of implementing orders. For the most important decisions on appropriate procedure, see *Bandua Mukti Morcha* v *Union of India* AIR 1984 SC 802, and *Sheela Barse* v *Union of India* (1988) 4 SCC 226. There is much literature on public interest litigation in India. The most important analyses include: Baxi U, "Taking Suffering Seriously" in Dhavan R, Sudarshan R, and Khurshid S, eds, *Judges and the Judicial Power*, Bombay, Tripathi, 1985; Bhagwati PN, "Judicial Activism and Public Interest Litigation" (1985) 23 *Columbia Journal of Trans Law* 561; Peiris GL, "Public Interest Litigation in the Indian Subcontinent: Current Dimensions" (1991) 40 ICLQ 66; and Breman J, "From Cane Fields to Court Rooms" in Shah G, ed, *Capitalist Development: Critical Essays*, London, Sangam, 1990. For a recent overview, see Hurra S, *Public Interest Litigation: In Quest of Justice*, Ahmedabad, Mishra, 1993.

[31]The term is adapted from Baxi U, "The Bhopal Victims in the Labyrinth of the Law: An Introduction" in Baxi and Dhanda *op cit* n 3 at xxiv.

[32]*Board of Trustees, Port of Bombay* v *DR Nadkarni* 1983 (1) SCC 124. The right to life has been interpreted to include, *inter alia*, a right to: livelihood (*Olga Tellis* v *Bombay Municipal Corp* AIR 1986 SC 180); legal aid (*Suk Das* v *Union Territory* AIR 1986 SC 991); and the enjoyment of clean air and water (*Subhash Kumar* v *State of UP* 1991 (1) SCC 598).

deprivation of life or personal liberty.[33] Of course, these remedies are only available against the state, but "the state" has been interpreted very widely to include parastatals, quasi-governmental authorities, and any organisation receiving substantial government aid or performing public functions.[34]

The relevance of these trends for the Bhopal case became evident in *MC Mehta* v *Union of India*[35] on an application for compensation following a leak of oleum gas from a factory in Delhi owned by the Sriram Food and Fertilizers company. It is worth noting that the case was brought by India's foremost environmental public interest lawyer, MC Mehta, and came before the court not as a suit for personal injury, but as an application for the enforcement of the right to life. In its judgment, the court took some steps to construe the Sriram company as an instrumentality of the state subject to the discipline of fundamental rights standards, but failed to make a definitive pronouncement on the matter. The five-judge bench went on, however, to evolve standards of liability which would apply to any enterprise engaged in hazardous or inherently dangerous activity. Developing a rule of liability based upon constitutional standards, the court discarded the principles of strict liability following *Rylands* v *Fletcher*, and pronounced a standard of *absolute liability* "not subject to any exceptions which operate *vis-à-vis* the tortious principle of strict liability".[36] Other aspects of the new principle, including its application to entire economic enterprises (such as a multinational enterprise) rather than individual corporations, and the pronouncement that the quantum of damages should increase proportionate to the size of the enterprise in order to provide a deterrent effect, suggest that it was tailor-made for the impending Bhopal litigation. Such jurisprudential innovation relied heavily upon the fundamental rights framework, because it would have been difficult to achieve within a construction of tort principles based on precedent. The relevance of absolute liability to Bhopal was never full explored. Although the principle was applied to Carbide in the Madhya Pradesh High Court in its decision on interim compensation, the 1989 settlement precluded either a hearing on the merits or a definitive pronouncement by the Supreme Court.

The combination of the *Mehta* principle and the *parens patriae* power of the central government provided ample opportunities for challenging the settlement by way of constitutional writ petitions, as we have seen. A large number of petitions were filed challenging the settlement on a variety of fundamental rights grounds. In the end, these petitions failed to attain their objects, since the 1985 Act was declared constitutional and the civil side of the

---

[33]*Rudul Sah* v *State of Bihar* 1983 (4) SCC 141; *Bhim Singh* v *State of J & K* 1985 (4) SCC 677; the recent decision in *Nilabati Behera* v *State of Orissa* 1993 (2) SCC 746 is important for the distinction it develops between a claim for compensation under public law and a remedy in tort for damages.
[34]*Ajay Hasia* v *Khalid Mujib* AIR 1981 SC 481; *Tekraj* v *Union of India* AIR 1988 SC 469.
[35]1987 (1) SCC 395.
[36]*Ibid* at 421.

1989 settlement was upheld.[37] Nevertheless, the fundamental rights procedures provided the activist groups and their lawyers with a powerful set of
tools for challenging government actions in what were essentially matters of
tort litigation. This has permanently modified the landscape of tort jurisprudence in India, so that toxic torts and other environmental claims are now
much more likely to be addressed through fundamental rights procedures.

The vocabulary of fundamental rights has been taken up by groups in
Bhopal, no doubt because it has an intuitive appeal, but also because it has
served as the basis for their court actions since 1989. Nevertheless, as an idiom
of protest and local understandings of justice, it is not as popular as that of the
criminal law. On balance, the rights violation approach has been largely
lawyer-led rather than activist-led. A human rights approach to the Bhopal case
was developed more fully by the Permanent Peoples' Tribunal, an NGO based
in Rome which held hearings in Bhopal during October 1992. Although the
Tribunal has no legal authority, the judgment is worth noting for the way it
attempts to build a human rights understanding of the Bhopal case:[38]

> "Human rights standards have too often been narrowly interpreted to exclude
> from their purview the anti-humanitarian effects of industrialisation and
> environmental damage . . . It is of little difference if the death which comes to the
> sleeping victim in the middle of the night is caused by a politically-motivated
> death squad or by a cloud of poisonous gas. In either case, the right to life of an
> innocent person is violated in an inexcusable manner . . . [A]nd in either case the
> international community has a profound interest in taking steps to ameliorate
> the effects of the violation and to prevent its repetition."

It is not surprising that this view resonates with those of many local activists.
Casting the Bhopal injuries in terms of human rights violations underscored
the sense of irreparable harm. If the right to life is absolute and inalienable, it
cannot be bought and sold on the open market of civil liability. This assertion
assumes additional importance where the prospect of low tort damages
encourages companies to risk accidents rather than investing in safety
equipment. The human rights language also holds the appeal of universality,
so that a human who is injured by industrial hazards should have the same
rights to care and compensation no matter where the injury occurs. Within a
human rights framework, a toxic death in India should carry the same legal
consequences as a similar death in Germany or the United States. The claim to
a universal standard of compensation runs directly counter to the tort
principle of awarding damages according to pecuniary loss calculated in terms
of local wages. Hence, the law of human rights, however blunt and ineffective a

---

[37]*Charan Lal Sahu* v *Union of India* AIR 1990 SC 1480; *Union Carbide Corporation* v *Union of India* AIR 1992
SC 248.
[38]Permanent Peoples' Tribunal (Third Session on Industrial and Environmental Hazards and Human Rights),
Findings and Judgements at 14. The judgment of the Tribunal is available from: The Permanent Peoples'
Tribunal, Via Della Dogana Vecchia 5, 00186 Roma, Italy.

tool in private litigation, offered a way to criticise the dominant discourse of tort law.

C. **Criminal law approaches**

Whatever the appeal of human rights concepts to lawyers and activists, there is no doubt that the most popular approach to the Bhopal case among BGPMUS members is through the categories of criminal law, particularly that of murder. Within the women's group, it is commonly pointed out that if the government could execute two men for the 1984 assassination of Prime Minister Indira Gandhi, then there is no reason why the former Chief Executive Officer of Union Carbide, Warren Anderson, should not be executed for his part in bringing about the deaths of over 3,000 innocent victims. The legal niceties of *mens rea* have no place in this demotic voice: the Bhopal gas leak is viewed as an inexcusable crime committed on a massive scale. Bhopal activists point out that the last time so many people died at once due to exposure to toxic chemicals was in the gas chambers of Nazi Germany. Bhopal is readily likened to genocide. Many argue that no amount of money, paid from the pockets of insurance companies and wealthy corporations, can begin to erase the personal guilt of the managers responsible for deaths on this scale. With an emphasis on manager liability, the notion of a corporation as a legal person has come under considerable attack in Bhopal. While there have been consistent demands to hold Union Carbide responsible for the gas leak, there has been a parallel movement focusing not on the corporation, but on the person of Warren Anderson. Whereas a corporation is by definition not a natural person, and is, therefore, impossible to confront in a personalised manner, Anderson is emblematic of the entire corporate structure employing over 100,000 people. Repeated calls to try Anderson for murder are partly rhetorical devices, but they are also efforts to reconceptualise the legal situation. There can be no doubt about the sincerity of these views, no matter how shocking they may seem to observers opposed to capital punishment.

For many activist lawyers, a criminal law approach has ideological appeal, but offers few practical opportunities. India's Criminal Procedure Code 1973 does not provide for private prosecutions, so the pursuit of criminal charges lies wholly in the hands of the state. Although Warren Anderson and a number of Indian managers were charged with a range of offences including culpable homicide shortly after the leak, prosecutions were not pursued while the issues of civil liability were before the courts. Rather, the threat of prosecution was used as a bargaining chip in the negotiation of the 1989 settlement. When the settlement order quashed all criminal proceedings, evidently in partial consideration for $470 million, the prosecutions were withdrawn. However, this appeared to be in clear violation of the Criminal Procedure Code provisions regarding non-compoundable offences,[39] so the illegality of the quashing became one of the central arguments of the review petitions.

When the Supreme Court issued its review judgment in October 1991,[40] the quashing of the criminal orders was set aside on the grounds that alleged offences of such gravity and magnitude should not be left uninvestigated. Criminal prosecution resumed shortly thereafter. In February 1992, Warren Anderson failed to appear before the Bhopal magistrate, and a warrant was issued for his arrest.[41] After it became clear that the Government of India was not willing to pursue extradition, the criminal trial was split into two parallel trials: one for Anderson and three other executives outside of India, and another for UCIL and nine of its employees.[42] In April 1993, formal charges were framed against UCIL and its employees under the Indian Penal Code provisions for: culpable homicide not amounting to murder (s 304); voluntarily causing hurt and grievous hurt (ss 324, 326); and mischief by killing cattle and other animals (s 429).[43] Under section 304, culpable homicide committed without any intention to cause death is punishable by fine and imprisonment extending up to 10 years.

While proceedings against the nine Indians are underway, the government has not yet initiated extradition proceedings against Anderson or the other non-Indian executives. Throughout 1993, the BGPMUS and other groups called repeatedly for extradition,[44] but officials have refused to act or comment. For the activist groups and their lawyers, the criminal proceedings are another example of their exclusion from the mechanisms of accountability. There is no procedural scope for public interest lawyers to initiate or support criminal prosecutions, even though criminal charges represent one of the most effective methods of deterring corporate negligence. If public interest lawyers in India and elsewhere are to represent the views of their client groups effectively, the substantive and procedural aspects of corporate crimes will require elaboration.[45] Above all, there is a need for better procedural vehicles to allow the expertise of public interest lawyers to influence criminal trials.

It is ironic that just as the criminal trials commenced, the BGPMUS and other groups became preoccupied with matters of monetary compensation. After the Supreme Court judgment of October 1991 opened the way to distribution of compensation under the 1985 Act, claimants in Bhopal were left scrambling to assemble evidence for the Claims Courts. In June 1992, the Supreme Court

---

[39]Sections 320, 321, 482.
[40]*Union Carbide Corporation* v *Union of India* AIR 1992 SC 248.
[41]*Financial Times*, 28 March 1992.
[42]*Financial Times*, 12 November 1992.
[43]Charge Sheet, Sessions Trial No 257/92, Bhopal Court of Sessions, 8 April 1993.
[44]"Bhopal: The Tragedy Continues" 10 *Lokayan Bulletin* 29 (July-August 1993).
[45]See the excellent study by David Bergman, *Disasters: Where the Law Fails – a new agenda for dealing with corporate violence*, London, Herald Families Association, 1993.

169

established guidelines for compensation, fixing lump-sum payments in a range between Rs 50,000 to Rs 300,000 (£1,080 to £6,500) as full and final compensation for relatives of the deceased.[46] The first awards were made three months later.[47] Unfortunately, the processing of claims has been characterised by corruption, unreasonable burdens of proof, and miserly assessment of damages. The Claims Courts require claimants to prove "beyond reasonable doubt that the death for which compensation is sought is attributable to gas exposure."[48] Even though most of the people who died in the first few days after the leak were buried in mass graves or cremated without post-mortem examinations, the Claims Courts have required claimants to produce post-mortem reports in order to qualify for compensation. Consequently, by June 1993 the Claims Courts had rejected about 70% of the 3,849 death claims which they had heard.[49] In such circumstances, even legitimate claimants are often forced to resort to bribery and forged post-mortem reports in order to secure compensation. Moreover, due to a lack of experienced district magistrates, new recruits with little or no experience in tort law have been brought in to make awards. One astonishing feature of the awards to date is that in assessing the quantum of damages, most have relied exclusively upon estimates of pecuniary loss, thus ignoring entirely the question of damages for non-pecuniary loss.

The activist groups in Bhopal have done their best to provide claimants with medical and legal advice, but the challenges of graft and judicial ignorance are large indeed. One of the problems which the Bhopal claimants share with plaintiffs in other toxic torts is the extreme difficulty in proving a causal link between exposure and chronic illness. Like many toxic substances, MIC produces idiosyncratic health effects which are subtle in manifestation and complicated or opaque in causation. The available epidemiological evidence is scanty, and riddled with methodological difficulties. Even where clear medical evidence exists – for instance in the link between MIC exposure and increased susceptibility to tuberculosis – the Claims Courts have generally refused to acknowledge its relevance to the quantum of damages. In an attempt to assemble independent medical evidence for the courts, the Bhopal Group for Information and Action, in collaboration with support groups in the United States, the United Kingdom and Canada, raised funds to sponsor an international medical commission to evaluate the health status of selected individuals in early 1994. However, even armed with better medical evidence,

---

[46]*Financial Times*, 22 June 1992. Activists and lawyers note that these amounts are only a tiny fraction of what probably would have been secured in US tort litigation.

[47]It is probably no coincidence that these were announced at the same time as the hearings of the Permanent Peoples' Tribunal *op cit* (n 38).

[48]Sarangi S, "It seems that we, not Union Carbide, are the culprits", *Times of India*, 30 March 1993.

[49]Singh NK, "No Succour in Sight", *India Today*, 30 June 1993. The courts have even rejected a large number of claims which were previously verified by a government committee of experts.

the activist groups may have to rely upon protests, lobbying and press coverage to secure better treatment before the Claims Courts.

v. **Conclusion**

Bhopal activists, like those in many other public interest movements, have used law as only one tool in a larger struggle involving campaigning, lobbying and grassroots welfare work. For the most part, they take the view that while the law is sometimes useful to secure minor gains, it has proved to be a failure in providing an adequate measure of justice to the victims of the gas leak. Nevertheless, the work of the activists and public interest lawyers has not only helped protect the interests of Bhopal victims, it has also had an impact on the evolving shape of environmental laws in India. The pace of legal change, to paraphrase Max Weber out of context, is often akin to the slow boring of very thick planks. However, the gas-affected people of Bhopal have not had the luxury of time: they had immediate need for a comprehensive and flexible regime that could cope with complex medical, legal and social issues with a minimum of bureaucratic hassle. They have also voiced another need: a need for justice. The Bhopal groups have been consistent in their view that ample medical care and economic relief are not adequate alone. They will continue to demand that liability for the leak be determined, and those found responsible punished. One would not wish to endorse their call for capital punishment, but their strong views are an instructive caution against unthinking reliance upon the law of tort.

A question for further exploration, in Bhopal and elsewhere, is the nature of the interaction of popular and official conceptions of justice. The activist groups in Bhopal were clearly influenced by legal understandings of liability, and yet they have retained a distinct autonomy from those understandings and were able to provide a sophisticated and compelling critique of many legal concepts. By shifting the idiom from one of civil responsibility to one of criminal responsibility and human rights violations, groups in Bhopal were able to articulate strong demands in ways which were more immediately accessible to demotic understandings. Of course, the ability of lawyers to translate popular understandings of justice into effective legal language is constrained by judicial attitudes and existing procedures. But to ignore popular notions of justice entirely would be a disservice both to client groups and the broader interests which the legal system is meant to serve.

Section II
UK Responses

Contents of Chapter 8

Citizen Suits – Can We Afford Them and Do We Need Them Anyway?

Chapter 8

Citizen Suits — Can We Afford Them and Do We Need Them Anyway?

Paul Bowden

I. Introduction

Not even the most complacent cynic could maintain that many, or indeed any, countries have yet achieved the right balance in their economic and legal structures between the competing interests and expectations of those with a stake in environmental issues. Nor could it be denied that there is a need for the reform of the rights of citizens to have their voices heard in relation to schemes and activities affecting them and the environment or to seek redress for the consequences of such activities. In Chapter 9 Martyn Day presents his personal agenda for such reform in this country.

Real reform, however, will only come about if we are pragmatic. All our hopes and arguments for reform will produce nothing more than a supportive editorial in the next issue of the *New Law Journal* unless we are able to carry with us all those who have a stake in such reform. We will need to measure their interests and address their concerns.

II. Stakeholders

Who are the stakeholders in this reform programme? Of course, they include environmental and citizen groups, both "established" and *ad hoc*, as well as the regulators and those who make policy. However, the list does not stop there. It includes industry (particularly manufacturers and waste disposal and treatment companies), commercial developers and the construction industry and it also includes the bankers and insurers of industry, workforces and workers' representatives.

---

*Paul Bowden** is a litigation lawyer and head of the environment group in the London office of Freshfields solicitors.

We may not trust industry or those who back it and depend on it for their livelihood. We may suspect that the basic instinct of industry is to pollute and to try to evade the consequences. However, without industry's support no reform programme – no matter how well-reasoned and well-intentioned – will work. Therefore, it is necessary to look at the interests and concerns of a hypothetical stakeholder from the industrial sector.

III. Interests and concerns of industry

A. Legal challenges to government and regulatory decisions permitting development and industrial emissions

In England the law on the *standing* of a person to bring a challenge against regulatory decisions affecting the environment is confused and unsatisfactory. For example, a body of distinguished scholars and actors who have devoted their careers to Elizabethan drama and literature will, apparently, not be heard by the courts in a challenge to preserve the most important and tangible relic of Shakespeare's life and work which has been discovered in recent years.[1] The law will not accord the necessary standing. On the other hand, a huge environmental campaigning organisation with interests and support which embrace, quite literally, the whole planet is granted its day in court in relation to the activities of a soap factory in North West England.[2]

Present judicial trends are towards the granting of rights of challenge on public interest grounds to a wide range of interested parties. The programme of reform suggested here must include the clear establishment of such rights. But what does a hypothetical stakeholder from industry make of this? His thoughts will include the following.

1. *Certainty*

There must be certainty as to the classes of person who can bring a challenge in furtherance of the public interest. There cannot be a "free-for-all". The court system cannot accommodate regiments of aggrieved objectors bringing judicial review proceedings in the public interest. We cannot enfranchise "recreational litigants".

What is needed are clear guidelines and criteria on the standing to challenge regulatory decisions in the courts, or a central co-ordinating figure such as the "Director of Civil Proceedings" suggested by Lord Woolf in his recent Hamlyn lecture.[3]

---

[1] *R v Secretary of State for the Environment, ex p Rose Theatre Trust Co* [1990] 1 QB 504.
[2] *Greenpeace v Albright & Wilson* [1992] 4 LMELR 56, [1991] 3 LMELR 170.
[3] Woolf, Sir Harry, "Are the Judiciary Environmentally Myopic?" [1992] *Journal of Environmental Law* 1.

2. Standards of science

We plan our businesses, say our industrial stakeholders, in accordance with those standards (*e.g.* as to maximum permissible discharges, environmental concentrations and assumed health effects) which are established in law or set by the regulators empowered to do so by Parliament. If, by increasing the pool of those who may challenge the regulators' decisions in court, the regulators themselves fall increasingly subject to judicial regulation, we need certainty as to whose environmental standards we have to work to in running our business operations. Public interest challenges provide an opportunity for environmental campaigning by other means. If environmental campaigners bring their full panoply of arguments into the courtroom we will see many more judicial review proceedings mounted on the basis of wide-ranging issues – not on the more usual and formal basis that the regulators have made some error in law or some procedural slip in their decision-making processes. The challenges will involve debates on "environmental theology". There will be argument that the regulators' own standards are suspect or inadequate and that so-called "conventional" views on the health effects of a particular environmental exposure are overly conservative and protective of industry's position. Spare us, would say our hypothetical industrial stakeholder, from having to accommodate, in the carrying on of our businesses, not only the standards set by our regulators, but the competing standards of those who seek to challenge what we do; spare us from having to plan our activities by reference to every current scientific fad; spare us, and our regulators, from having to meet endless challenges based on "junk science".[4]

3. Financial costs

If public interest challenges to regulatory decisions and the activities which they permit become a regular feature of life and business our industrial stakeholder will (as will his workers and customers) want protection from the financial and economic costs which he will incur as a result of not being able to use his planning permissions or process authorisations in the event that he is prevented from doing so whilst the challenge is pending. When judicial review proceedings are accompanied by applications for a stay of the authorisations or permits which the stakeholder requires to operate, then those who bring a challenge should hold him harmless against the interruption costs to his business if they fail ultimately in their attack. In this regard, the recent

---

[4][Ed. note] For a recent debate on "green science", from the perspectives of Greenpeace and an industrial scientist respectively, see Wynne B and Mayer S, "How Science Fails the Environment", [1993] 1876 *New Scientist* at 33; and Milne A, "The Perils of Green Pessimism" [1993] 1877 *New Scientist* at 34; and the special newsletter of ensuing correspondence, "Science and the Environment" issued subsequently by *New Scientist*.

judgment of the Court of Appeal in a case involving Greenpeace is very welcome.[5]

Moreover, if public challenges to regulatory decision-making increase the overall lead-time necessary for initiating a business development, then it could be argued by the stakeholder that is not unreasonable for the "up-front" delays which are inherent in the present planning and process control regimes to be reduced. There should be shorter, and more focused planning and permitting procedures. Local and public inquiries should be run on a tighter basis.

B. **Civil litigation for compensation**

The hypothetical stakeholder also has concerns about the present regime under which he may have to face claims for compensation in the courts brought by those who consider themselves to be "victims" of his operations. Reform in this area must also take account of his position.

1. *Legal aid*

One of the major bars to justice in the United Kingdom, as in many other countries, is legal costs. The United Kingdom's present system of civil legal aid is one of the most honourable and successful attempts which has been made in any developed jurisdiction to relieve the problem. However, in seeking to redress the financial inequality between private claimants and corporate defendants, the system is, in particular cases, liable to create fresh injustices.

The hypothetical stakeholder is often bewildered by a system which seems to have created a class of claimants against whom he can never recover his costs, no matter how convincingly he has won his case. Large international corporations with multi-billion dollar balance sheets may be able to take this in their stride, but smaller businesses (whose insurers may take every step available on general liability and environmental policy wordings to avoid cover) find themselves staring down into the "ultimate deep pocket" of the legal aid fund. Practice indicates that the legal aid system may keep plaintiffs' lawyers on a tight financial rein, but once committed to a major multi-party public health action, there are few corporate concerns which can match the "spend" of the legal aid fund. In these circumstances the temptation to settle even the most unmeritorious claim becomes irresistible.

If the best which a hypothetical stakeholder can expect by a way of an order for costs, if he is successful in his defence against a legally aided claimant, is a "football pools order" (*i.e.* an order for costs with an indefinite stay on enforcement with liberty to apply for enforcement contingent on a significant change in the financial circumstances of the claimant) and if, in effect, the

---

[5]*R* v *Inspectorate of Pollution and Another ex p Greenpeace Ltd* [1994] 1 WLR 570; [1994] Env LR 77.

claimant can bring his claim with state support and at no real risk to himself, then there must be a fairer and more open system for the granting and continuation of legal aid funding. What is needed is:

(i)   a more transparent system for the granting of legal aid where the prospective defendant has the right to make his own observations on the claim so that the legal aid officers can carry out an informed cost-benefit analysis of the claim which the state is being asked to fund – not just relying on analysis of the case and the science provided by the lawyers and experts of the claimant; and

(ii)   a proper filtration system, including advice from independent scientific experts where necessary, with which the Legal Aid Board can weed-out claims with little merit or prospects or where the claimant's case and application may be based on an incomplete view of the relevant science.

The "direct action", to which prospective defendants increasingly resort by writing to legal aid committees with their representations on the claim, is not a bullying tactic; it is a measure of frustration at the partial way in which the present system appears to operate in cases where the science is complex and where the legal aid officers and committees are wholly dependent on what they are told by others about its nature and significance.

2. *Strict liability*

There are judicial and legislative trends towards strict liability in environmental torts and against a negligence-based system. This can be seen in the Environmental Protection Act 1990, the European Commission's "Green Paper" recommendations[6] and the strict duties under various particular industry statutes.

The hypothetical stakeholder would argue that, if a move is made towards a comprehensive system of strict liability in relation to environmental harm, then it is necessary to reflect on whether industry can afford the cost of the increased insurance premiums and whether banks and other financial institutions will be prepared to continue lending the money which industry needs to continue its operations. The hypothetical stakeholder would argue for time to rationalise his businesses (including, if necessary, cutting jobs) so that he can afford the new burden of comprehensive strict liability.

There must also be trade-offs and a change of the procedural rules requiring automatic discovery of documents – along the lines suggested by the Heilbron Committee.[7] It is this automatic discovery obligation which makes litigation so costly to the defendant and which protracts litigation. If liability in the

---

[6]*Green Paper on Remedying Environmental Damage* Com(93), 47 final, 14 May 1993.
[7]"Civil Justice on Trial – The Case for Change" (June 1993).

environmental torts is to be centered on the issue of causation and nothing more, then a system of selective and specific discovery, rather than automatic discovery, is much more appropriate.

3. *Reversing the burden of proof*

Many would contend, in this reform programme, for the reversal of the burden of proof in civil cases. The argument is that it is the defendant, rather than the claimant, who knows, or at least should know, what effects his operations are having on the environment and the local population. Anecdotal evidence, or more reliable statistical research, may point, for example, towards the plant's operations giving rise to particular health effects in the local community. However, the present system requires the claimant to show that his particular condition is one which is being caused by those operations, rather than by some other exposure or, indeed, are simply a chance occurrence. Taking into account the balance of resources and knowledge, it should be for the defendant to demonstrate that the cause of the health effect lies elsewhere.

The hypothetical stakeholder from industry, however, will not be attracted to the idea that because he is supposedly large, rich, a corporate entity and not well-loved, it should be for him to "prove his innocence". The view he will take is that if this reform programme is going to change a century of English jurisprudence in relation to the burden of proof, then there must be some compelling reason for doing so. The key question is – are there any good and meritorious claims which are being lost because of the technical requirement that the claimant must prove his case on the balance of probabilities? The following may be considered:

(i)   Legal aid funding gives a claimant as much resources, and as great a capability as any corporate defendant, to seek expert advice and evidence to formulate and pursue his claim.

(ii) The present rules as to discovery, discussed above, give the claimant access to the defendant's internal papers (and in the case of health claims, where third-party discovery orders may be available, access to the files of the entire industry sector in which the defendant operates).

(iii) In reality, a defendant who is well-advised, does not simply rely in defending his claim upon the technicalities of the burden of proof. He deploys every shred of evidence and argument available to him to show positively that he is not responsible for the injury or damage in question.

What those who propose a reversal of the burden of proof argue is that they would like the courts to take a less rigorous view of evidence; to reach "common sense" conclusions rather than tackling the detail of the basic scientific issues; and, overall, to adopt a "tabloid" approach – to take a "quick gut feel" as to causation issues.

IV. **Conclusion**

No matter how partial and sectional the observations made above may seem to be, the truth is that unless industry can be persuaded that the issues which have been highlighted are being addressed as we push forward with our reform programme, it will be hard to secure the support of industry for that reform. If its views are not addressed, then industry will not be persuaded that citizen suits are something that it can afford or that it needs. If industry is unpersuaded, there is little hope for our reforms.

Contents of Chapter 9

Shifting the Environmental Balance

Chapter 9
Shifting the Environmental Balance

Martyn Day

I. Introduction

Citizens' rights have become a central theme of the 1990s, across the political spectrum. One area where citizens' rights are pitifully few is that of the environment. The Environmental Protection Act 1990 was a prime example of this, creating powers and structures for the control of pollution but giving virtually no additional rights to the individual.

At present there is no question that the industries of Britain hold all but a very few cards in their hands in any environmental situation which brings the citizen up against them. When objectors attempt to prevent the construction of an industrial plant on the ground of potential ill-health effects, industry is able to flood the planning system with experts and lawyers, whereas the objectors have no tools other than the strength of their own convictions and the possibility of raising the issue in the media.

Further, in any case where citizens allege that an existing industrial process has actually caused them injury, companies are not only able to turn to scientists and lawyers, but are able to pour major resources into defeating the claim. In addition, they have the enormous advantage of knowing that although scientists are clear that, in general, environmental pollution is likely to cause a sizeable proportion of cancers and other serious illnesses in Britain today, the difficulty in ascribing any one illness to any one pollutant is great. For example, it is known that the radioactive emissions from Sellafield are likely to have killed hundreds if not thousands of people outside the plant during its 40 years of operation, but no claim against British Nuclear Fuels related to those injuries has, as yet, succeeded.

Martyn Day is a partner of Leigh Day & Co, London and specialises in representation of plaintiffs in toxic tort and environmental pollution cases.

II. **Legal aid**

One of the few weapons in the hands of citizens in damages claims (but usually not for objectors to proposed developments in planning cases) is legal aid. Legal aid allows the citizen to build up a team of experts and lawyers to fight on at least the semblance of an even playing-field, and is a fundamental component of protecting citizens' rights in this field. However, in what is a very worrying trend, the last few years have seen defendants and City law firms making increasing efforts to remove this one significant card from the plaintiff's hand.

This trend, allied to government cut-backs in legal aid, has meant that the prospect of citizens being awarded legal aid in these complex cases has become increasingly slim. This is a matter of great concern.

My firm specialises in medical negligence and ordinary accident cases (such as those occurring on the roads or at work), as well as environmental damage claims. In the former two areas, we rarely have the slightest problem in obtaining legal aid from the Legal Aid Board. In environmental claims, however, it is depressingly rare for the Board to grant legal aid, which has meant that we are having continually to appeal against the Board's decision to the Area Committee. I am pleased to say that apart from tobacco-related cases, we have not, as yet, lost an appeal. This, perhaps, simply goes to show the negative attitude taken by the Board itself to these complex claims, which the Area Committee is showing to have merit.

Further, in a large number of cases defendants are now attempting either to prevent legal aid being granted in the first place, or stop it once it has been granted. In the Sellafield case,[1] British Nuclear Fuels' lawyers sent to the Board a lengthy letter setting out why they thought legal aid should not be granted.[2] As far as I know this was the first time such an attempt had been made under the legal aid system. Such a practice is now common, however, as the 15-page letter in 1992 from the tobacco companies' lawyers, attempting to stop the granting of legal aid in those cases, illustrates.

Where legal aid has been granted, the latest ploy, as seen in the London Docklands litigation, is to attempt to judicially review the Board's decision to grant legal aid.

Although it is understandable that defendants and their lawyers are now intervening at this very early stage of the process, in an attempt to nip litigation in the bud, the problem is that it threatens to take all the remaining remedies out of the hands of the individual and place them solely at the disposal of the company. As such, defendants who have the resources in terms of in-house expertise, tame scientists and expensive City lawyers who are given wide scope to devote time to oppose the plaintiffs' case, are able to put forward a

---

[1] See Chapter 16 n 21 at p 299.
[2] Bowden defends this practice in Chapter 8, Section III(B)(1) "Legal aid".

very strong case opposing the plaintiffs' application right from the start. The plaintiffs, on the other hand, will have little, if any, opportunity of obtaining expert assistance at this early stage, and their lawyers will usually have only a basic understanding of the complexities of the case. That is the nature of these type of actions.

The problem lies in the fact that the expectations of the Legal Aid Board are being increasingly raised as to the amount of evidence required to support the case put forward by the plaintiffs at the application stage. This has led, consequentially, to the position that unless the plaintiffs are able to show to the Board from the outset that the case is strong, the Board is not prepared to grant legal aid even to allow preliminary investigations to be undertaken.

The iniquities of this position can best be shown by comparing what happens in environmental cases with what happens in medical negligence cases. In medical negligence cases it is rare for the plaintiffs' solicitors to be clear about the chances of the claim succeeding at the initial stage, and, almost always, legal aid is granted for the solicitors to investigate, to obtain experts' opinions and, subsequently, to obtain an opinion from counsel. It is only at this stage that the strength of the case can be properly assessed by all concerned and a decision be made as to whether the case can be proved at trial. If a health authority contacted the Legal Aid Board, with the benefit of their in-house expertise, opposing the grant of legal aid at the investigative stage, saying that there was no case to answer, there is no question but that the public would say that this was an abuse of the health authority's power. Environmental cases should not be dealt with differently. Legal aid should almost always be granted for the investigation phase of the case, when a decision can be made as to the real chances of the claim succeeding.

In a country which prides itself on its sense of fair play, it is difficult to see how the way in which the current system operates is at all just. It leaves plaintiffs having to find lawyers who are prepared to agree to do increasing amounts of preparatory work for free, or at best on the paltry rates offered by the "green form" scheme. The reality is that most lawyers are not prepared to accept these losses and therefore the pool of firms to whom plaintiffs can turn in this field has remained extremely small.

If citizens are to have full environmental rights we need to ensure not only that key cards like legal aid are not taken away but, further, that legal aid is granted more readily at an earlier stage in the process. We also need to redress the existing imbalance by providing the citizen with further cards.

For the objector to a development the subject of a planning appeal, the key issue is for legal aid to be extended, particularly in those cases where there is a *prima facie* risk of harm, to obtaining legal representation and to enable experts to appear on behalf of the objectors against representatives of the developers. It is a real problem for objectors that the only experts who will be prepared to attend a hearing on their behalf, for little or no recompense, are often those who are campaigning for the particular cause, which, in itself, will usually undermine their impartiality at the hearing. The availability of paid, clearly independent experts may well ensure a greater degree of success for the objectors.

III. **Costs**

Another central issue in relation to the problem facing individuals in environmental cases is that of costs in those actions involving judicial review. Being able to obtain a judicial review of the administrative decisions of central or local government, or other parts of the establishment, is of great importance in keeping a check on executive decision-making. Legal aid is rarely available for such review because almost invariably, persons other than the applicant benefit (this being the nature of public interest litigation) and, as a result, legal aid is refused.[3] This criterion should be discarded to ensure that the poor are just as able as the rich to review decisions which impact on their environment.

Further, and in some ways more importantly, is the problem of the current system where costs follow the event. This means that if applicants lose a case, they have to pay not only their own costs, but also those of the defendants. The result of this rule is that any individual or group of individuals considering reviewing a decision must contemplate not just finding a lawyer who is able to act cheaply or for free, but also paying the costs of what will often be a "Rolls Royce" defence. Most defendants in these types of cases will employ the top, City law firms where charges are often in the region of £350 per hour, who will then go on to employ some of the most expensive QCs in the country to defend the action. Whether or not this is done with the purpose of specifically dissuading potential litigants, the effect is the same.

If defendants succeed in defending a judicial review case, the normal order should be "no order as to costs", that is, both sides simply bear their own costs. It could be said that this is unfair on the defendants and that they will face a myriad of vexatious claims. The reality is very different. The potential litigant must not only locate a solicitor who is prepared to take on the case for little or no money, but also counsel who will act on a similar basis. Further, before proceedings are served on the defendants, the plaintiff must obtain leave from a High Court judge to bring the proceedings. This is a significant filter in ensuring that only those cases with real merit actually go ahead.

Understandably, defendants argue that it would be unfair for them to have to bear their own costs where plaintiffs fail. The simple question is, however, where should the imbalance lie? A democratic society should ensure that the "Davids" are fully able to take on the "Goliaths" in the courts. Defendants are far more able to cope with any financial imbalance than plaintiffs. Indeed, the

---

[3]See Chapter 10 n 41 and accompanying text. Contrast legal aid available for public interest environmental cases in New South Wales (discussed in Chapter 16 at n 21 and accompanying text).

position of a defendant in a non-legally aided, judicial review case should be no different to that in a legally aided case, where the defendant is usually unable to reclaim costs, even in the most expensive claims.[4]

IV. **Standing**

In the recent judicial review proceedings by Greenpeace over the government's authorisation to allow British Nuclear Fuels Plc (BNFL) to go ahead with the initial testing of their THORP Plant at Sellafield, BNFL questioned Greenpeace's standing in making the application. Although Greenpeace lost the review itself, they received a glowing commendation from Mr Justice Otton, the trial judge, for their role in the defence of the environment, knocking the BNFL proposition for six. It is heartening to see the judiciary take such a positive line on this important issue of standing, and it may be that no change is needed to the current rights of individuals or groups to take this type of action. It is, however, a matter that should be kept under close review, as other judges may not take such a liberal view.

V. **Protecting the environment**

A real shortcoming at present in the current law is the lack of a cause of action where there is damage to the environment but where no specific individual or organisation is damaged. Examples might be damage to wildlife caused by an oil spillage at sea and damage to life in rivers and seas caused by the pumping of sewage and other industrial pollutants. It should be open to groups like Greenpeace and Friends of the Earth to take legal proceedings on behalf of such wildlife, and even on behalf of flora, where pollutants are killing off plant-life. Protecting our environment and passing on to our children a less polluted world should be a key feature of our legal system.

For those injured by environmental pollution there are two key hurdles to overcome. The first is the enormous difficulty in proving causation, for example showing that any complex cancer has been caused by the environmental pollutant in question, rather than by any other possible causes. The second is in showing fault. These two hurdles, in most cases, are almost impossible to overcome.

---

[4]An important aspect of the legal aid system is that assisted plaintiffs have the benefit of an indemnity against adverse costs orders – hence the comment that prevailing defendants cannot recover costs.

A. **Strict liability**

Looking first at the issue of fault, the consultation process has recently been completed for the EC Green paper on the imposition of strict liability on polluters,[5] and this would largely abolish the hurdle of fault. The strength of the arguments in favour of such European legislation is overwhelming. Where, in years to come, it becomes possible to show that a particular child's cancer has been caused by a particular process, it would ill behove a company to say: "Ah, but we were not clear that the pollution we were pushing out could cause that particular harm and it would be unfair to make us pay". The child is a totally innocent victim and it is entirely right that it is the polluter, being the party who has profited from the polluting activities, who must take the burden of the risk and not the individual.

Using the work which my firm is undertaking on electro-magnetic fields as an example, we are acting for a family who live in Bury, next door to an electricity sub-station. Within a year or so of moving into this house their eldest son had developed leukaemia, and their daughter suffered epileptic fits. On making enquiries it was discovered that the children's bedroom was subject to a level of electro-magnetic fields some 10 times greater than that, on epidemiological evidence, producing up to a five-fold increase in risk of children contracting leukaemias and brain tumours.

When I wrote to the Electricity Board responsible asking them to reduce the level of electric field and to agree to pay compensation, they said they would do nothing until the link was proven. However, when I wrote to the Swedish equivalent, where one of the main epidemiological studies had been carried out, they responded by saying that it would take 10 years before scientists would be able to come to a conclusion, one way or the other, as to whether the suggested link was indeed causal, but that because of the significance of the damage which could be being caused where there are high levels of electro-magnetic fields, they would treat the link as being true unless the contrary position was proven.

The attitude of the Swedes is one which we should be following, and I would suggest that if the Electricity Board here was quite clear, through the imposition of strict liability, that if the link becomes proven they would have to compensate all those who had suffered in the past as well as the future, they would be much less bullish about refusing to acknowledge any responsibility until the link has been absolutely proven.

The current state of the law in relation to the importance of foreseeability was explained in the recent House of Lords' decision in the *Cambridge Water*[6] case. The House of Lords held that under the common law head of *Rylands* v

---

[5]*Green Paper on Remedying Environmental Damage*, Com (93), 47 final, 14 May 1993. For the UK response, see Chapter 16, n 6 and accompanying text at p 317.
[6]*Cambridge Water Company* v *Eastern Counties Leather Plc* [1994] 1 All ER 53, [1994] Env LR 105, (1993) 227 ENDS Report. Also discussed in Chapter 16 at text following n 2, p 316.

Fletcher[7] it was still necessary to show that at the time of the pollution of the environment, the potential problem which resulted in the case was reasonably foreseeable. The court, therefore, refused to agree with the strict liability principle, which was the Court of Appeal's earlier decision in the action. The prime rationale behind the House of Lords' decision was that whilst they gave support to the general principle of "the polluter pays", they considered it a matter for parliament rather than the common law to abandon the foreseeability principle. I agree. It is a political decision as to where loss lies and the matter should be dealt with at a political level rather than by the judiciary.

It may well be that because of vigorous opposition by the Confederation of British Industry (CBI) to the strict liability principle being proposed in Europe, the British Government will strongly oppose the principle, but I am hopeful that with other countries, such as Germany, which have already taken this principle on board, and with Britain's poor record in controlling land and sea pollution, the strict liability proposal will eventually become law. Whether it will be applied retrospectively remains to be seen.

Despite media criticism of the House of Lords' decision in the *Cambridge Water* case, it contains some significant steps forward. First, Lord Goff declined to follow an earlier decision regarding what constitutes non-natural user of land. In *Read* v *Lyons*[8] it had been suggested that the term "natural user of land", as originally stated in *Rylands* v *Fletcher*, could cover a wide variety of activities on the land, such as the manufacturing of explosives. In *Cambridge Water*, however, Lord Goff suggested that the storage of substantial quantities of chemicals should be regarded as a classic case of *non-natural* use. This certainly puts a few more teeth in the rarely used, *Rylands* v *Fletcher* head of action.

The second important development is related to the use of *Rylands* v *Fletcher* to claim personal injuries. The issue whether personal injury claims can be brought in nuisance-type claims, rather than just in negligence, is one which has been unresolved for many years. In the *Cambridge Water* case Lord Goff referred to this in passing and stated that as this case did not include an aspect of personal injury, he did not need to make any specific ruling. However, in referring to the earlier case of *Read* v *Lyons*, which had restricted the use of nuisance to claim personal injury, he interpreted it in a restricted manner, suggesting that there is at least a possibility of pursuing a personal injury claim alongside a nuisance action.

B. Causation

On the issue of causation, the key problem for the plaintiff lies on the level of proof. The fact that current scientific knowledge does not extend to genetic

---

[7](1865) 3 H&C 774.
[8][1947] AC 156.

proof that a particular pollutant has caused a particular cancer means that the main proof of causation lies at the door of epidemiology. The problem here is that with the onus being on the plaintiff to prove the case "on the balance of probabilities", the hurdle for almost all cases becomes almost insurmountable.

In years to come it may well be that this position will alter in that our geneticists may be able to look at a particular cancer, determine the mutation of the particular gene or genes which started or progressed the cancer's development, and may further be able to identify the type of insult (such as radiation, a specific chemical or virus), which is likely to have caused that particular type of mutation. Further, the last decade has seen major advances in epidemiological research, and it may well be that as that research expands and is refined, it will be more possible to ascribe particular pollutants to particular clusters of cancers. In both cases this should put the plaintiff in a far stronger position to point the finger at a particular pollutant and a particular defendant as being the cause of complex ailments such as cancers. However, this is looking, perhaps, 10 to 20 years into the future.

The only way of putting more cards into the hands of the plaintiffs on this issue is to alter the level of proof. A far more equitable system would be for the plaintiff to have to show that there is a *prima facie* case that the injury has been caused by the defendants, but that thereafter the onus should shift to the defendants to show that they are not responsible, rather than being on the plaintiffs to show the defendants are responsible.

This would not open up the floodgates, but would mean that defendant companies were put far more on their mettle and would give plaintiffs a real chance of succeeding in their claims.

VI. **Conclusion**

One of the key functions of the law is to provide a proper balance in society. It is my view that in the field of the environment that balance is very far from being achieved. With a government and Prime Minister supposedly committed to a citizen's charter, I would have hoped that the proposals I have set out above for empowering the individual in the environment would fit well within their ideology. Whether their deeds match their rhetoric is, however, another matter.

Contents of Chapter 10

Access to Environmental Justice
in Public Law

Chapter 10

Access to Environmental Justice in Public Law

Stephen Grosz

I. Introduction

This chapter seeks to examine some of the problems of access to justice encountered in environmental litigation in the public law field in the United Kingdom.

Public law is already one of the principal battlegrounds for environmental litigation, although the success of applicants so far is only limited. The volume of litigation is likely to grow: the regime established by the Environmental Protection Act 1990, the introduction of regulation consequent on privatisation of the energy and water[1] industries, the development of environmental impact assessment[2] and the new right of access to information on the environment[3] are likely to ensure an increasing recourse to public law remedies in environmental law questions. The influence of European Community law is responsible for many of these developments, and its effects will be felt increasingly in the face of continuing failure to implement European obligations. The current enthusiasm for road-building within the Department of Transport is destined to generate increased legal activity (although some of this may be in the field of public order).

The chapter concentrates on two areas of concern as potential barriers to environmental justice: standing to sue and costs.

For the reasons which follow, my views are that:

---

*Stephen Grosz is a partner of Bindman & Partners, London. He specialises in public and administrative law and European Community law. He has acted for the Friends of the Earth, the Oxleas Nine and the World Development Movement.

[1] See Water Resources Act 1991 and the Water Industry Act 1991.

[2] See Directive 85/337/EEC on the Assessment of the Effects of Certain Private and Public Projects on the Environment 85/337 OJ 1985 L175 at 40, implemented in the UK by s 71A of the Town and Country Planning Act 1990 and the Town and Country (Assessment of Environmental Effects) Regulations 1988.

[3] See Directive 90/313/EEC on Freedom of Access to Environmental Information, implemented in the UK pursuant to the European Communities Act 1972 through the Environmental Information Regulations 1992 (SI 1992/3240).

194

(i)   standing to sue is unlikely to present serious problems, in particular for established environmental interest groups, if an application otherwise has merit; and

(ii) by contrast, the cost of litigation, and the risks associated with losing, are likely to present a major barrier to access to environmental justice.

II. **Standing to sue**

"When everyone is somebodee,
Then no one's anybody" (WS Gilbert, *The Gondoliers*).

"I am a concerned member of society, you are a one-man pressure group, he or she is a busybody" (Sir Konrad Schiemann, "*Locus Standi*" (1990) *Public Law* 342 at 351).

The requirement for standing arises from section 31(3) of the Supreme Court Act 1981, which provides that the High Court shall not grant leave to apply for judicial review "unless it considers that the applicant has sufficient interest in the matter to which the application relates". Discussion of the application of this provision has generated much heat, but little light, so that its true effect remains obscure. However, I have found no reported case in which an applicant with a sound point of law has been denied relief on the ground that he does not have sufficient interest. Cases where standing has been denied have also failed on substantive grounds.

Most concern in the environmental field has focused on the decision in the *Rose Theatre Trust*[4] case, in which Schiemann J decided that the Trust did not have sufficient interest to challenge the refusal of the Secretary of State for the Environment to schedule the remains of the theatre as an ancient monument. In that case, he raised the possibility that there might be decisions, which affected everyone equally and no one in particular, which were effectively immune from challenge by judicial review.

Schiemann J returned to his theme in *R* v *Poole Borough Council ex p Beebee*,[5] a challenge to the grant of planning permission to build houses on Canford Heath in Dorset. The two applicants in that case represented the Worldwide Fund for Nature (WWF) and the British Herpetological Society (BHS). The judge considered that BHS did have *locus standi*, since it had had "a continuing and genuine interest in the subject sites for years". Poole Borough Council had recognised their interest by including a condition in the planning permission to the effect that notice should be given to BHS before development started to enable it to catch and relocate rare species on the site. By contrast, although WWF had been involved in the conservation of Dorset

---

[4] *R* v *Secretary of State for the Environment, ex parte Rose Theatre Trust Co* [1990] 1 QB 504.
[5] [1991] 2 PLR 27.

heathlands for over 15 years and had made grants to BHS, and in spite of its more general objects, he considered that they would not have had sufficient interest if they had stood alone. The judge was particularly impressed with the submission that he should be slow to find that others had sufficient interest where Parliament had created a body (in this case the Nature Conservancy Council) to protect the interest in issue in the proceedings.[6]

These cases appear to demote the importance of the public interest in conservation, which may exist independently of, for example, property rights or personal freedoms. So, for example, the preservation of a wilderness or of open moorland will be of interest to many who will nonetheless be unable to point to any particular interest over and above that of everyone else. The judgments also fail in part to recognise that bona fide interest groups, with no personal axe to grind, represent a considerable force in society.

However, the above cases represent the low point of the standing issue,[7] and others are more encouraging. The Child Poverty Action Group (CPAG) was held to have sufficient interest to make an application in relation to a practice which clearly affected a large number of unidentifiable supplementary benefit claimants – members of its client group.[8] More recently, in February 1993 the Divisional Court heard an application in which the Alcohol Recovery Project (ARP), a charity which provides help for people with alcohol-dependency problems, challenged the Health Secretary's decision not to ring-fence funds for residential drug and alcohol care, such as that provided by ARP. The Secretary of State contended that as ARP was not itself the ultimate beneficiary of the funds in issue it had no standing. The court held that as a provider of services, ARP was clearly affected by the decision and "certainly has sufficient interest to bring these judicial review proceedings".[9] ARP might be said to have an interest on three levels: it was a recipient of the funds which were to have been ring-fenced; it had been involved in consultation with the Secretary of State about the way in which the funds were to be distributed and the guidance which was to be given to local authorities; and, at its widest, it also brought the application in the interests of the ultimate beneficiaries of the funds, those to whom ARP provided its services. The decision does not distinguish between these grounds.

---

[6]See for example *R v Secretary of State for Employment ex p Equal Opportunities Commission* [1994] IRLR 176, in which the House of Lords held that the Equal Opportunities Commission had standing to apply for declarations that certain aspects of English employment protection law contravened sex equality provisions of European Community law.

[7]At least I thought so, until I was told of the unreported decision of a single judge on an application for leave to apply for judicial review on 25 August 1993 in *Re Elliot*, in which the judge expressed the opinion that the son of a woman detained under the Mental Health Act 1983 had no *locus standi* to challenge a decision to administer electro-convulsive therapy to her, on the ground that he had been deprived of the status of her nearest relative in accordance with the Act.

[8][1989] 1 All ER 1047 at 1056, per Woolf LJ. However, the Court of Appeal held that the first instance judge, Schiemann J, had been wrong to accept the respondent's concession that CPAG had standing.

[9]*R v SS for Health ex p Alcohol Recovery Project Ltd*, QBD, draft judgment dated 15 February 1993, p 8.

In *R* v *Lord Chancellor ex p the Law Society*,[10] the Divisional Court considered an application for judicial review of the Lord Chancellor's changes to the rules governing financial eligibility for legal aid, advice and assistance. It was argued on behalf of the Lord Chancellor that, except as to its alleged right to be consulted, the Law Society had no sufficient interest in the matter. Interestingly, counsel for the Lord Chancellor submitted that the position might have been different if the proceedings had been brought by a group such as CPAG. Neill LJ (with whom Mantell J agreed) rejected this submission, reasoning that:[11]

> "The Law Society has enormous knowledge and expertise of the workings of the legal aid scheme. It is difficult to imagine any body of persons which has a greater interest in the proper and fair working of legal aid. In addition, on a different level, the Law Society have an interest because their numbers are directly affected by legal aid and not least by the workings of the Green Form scheme."

Once again, there are different bases on which this decision confirming *locus standi* may be understood. In context, it is clear that the Law Society had been engaged in consultation with the Lord Chancellor about the proposed changes before they were introduced; changes in eligibility (and in the case of Green Form changes, method of payment) would clearly affect the Law Society's members; but on a more general level, the court recognised that as an established body with a long interest in the administration of justice, the Law Society was clearly entitled to represent a more general interest beyond the sectional concerns of its members. It had an interest in access to justice, in particular for those of its members' clients who would be denied it.

The courts have also traditionally entertained applications from a certain type of public-spirited individual.[12] The most recent example is Lord Rees-Mogg, whose application for judicial review relating to the Maastricht Treaty was dismissed by a strong Divisional Court.[13] *Locus standi* was dealt with very briefly as follows:[14]

> "There is no dispute as to the applicant's *locus standi*, and in the circumstances it is not appropriate to say any more about it, save to refer to the observations of Slade LJ in *Ex parte Smedley*[15] at page 669. It was suggested by [counsel for the Crown] that the proceedings are no more than a continuation by other means of arguments ventilated in Parliament. Be that as it may, we accept without question

---

[10]Unreported, judgment of 21 June 1993.

[11]Transcript, pp 64–65.

[12]For example Mrs Gillick, a concerned parent, in *Gillick* v *West Norfolk and Wisbech Health Authority and the DHSS* [1986] AC 112. In fact, she brought her application in private law, a proceeding which also escaped criticism.

[13]Consisting of Lloyd, Mann and Auld LJJ; *R* v *SS for Foreign and Commonwealth Affairs, ex p Lord Rees-Mogg*; judgment of 30 July 1993, *The Independent*, 3 August 1993.

[14]Transcript, pp 3–4.

[15][1985] 1 QB 657.

that Lord Rees-Mogg brings these proceedings because of his sincere concern for constitutional issues."

There are two other cases dealing specifically in environmental law which are worth mentioning.

In July 1987 Friends of the Earth (FoE) sought leave to challenge the decision of the Energy Secretary to give consent for the construction of the Sizewell B nuclear power station.[16] Kennedy J refused leave on the ground of delay; the Court of Appeal refused leave principally on the ground that there was no arguable point of law. *Locus standi* was not challenged or discussed, but Ralph Gibson LJ concluded that he would have granted leave if there had been an arguable point of law in view of the importance of, and public interest in, the matter to which the application related. In that case again, FoE had taken part in the inquiry which had preceded the grant of consent, which may have been the basis on which *locus standi* was tacitly conceded.

In *R v Swale BC ex p Royal Society for the Protection of Birds*,[17] the RSPB challenged the grant of planning permission for land reclamation of mud-flats which were used as feeding grounds by a significant proportion of the wintering populations of various species of birds. The grounds of challenge were that they had been promised consultation before any decision was made and that the council had misdirected itself in failing to conduct an environmental impact assessment. The RSPB claimed no particular connection with the subject site in the way that BHS did with Canford Heath. They had, however, corresponded with the council before the decision was made and had extracted a promise of consultation, which promise was not honoured. Their *locus standi* was not challenged and Simon Brown J said of RSPB only that "The applicants are, of course, well known. They are the largest conservation charity in the United Kingdom, with over half a million members".[18] Dealing with the substance, he said "once one postulates a promise of consultation in advance of a decision *in which the promisee has a sufficient interest*, that of itself founds a legitimate expectation".[19] The judge was not deterred by the fact that the Nature Conservancy Council had not chosen to apply for judicial review, a consideration which had weighed with Schiemann J in *Ex p Beebee* (*supra* n 5).

The issue of the standing of environmental pressure groups and the effect of the *Rose Theatre Trust* case were considered directly in an application brought by Greenpeace in respect of authorisations relating to the thermal oxide

---

[16]Unreported, judgment of 21 July 1987.
[17][1991] 1 PLR 6.
[18]*Ibid* at 8C.
[19]*Ibid* at 13G (emphasis added). Relief was refused on the ground of delay.

reprocessing plant at Sellafield in Cumbria.[20] British Nuclear Fuels plc (BNFL) contended that Greenpeace did not have sufficient interest in the matter.

Otton J referred to several considerations in concluding that Greenpeace did have standing. Put on the narrowest basis, he noted that the organisation had been treated as one of the consultees during the consultation process. On its widest basis, he referred to the fact that Greenpeace was "an entirely responsible and respected body with a genuine concern for the environment", which therefore had "a bona fide interest in the activities of BNFL at Sellafield and in particular the discharge and disposal of radioactive waste from their premises". Thirdly, he referred to the fact that 2,500 of Greenpeace's supporters came from the Cumbria region and – although they were not necessarily near neighbours or BNFL employees – they were inevitably concerned about the health and safety aspects of the discharges: "If I were to deny standing to Greenpeace those they represent might not have an effective way to bring the issues before the court".

Otton J also took into account two discretionary considerations. The first was that if the unsuccessful applicant had been legally aided, the respondents and BNFL might have been left with no effective remedy in costs. Secondly, he considered that Greenpeace, with its particular experience and access to experts in environmental matters, was especially well placed to mount a "carefully selected, focused, relevant and well argued challenge".

Distinguishing the *Rose Theatre Trust* case, the judge said that in that case "the interest group had been formed for the exclusive purpose of saving the Theatre site and no individual member could show any personal interest in the outcome". He also made clear that the question of standing was to be considered on its merits in each case, and that it should not be assumed that Greenpeace or any other pressure group would automatically be accorded standing as a result of his judgment.

On 29 March 1994, Schiemann J gave judgment[21] in an application for judicial review brought by Friends of the Earth and their Campaigns Director, Andrew Lees, in which the applicants challenged the Environment Secretary's alleged failure to enforce the standards laid down in the EC drinking water Directive.[22] During the course of argument, the judge himself raised the question of the applicants standing. The respondent declined to advance any argument to the effect that either of the applicants lacked the necessary standing, whilst reserving the right to argue the matter on another occasion. Clearly unhappy with the respondent's stance, the judge said that he had

---

[20]*R v Her Majesty's Inspectorate of Pollution and MAFF, ex p Greenpeace Ltd* (No 2); (1993) *The Times*, 30 September; [1994] COD 116, [1994] Env LR 77 [1994] 4 All ER 329 at 349B–351J.

[21]*R v SS for the Environment, ex p Friends of the Earth*, *The Times*, 4 April 1994, *The Independent*, 12 April 1994. See also *R v SS for Foreign Affairs, ex p World Development Movement Ltd*, QB, oral judgment of 10 November 1994 – held pressure group had sufficient interest to challenge decision of SS to approve aid for the construction of the Pergau Dam in Malaysia.

[22]Directive 80/778/EC relating to the quality of water intended for human consumption; OJ (1985) L229 at 11.

nonetheless to consider the matter at the outset. The judge had, in particular, raised the question whether the existence of the European Commission, as guardian of observance of European law, might deprive other applicants of sufficient interest. This was an echo of his attitude to the Nature Conservancy Council in *Ex parte Beebee*.[23] The judge noted that Andrew Lees was a resident of the Thames Water supply area and that Friends of the Earth was "a company of high repute limited by guarantee founded in 1971 and accepted as having relevant expertise". Noting that leave had twice been granted, and in the absence of contrary argument, the judge held that the court had jurisdiction to embark on the enquiry as to whether the respondent had acted unlawfully. However, he expressly stated that the applicants' status would have to be reconsidered if unlawfulness were made out and he had to decide whether to grant relief. The matter, therefore, remains unsettled.

On 10 November 1994, in *R v SS for Foreign Affairs, ex p World Development Movement Ltd*[24] (the *Pergau Dam* case), the Divisional Court accepted that although it could not directly claim a client group affected by Mr Hurd's decision, the WDM had an interest in ensuring that aid money was spent legally in view of its track record in the field. The court had in mind particularly that if the WDM could not bring a case, it was difficult to see who could. The judges were also influenced by the seriousness of the allegation that the SS had acted unlawfully, by the importance of the issue raised and also the public interest in vindicating the rule of law (judgment as yet unreported, CO/1455/94).

Despite some judicial reservations, it is now possible to discern certain criteria from the cases discussed.

Certainly a person or body which has made representations or been involved in the planning process will have *locus standi*, as will those who have been more specifically involved, in the past, with the site which is the subject of the decision or policy under challenge. Those with an established track record of interest in the area of policy to which the decision relates should have sufficient interest; those with a recognised client group which is affected by the decision, but which may be unable to bring a claim (*e.g.* benefit claimants, seekers of legal advice, alcohol abusers, reptiles or birds), would appear to be sufficiently interested; in exceptional cases, an individual with a "sincere concern" for the matters in issue will have standing.

The case law of the European Court of Justice has so far had little to say on the subject of standing in national law, as it has traditionally left to national law the question of remedies for breach of Community norms.[25] However, recent cases have seen a greater tendency to become involved in the question of

---

[23]See n 5 *supra*.

[24][Ed note] The case is significant both because of the grant of locus standi to WDM, and because of the affirmation that explicit statutory criteria must be objectively satisfied (*e.g.* determining where funds for environmental and development projects should be allocated).

[25]See, for example *Rewe v Landwirtschaftskammer Saarland* [1976] ECR 1989.

effectiveness of national enforcement,[26] and questions of standing may well be referred to the European Court of Justice, particularly in a case where restrictive notions of standing might deprive anyone of sufficient interest to apply for judicial review.[27] One other slight indication of the European judicial approach may be found in *Commission* v *Federal Republic of Germany*,[28] which concerned Directive 80/68/EEC on the protection of groundwater against pollution caused by certain dangerous substances and, in particular, whether implementation might be effected by mere administrative means. In his Opinion, Advocate-General van Gerven said:[29]

> "The purpose of the directive is to protect groundwater from pollution by prohibiting or restricting the discharge, tipping or other treatment of a range of substances. To that end the Member States must provide in national law for a range of prohibitions, authorisations and monitoring procedures. In other words, the Directive requires the Member States to introduce a set of rights and duties as between national authorities and those concerned with the substances referred to by the Directive, and therefore is designed to create rights for individuals. Clear and precise implementation of the Directive's provisions may also be important for third parties (*for instance environmental groups or neighbourhood residents*) seeking to have the prohibitions and restrictions contained in the Directive enforced as against authorities or other individuals."

In at least one case, a Directive has specifically dealt with the issue of standing. Article 3(1) of the Access to Information Directive[30] obliges a Member State to make available information relating to the environment to any natural or legal person on request "without his having to prove an interest". The Environmental Impact Assessment (EIA) Directive[31] requires Member States to ensure that "the public concerned is given the opportunity to express an opinion before the project is initiated" (art 6(2)). It is unlikely, however, that a Member State is left entirely free to determine the public concerned. Nor should the existence of the Commission as enforcer of EC law be a ground for excluding individual

---

[26]*UNECTEF* v *Heylens* [1987] ECR 4097 (duty to give reasons and availability of judicial review); *Emmott* v *Minister of Social Welfare* [1991] ECR I-4269 (time-limits); *Danfoss (Handel-OG Kontorfunktionaerernes Forbund I Danmark* v *Dansk Arbejdsqiverforening)* [1989] ECR 3199 (burden of proof); *R* v *Secretary of State for Transport, ex p Factortame* [1990] 3 CMLR 1, [1990] ECR I-2433 (national courts must set aside national procedural laws if the latter prevent the implementation of EC law; availability of interim relief); *Francovich* v *Italian Republic* [1991] ECR I-5357 (damages for loss caused by non-implementation of European Community norms); *Marshall* v *Southampton and SW Hampshire Area Health Authority (Teaching) No 2* [1993] IRLR 445 (limits on the amount of damages, and availability of awards of interest).

[27]For example, the European Court of Justice might well have had something to say about the judgment of 26 October 1990 in *Twyford Parish Council* v *Secretary of State for the Environment* [1992] 1 CMLR 276 ("*Twyford Down*") in which McCullough J held that an individual could not complain about failure to implement a Directive properly unless he had suffered as a result of that failure.

[28]Case C-131/88, [1991] ECR I-825.

[29]*Ibid* at 850 (emphasis added).

[30]See n 3 *supra*.

[31]See n 2 *supra*.

access to the courts. In a very early case dealing with the direct effect of articles of the EC Treaty, the European Court of Justice rejected such an argument, holding that "the vigilance of individuals concerned to protect their rights amounts to an effective supervision in addition to the supervision entrusted by Articles 169 and 170 to the diligence of the Commission and of the Member States".[32]

There are two sets of law reform proposals which touch on the question of standing. The Law Commission's report on Administrative Law that proposes a broader test of standing, so that an application might be brought by an applicant who is not adversely affected where the court considers that "it is in the public interest for an applicant to make the application".[33]

The European Commission has before it a proposal for a Directive concerning access to justice in environmental matters, which specifically provides that an environmental association should be able to apply for judicial review of an administrative act which it considers to be in breach of a rule of national or Community environmental law without having to show impairment of its own interests or prior participation in administrative proceedings relating to that act (unless such participation could reasonably be expected).[34]

The growing amount of environmental protection legislation and the continued popularity of public law proceedings are likely to lead to an increase in the amount of litigation. It is in the nature of much environmental law that it does not deal necessarily with individual rights or interests, but with the interest which the community at large has in protection and conservation. A decision affecting the environment should not be allowed to go unchallenged simply because it is not possible to identify an individual whose interest is greater than that of the generality of people. In particular, the courts appear to be ready to recognise that well-established environmental pressure groups, such as FoE, Greenpeace or WWF, are a manifestation of public concern about the environment. They should further recognise that statutory bodies such as English Nature may have their own reasons for not applying to court, and the existence of such bodies is not a reason for denying standing to other applicants. They should also be aware of the financial reality that individuals with a sufficient interest may have insufficient funds. The requirement of a sufficient interest should be used only to exclude applicants who manifestly have no legitimate interest in the decision under challenge. If this approach is adopted, it ought to be dealt with at the leave stage so that an applicant does not have to incur the considerable cost of a substantive hearing only to be told that he has no standing.

---

[32]Case 26/62 *Van Gend en Loos* v *Nederlandse Administratie der Belastingen* [1963] ECR 1 at 13.
[33]*Administrative Law: Judicial Review and Statutory Appeals*, Law Com No 226, HC 669, para 5.22.
[34]See Chapter 3.

III. **Costs**

"You want justice, but do you want to pay for it? When you go to a butcher, you know you have to pay, but you people go to a judge as if you were off to a funeral supper" (Bertolt Brecht, *The Caucasian Chalk Circle*, Act I).

When vast sums of money are involved in a major project, in terms of development cost, expected direct income and potential indirect economic benefits, the cost to the proposer of the project of participating in even a lengthy public inquiry is trivial. The state has a bottomless pocket for these purposes, and from the developer's point of view it is certainly worth pulling out all the legal stops to ensure that the proposal is accepted and quickly. Speed is of the essence, and no expense need be spared on legal representatives and technical expertise.

Contrast this with the position of the individual, the neighbourhood group or even the environmental organisation or local authority. Legal aid is not available for statutory inquiries. An individual cannot begin to match the resources available to, for example, the Department of Transport or the Central Electricity Generating Board. Neither local authorities nor environmental groups have the staff or the funds to fight such major developments adequately. Inspectors at public inquiries are obliged to make their decisions on the basis of the evidence before them. Whilst objectors may contend, for example, that building a new road generates more traffic, an inspector will not accept such an assertion without evidence to support it. If the proponent can produce contrary evidence, objectors will lose their point without rebutting evidence, which they cannot afford to muster. Planning battles are thus fair in form only, while in reality it is rare that effective opposition can be mounted at the inquiry stage. After that it is usually too late.

Legal complaint has been made about this state of affairs. In their ill-fated Sizewell application for judicial review, Friends of the Earth complained that they could not afford to be represented throughout the inquiry, that the Central Electricity Generating Board consistently placed new documents before the Inspector, and that since no one would pay the costs of their returning to deal with new documents, the inquiry was unfair. The Court of Appeal rejected that contention as being unarguable.[35] In *R v Legal Aid Area No 8 (Northern) ex p Sendall*,[36] complaint was made that by failing to grant the applicant legal aid to be represented at a public inquiry for a proposed clinical-waste incinerator, the Legal Aid Board had failed to comply with the requirement of Article 6.2 of the EIA Directive[37] that the public concerned should be given an opportunity to express an opinion before the project is

---

[35]See n 16 *supra* (transcript p 10).
[36]203 *ENDS Report* at 27.
[37]See n 2 *supra*.

initiated. Kennedy J refused leave to apply for judicial review, as did the Court of Appeal, to whom the application was renewed.

Although legal aid is available for applications for judicial review, and for statutory appeals, there are several limitations. First, the recent changes in the rules relating to financial eligibility have reduced considerably the number of people who are eligible for legal aid. Secondly, the potential applicant must satisfy the Legal Aid Board that he has reasonable grounds for taking the proceedings,[38] and legal aid is to be refused "if in the particular circumstances of the case it appears to the Board . . . unreasonable that he should be granted representation . . . ",[39] for example because the applicant would secure no personal benefit out of the proceedings.[40] Thirdly, legal aid may also be refused "where it appears to the Area Director that . . . only a trivial advantage would be gained by the applicant from the proceedings to which the applicant relates".[41]

However, perhaps one of the most difficult obstacles for local action groups, particularly in public law and statutory appeals relates to financial contributions. The relevant parts of reg 32 of the Civil Legal Aid (General) Regulations 1989 provide as follows:

"(1) When determining an application, the Area Director shall consider whether it is reasonable and proper for persons concerned jointly with or having the same interest as the applicant to defray so much of the costs as would be payable from the fund in respect of the proceedings if a certificate were issued.

(2) In determining an application made by, or on behalf of, a person in connection with an action, cause or matter in which –

(a)   numerous persons have the same interest; and

(b)   in accordance with rules of court, one or more persons may sue or be sued, or may be authorised by a court to defend any such action, cause or matter on behalf of or for the benefit of all persons so interested,

the Area Director shall consider whether the rights of the applicant would be substantially prejudiced by the refusal of his application.

(3) Where an application has been approved and the Area Director considers that it is reasonable that persons concerned jointly with or having the same interest as the applicant should contribute to the cost of the proceedings, he shall add the amount which would be payable by such persons to the sums (if any) payable by the applicant under regulation 31 and shall so notify him under regulation 43(2).

(4) The Area Director may subsequently redetermine the amount of any additional sums payable under paragraph (3) where he is satisfied that the

---

[38]Legal Aid Act 1988, s 15(2).
[39]*Ibid*, s 15(3).
[40]Notes for Guidance issued by the Legal Aid Board, para 6-08 (i); *Legal Aid Handbook* (1992) at 50.
[41]Civil Legal Aid (General) Regulations 1989, reg 29.

applicant has, without success, taken all reasonable steps (including permitting the Area Director to take those steps on his behalf) to obtain such payment."

The meaning of these provisions is fairly impenetrable, and their impact on public law environmental litigation can be serious. Let us assume, for example, that an individual lives near an ancient woodland in south London, through which the Department of Transport proposes to run a road. This person is one of a group which has objected to the road and made representations at the public inquiry. Certain members of the group, including this individual, appeal against the Environment Secretary's Exchange Land Certificate under section 19 of the Acquisition of Land Act 1981 in an effort to prevent the compulsory purchase of part of the wood. Is it reasonable, in the circumstances, that the applicant should have legal aid? Does he receive any personal benefit; and is it more than trivial? Are the other appellants concerned jointly, or do they have the same interest as the applicant? If so, is it reasonable and proper to expect them to defray so much of the costs as would be payable by the legal aid fund? If not, would the applicant's interest be substantially prejudiced if legal aid were refused (*i.e.* would the appeal continue in any event)? If legal aid is granted, should anyone else, such as a local amenity group, be made to contribute, and if so how much?

These were precisely the problems faced by two of the Oxleas 9,[42] whose appeal was supported, but not funded, by People Against the River Crossing. Two of the nine were eligible for legal aid. For the proceedings at first instance, the Area Committee granted their applications but decided to require a contribution of £5,000 from people who were *not* parties to the litigation. For the appeal, another Area Committee decided that the appeal would continue even if legal aid was not granted. They therefore refused legal aid altogether. Whilst it may be wrong to set up only applicants or appellants who are financially eligible for legal aid, it also seems wrong that, where there is a mixed group, those who are entitled to legal aid should not have it and should effectively be funded out of the pockets of those who are slightly better off.

The present system, therefore, places a great burden of fund-raising on such groups. However, the courts take little notice of this. For example, in the *Oxleas Wood* case the Department of Transport applied to expedite the hearing of the appeal to the Court of Appeal. The appellants countered that they needed time to raise funds for the appeal, but this contention was rejected, on the basis that parties must come to court with the means to pursue the litigation. Similarly, in the *Twyford Down* case,[43] McCullough J acceded to the Department's request that he abridge time for appealing to 21 days, even

---

[42]*Mayor and Burgesses of the London Borough of Greenwich and Yates* v *Secretaries of State for Transport and the Environment (Oxleas Wood Case)* (CO/2863/91 and 35/92), unreported judgment of Hutchison J dated 19 February 1993.
[43]*supra*, n 27.

though the applicants asked for more time to see whether they could raise the necessary funds.

Further, the requirements of personal benefit and the interpretation of "trivial" may well prevent the public-spirited individual from bringing proceedings. What of the person seeking environmental information? Is his or her right to know "trivial", and does knowing confer any benefit on the applicant?

Where an applicant does not obtain legal aid, he or she runs the additional risk of being ordered to pay the other side's costs. The combination of one's own legal costs and the risk of having to foot the opposition's bill can act as a serious deterrent to bringing proceedings at all.

In practice, our present inquiry and public law systems fail to recognise or take account of the distorting effects of legal costs. Costs represent both a bar to access to the courts – as some people cannot afford to litigate at all – and as a source of inequality in court. Both these vices may, in certain circumstances, be contrary to Article 6 of the European Convention on Human Rights, which guarantees the right to a fair trial "in the determination of a civil right". This guarantee includes a practical right of access to a court and "equality of arms" in court. These principles will become more important now that our own courts have begun to recognise the importance of the Convention in interpreting national law. The European Court of Justice has frequently referred to the principles enshrined in the Convention to support its reasoning, and this trend will undoubtedly increase now that the Treaty on European Union has entered into force.[44]

The Law Commission's report[45] proposes that in public interest cases, the judge should have a discretion to award the successful party's costs out of central funds rather than against the loser, and that in such cases the losing party's costs might also be met out of central funds. The Commission also recommends that when it is considering whether to grant legal aid, the Legal Aid Board should be empowered to consider the wider public interest in having a case heard.[46] Potts J decided that there should be no order for costs in the *Greenpeace* case,[47] in part relying on the fact that the case was one of substantial public interest. Lord Woolf adopted a similar approach in the Privy Council decision in *New Zealand Maori Council* v *Attorney-General of New Zealand*.[48] The proposed draft Directive before the Commission of the EU on access to justice in environmental matters makes similar proposals, adding an obligation on Member States to ensure that costs should not cause a barrier

---

[44]Article F (2) provides that the European Union will respect the rights guaranteed by the Convention and as they result from the constitutional traditions common to the Member States as general principles of Community law.
[45]See n 33 *supra*.
[46]*ibid*, paras. 10.5, 10.6 & 10.7.
[47]*R* v *Secretary of State for the Environment, ex p Greenpeace*; *The Independent*, 8 March 1994, (1994) 6 *Environmental Law and Management* 44 and (1994) *ENDS Report* 230.
[48][1994] 2 WLR 254.

to the commencement or continuation of administrative or judicial proceedings.[49]

IV. Conclusions

The present uncertain law of standing fails to recognise the importance of public interest and group rights, concentrating on the rights and interests of the individual. A proper appreciation of the importance of pressure groups as part of the political system could lead to a more coherent judicial policy on *locus standi*. The courts have given little attention to the principles on which the standing of groups should be recognised and the exceptional circumstances when it should be denied. This question should always be determined at the leave stage, so that parties do not have to bear the cost of preparation for a full substantive hearing, only to lose on standing.

The cost of litigation and the risk of losing are the most serious barriers to fair and effective environmental litigation. The costs regime *inter partes* must recognise and seek to redress the fundamental inequality which exists between the proponent of a scheme or a public authority on the one hand and the objectors on the other. Individuals and groups also need better access to experienced practitioners willing and able to undertake environmental advocacy. At present, a body of lawyers with the relevant experience does not exist; nearly all the firms listed as environmental lawyers advise corporations. Legal aid is not available in many cases of this kind, and the trend is decidedly against any extension of its availability. Environmentalists must seek to establish alternative resources which can provide the necessary support for objectors and redress the current inequality of legal fire-power.

---

[49]See Chapter 3 section IV (proposed art 8 – costs).

Contents of Chapter 11

Legal Standing in Scotland

Chapter 11
Legal Standing in Scotland

Colin T Reid

I. Introduction

The position of an individual or group seeking to raise an action before the Scottish courts is much the same as that facing a potential litigant in England and Wales. Rules exist to prevent the "mere busybody" from interfering in the business of others by raising actions in the courts. In the two jurisdictions the general approach is largely the same, but there are a number of differences which might be significant in particular cases. The general problem for environmentalists is that in deciding whether somebody is a "busybody" or has a genuine interest in the matter, the law recognises only a limited range of interests, for example property rights, without taking cognisance of what might be claimed as the "environmental rights" of the public which are infringed whenever environmental harm is done.

II. Criminal law

In Scotland, there is only a very limited possibility of starting a private prosecution. In all but the most exceptional cases, prosecutions are in the hands of the procurators fiscal and the Crown Office, and it is very rare indeed for private prosecutions to take place. It is legally possible for a private prosecution to be mounted, but only by an individual who can show a particular and special interest in the matter,[1] in essence that he or she has been personally wronged by the alleged crime.[2] Where the crime is primarily a matter of public interest, only the Crown can prosecute.[3] In the environmental context, therefore, it would seem that there is no possibility of a private prosecution for pollution or other environmental offences, and it would take the most unusual circumstances, where malicious mischief, assault or culpable

---

*Colin T Reid** is a Senior Lecturer in the Department of Law at the University of Dundee. His book on *Nature Conservation Law* (GB) was published in 1994.
[1]*McBain* v *Crichton* 1961 JC 25.
[2]*e.g.* the victim of alleged rape in *X* v *Sweeney* 1982 JC 70.
[3]*e.g.* obscene publications (*McBain* v *Crichton supra*) or perjury (*Trapp* v *M* 1971 SLT (Notes) 30; *Meehan* v *Inglis* 1975 JC 9).

homicide can be alleged and the prosecuting authorities take no action, before an individual could begin criminal proceedings.

Reliance on the prosecuting authorities can be a source of frustration to the regulatory bodies seeking to enforce environmental law as it is felt that procurators fiscal tend to give such offences low priority and may lack the expertise to present the best case in an area of law which is unfamiliar to them. On the other hand, fiscals have complained that the preparation of the cases referred to them is often inadequate so that it is not feasible for proceedings to be taken.[4] The Crown Office is responding to these difficulties by producing guidance to assist fiscals in dealing with the legal complexities in this field and to assist regulatory bodies in presenting cases in a way which will enable successful prosecution.

III. **Delict**

For actions based in delict (tort), the pursuer must be able to establish that a wrong has been committed against his or her legally protected interests. Therefore, personal injury or damage to property may form the basis of an action, but if no one with a legally recognised interest comes forward, the courts will not entertain any proceedings. This is one of the traditional limitations of using the common law to deal with environmental issues; for example, so long as nobody's health and no neighbouring land are affected, landowners can do what they like on their land and no one else is in a position to intervene. Moreover, even though neighbours may be entitled to take action, the social or economic relationship between them and the offending landowner may be such that no qualified pursuer is in fact likely to come forward.

In the absence of any willing pursuer enjoying legal standing, certain forms of environmental harm effectively lack a legal remedy at common law. In particular, as wild animals are not the legal property of anyone, no one is in a position to raise an action if they have suffered harm, and any attempt to prevent activities harming wild animals must be based on a threat to human health or legally owned property.

This is not to say that the common law does not have a place in environmental litigation. In the event of pollution causing or threatening personal injury, the potential for actions is obvious. Moreover, there is a wealth of authority on the rights of riparian proprietors to receive from those

---

[4]Rowan-Robinson J, Young E, McLarty I, *The Enforcement of Planning Control in Scotland* (Edinburgh, SDD, 1984) at 111–124; Rowan-Robinson J, Watchman P, Barker C, *Crime and Regulation* (Edinburgh, T & T Clark, 1990) at 259–261.

upstream waters which have not been severely diminished in either quantity or quality.[5]

Fishing and game rights may also offer legal standing to intervene in the case of activities or incidents which would otherwise be purely a matter for the owner of the land directly affected. Any disturbance of the land or interference with its flora and fauna will affect the exercise and value of such rights and entitle the holder of them to sue. For example, it has been held that every owner of salmon-fishings on a river is entitled to sue in respect of harm caused to the spawning beds.[6] Even though there is no desire to exercise them and the main concern is to protect species other than those covered by such rights, the acquisition of fishing or game rights may provide the legal standing to intervene in situations where otherwise no such outside intervention is possible.

In Scotland there are no special procedures for representative or class actions, although certain actions are in practice treated in this way.[7] There has however been considerable experience of multi-party actions co-ordinated by solicitors' groups,[8] but the legal aid arrangements for these are not as developed as those in England and Wales.[9] In such cases it may be useful that in any action issues of liability can be determined separately from issues of quantifying the loss, allowing the broader issue to be determined to some extent independently of the pursuer's individual circumstances.[10] Actions taken on a contingent fee basis are not allowed, but fees can be charged on a speculative basis, with an agreed fee, up to a maximum of twice that normally charged, due only in the event of success.[11]

IV. **Public rights**

In certain circumstances Scots law recognises an *actio popularis*, the right of any member of the public to sue in vindication of public rights. There is no need for the individual raising the action to show any special interest or that he or she has been particularly affected by the infringement of the public right;

---

[5] *e.g. Duke of Buccleuch* v *Alexander Cowan & Sons* (1866) 5 M 214; see generally Lyall F, "Water and Water Rights" in vol 25 of *The Laws of Scotland: Stair Memorial Encyclopaedia* (Edinburgh, Law Society of Scotland/ Butterworths, 1989).

[6] *Countess Dowager of Seafield* v *Kemp* (1899) 1 F 402.

[7] *e.g. McColl* v *Strathclyde Regional Council* 1983 SLT 616, where the proposed fluoridation of water was successfully opposed by an "elderly edentulous inhabitant" of Glasgow.

[8] See generally Barker, Willock and McManus *Multi-party Actions in Scotland* (Edinburgh, Scottish Office Central Research Unit, 1994).

[9] See Barker *et al op cit* (n 8); on the use and abuse of legal aid see Lord Jauncey's comments in *McColl* (*supra* (n 7) at 617–618).

[10] Rule of Court 36.1 (Act of Sederunt (Rules of the Court of Session 1994) 1994, SI 1994/1443); Sheriff Court Ordinary Cause Rule 29.6 (Act of Sederunt (Sheriff Court Ordinary Cause Rules) 1993, SI 1993/1956).

[11] Act of Sederunt (Fees of Advocates in Speculative Actions) 1992, SI 1992/1897; Rule of Court 42.17 (Rules of the Court of Session 1994 *supra*).

the right to sue is commensurate with the right to use.[12] The main examples of such actions are in relation to public rights of way,[13] public rights of navigation,[14] and the use of public land.[15] These may benefit those concerned with access to the countryside, but offer little encouragement for those concerned with preventing environmental harms as there is usually no general public right which can be vindicated. However, it has been stated that a member of the public has the right to sue to prevent a danger to those exercising public rights,[16] so that action might be possible against potential health hazards facing those on public roads or the foreshore.

In practice there is no equivalent of the relator action in England in Wales, and it is unclear to what extent the Lord Advocate may take action to protect public rights.[17]

V. **Judicial review**

Anyone seeking to invoke the Court of Session's powers of judicial review must demonstrate title and interest to sue. This is generally treated as a preliminary issue, to be determined before any consideration of the substance of the case, and both title and interest must be shown – it is quite possible for a party who is recognised as having title to sue to be denied access to the courts on the basis that he or she has no interest in the particular circumstances.[18] If individuals are entitled to sue in their own right, a club or association of which they are members will also have the right to sue.[19]

No comprehensive definitions exist, but as far as title is concerned, reference is made frequently to Lord Dunedin's comment that to have title a person "must be a party (using the word in its widest sense) to some legal relation which gives him some right which the person against whom he raises the action either infringes or denies".[20] This idea has been given a broad interpretation and it has been held that when a statutory body owes a duty to the public, individual members of the public may have title to sue,[21] and also that all members of the public have title (if not necessarily interest) to

---

[12]*Torrie* v *Duke of Atholl* (1852) 1 Macq 65.

[13]*e.g., Torrie (supra)* (existence of public right of way); *Ogston* v *Aberdeen Tramways Co* (1896) 24 R (HL) 8 (obstruction of roads by snow cleared from tram lines).

[14]*Colquhoun's Trustees* v *Orr Ewing & Co* (1877) 4 R 344 (bridge obstructing navigation).

[15]*Wallace-James* v *Montgomerie & Co Ltd* (1892) 2 F 107 (encroachment on public ground in burgh).

[16]*Fergusson* v *Pollock* (1900) 3 F 1140 (danger to public on foreshore from firing range).

[17]See, *e.g.,* Lord President Clyde's *dicta* in *Glasgow Corporation* v *Barclay, Curle & Co Ltd* 1922 SC 413 at 427 and *Magistrates of Buckhaven* v *Wemyss Coal Co* 1932 SC 201 at 214; it is also suggested that the procurator fiscal may have the power to take action on behalf of the public (Whitty N, "Nuisance" in *The Laws of Scotland: Stair Memorial Encyclopaedia* vol 14 para 2161 (Edinburgh, Law Society of Scotland/Butterworths, 1988).

[18]*Scottish Old People's Welfare Council, Petitioners* 1987 SLT 179.

[19]*Ibid.*

[20]*D & J Nicol* v *Dundee Harbour Trustees* 1915 SC(HL) 7 at 12.

[21]*Wilson* v *Independent Broadcasting Authority* 1979 SLT 279 (duty to maintain proper balance in broadcasting).

challenge the rules governing entitlement to social security benefits.[22] It has also been extended to allow a party to challenge the rules governing permission to fly to and from Scottish airports even though the party at that stage had not yet lodged any application for permission which would be affected by the portion of the rules in question.[23]

The court must also be satisfied that the party has an interest to invoke the court's jurisdiction in the particular circumstances. This requires the issue to be of some real concern to the party, not an academic issue or something raised simply as a matter of general public-spirited concern. Thus, despite having title, a pressure group was held not to have an interest in challenging aspects of the social security system at a time when none of those involved were actual claimants for the benefit subject to dispute.[24] The interest need not be a formal legal or property interest, for example a local authority has been allowed to sue on the basis of its "reasonable concern with a major project in their area which may affect the economy or amenity of the area generally",[25] but there must be some direct connection with the issue.

One way of securing title and interest to challenge decisions is to become involved in the relevant proceedings at an early stage, for example by taking advantage of the opportunity which exists in many administrative procedures for members of the public to make objections or representations when official permission is being sought for some project. It is accepted that objectors are entitled to ensure that their objections are properly considered, and accordingly by becoming involved in proceedings in this way parties can ensure that they have both title and interest to seek a remedy for any flaw in the procedure. In this way a company, by making an objection when a rival company's application for a gaming licence was advertised, was able to demonstrate that as an objector it had title and interest to challenge the grant of the licence, whereas as a mere rival trading concern it would have had no standing to seek judicial review.[26]

In statutory matters, the right to challenge decisions etc. is often reserved to "persons aggrieved". In recent decisions this phrase has been given a broad definition, extending to an individual who did not in fact make any representations against an application for planning permission because he was misled as to the exact nature and extent of the proposal by the description in the public advertisements required by its classification as a "bad neighbour" development.[27]

---

[22]*Scottish Old People's Welfare Council, Petitioners (supra* n 18).
[23]*Air 2000 Ltd* v *Secretary of State for Scotland (No 2)* 1990 SLT 335.
[24]*Scottish Old People's Welfare Council, Petitioners (supra* n 18).
[25]*Kincardine & Deeside District Council* v *Forestry Commissioners* 1992 SLT 1180.
[26]*Patmor Ltd* v *City of Edinburgh District Licensing Board* 1987 SLT 492 (aff'd 1988 SLT 850).
[27]*Cumming* v *Secretary of State for Scotland* 1993 SLT 228.

VI. **Conclusion**

In both Scotland and England the rules on legal standing operate to prevent outsiders meddling in the affairs of others by raising actions in the courts. Although the general approach in both jurisdictions is similar, there are differences. The absence of the general availability of private prosecutions puts the environmentalist in Scotland at a disadvantage in employing the criminal law, but this may be balanced by the presence of an *actio popularis* to vindicate public rights and an arguably more generous approach in relation to judicial review.

In both jurisdictions, however, the law will usually operate to prevent individual environmentalists and pressure groups from invoking the assistance of the courts unless they can show that their own health or property is being affected in some fairly direct way. An interest in the quality of the environment does not of itself qualify as a legal interest sufficient to confer legal standing. There is scope for the courts to take a less restrictive approach on this issue, but statutory intervention is likely to be necessary before members of the public are recognised as having broad "environmental rights" which they can vindicate in the courts.

One possible source of such rights is the law of the European Community. Already, the Directives on environmental assessment[28] and freedom of access to environmental information[29] have conferred certain rights on the public at large. Although these have so far been limited to the rights to be consulted and to have access to information (matters of procedure not substance) these rights do give members of the public some standing in the process of environmental regulation.

More far-reaching is the suggestion that some Community legislation may in effect confer substantive rights on individuals.[30] In *Commission* v *Germany*,[31] Advocate-General Mischo stated:[32]

> "It may be seen from the preambles to the contested Directives that, in addition to protecting the environment, they are intended to protect human health and to improve the quality of life. The obligation of the Member States to ensure that the concentrations in air of the substances in question do not exceed the levels

---

[28]Directive 85/337/EEC, implemented by the Environmental Assessment (Scotland) Regulations 1988 (SI 1988/1221) and other parallel regulations.

[29]Directive 90/313/EEC, implemented by the creation of public registers as part of many regulatory schemes (*e.g.* Environmental Protection Act 1990, ss 20, 64 & 122) and the Environmental Information Regulations 1992 (SI 1992/3240).

[30]See Krämer L, "Implementation of Community Environmental Directives within Member States: Some Implications of the Direct Effect Doctrine" (1991) 3 JEL 39, esp at 52–54; Geddes A, "*Locus standi* and EEC Environmental Measures" (1992) 4 JEL 29.

[31]Case C-361/88, [1991] ECR I-2567; the case concerned whether Germany had properly implemented Directive 80/779/EEC setting air quality limit values for sulphur dioxide and suspended particulates.

[32]At para 23.

deemed permissible, has, as its corollary, the right of individuals to rely on those quality standards when they are infringed . . . "

This would seem to raise the possibility that, in some cases at least, Community environmental legislation might be regarded as conferring rights on individuals, rights which could then be enforced by legal action in the courts.

At present, however, the potential environmental litigant must learn to cope with the existing rules on title and interest to sue. These may prove to be a considerable obstacle to invoking the assistance of the courts, but by thinking ahead and taking advantage of opportunities to acquire some legally recognised interest in the matter, the position can be considerably improved.

Contents of Chapter 12

Do Public Interest Environmental Law and the Common Law Have a Future Together?

Chapter 12

Do Public Interest Environmental Law and the Common Law Have a Future Together?

Andrew Harding

I. **Introduction**

The environment represents probably the single most important challenge of all those facing modern legal systems, and is a particularly great challenge to the common law. The common law is a system which has, over several centuries, proved amenable to adaptation, and this is, in part, probably due to its predilection for procedure and its distrust of explicit fundamental premises. However, this adaptation is usually very gradual, and we do not have the luxury of being able to await the dawn of a new era in which the common law turns slowly green. That being the case, we must rapidly and fundamentally improve on our common law inheritance.[1] The question which now arises is whether the common law can embrace a concept of public interest environmental law.

The first problem is, what exactly is meant by "public interest environmental law"? This term can be taken to be the equivalent of "public interest law in environmental cases", because public interest law is unlikely to develop in such a way as to provide significantly different legal rules for environmental cases. If this is right, then it follows that public interest environmental law represents a particular application of, or a sub-set of, public interest law. This

---

*__Andrew Harding__ is a Senior Lecturer with the School of Oriental and African Studies, University of London with interests in environmental law and comparative public law, particularly in South East Asian countries.
[1]This chapter is addressed to English law, and "we" and "our" should be construed accordingly. My apologies to Scots lawyers for the constant use (for convenience) of the terms "common law" and "our legal system" in this chapter. However, *mutatis mutandis*, much of what I have to say applies to Scots law as well as English law (see Colin Reid's Chapter 11 in this book) and the context sometimes requires reference to Britain rather than England. It is, of course, outside the scope of this chapter to suggest how civil law might contribute to public interest environmental law in the UK. Naturally, some of the contents of this chapter may be applicable to other common law jurisdictions.

does not solve the problem of definition entirely, because the term public interest law itself has different meanings. Much discussion about public interest law is devoted to the issue of standing in judicial review cases.[2] This is, of course, a crucial issue, and will be addressed. However, it is not the only crucial issue. I would prefer to adopt a view of public interest law which embraces a radical approach not only to litigation in judicial review cases, but to the legal system itself, the whole tradition of legal practice and, of course, to legal education. Such a broad definition will help us to explore ways in which our common law traditions can be developed usefully.

Public interest law in India has taken the form of relaxing or interpreting both substantive and procedural rules to enable the courts to intervene on behalf of large, especially disadvantaged, groups of people. Thus, some prefer the term "social-action litigation". In the Indian context this is quite correct, even though "public interest litigation" has acquired a technical procedural meaning. In Britain, however, social action is seen as the task of government, and there are great obstacles in the way of courts presuming to second-guess government policy on these matters. Even the US model of public interest law, which is not necessarily always "social-action litigation" in the Indian sense, assumes the legitimacy of a constitutional role which US (and indeed Indian) judges have acquired, but British judges have not.

II. **Limiting factors**

A. **The Constitution**

There appears to be a major constitutional inhibition which, in Britain, restricts the growth of public interest law in the broader sense of the term. Britain does not yet seem to be politically ready for a constitutional overhaul, much as such an overhaul is urgently needed. There is a prevailing sense in the corridors of power that our institutions are adequate to the constitutional challenges they face, even though they are demonstrably inadequate. The view in both the Conservative and Labour parties is that what is needed is for their party to attain or keep power, and the Constitution will then be preserved; as for everything else, minor tinkering will suffice. Until, therefore, we face such an environmental or social catastrophe that a desire for constitutional change becomes paramount, or until we have a hung Parliament and constitutional "horse-trading" begins, the present notions of judicial and legislative power will remain.

---

[2]Indeed, for some people the term is synonymous with broad standing rules.

B. **The legal system**

This observation extends to current notions of legal practice. The legal profession now has an opportunity, since the Courts and Legal Services Act 1990, to make significant changes in its modes of practice. For example, the Legal Aid Board's powers to contract-out legal aid work to particular law firms could be used to encourage environmental-litigation specialism;[3] the new opportunities for international practice could also be used to the same end. The market-oriented reforms of the 1990 Act have received a frosty reception in some professional quarters; but if lawyers want to be loyal servants of the public and agents of legal change, rather than mere efficient providers of services in an expanding market-place, they would do well to consider the nature of their own professional practices in a broader perspective. The same applies to the academic branch of law. Major changes in legal thinking must either originate or be encouraged by the law schools and teaching pro-grammes should reflect this.[4] Only when these changes occur will a legal and constitutional environment exist in which our judges can assume a more activist stance capable of embracing public interest environmental law. Academics should ask: how green is our curriculum? Practitioners should likewise ask: how green is our practice? Public interest environmental law cannot await a constitutional millenium. On the other hand, it must grow out of, and use, the traditions of the common law. It is no use, in the short-term at least, pursuing a regime of public interest environmental law which founders instantly on those dangerous sunken wrecks, the common law tradition and our ancient and creaking constitution.

There are several interlocking features of our legal system which are actually inimical to public interest environmental law.[5] Because our legal system is adversarial rather than inquisitorial it has come to be an effective weapon for the safeguarding of individual rights, especially property rights, rather than group rights (environmental rights are, of course, group rights *par excellence*). Thus, our legal system is shot through with substance and procedure which reflect this ideological bias. There is much to be said for it, but it does not assist in environmental cases, except in those instances where property rights and environmental protection happen to coincide (and not always even then if the judges detect a group right lurking ominously in the background). Group rights are regarded traditionally as "political" matters, where the remedy is through the ballot-box. This perception has changed,

---

[3] Legal Aid Act 1988, s 4(1),(5); see also n 23 *infra* and associated text.
[4] Most law schools now have courses on environmental law, and a Master of Laws degree in environmental law is offered by the University of London. Environmental law also features prominently in research programmes. SOAS, for example, offers three LLM courses in environmental law, and is engaged in a major ESRC research project on access to environmental justice in cities in Asia and Africa.
[5] See, further, Chapter 16 at Section II(A) "Public Interest Environmental Law and the UK".

marginally one might say, over the last 20 years or so, but it still motivates most administrative law decisions.

1. *Default powers*

A classic example is the law on the use of default powers, which is of great importance with regard to the environment. Approximately 100 years ago the House of Lords refused a remedy to a riparian owner affected by industrial pollution when he sued the local authority to compel them to take action under the Public Health Act 1875, because the central government had been given default powers to act where the local authority failed to do so.[6] In a 1984 case the Court of Appeal adopted a similar approach in a case involving settlement of gypsies under the Caravan Sites Act 1968, but conceded that the exercise of default powers was itself reviewable.[7] This is movement of a sort, but glacial movement. Much the same can be said of the rule which denies judicial review where there is an alternative remedy.[8] This rule has always seemed odd, and is crucial in environmental cases where there are usually alternative remedies. It is open to the objection that if other remedies were actually beneficial, the litigant would surely have pursued them.

2. *Standing*

Another important example of this glaciality is the rules of standing in public law, which still reflect a bias towards private property interests. Traditionally, public law remedies were not available except at the instance of those who sought to protect their property. Ratepayers and taxpayers, for example, were treated with care; those with more intangible interests were not generally given standing unless a clear commercial interest could be shown or statute had conferred a right of objection. Lest we be complacent that these are only the attitudes of the past, it is worth reflecting on recent cases.

In the *Fleet Street Casuals* case in 1981 standing was denied to a group of taxpayers even as the House of Lords declared itself in favour of liberalisation of the rules;[9] while in *R v HM Treasury, ex p Smedley* in 1985 standing was granted to an individual taxpayer, albeit one with no greater interest than all other taxpayers;[10] and in the *Rose Theatre Trust* case in 1990 standing was

---

[6]*Pasmore v Oswaldtwistle UDC* [1898] AC 387.
[7]*R v Secretary of State for the Environment, ex p Ward* [1984] 1 WLR 834, [1984] 2 All ER 556.
[8]The most recent example is *R v Birmingham CC, ex p Ferrero Ltd* [1993] 1 All ER 530, CA.
[9]*IRC v National Federation of Self-Employed* [1982] AC 617.
[10][1985] QB 657, [1985] 1 All ER 589.

denied to a public interest group with no property interest but only an intellectual or historical interest.[11]

Even though Parliament has decreed a single test for standing: "a sufficient interest in the matter to which the application relates" (Supreme Court Act, s 31) and the House of Lords has asserted its right to adopt a flexible interpretation of the standing rules, the actuality, in terms of judicial decisions conferring standing, gives no firm juridical basis for those with no property or commercial interest to claim standing as of right. The cases amount to a kind of conspiracy to give standing to favoured litigants without giving a sufficiently broad *right* to standing.[12] This is a defect in the law which should be rectified. At the very least the term "interest" should be construed broadly to include interests which are no greater than those of the public in general, including, for example, the intellectual interest of the Rose Theatre Trust in the resurrection of the Tudor theatre of that name. Some decisions cannot, effectively, be challenged at all if an interest greater than that of any other citizen is required. This is true of environmental decisions above all, since of their very nature the interest each one of us has in the environment, in most cases, is similar to that which others have in it; the difference is one of degree but not kind, unless one measures environmental interests purely in terms of the effect on property values, which is clearly retrograde.

Standing rules appear to serve no real purpose. To summarise briefly, the only purposes which standing rules seem to serve are:

(i)   to keep unmeritorious actions out of the courts;
(ii)   to prevent those unaffected or indirectly affected by administrative action from disturbing that which is acquiesced in by those directly affected; or
(iii) to ensure that the best arguments are put against administrative action.[13]

The first point is dealt with adequately by the leave requirement. The lack of merit of a case bears no relation to the identity of the litigant. A person with a sufficient interest is as capable of being idiotic as a person without a sufficient interest. The remarks of Popplewell J in *R v Wychavon DC & Secretary of State for the Environment, ex p Saunders*[14] indicate that the state of the court lists is

---

[11]*Rose Theatre Trust v Secretary of State for the Environment* [1990] 2 WLR 186. However, standing has been accorded to non-governmental organisations (NGOs) in some cases; see *e.g. Covent Garden Community Association v GLC* [1981] 183; *R v Secretary of State for the Environment, ex p Ward* [1984] 1 WLR 834; *R v Poole BC, ex p Beebee* [1991] COD 264. In *R v HM Inspectorate of Pollution and the Minister for Agriculture, Fisheries and Food, ex p Greenpeace Ltd* [1994] 1 WLR 570 Otton J accorded standing on the basis of members of Greenpeace being personally affected by BNFL's THORP proposals at Sellafield. The learned judge distinguished the *Rose Theatre* case.
[12]See *R v MPC, ex p Blackburn* [1968] 2 QB 118, CA; *R v GLC, ex p Blackburn* [1976] 3 All ER 184; *R v GLC, ex p McWhirter* [1976] 1 WLR 550; *R v Secretary of State for Social Services, ex p GLC and CPAG, The Times*, 16 August 1984; *R v Secretary of State for Social Services, ex p CPAG* [1989] 1 All ER 1047.
[13]Harding, *Public Duties and Public Law*, Oxford, Oxford University Press, 1989 at 221 *et seq*.
[14]Unreported.

still attributed to the number of "unmeritorious claims" being brought; if so, then clearly judges in Order 53 cases[15] have been granting leave too readily.

The second point ignores the fact that illegality is illegality whoever acquiesces in it. It is, in any case, irrelevant to environmental issues, which affect all of us, not just those who live near a development site or have statutory notices served on them.

The third point is simply nonsense, and egregious nonsense in environmental cases. Environmental groups are often better able to fight the case than individuals; again, capacity to argue the case does not depend on having a sufficient legal interest in the matter, but on the resources and expertise at one's disposal. Is it seriously thought that only those with property or commercial interests have the tenacity and motivation to pursue litigation effectively? In the recent *Greenpeace* case,[16] it is pleasing to note, Otton J has exposed this argument very convincingly.[17]

Standing rules, therefore, should simply be done away with, so that a litigant need only show that he has an arguable case on the law. In view of the uselessless of legal aid in this area, it seems an essential component of our democracy that interest groups and individuals who are, in reality, suing on behalf of the community should be allowed into court. If not, there is a danger that official and commercial interests will stitch up administrative decisions between them, leaving the rest of the community with nothing but political remedies which our Constitution is ill-adapted to give them in full measure.

III. **Areas of potential growth**

Slowly, the old premises of the legal system are giving way before some recognition of the need to relax procedural obstacles in favour of group interests. These may be regarded as areas of potential growth.

Some cases actually fail or succeed only because standing has been conceded as a tactical gesture. Often, the publicity gained is sufficient to secure the object of the litigation, as in the *Ocean Island* case,[18] and the action brought by haemophiliacs against the government in respect of HIV-contaminated blood. The more such litigation is perceived as legitimate, the more likely it is that it will result in legal change.[19]

The practical effect of rules can be altered by collective action. For example, if a field adjoining a proposed road is sold to 100 environmentalists as small

---

[15]*i.e.* "application for judicial review" cases under the reformed Rules of the Supreme Court, Ord 53.
[16]See n 11 *supra*.
[17]His point is that there are advantages in litigation being conducted by an NGO; it prevents a multiplicity of claims, and facilitates the definition of issues. *Cf. Environmental Defence Society* v *Agricultural Chemicals Board* [1973] 2 NZLR 758, where the EDS was said to have more of the relevant expertise than the government, but standing was still refused.
[18]*Tito* v *Waddell (No 2)* [1977] 2 WLR 496.
[19]See Hedley, "Group Personal Injury Litigation and Public Opinion" (1994) 14 *Legal Studies* 70.

clods of earth, there exist 100 rights of objection. Inhabitants of some rural middle-class areas have secured their environment by lobbying a member of the House of Lords to secure the passage of an Act of Parliament imposing a kind of collective restrictive covenant. This is not what Indian lawyers would call social action, but it is effective all the same.

Representative actions may be brought under RSC Order 15, rule 12. So far, this rule has not proved a suitable vehicle for public interest environmental law, and has been confined to instances where plaintiffs have a common property or commercial interest. Its usefulness in mass tort claims is limited by the fact that plaintiffs suffer different degrees of damage, rendering their interests different.

Rules of procedure can be relaxed to accommodate an advancing tide of litigation. In *Chrzanowska* v *Glaxo Laboratories*,[20] a tort case involving the drug Myodil, Steyn J granted an order under RSC Order 14, rule 12, that any costs falling on the plaintiff would be shared equally by all plaintiffs, and directed that all pleadings and affidavits should be marked "Myodil litigation", and all Myodil cases on the Northern Circuit should be heard by himself or another judge.[21] These orders are new[22] and welcome. They could also be invoked in cases of mass environmental damage, such as occurred in the Shetlands when the ship the "Brer" went aground.

The same applies to modes of professional practice. The trend towards particular firms of solicitors representing multiple plaintiffs in mass accident cases assists the pursuit of group rights. The utility of this development is implicitly recognised in Legal Aid Act 1988, section 4(1), (5).[23]

Some judicial review cases have involved large groups of people.[24] Environmental litigation has not been as prominent in this area as one would expect when one compares Britain with India, the United States, Australia, Canada and New Zealand, for example. However, a number of recent cases has shown that this kind of litigation is developing, as is evidenced by cases such as *Greenpeace*, discussed above.

In the sphere of enforcement of public duties – an area of peculiarly great importance to public interest environmental law – British law lags behind that of other common law countries. There are no clear British decisions stating that the courts will grant mandamus to compel enforcement of environmental

---

[20](1990) *The Times*, 16 March, (1990) *The Independent*, 13 March.
[21]The plaintiff's solicitors had also been consulted by 700 claimants who alleged that they had suffered side-effects from being injected with Myodil; the plaintiff was legally aided but 25% of the 700 claimants were not.
[22]See, however, *Davies* v *Eli Lilly* [1987] 1 WLR 1136, CA.
[23]These provisions, in effect, allow the Legal Aid Board to contract-out to a particular firm or firms representation of plaintiffs in class actions.
[24]*e.g. Congreve* v *Home Office* [1976] QB 629, [1976] 1 All ER 697; *Gillick* v *West Norfolk and Wisbech Health Authority* [1986] AC 112, [1985] 3 WLR 830; *R* v *Liverpool Corporation, ex p Liverpool Taxi Fleet Operators' Association* [1972] 2 QB 299, [1972] 2 All ER 589, CA; *Meade* v *Haringey LBC* [1979] 1 WLR 637, CA; *W Glamorgan CC* v *Rafferty* [1987] 1 All ER 1005, CA.

legislation. The excuses for not intervening, apart from standing, are legion.[25] There are, however, some decisions[26] which indicate that this approach may be changing.

Criminal law can also embrace public interest environmental law. But only if a broad approach to statutory interpretation is taken. A recent case suggests this is not being done.[27]

Tort law can be developed so as to assist in the creation of public interest environmental law. Two recent examples, the *Cambridge Water* case[28] in the House of Lords, and the *Asian Rare Earth* case[29] in the Malaysian Supreme Court, indicate, tantalisingly, the possibility of developing tort law (nuisance and *Rylands* v *Fletcher*[30] particularly) along public interest lines, but also the unwillingness of the courts to undertake such development when statutory developments appear to them to be more suited to environmental purposes. In the former case, which concerned the leakage of toxic solvents into the municipal water supply, a unanimous House of Lords advanced the existence of statute law as a reason for not developing *Rylands* v *Fletcher* liability, precisely because the environment is so important.[31] In the Malaysian case, which concerned the dumping of radioactive waste, the existence of statutory controls was advanced as a reason for refusing an injunction. The judgments in both cases are open to serious objection, however, and reversed notable judgments in the lower courts.

IV. **Conclusion**

There are many possibilities for doctrinal development. Public interest environmental law can lie down with the common law, but the urgency of environmental law reform requires Parliament to intervene on a grand scale. Only then, it seems, will our judges follow suit.[32] The notion that *either* the common law *or* statute law, but not both, can achieve environmental objectives, seems mistaken and contrary to the entire history of the common law.

---

[25]"There is an alternative remedy"; "it is a duty of imperfect obligation"; "the duty is not absolute, only a duty to act reasonably"; "the court can refuse an order in its discretion"; "mandamus will not lie against the Crown", etc.

[26]In non-environmental cases, however. See *R* v *Thamesdown BC, ex p Pritchard, The Independent*, 29 December 1988, CA; *R* v *Camden LBC, ex p Gillan*, (1988) *The Times*, 13 October.

[27]*Wychavon DC* v *National Rivers Authority* [1993] 2 All ER 440.

[28]*Cambridge Water Co Ltd* v *Eastern Counties Leather plc* [1994] 1 All ER 53.

[29]*Woon Tan Kan and 7 Others* v *Asian Rare Earth Sdn Bhd*, Civil Suit No 02-313-92. The case is not reported at the time of going to press. It was decided by the Supreme Court of Malaysia on 23 December 1993.

[30]*Fletcher* v *Rylands* (1866) LR 1 Ex 265; affirming *Rylands* v *Fletcher* [1861-73] All ER Rep 1.

[31]Per Lord Goff, [1994] 1 All ER 53 at 76e-g. Further discussed in Chapter 16 at text following n 2, p 316.

[32]The creation of participatory rights in planning legislation, which are enforced by the courts routinely these days, show what can be done. See *Save Britain's Heritage* v *Secretary of State for the Environment* [1991] 2 All ER 10, HL; sub nom *Save Britain's Heritage* v *Number 1 Poultry Ltd* [1991] 1 WLR 153. See, further, Lomas O (ed), *Frontiers of Environmental Law*, London, Wiley Chancery, 1992.

In Britain a massive effort of will is required. It is not enough to discuss endlessly the pros and cons of reform. The nature of our constitutional system is that a political lead is required. Ultimately, therefore, the only real remedy for the environment and catalyst for legal reform is votes cast for parties promoting green policies and constitutional changes.

Contents of Chapter 13

Pollution Control: A Preventive Approach for Urban Communities

Chapter 13

Pollution Control: A Preventive Approach for Urban Communities

Phil Shiner[1]

This chapter is concerned with pollution control, being the aspect of environmental law most affecting deprived urban communities. The focus is on the potential pollution effects to air and water of proposed developments. Other aspects of environmental law affecting urban communities include land contamination, waste disposal, radioactivity, pesticides, consumer protection, product liability and health and safety. After exploring the context of environmental law, guidelines are suggested for a preventive approach to pollution control.

It is presumed that those concerned with environmental law on behalf of urban communities – rather than developers – are motivated by a desire to assist the communities in their struggle against potential developers and, to some extent, against central and local government and enforcing agencies such as Her Majesty's Inspectorate of Pollution (HMIP). The aim is to help the communities to achieve a long-term qualitative change in their environment and quality of life.

I. Environmental law in context

A. Law and practice of urban regeneration

Environmental law does not exist in a vacuum. It is part of a complex jigsaw which includes the law, practice and policy of:

– planning and land-use and property development;

Phil Shiner is a solicitor with the Birkenhead Resource Unit, England and specialist planning lawyer particularly concerned with the effects of urban regeneration on local communities.
[1] I acknowledge the assistance of David Robinson in commenting upon earlier drafts of this chapter.

- housing, including urban renewal, housing associations and housing finance;
- local government law and finance;
- urban funding regimes;
- local economic development, including social security law and how to maximise people's income;
- transport and highways;
- health and public health.

In short, environmental law is concerned with the law, practice and policy of urban regeneration and, to be effective, it is essential to grasp the fundamentals of urban policy as well as having a good understanding of the various areas of law concerned. A practitioner does not have available a single book on this subject but must look to a whole range of materials from different specialised areas of law.[2]

The environmental issues for a particular community will reflect the state of the regional and local economy. A depressed area, for example, will tend to be prey to "dirty industries"[3] and a polluted area is less likely to attract high-quality inward investment. Clearly, a local planning authority (LPA) in a depressed area will tend to think that any development is to be welcomed, even if it is unattractive or simply unhealthy. This tendency is particularly enhanced when there is high unemployment. A developer may be tempted to make use of these pressures. Thus there exists a vicious circle for some communities. The major challenge for a community is how to insist that, in the absence of a people-led approach to regeneration,[4] the local authority's access to funds for urban regeneration should be used to achieve long-term sustainable regeneration which improves the state of the economy and the quality of lives of local people.[5]

Given the emphasis of the government on property-led regeneration, and how this has been reflected in the rules of funding regimes for urban

---

[2]Planning – *Encyclopedia of Planning Law and Practice*, Sweet and Maxwell; *Butterworths Planning Law Service*, Butterworths. Environmental Law – *Encyclopedia of Environmental Law*, Sweet and Maxwell; *Garners Environmental Law*, Butterworths. Housing – *Encyclopedia of Housing Law and Practice*, Sweet and Maxwell. Local Government – *Encyclopedia of Local Government Law*, Sweet and Maxwell; *Cross on Local Government Law*, Sweet and Maxwell. Local Government Finance – Arden and Hunter, *Local Government Finance: Law and Practice*; Longman. *The Local Government Information Guide to Local Government Finance*, London, Local Government Information Unit, 1993. Housing Finance – Garnett D *et al*, *Housing Finance*, London, Longman, 1991. Urban Renewal – *Encyclopedia of Compulsory Purchase Law*, Sweet and Maxwell; Alder J and Handy C, *Housing Association Law*, London, Sweet and Maxwell, 1991.
[3]It is worth noting the recent creation of an Interagency Working Group on Environmental Justice in the United States to counter this tendency.
[4]Nevin B and Shiner P, "Britain's Urban Problems: Communities Hold the Key" (1993) 50, *Local Work*.
[5]Sustainable regeneration policies will link physical economic and social regeneration, and will produce a thriving, healthy local community integrated with the outside world.

regeneration, public funds have been disposed of in schemes of little, if any, long-term benefit to the indigenous population.[6]

In considering the future of the local economy and, therefore, the likely environmental impact of new development, one must look at the paucity of funds presently available to local authorities.[7] Furthermore, the ability and willingness of a local authority to enforce environmental protection legislation against existing polluters will be constrained and affected by at least five factors:

–   the strength of the local community;
–   the amount of the local authority's standard spending assessment.[8] The amount of monies available to a local authority will determine the numbers of enforcing officers, the salaries paid and, therefore, the quality of those officers;
–   the commitment of officers, especially the chief officer;
–   the access of the local authority to urban funds – the more funds available to a local authority the more likely it is that it will be able to co-ordinate a coherent strategy to attract high quality investment to the area, that it will wish to repel any potentially polluting development or environmental problem which may serve to deter potential investors, and that, generally, the factors which tend to attract "dirty industries" will either not be present or will be on the decline;
–   the political commitment of the council members to environmental matters.

B. **Environmental law in the context of the planning system**

There have been fundamental shifts in the planning system since 1979. The planning system is crucial to the question of whether a polluting development is allowed to operate. These changes have, to a large extent, reflected the needs of developers and the thinking of the "New Right".[9] These changes include:

–   a shift from local authorities to central government as strategic planners. Thus, whilst one sees a major shift from a "providing" to an "enabling"

---

[6]Colenutt B, "After the Urban Development Corporations? Development Elites or People-Based Regeneration?" in Imrie R and Thomas H (eds), *British Urban Policy and Development Corporations*, London, Paul Chapman Publishing Limited, 1993 at 175–185; Loftman P and Nevin B, *Urban Regeneration and Social Equity; a case study of Birmingham 1986–1992*, Research Paper series No 8, Faculty of the Built Environment, University of Central England in Birmingham, October 1992.
[7]Shiner P and Nevin B, "Behind the Chimera of Urban Funding" (1994) 52 *Local Work*.
[8]A standard spending assessment (SSA) is the amount central government determines a local authority should spend in order to provide a standard level of service.
[9]Thornley A, "*Urban Planning under Thatcherism*", London, Routledge, 1993.

role for local authorities which presupposes an increased strategic influence, the reverse is, in fact, the case;

–   increasing centralisation with greater reliance on parliament and central direction and control;
–   a greater status given to market trends and allowing the market to dictate which development should proceed within a flexible development plan system;
–   a shift from a developer-led to a plan-led system[10] (apart from urban development corporations (UDCs));
–   increasing deregulation, for example enterprise zones (EZs),[11] simplified planning zones (SPZs)[12] and changes to the General Development Order[13] and Use Classes Order.[14]
–   a reduction in public participation.

A closer examination of these changes shows the emergence of clear trends. At first glance it may appear that the community has never had it so good. Murdie notes that in a government publication,[15] John Major expresses the view that the protection of the environment is not a matter for the state alone but one in which citizens are to become partners. In Murdie's view,[16] this is not mere rhetoric:

" . . . it is backed up by legal changes which place individual citizens in a better position than ever before to have an influence in matters ranging from Town and Country Planning to Genetically Modified Organisms."

The evidence for this optimism appears to be sound.

(i)   The new emphasis on development plans (Local Government Act 1985 and Town and Country Planning Act 1990 (TCPA 1990)) includes statutory rights for the public to be consulted and participate, if necessary, at a public local enquiry.

---

[10]Department of Environment, *Planning Policy Guidance 1, General Policy and Principles (PPGI)*, March 1992 at paras 25–28; *Encyclopedia of Planning Law and Practice*, Sweet and Maxwell at 2-3150/39.
[11]Established by s 179 of and Sched 32 to the Local Government and Land Act 1980, an EZ is a site in which business is freed from much detailed planning control and from rates. An EZ may last for 10 years.
[12]An SPZ is a new type of planning regime applied by an LPA to a particular area. The LPA specifies that particular types of development are allowed in the area so that developers can then carry out development which conforms to the scheme without the need for a planning application and a related fee. See ss 82–87 of and Sched 7 to the Town and Country Planning Act 1990 (TCPA 1990).
[13]The General Development Order 1988 authorises automatically the carrying out of 76 classes of development (ss 58(1)(a), 59 of the TCPA 1990). There is no need for a developer undertaking these types of development to make any application for planning permission in respect of it.
[14]The Town and Country Planning (Use Classes) Order 1987 specifies 16 different classes of use. Article 3 provides that, generally, the use of a building for any purpose specified in one of the 16 classes may be changed to any other purpose falling within the same class, without the need to obtain planning permission.
[15]UK Government, *This Common Inheritance – A First Year Report*, Cmnd 1655, London, HMSO, 1991.
[16]Murdie A, *Environmental Law and Citizen Action* London Earthscan, 1993 at 3.

(ii) The Environmental Information Regulations 1992[17] give new rights to any person seeking environmental information to obtain it from any public body which holds it, subject to certain exceptions.

(iii) The new systems of integrated pollution control (IPC) and local authority air pollution control (LAAPC) introduced by Part I of the Environmental Protection Act 1990 (EPA 1990) provide for wide opportunities for public consultation and involvement in the grant of authorisations to certain processes.

(iv) New proposals from the European Union, including the Draft Directive on Civil Liability for Damages caused by Waste[18] would impose a wide civil liability for damage, including environmental damage.

However, great caution is needed. It is true, for example, that there is a new shift from a developer-led to a plan-led system. However, the extent of public participation has been reduced quite deliberately. Thornley notes that a White Paper[19] reflected some of the proposals of two vested interest groups[20] and adds:

> "The Government's proposals on local plan participation have been criticised for concentrating participation on a stage that experience has shown produces little response. Thus the proposals are likely to result in a major reduction in involvement as this would be concentrated on the formal stage after the plan had been produced. It must be assumed therefore that the government desires less participation although the reasons for this are not made explicit."[21]

C. Community participation and consultation

The apparent opportunity for participation and consultation for the community is further diminished by two Ministerial policy documents. First, paragraph 9 of Ministerial Circular 2/87[22] is as follows:

> "Planning authorities are expected to take into account the views of local residents when determining a planning application. Nevertheless, on its own, local opposition to a proposal is not a reasonable ground for the refusal of a planning application unless that opposition is founded upon valid planning

---

[17]SI 1992/3240.

[18]Com 91.219 final.

[19]Department of the Environment, *The Future of Development Plans*, Cmnd 569, HMSO, 1989.

[20]The two groups are the Royal Institution of Chartered Surveyors (RICS), *A Strategy for Planning*, London, RICS, 1986 and the British Federation Property (BPF) Report, *The Planning System – A Fresh Approach*, London BPF, 1986.

[21]Thornley *op cit* (n 9) at 142.

[22]Department of the Environment (DoE) *Awards of Costs incurred in Planning and Compulsory Purchase Order proceedings*, Circular 2/87, DoE, 1987.

reasons which are supported by substantial evidence. While the planning authority will need to consider the substance of any local opposition to the proposal their duty is to decide a case on its planning merits. They are unlikely to be considered to have acted reasonably in refusing an application if no material departure from statutory plans or policies is involved and there are no other planning reasons why permission should be refused."

These fears are reinforced by the wording of paragraph 42 of Planning Policy Guidance 1:[23]

"In general, the elected members of the local planning authority represent the interests of the community in planning matters. But when determining planning applications they must take into account any relevant views on planning matters expressed by neighbouring occupiers, local residents and any other third parties. For example, opponents of a development proposal may highlight factors, such as traffic problems or the scale of a proposed development in relation to its surroundings, which are land-use planning issues and thus comprise material considerations; these must be taken into account, along with all other material considerations, in deciding the case. Nevertheless local opposition to a proposal is not in itself a ground for refusing planning permission, unless that opposition is founded upon valid planning reasons which can be substantiated. While the substance of local opposition must be considered, the duty is to decide each case on its planning merits."

It is vitally important that the community's views are represented in the draft development plan, and taken into account in considering an application for planning permission. However, it should be noted that the rights of consultation and participation in the former instance are limited. In the latter, as discussed below, if an LPA decides to grant a consent, a third party has no right to object except by proceedings for judicial review.

Similarly, the Environmental Information Regulations 1992 (above) appear to offer unbounded opportunities for the public to gain access to important information about the environment. However, regulation 4 contains a number of important exemptions to the duty to release information. There is a discretion to refuse if the information is capable of being, or must be classified as "confidential". Regulation 4(2) defines various categories of confidential information which includes "information relating to, or to anything which is or has been the subject matter of, any legal or other proceedings (whether actual or prospective)". Regulation 4(5) defines "legal or other proceedings" as including "any disciplinary proceedings, the proceedings at any local or other public enquiry and the proceedings at any hearing conducted by a person appointed under an enactment for the purpose of affording an opportunity to persons to make representations or objections with respect to any matter". This is an extremely wide definition which could, in theory, catch

---

[23] *op cit* n 10 *supra*.

controls for pollution authorisation, town and country planning matters, enquiries etc. Murdie has written:[24]

"much will depend on how the courts interpret the words 'actual or prospective' since it will always be open for a public official to suggest that proceedings on some matter may be prospective and anticipated all along!"

When one considers also that regulation 3(4)(b) allows the person supplying the information to make a charge for it, these regulations may have a limited practical effect. Charging for copies of documents, such as draft local plans or planning agreements, may tend to exclude the public.

D. **Planning and pollution control**

Pollution control must be a central concern of the planning system. This is because of problems with enforcing pollution legislation. Even assuming that new public rights to consultation and involvement in pollution authorisations lead to tougher pollution controls,[25] pollution enforcement agencies may not be able or willing to rigorously enforce the law. Three trends in the planning system give cause for concern regarding pollution control.

First, the "New Right", which has influenced government policy over the period since 1979, is anxious to dismantle the planning system to allow the market to decide which development should proceed in a particular area. To that end one can see a move to other control mechanisms: economic forces, the law of nuisance, central regulation and private institutional controls. As Thornley[26] notes:

"a strengthened law of nuisance and its enforcement would ensure that planners do not need to concern themselves with the problem of 'externalities' or neighbour conflicts."

The shifting of planning controls into the legal arena of civil or criminal actions is an unlikely panacea for environmental ills for deprived communities.

---

[24]Murdie *op cit* (n 16) at 34.
[25]Schedule 10 to the Water Resources Act 1991 sets out the various procedures to be followed on the application for a consent to discharge to water. There is an opportunity for the public to make representations or objections and request the Secretary of State to give a direction.
[26]Thornley *op cit* (n 9) at 115.

Secondly, the Conservative Government has systematically attacked the basis of the planning system in particular localities by the setting up of UDCs, EZs, SPZs and the establishment of the City Challenge scheme and the Urban Regeneration Agency. There has been much criticism of the property-led approach to urban regeneration as represented by UDCs. Land in the designated area of a UDC passes out of local authority control and vests in the UDC, which becomes the LPA.[27] What is not so generally known is that the City Challenge scheme contains within it worrying attacks on the very basis of a locally accountable planning system. Even though it is apparently local authority led it is, in fact, very much a reflection of the vision and needs of the private sector. When the scheme was announced the seven general criteria in the government guidance which local authorities were to meet included:[28]

–   proposals for imaginative management and organisational arrangements offering rapid and flexible delivery . . . ; and
–   commitment of private sector and willingness of public authorities to promote private sector enterprise.

Thus, local authorities were being urged to provide a fast track for City Challenge schemes through the planning system. A typical local authority approach may be to establish an executive body which would approve a development in principle. This development will then go through planning committee "on the nod" shortly after the executive bodies decision, with no opportunity for the community at large to influence that decision, the whole process taking less than eight weeks. If that development happens to be a polluting one which later gains the appropriate authorisation (if necessary) it can be seen that these trends are effectively circumventing the local participation, consultation and politically accountable elements of the planning system. These moves will be taken to their logical conclusion if, and when, central government moves to deregulate systematically both the planning and pollution control systems. Part of this process of deregulation may involve passing responsibility for various prescribed processes from local authorities to HMIP (see s 4(4) of EPA 1990). As Murdie notes, this is "one of a number of signs which do not bode well for the future of local government as a major influence for environmental protection".[29]

The third, and the most worrying, trend of all in terms of pollution control is the increasing emphasis that matters of pollution control should not be dealt with through the planning system at all. The government's current approach is

---

[27]Centre for Local Economic Strategies (CLES) *Social Regeneration: Directions for Urban Policy in the 1990s*, Manchester, CLES, 1992.
[28]Department of the Environment, *City Challenge, Government Guidance*, DoE, 1991 at 5.
[29]Murdie *op cit* (n 16) at 25.

set out in Planning Policy Guidance 23 issued in July 1994.[30] Paragraph 1.34
urges LPAs as follows:

"Planning authorities will need to consult pollution control authorities in order
that they can take account of the scope and requirements of the relevant
pollution controls. Planning authorities should work on the assumption that the
pollution control regimes will be properly applied and enforced. They should
not seek to substitute their own judgement on pollution control issues for that of
the bodies with the relevant expertise and the statutory responsbility for that
control."

However, there are clear dangers in leaving matters of pollution control to be
determined by the enforcing authorities. There is a danger of a lack of
coherence and rationality in this approach. HMIP does not have the
commitment to enforce the existing legislation against polluters. People in
areas such as the Mersey Basin will attest to that fact. Furthermore, HMIP and
other enforcing agencies are not accountable to the local community. The
point can be illustrated by a hypothetical example. Let us assume that an LPA
was being asked to make a decision on an application for planning permission
in respect of a development containing a prescribed process.[31] Suppose also
that the proposed development is of a type for which there must be an
assessment in environmental terms before permission is granted[32] (for
example, a clinical waste disposal incinerator) but that the Environmental
Statement report does not satisfy the LPA that there will be no demonstrable
harm to nearby residents. The LPA asks the applicants for more information
about various aspects with which they are unhappy, but the applicants refuse
to disclose more, saying that this is a matter for HMIP. The LPA then approaches
HMIP to take initial soundings on whether an authorisation is likely to be
forthcoming and are told that it is likely, provided that standard conditions on
the operations of such incinerators are met. If the LPA refuses permission
subsequently on the grounds of the likely adverse environmental effects in the
vicinity of the particular site proposed and the applicants appeal it is suggested
that the LPA would be at real risk of losing the appeal and possibly having costs
awarded against it.[33] In other words, the HMIP approach of making

[30]Department of the Environment, *Planning Policy Guidance: Planning and Pollution Control*, HMSO, July
1994.
[31]Schedule I to the Environmental Protection (Prescribed Processes and Prescribed Substances) Regulations
1991 (SI 1991/472), as amended by SI 1991/836, SI 1992/614 and SI 1993/1749.
[32]The Town and Country Planning (Assessment of Environmental Effects) Regulations 1988 (SI 1988/1199) which
brought into effect the provisions of EC Directive 85/337/EEC.
[33]DoE Circular 2/87 (n 22 *supra*) and Department of the Environment, *8/93 Award of Costs incurred in
Planning and Other (including Compulory Purchase Order) Proceedings*, DoE, 1993.

incinerators as clean and safe as practicable pre-empts the essential planning consideration of whether any incinerator at all is appropriate for the site.[34] The right to make representations to HMIP on the granting of an authorisation is cold comfort if the issue is whether this particular clinical waste disposal incinerator should be given planning permission.

II. **Towards a preventive approach**

It is preferable to try to prevent a development with unacceptable pollution risks from obtaining planning permission and starting operation, rather than suing or prosecuting the owners once the health effects become evident after the event. This is not radical, it is plain common sense. Of course, many communities are already affected by existing polluting developments which have both planning permission and authorisations to discharge. In these cases, communities must focus their energies on trying to limit any harm by taking legal proceedings. However, in this section the pollution control issues are discussed in the context of developments which are yet to begin their operations.

Pollution control legislation typically proceeds by imposing upon defined activities the requirement of a licence, or other form of authorisation which may include conditions governing the activity. The activity controlled in this way may be defined by reference to a particular act or a particular process, for example, under Part I of EPA 1990. This creates two parallel systems of pollution control, first, over processes prescribed for control at central level, that is, the system of IPC enforced through HMIP, and, secondly, those prescribed for control at local level through local authorities known as LAAPC.

Once a potentially polluting development has commenced operation, the community has lost the battle. This section argues, therefore, for a preventive approach to pollution control which focuses on possibilities to intervene in the decision-making process prior to an authorisation to discharge being granted, or, if an authorisation is not required, the decision to grant planning permission with or without conditions or obligations.

An alternative to a preventive approach is, of course, to sue at common law for damages caused by historical pollution if one can establish liability as a toxic tort and, in particular, under the rule in *Rylands* v *Fletcher*.[35] In that respect the recent House of Lords' judgment in *Cambridge Water Company* v

---

[34]See the discussion *infra* accompanying n 69 on *Gateshead Metropolitan BC* v *Secretary of State for the Environment*.
[35][1861–73] All ER Rep 1.

Eastern Counties Leather plc[36] is unhelpful, establishing that reasonable foreseeability is a necessary pre-requisite to any claim for damages in nuisance and *Rylands* v *Fletcher*.

Planning law is of crucial significance to such a preventive approach and there are various opportunities for the community to influence the outcome of whether or not particular types of development are allowed to proceed in the locality. To the extent that activity constitutes "development" requiring planning permission – either as building, engineering or other operations, or as a material change in the use of land[37] – the planning system can be effective. Its effectiveness lies in the ability to take into account as "material considerations" pollution and other environmental impacts, and either to refuse permission for development on such grounds or to impose conditions on the permission so as to reduce adverse effects.

This section is no more than an introduction to a preventive approach to pollution control.[38] It concentrates on establishing the possibilities of feeding information obtained, either from public registers or through the use of the Environmental Information Regulations 1992 into later stages of the planning system including the emerging development plan process, representations on an application for planning permission and on applications for pollution authorisations.

A. **The campaign**

There are many environmental pressure groups. Their expertise, knowledge and commitment should be brought to bear on any local issues. If there is a proposal to site a particular type of development in a locality there will be national groups able to assist with the provision of information, speakers, sources of funding and other local groups elsewhere in Britain who have fought successfully against similar developments. Furthermore, there is a need to ensure that this expertise and knowledge influences the local political scene. For example, a local environmental pressure group can force candidates at local elections to commit themselves on various environmental concerns. Generally, the earlier a campaign group can intervene in the political and planning processes the better.

---

[36][1994] 1 All ER 53.
[37]For the definition of "development" see TCPA 1990, s 55.
[38]For more information see *Encyclopedia of Environmental Law*, Sweet and Maxwell; *Encyclopedia of Planning Law*, Sweet and Maxwell; *Garners Environmental Law*, Butterworths; *Butterworths Planning Law*, Butterworths; Ball S and Bell S, *Environmental Law*, London, Blackstone Press Limited, 2nd ed 1994; *Journal of Planning and Environmental Law*, Sweet and Maxwell.

B. **General sources of information**

Community groups seeking general information about a particular type of development or process may wish to consult general texts, pamphlets, journals and data-bases. A useful guide to sources of environmental information has been published by the British Library.[39] Some academic institutions publish inform-ative surveys and periodical reports.[40] Local authorities motivated on environ-mental matters produce their own general reports, such as the Cheshire District Councils' review of pollution.[41] Reports from government depart-ments are also published periodically and contain general national data.[42]

C. **Use of public registers**

Specific information on particular developments can be obtained from statutory public registers. The general public has the right to consult the registers, which must be kept open for inspection at reasonable hours. Photocopies may be taken of any information found on the registers, subject to a reasonable charge. There are several types of register in existence, and those which will most concern inner-urban or deprived communities relate to planning permissions, water pollution, IPC, LAAPC and other atmospheric emissions (see *Table 1*).

These registers are maintained by HMIP, local authorities, the National Rivers Authority (NRA), privatised water companies and the port health authorities. In addition, local authorities keep on their registers information from the register of HMIP relating to centrally controlled processes in their area, thereby making such information available locally.[43]

The existence of some of these registers is not well-publicised and there is some confusion as to where they may be found, partly because of the numerous and decentralised enforcement agencies involved.[44] Physical access may be difficult because of the geographical situation of the registers, particularly with water registers kept by the NRA. The evidence to date suggests that little use has been made of the registers, particularly by the public,[45] but environmental pressure groups have, at times, made effective use of the registers. The Anglers Co-operative Association based their prosecution of Thames Water Authority for breaching their discharge consent standards on evidence gleaned from the registers.

---

[39]Lees N and Woolston H, *Environmental Information – A Guide to Sources*, British Library, 1992.
[40]*e.g.* the report on an epidemiological study of health and pollution, Hussey RM, Ashton JR and Sainsbury P, *Health in the Mersey Basin*, Department of Public Health, University of Liverpool, March 1991.
[41]Cheshire District Councils, *A Review of Pollution 1986–1990*.
[42]*e.g.* Department of Environment, *Digest of Environmental Protection and Water Statistics*, No 15, DoE, London, HMSO, 1993.
[43]EPA 1990, s 22.
[44]Ball and Bell *op cit* (n 38) at 123–127.
[45]Burton T, "Access to Environmental Information – the UK Experience of Water Registers" (1989) 1 JEL 192.

*Table 1 – Public registers containing information
relevant to pollution control*

Type of Register	Statutory Provision	Authority
Planning	Section 69 Town and Country Planning Act 1990 (applications and decisions) Section 188 Town and Country Planning Act 1990 (enforcement and stop notices) Articles 7, 27 and 28 Town and Country Planning General Development Order 1988 (SI 1988/1813) Section 28 Planning (Hazardous Substances) Act 1990	LA
Water pollution	Section 190 Water Resources Act 1991 Control of Pollution (Registers) Regulations 1989	NRA
Local authority air pollution control and integrated pollution control	Section 20 Environmental Protection Act 1990 Environmental Protection (Applications, Appeals and Registers) Regulations 1991	HMIP/LA
Other atmospheric emissions	Health and Safety at Work Act 1974 Health and Safety (Emissions into the Atmosphere) Regulations 1983 Health and Safety (Emissions into the Atmosphere) (Amendments) Regulations 1989 The Alkali Works Etc. Act 1906 Control of Industrial Air Pollution (Registration of Works) Regulations 1989	HMIP/LA

In relation to planning applications, IPC and atmospheric emissions, physical access is relatively easy. Either the original register or, as with IPC, a copy, will be found at the planning and environmental departments of the local authority. Once a register has been located, other important considerations are whether the data contained in it is comprehensible, what help is available from the staff and what facilities are provided for public inspections.[46]

The type of information found on the registers includes applications for IPC and LAAPC authorisations, water discharge consents and planning permissions, together with the authorising documents themselves once they are passed by the relevant regulatory body. An application to obtain, for example, an IPC authorisation should give a full description of the process, techniques to be used, volume and composition of emissions and how sampling and analysis is to be carried out. Section 20(1) of EPA 1990 provides that it is the duty of each enforcing authority to maintain a register containing particulars of, amongst other things, the following:

– applications for authorisations made to that authority;
– authorisations which have been granted by that authority or in respect of which the authority has functions;
– variation notices, enforcement notices and prohibition notices issued by that authority;
– convictions for offences under section 23(1) of EPA 1990 as may be prescribed;
– information obtained or furnished in pursuance of the conditions of authorisations.

Some new projects will require an environmental assessment (see below). An environmental statement must be lodged with the planning application and a reasonable number of copies must be kept for public use.

D. **The Environmental Information Regulations 1992**

The Environmental Information Regulations 1992[47] establish a positive right for any persons seeking environmental information to obtain it from any public bodies, subject to certain exceptions. The Regulations implement EC Directive 90/313/EEC on the Freedom of Access to Information on the Environment which came into force on 31 December 1992. They also apply to prior information held on statutory registers and may go back several years. The objective is to impose a duty on all public bodies who process

---

[46]Association of Public Injury Lawyers (APIL), *An Investigation into the Facilities for Public Access to Environmental Registers*, APIL, 1992.
[47]SI 1992/3240.

environmental information to make it available on request to anyone, without the need to prove an interest. The information should be provided as soon as possible, but, in any event, within two months. Any refusal must be in writing and accompanied by reasons. The type of information targeted relates to air, water, flora, fauna, soil and natural sites or other land, activities adversely affecting or likely to affect them, and measures designed to protect them.

There are some obvious criticisms of the Regulations. These include, first, that central government has left it to individual bodies holding the information to make their own arrangements for access instead of imposing a uniform arrangement; secondly, the Regulations deal only with availability of information – not with its publication; thirdly, the body providing the information can make a reasonable charge for supplying it – unlike access to the information held on public registers; fourthly, it is not clear which organisations are subject to the duty;[48] fifthly, there is a possible exception to the duty if the request is worded too broadly or vaguely or where it is "manifestly unreasonable"; and, finally, a number of important exemptions to the duty to release information are made in regulation 4.[49]

The Regulations have not yet been tested and, to date, they appear to have had little impact. They are drafted in such a way as to leave much room for discretion, particularly in relation to the exceptions in regulation 4. The "legal proceedings" exception is, potentially, very damaging to the essential aim of the Regulations and it is difficult to see why such information should not be disclosed, particularly when the body concerned is not a prospective party to proceedings.[50]

E. **The Local Government Act 1972**

Section 1 of the Local Government (Access to Information) Act 1985 inserts a new Part VA (sections 100A–100K) in the Local Government Act 1972. Part VA provides for much greater public access to the machinery of local government. Normally, the meetings of committees and sub-committees should be open to the public, and copies of the agenda and any reports for a meeting must be open to public inspection at least three clear days before the meeting.[51] After a meeting, certain documents must be open to public inspection for six years.[52] Certain information is exempt and the public may be excluded from that part of the meeting whenever it is likely that "exempt information" would

---

[48]Department of Environment, *Guidance on the Implementation of the Environmental Information Regulations 1992 in Great Britain*, DoE, 1992; and *The Government's Proposals for the Implementation in the UK of the EC Directive on the Freedom of Access to Information on the Environment*, June 1992.
[49]See text preceding n 24 and Murdie *op cit* at 28–36.
[50]Birtles W, "A Right to Know: The Environmental Information Regulations 1992" (1993) *Journal of Planning and Environment Law* at 615–626.
[51]*R v Swansea City Council, ex p Elitestone* (1993) *The Times*, 13 May.
[52]Local Government Act 1972, s 100C.

otherwise be disclosed to members of the public.[53] However, in that case there must be available a summary which provides a reasonably fair and coherent record of proceedings without disclosing exempt information. Background papers must also be available for inspection.[54] Community groups concerned with environmental issues should concentrate on the proceedings of the planning and the environmental protection committees and sub-committees.

F. Other useful information

Other useful information includes convictions and enforcement actions against a particular company and taken generally by an enforcement agency.

The authority to seek an application for such information is regulation 15 of the Environmental Protection (Applications, Appeals and Registers) Regulations 1991.[55] These Regulations will enable information to be obtained about processes subject to Part I of EPA 1990.[56]

It should be possible for a member of the public to find out what action their local authority has taken in any one year against polluting industries by examining this register or, alternatively, by making a specific request for that information under the Environmental Information Regulations 1992.

A community group may wish to obtain general information about air and water quality in the local environment. The critical loads approach recognises that a particular environment can sustain only a limited amount of pollution and this approach, referred to in *This Common Inheritance*[57] has led to the production of maps and monitoring data to show the sensitivities of different parts of Britain to various pollutants.[58] This information should assist a community in its representations to the LPA on planning matters and also to HMIP over authorisations.

---

[53]Local Government Act 1972, s 100A(1)–(5) and Sched 12A.
[54]Local Government Act 1972, s 100D; the Council for the Protection of Rural England (CPRE) found that 25% of authorities were in breach of this provision by failing to list the background papers which support reports made by officers to Council Committees (*Public Access to Planning Documents*, CPRE, January 1994).
[55]SI 1991/507.
[56]See also *Environmental Protection (Prescribed Processes and Prescribed Substances) Regulations* (SI 1991/422). A register in accordance with reg 15 will contain details of, amongst other things, all particulars of any variation notice, enforcement notice or prohibition notice issued by the authority (either HMIP or local authority), all particulars of any revocation of an authorisation effected by the authority, and details of any conviction of any person or any offence under s 23(1) of EPA 1990.
[57]UK Government, *This Common Inheritance: Britain's Environmental Strategy*, Cmnd 1200, London, HMSO, 1990.
[58]Quality of Urban Air Review Group, *Urban Air Quality in the United Kingdom, First Report*, January 1993; Quality of Urban Air Review Group, *Diesel Vehicle Emissions and Urban Air Quality, Second Report*, December 1993; Critical Load Advisory Group, *Critical Loads of Acidity in the United Kingdom*, Summary Report, February 1994.

G. **Representations on development plan**

A community group suitably armed with all available information about the local environment, specific polluting industries and particular local companies will need to ensure that the development plan makes it clear that an LPA intends to protect the environment as appropriate. Most areas will have a development plan that has not yet been adopted and there are clear opportunities for public participation and representation.

Development plans outline the main considerations on which planning applications by developers will be decided by the LPA. There have been a number of important changes recently to the development plan system. What must be understood at the outset is the crucial significance of the development plan following the insertion of section 54A into TCPA 1990.[59] Section 54A provides:

"Where, in making determination under the planning Acts regard is to be had to the development plan, the determination shall be made in accordance with the plan unless material considerations indicate otherwise."

Thus, there is a presumption in favour of development that accords with the plan and a presumption against development that does not. An applicant proposing a potentially polluting development which is in conflict with the development plan would need to produce convincing reasons, on planning matters, to demonstrate why the plan should not prevail.[60]

This chapter cannot examine in detail how communities can influence an emerging development plan, make representations at a public local inquiry (PLI) or, after adoption of the plan, make representations for it to be altered or modified.[61] However, in terms of a preventive approach to environmental law, ensuring that the development plan provides for a lawful but effective policy towards maintaining a clean environment is the single most effective step which a community group can take.

It is not lawful for an LPA to state that it will never consider that certain types of development are an appropriate land-use,[62] but it is allowable to make clear that the LPA would not, in normal circumstances, consider them to be so.[63]

By way of a practical example, in Wirral there was an application by a developer to build a new municipal waste incinerator on a particular site. The draft unitary development plan (UDP) for consultation made specific reference to that site as being appropriate for such a development, and made no references to policies against incineration of waste. The draft UDP was a

[59]Planning and Compensation Act 1991, s 26, brought into force on 25 September 1991 by SI 1991/2067.
[60]*PPG1 supra* n 10 at para 25.
[61]Murdie *op cit* n 16 at Chapter 27; *Butterworths Planning Law Service*, Butterworths at C433–488 and Shiner P "Affordable Housing and Development Plans" *Legal Action*, May 1993 at 11–14.
[62]*Stringer* v *Minister of Housing and Local Government* [1971] All ER 65.
[63]*R* v *Exeter City Council ex p Thomas & Co* [1991] 1 QB 471.

"material consideration" for the purposes of section 70(2) of TCPA 1990, which meant that if the reference remained and the LPA refused planning permission the developers were likely to succeed on appeal. The community made effective representations so that not only was the particular reference to the site being suitable for an incinerator removed, but also a stronger policy in favour of recycling and a reasoned justification expressing serious doubts about the technology involved in incineration were inserted in the draft to go on deposit.[64] The various community groups have helped to ensure that the district of Wirral should remain incinerator-free for at least the lifetime of the UDP.

1. *Development plans and environmental considerations*

An LPA should include in the plan's written justification the attention it has paid to environmental considerations in formulating its Part 1 (in the case of a unitary development plan) or structure plan policies.[65]

Furthermore, in formulating the policies in Part 1 or the structure plan the LPA must pay attention to, amongst other things, any planning policy guidance (PPGs) and current national policies.[66] Current national policies include all the PPGs and circulars listed in PPG12.[67]

Section 6 of PPG12 provides detailed guidance to LPAs on development plans and the environment including with regard to the matters listed below.

–   An LPA should base the draft plan on the outcome of an environmental appraisal. The outcome of that appraisal should be set out in the explanatory memorandum or reasoned justification for the policies proposed (para 6.2).
–   The government states that "environmental concerns weigh increasingly in the balance of planning considerations. Increased scientific understanding and better estimating are showing us that the cost to the community of many forms of pollution are more substantial that we had been accustomed to think" (para 6.7). Thus, if an LPA collects scientific and other evidence that certain types of development are likely to have unjustified costs to the community, and these policies are written into Part 1 (or the structure plan), with a reasoned justification, a great deal of weight should be attached to them. There would be two "material considerations" to take into account, namely, PPG12 and the policies in the development plan.

---

[64]The appeal to a public local inquiry was withdrawn by the developers at a late stage and costs were awarded against them.
[65]Town and Country Planning (Development Plan) Regulations 1991 (SI 1991/2794), reg 9(1).
[66]TCPA 1990, s 12(6).
[67]Department of Environment, *PPG12, Development Plans and Planning Guidance*, annex F , DoE, February 1992, as updated.

– "Plans may also include policies designed to control pollution and to limit and reduce nuisances such as noise, smells and dirt" (para 6.18).
– Part 1 (or structure plans) should reflect national policies clearly set out in *This Common Inheritance* (para 6.24). This enables LPAs to reference some wide-ranging and radical policies, for example that the government believes in a critical loads approach to pollution and is committed to supplying the monitoring data.

It is clear that an LPA must have a clear, relevant and up-to-date plan which is consistent with national and regional policies. Such a plan will be given considerable weight.[68]

H. Representations on applications for planning permission

The relationship between planning control and the specific environmental controls under EPA 1990 is difficult and there is clear overlap between the two. In *Gateshead Metropolitan BC* v *Secretary of State for the Environment*,[69] the High Court accepted that there was no doubt that the environmental impact of atmospheric emissions was a material consideration in determining a planning application for a clinical waste incinerator. So, too, was the existence of the controls under EPA 1990. It was not helpful to try to define where one ended and the other began in terms of abstract principles. The court stressed that it would be wrong for applicants for planning permission to ignore the pollution implications of their proposed development, and that there might be cases where there was positive evidence of a serious risk of harm, where it would be right to refuse planning permission.[70] In a ministerial appeal the minister indicated that planning controls could be used to supplement standards under air pollution controls in that the former provided long-term protection which could be reasonably easily enforced.[71]

Members of the public may wish to make representations against the application itself in an effort to ensure that permission is refused, or, assuming that permission is to be granted, about the conditions which should be attached[72] or the obligations which should be entered into to restrict or regulate the use of land.[73]

---

[68]*PPG1 supra* at paras 25–34.
[69][1993] 225 ENDS Report 44; [1994] JPL 255.
[70]See also *Esdell Caravan Parks* v *Hemel Hemstead RDC* [1966] 1 QB 895.
[71]*Ferro Alloys and Metals Smelter, Glossop* [1990] 1 LMELR 175. *Cf.* Department of Environment draft Planning Policy Guidance note on planning and pollution control, *supra* n 30 which states that it is not the job of the planning system to duplicate controls which are the statutory responsibility of other bodies and that LPAs should not substitute their own judgment on planning control issues for those of bodies with the relevant expertise and responsibility for statutory control over such matters.
[72]TCPA 1990, s 72.
[73]TCPA 1990, s 106.

1. *Material considerations*

Apart from the requirements of section 54A of TCPA 1990, in dealing with planning applications LPAs must "have regard to . . . any other material consideration" (s 70(2)). Thus, apart from the policies in the development plan, which carry the presumption of section 54A, statements of national and planning policy will also be material whether or not referenced in the plan. The material or relevant considerations will include consultations with affected bodies and the representations received in respect of planning applications publicised.[74] The Court of Appeal has ruled recently on the question of "material considerations" in the *Plymouth* case.[75]

Community groups and members of the public have no right to object to an application for planning permission, nor is the LPA obliged to consult the public.[76] However, the LPA has a discretion to consult with bodies and individuals likely to be affected by a proposed development. Views received are then relevant considerations. The LPA would be wise to consult with community groups representing those people likely to be affected by a proposal. Furthermore, the courts will intervene if the LPA does not act fairly on the issue of consultation. The courts require authorities to conduct their planning functions fairly and not mislead objectors to proposed developments by conduct or representation. What is "fair" is a question of fact in each case. A judge might well find a "breach of fairness" where the LPA knows that a leading objector would wish to press a case to any appeal and it fails to inform of the appeal.[77] The notion of "legitimate expectation" is helpful and assurances that consultation would take place before development was permitted will give rise to a legitimate expectation on the part of the would-be consultee and give it *locus standi* to make a challenge.[78]

It is arguable that an LPA will be acting fairly if it decides to exercise its discretion to consult the community in respect of certain types of development, for example all those requiring an environmental assessment (EA) or major urban and housing developments. It might give an assurance to community groups that it will consult, thus giving rise to a legitimate expectation. The result of that consultation will be a material consideration.[79] The community may assist the LPA to substantiate a refusal on "valid planning

---

[74]See *Encyclopedia of Planning Law and Practice*, Sweet and Maxwell at 2-3275-3278 for a discussion of the case law.

[75] *R* v *Plymouth City Council, J Sainsbury plc and others ex p Plymouth & South Devon Co-operative Society* [1993] JPL B81. Shiner P, "Planning Obligations and the Community," Faculty of the Built Environment Research Paper series No 12, University of Central England in Birmingham, 1994.

[76]*R* v *Sheffield City Council ex p Mansfield* (1978) 37 P & CR 1.

[77]*R* v *Torfaen Borough Council ex p Jones* [1986] JPL 686; *Wilson* v *Secretary of State* [1988] JPL 540.

[78]*R* v *Swale Borough Council ex p RSPB* [1991] JPL 39.

[79]For guidance on the extent of the duty to consult see *R* v *Secretary of State for Social Services ex p Association of Metropolitan Authorities* [1986] 1 WLR 1.

reasons".[80] This is likely if those reasons reflect the views, concerns and evidence that formed the environmental appraisal upon which the development plan is based, and if the plan references clearly the relevant planning and national policies.

There may be a variety of matters which community groups may wish to see made the subject of planning conditions or obligations. If the LPA considers that a particular matter should be a condition precedent to the granting of permission, this may be covered by a "Grampian" that is, negative, condition.[81] Otherwise, it may be appropriate to restrict or regulate development by means of a planning condition or obligation.[82]

If the community does wish to make representations on the application, any information obtained about the likely effects of this type of development, or the track record of similar developments elsewhere or even of this particular developer will be helpful. Notwithstanding the discretion to consult it is advisable that the community make its intervention early and decisively, particularly as negotiation with developers on conditions or obligations takes place outside the public forum of development control.

2. *Environmental assessments*

The Town and Country Planning (Assessment of Environmental Effects) Regulations 1988,[83] implement, in part, the EC Directive on the assessment of certain public and private projects on the environment (Dir 85/337/EEC).[84] Certain major projects, as defined in Schedules 1 and 2, are subject to a process in which the likely environmental effects must be considered before permission is granted for them. Schedule 1 defines major projects where an EA is mandatory and Schedule 2 defines relevant planning projects where an EA is required if the project will leave "significant effects on the environment by virtue of factors such as its nature, size of location" (reg 2). Thus, environmental factors are considered as an integral part of the decision-making process. The developer must submit an environmental statement to the "competent authority", which should identify the potential environmental effects and the steps that are envisaged to avoid, reduce or remedy these effects. This environmental statement will include a non-technical summary.

---

[80]*PPG1 supra* (n 10) at para 42 states: " . . . local opposition to a proposal is not in itself ground for refusing planning permission, unless that opposition is founded upon valid planning reasons which can be substantiated".

[81]In *Grampian Regional Council* v *City of Aberdeen* [1984] JPL 590 the House of Lords decided that a planning condition would not be invalid merely because it prevented development proceeding, unless and until an event had occurred which prevented the applicant from satisfying the condition.

[82]For more on planning conditions and obligations, see *Butterworths Planning Law Service*, Butterworths at 2-3293-3306 and 2-3416-3429, and Shiner P, "Planning Obligations and the Community" *op cit* (n 75).

[83](SI 1988/1199), as amended by SI 1990/367 and SI 1992/1494.

[84]See also Department of Environment, *Circular 15/88, Town and Country Planning (Assessment of Environmental Effects) Regulations*.

The authority must then consult with various public bodies, and give the public an opportunity to express an opinion. The developer's environmental statement must be made publicly available and copies must be sent to the consultees. The competent authority must prepare an EA of the proposal before deciding whether it may go ahead. This should take into account the views of the public and consultees. It should be noted that although an LPA is not required to consult the public it must, in all matters, act fairly.[85] There are opportunities for the community to influence this process as shown in the "*Good Practice*" *checklist* (Table 2, below).

I. **Representations on applications for pollution authorisations**

Pollution control involves a system of authorisations, consents and licences to discharge from certain processes into the environment. The most important are authorisations required to carry on a "prescribed process" after 1 April 1992. Processes falling within Part A of Schedule I to the Environmental Protection (Prescribed Processes and Substances) Regulations 1991[86] are matters for IPC and are enforced by HMIP. Those in Part B are the responsibility of the LAAPC. It is an offence to carry out Schedule I processes without an authorisation.[87] Industry is expected to use "best available techniques not entailing excessive costs" (BATNEEC) to keep up with technological improvements. There are procedures for the variation of authorisations by the enforcing authority,[88] or on application by the holder of the authorisation.[89] The National Rivers Authority is responsible for granting consents under the Control of Pollution Act 1974 and the Water Resources Act 1991 (Schedule 10) to allow discharges of polluting substances into "controlled waters". With these, and other authorisations and consents, there is an opportunity for the public to participate in the process. Members of the public wishing to make representations on applications may wish to draw on information gleaned from public registers and by use of the Environmental Information Regulations 1992.[90]

---

[85] *R* v *Great Yarmouth Borough Council ex p Botton Bros Arcades Limited* [1988] JPL 18.

[86] SI 1991/422.

[87] EPA 1990, ss 6(1) and 23(1).

[88] EPA 1990, s 10.

[89] EPA 1990, s 11.

[90] SI 1992/3240. See also the Environmental Protection (Applications, Appeals and Registers) Regulations 1991 (SI 1991/507). [Ed note] Prior to the establishment of the NRA in 1989, regional water authorities publicised only about 10% of all applications received to discharge. The other 90% were anticipated to have "no appreciable effect" on the receiving waters. DoE Circular 17/84 suggests, amongst various indicators (such as whether there will be a significant effect on environmental amenity), a 10% rule of thumb to determine "appreciable effect" – whether the effect of the discharge would increase all relevant parameters by 10%. "It is objectionable that the operation of such an important procedure rests on a rather restrictive interpretation given in a Department Circular" (Ball and Bell, *op cit* (n 38) at 373). It is hoped that the NRA will adopt a more accountable approach.

J. **Other preventive measures**

There are other measures to prevent a polluting development from commencing its activities. For example, the public may wish to be represented at a public local inquiry following the decision of the LPA to refuse planning permission if the applicant takes the matter to an appeal, and that appeal is subject to an inquiry. In addition, in some cases the threat of a civil action for damages, or a private prosecution under section 82 of EPA 1990 may act as a deterrent to expanding and existing operation, and in that respect could be seen as being a preventive measure.

III. **Conclusion**

Environmental law is currently practiced by lawyers concerned principally with the interests of developers and local authorities. However, community groups and their advisers will be aware of the significance of planning law to their campaigns.

It is important to understand environmental law within the context of urban regeneration and of the planning system, and changes made to that system since 1979. Just as it is essential for lawyers concerned with principles of social justice to understand law in its socio-economic and political context, so is it important to be able to relate the law and practice of environmental and planning law to changing urban policy. This is especially important at the moment as we witness the government virtually abandoning the inner cities in terms of urban funding.[91] The idea of a preventive approach is not new; but it is largely undeveloped. This is for two main reasons. First, lawyers in private practice and also in law centres are concerned mainly with individual rights and with traditional areas of law. Secondly, at present the legal aid system does not enable lawyers to undertake public interest work.

Most environmental lawyers are presently not concerned with the interests of community groups. Without denying the funding problem, it is suggested that they should work more with urban community groups, addressing planning and pollution issues in the preventive ways described in this chapter.

Table 2

Good practice for community groups: pollution control and the planning system

1. Get to know the pieces of land, open space, countryside or potential developments which the community wants to protect or regulate and learn why.
2. Record any particular reasons for protecting an area of land or particular environmental concerns.

---

[91]Nevin B and Shiner P, "Behind the Chimera of Urban Funding" *op cit* (n 7).

250

3. Co-ordinate a district-wide register of areas of land and note which individual/groups have registered an interest or potential objection.
4. Ensure easy access to advisers when needed, for example, the Environmental Law Foundation, law centres and Earth Rights (a new, specialist environmental law and resource centre), the Association of Community Technical Aid Centres, Planning Aid, Friends of the Earth, Greenpeace, Communities Against Toxins and the Environmental Law Alliance Worldwide (E-Law).
5. Research the pollutants affecting the air, water and land in the area already.
6. Obtain any relevant epidemiological surveys and general information and data from health authorities.
7. Obtain a copy of the draft or adopted development plan and check the general policies on environmental issues, and the specific allocation of sites for particular land-uses.
8. Ensure that the LPA's general policies on environmental issues are adequate and make any representations as necessary.
9. Access in the LPA's library (or that of pressure groups such as the Council for the Protection of Rural England) any other LPA development plans to obtain examples of best practice on various policies.
10. Ensure that the LPA has included in its environmental appraisal (forming the basis of Part 1 of the UDP or structure plan) the environmental concerns of the community.
11. Ensure that the LPA has collected scientific and other evidence which indicates whether or not certain types of developments have unacceptable environmental costs.
12. If the development plan is inadequate on environmental issues and policies in respect of specific sites, consider making representations to amend it.
13. Influence the drawing up at an early stage of a site specific development brief to ensure that matters which should be regulated are subject to conditions or an obligation.
14. Obtain from LPA assurances that the community will be consulted in respect of applications for planning permission for certain projects and on all those requiring an environmental assessment, so that the community has a legitimate expectation of consultation.
15. Ensure that the LPA has clear public policies on procedures when the development proposed is its own and, in particular, that it is not enabled in potentially polluting developments to obtain permission unchallenged through the outline planning permission mechanism, and that there are procedures on EA.[92]
16. Arrange for regular and systematic scans of newspaper advertisements for planning applications, and ensure that the community is ready to make representations in writing as required following advertisement by the applicant in a local newspaper.[93]
17. Ensure that the LPA makes a decision where relevant as to whether an EA is necessary.[94]
18. Be prepared to show how the community will be prejudiced by any failure to carry out an EA.[95]
19. Inspect the register for any opinion, direction of Secretary of State, notification and other documents regarding the need or otherwise for an EA.[96]
20. If necessary, make representations to the LPA, prior to its decision as to whether an EA is required, as to why projects will have "significant effects". The community should address the question of whether as a matter of "fact and degree" it is so likely.[97]
21. Give evidence to the LPA as to likely effects of the project for the purpose of having the community's concerns and views reflected in the LPA's own environmental assessment of the proposal.
22. Make representations to the LPA, if appropriate, as to whether the developer is to be asked to provide further information after submission of an environmental statement.[98]
23. Obtain a copy of the LPA's Code of Practice on publicity for planning applications. (If one does not exist, suggest that it be prepared.)

[92]DoE Circular 15/88 (n 84 *supra*) at paras 45–48.
[93]Town and Country Planning (Assessment of Environmental Effects) Regulations 1988 (SI 1988/1199) reg 13.
[94]*R v Poole Borough Council ex p Beebee* [1991] 3 LMELR 60.
[95]*Twyford DC v Secretary of State* [1991] 3 LMELR 89.
[96]Town and Country Planning (Assessment of Environmental Effects) Regulations 1988, regs 5(5) and (7).
[97]*R v Swale BC ex p RSPB* [1991] JPL 39 and Circular 15/88 (n 84 *supra*) at paras 18–21.
[98]Town and Country Planning (Assessment of Environmental Effects) Regulations 1988, reg 21.

Public Interest Perspectives in Environmental Law

24. Ask to be added to the LPA mailing list for planning applications in respect of certain developments or in certain areas.
25. Make representations, as appropriate, either against the planning application itself, or on questions of which matters should be restricted or regulated through planning conditions or planning obligations.
26. Consider making representations that ongoing observance of controls set by the pollution agency should also be a condition for planning authorisation.
27. Ensure that all residents in the immediate locality or likely to be affected by the development are made aware of potential objections.
28. Ensure that a system exists for entering representations within statutory time-limits.
29. Ensure that elected representatives apply pressure on the LPA's officers so that the community's views, both on the application itself and on the need for conditions or planning obligations, are taken into account.
30. Ensure that community groups are aware of (and attend and make representation if necessary) the relevant planning and environmental protection committee meetings.
31. Ensure that the planning committee does not use provisions of Schedule 12A to the Local Government Act 1972 on exempt information without good cause and that meetings are in public.
32. Ensure that the text of any conditions or obligations meets with the needs of the community, and that a copy of relevant committee minutes, officers' reports, planning obligation, etc are made available.

Section III
Environmental Courts?

Contents of Chapter 14

A Specialist Environmental Court: An Australian Experience

Chapter 14

A Specialist Environmental Court: An Australian Experience

Paul Stein

I. **Background**

In many ways Australia's relative geographic isolation has made it the lucky continent in environmental terms. Unlike Europe and North America, we have not witnessed the destruction of inland waterways, had our forests denuded by acid rain, suffered major environmental disasters (such as Sandoz, Chernobyl, Exxon Valdez) or suffered the devastation of war (as in the Gulf and Eastern Europe).

However, in terms of the effects of global environmental pollution Australia is, perhaps, unlucky, and is a victim of its geographic proximity to the depleted ozone layer over the Antarctic. While it has not experienced the degree of environmental damage which has occurred in parts of the northern hemisphere, serious environmental problems are entrenched. In under 200 years of European settlement, we have managed to severely degrade our soils and pollute our waterways. Indeed, soil erosion and water salinity are major issues. It would not be an exaggeration to say that much of our soil has been permitted to blow away through over-grazing. Intensive coastal development has caused wholesale loss of wetlands and dunes. Our native forests and woodlands, including rainforest, have been reduced dramatically. Many unique flora and fauna are becoming endangered or extinct through habitat loss and the impact of feral and introduced animals. Air pollution and waste disposal problems are myriad.

In New South Wales, Australia's most industrialised and populous state, we face pressing environmental problems. An example from recent times was the extensive sewerage contamination of Sydney's famous beaches as a result of using the South Pacific ocean as a bottomless waste disposal pit! In many ways this was a fortunate incident because it had the effect of raising public

---

'**Justice Paul Stein** AM, Judge, Land and Environment Court, New South Wales, Australia.

awareness of pollution, the need for expenditure on environmental protection measures and stricter pollution legislation. As "beach culture" is virtually part of the Australian psyche, the pollution threatened not only human health but our way of life. Sydney (the state capital) will also have the dubious distinction of being the first city to stage the Olympic Games on a site contaminated by the dumping of toxic wastes.

Australia, and the state of New South Wales in particular, needs to be placed into context and perspective in order to understand the significance of environmental management systems and the role which the Land and Environment Court plays in the enforcement of environmental protection laws.

The Australian continent is some 7.7 million sq km, almost as large as the whole of Europe or the United States. Its population, however, is only 17.5 million, the large majority of whom live in the south-eastern corner, especially along the coast. New South Wales has a population of around 6 million and in this respect is comparable with Scotland, Switzerland or Denmark. However, a land area of 800,000 sq km makes it as large as Germany and France combined. Like much of the continent, a large percentage of the state is arid or semi-arid, although the eastern third experiences a moderate "Mediterranean" climate. Nonetheless, floods, bush fires and droughts are not infrequent occurrences.

II. **The establishment of the Land and Environment Court**

The innovative nature of the Land and Environment Court was stressed by the then Minister for Planning and Environment, the late Paul Landa, in his second reading speech in November 1979. In introducing a series of cognate Bills to completely reform the environmental planning system, which included the Land and Environment Court Act 1979 (LECA 1979), he said:

GOOD QUOTE

" . . . the proposed new court is a somewhat innovative experiment in dispute resolution mechanisms. It attempts to combine judicial and administrative dispute-resolving techniques and it will utilize non-legal experts as technical and conciliation assessors . . . The court is an entirely innovative concept, bringing together in one body the best attributes of a traditional court system and of a lay tribunal system. The court, in consequence, will be able to function with the benefits of procedural reform and lack of legal technicalities as the requirements of justice permit in accordance with clause 38. The court will establish its own body of precedents on major planning issues, precedents sorely sought by [local government] councils and the development industry but totally lacking in the now to be abolished local government appeals tribunal. The decision of the court in its civil jurisdiction is final, except for appeals to the Court of Appeal on questions of law . . ."

III. **Public participation**

One emphatic theme ran through the comprehensive package of legislation – the right of the general public to participate in the process of environmental planning. This is a specific objective under section 5 of the Environmental Planning and Assessment Act 1979 (EPAA 1979). The objective is strengthened by other provisions relating to environmental plan-making, third-party appeals and open-standing provisions to enforce compliance with environmental and planning laws. The legislation was an effort to progress from narrow, traditional town and country planning, largely based on the UK experience, to a wider concept of integrated assessment of environmental planning issues. It was also a recognition and acknowledgment of the importance of the environment and the developing area of environmental law, as well as the right of the general public to participate in the system.

The establishment of the Land and Environment Court, in 1980, was a crucial ingredient in the initiative. It was created as an integrated superior court of record of equal status to the State Supreme Court, with exclusive jurisdiction to determine disputes arising under more than 20 separate environmental laws. These statutes make provision for the protection of the environment and include, *inter alia*, planning, waste management, hazardous chemicals, coastal protection, ozone protection, heritage conservation, national parks and wildlife protection, marine pollution, biological control of organisms, air, water and noise pollution.

Under the LECA 1979 various fragmented jurisdictions were consolidated. Jurisdiction was no longer to be split between numerous different courts, boards, tribunals and authorities or simply lacking. Rather, the court was given a very broad jurisdiction to hear all civil and criminal (summary) enforcement matters, judicial review and merit appeals relating to land and environment matters.

For the first time, in the environmental context, non-judicial members were included alongside judges. The Court Act also contained significant procedural innovations in an attempt to make it more accessible and effective. A unique experiment had begun!

IV. **Jurisdiction of the court**

The wide-ranging jurisdiction is exercised by judges and technical assessors.[1] The latter are not required to have legal qualifications (although some do) but must be qualified in fields such as planning, local government, land valuation, engineering, architecture, environmental sciences, natural resources and

---

[1]Presently there are five judges, nine assessors, two registrars and a number of part-time Aboriginal assessors.

Aboriginal land rights. The work of the court is divided into five areas or classes.

Classes 1 and 2 include environmental planning and protection appeals and local government appeals. These comprise, *inter alia*, development and building appeals as well as appeals concerning pollution control licences and heritage determinations. The majority of these matters are heard by assessors unless questions of law are involved. Such questions, which must be identified shortly after an application is filed, are promptly referred to judges for determination. If an appeal is unusually complex or controversial, a judge will preside, often assisted by the advice of an appropriately qualified assessor.

Class 3 appeals concern land tenure, rating, valuation and compensation for compulsory land acquisition by governments – local and state. Again, assessors hear the majority of these matters, except the latter category. Aboriginal land rights appeals are also heard in this class, normally by a judge assisted by two Aboriginal assessors. Internal appeals are available from any error of law by technical assessors.

Class 4 includes civil enforcement of environmental laws and judicial review. Injunctions (restraining and mandatory) and declarations of right are among the remedies available. Judicial review of environmental decisions is an integral part of the court's jurisdiction. Open-standing provisions make this a reality for the general public who do not have to jump over the *locus standi* hurdle to gain access to the court.

Finally, there is the summary criminal jurisdiction of the court which covers all pollution and planning laws. Depending upon the offence, penalties may range up to $1,000,000 for corporations and $250,000 or a maximum seven years' imprisonment for individuals. The criminal jurisdiction (as well as Class 4) are the exclusive province of judges of the court.[2]

Recent amendments have created a new class of appellate jurisdiction – class 6 – which was proclaimed to commence on 4 July 1994. This redirects all appeals from prosecutions for minor environmental offences in the local (or magistrates) court from the District Court to the Land and Environment Court.

The court is a very public court – mainly because it deals with public law and issues which touch on the everyday concerns of those living in the state. The court has always strived to be accessible, is mandated to operate with as little formality and technicality as possible and is not bound by the rules of evidence in merit appeals.[3] In this regard it has abolished archaic wigs and robes and introduced procedural innovations in an endeavour to demystify the law and provide efficient resolution of disputes. In addition to the final determination of matters by judges and assessors, dispute resolution options of mediation

---

[2]However, the Land and Environment Court cannot determine criminal matters where a term of imprisonment of greater than two years is sought. Only the Supreme Court, on trial by indictment, may impose a sentence between two and seven years. It may be noted that no such proceedings have been brought.
[3]LECA 1979, s 38(1), (2).

and conciliation are also available to litigants, the former from May 1991 and the latter since the court's inception in 1980. Indeed, the Land and Environment Court was the first court to offer the option of conciliation conferences.

V. **Features of the court's operations**

The flexible structure of the Land and Environment Court has enabled the moulding of procedures to fit the public law nature of most environmental disputes, thereby facilitating public participation. To this end, the court has instituted a number of procedural initiatives. Some of the principal features and innovations of the court are listed below. *begin again (from the beginning)*

– Most appeals are heard *de novo* with the court having all the functions and discretions of the body or person appealed against. Its decision is final. As noted previously, the court is charged not only with acting with as little formality and as much expedition as is consistent with the proper consideration of matters, but is not bound by the rules of evidence in such appeals. It may also inform itself as it thinks appropriate and obtain the assistance of any person with relevant qualifications.[4] This power has been used on a relatively small number of occasions, although lack of a relevant budget item has curtailed any widespread utilisation.

– In determining appeals the court is directed to have regard to the public interest.[5]

– The court has no formal pleadings but will have issues (of fact and law) identified shortly after the application is lodged. In judicial review proceedings brief points of claim and defence will usually be required.

– The court maintains a tight control over its processes and procedures. This is necessary to meet the pressures of modern-day litigation and the need for efficient case management. Additionally, this control is required because the public interest is not always represented by the parties before the court.

– Careful case-flow management means that delays are contained and hearings are expedited for good cause. If a major controversy enters the court it is "fast-tracked" to a final hearing in a very short time – weeks not months. This keeps the lawyers and scientists on their toes but is necessary in the general public interest. Indeed, the court has the enviable reputation of being a delay-free court.

– The court has developed policies on legal costs, which, under the LECA 1979, are a matter of discretion. In administrative or merit appeals no

---

[4]LECA 1979, s 38(2), (3).
[5]LECA 1979, s 39(4).

costs will be ordered, except in exceptional circumstances. In civil enforcement and judicial review, costs will normally follow the event of the litigation. However, a number of cases have held that if the unsuccessful party can properly be characterised as representing the "public interest", it may be appropriate not to make an order for costs.[6]

While the court has developed criteria to determine what may be characterised as "public interest" litigation, the concept still involves an element of value judgment. It is not surprising, therefore, that judicial minds may vary in appellation of a particular piece of litigation. However, the concept has recently received recognition by the President of the Court of Appeal in *Maritime Services Board* v *Citizens Airport Environment Association Inc.*[7] While this case concerned an application for security for costs of an appeal from a public interest group and was guided by the Supreme Court Rules which only allow for such an order in "special circumstances", Kirby P made the following observation:

> "I do not believe that it is appropriate to consider this case as just another suit between ordinary litigants disputing claims of private interest only to themselves. When considering whether 'special circumstances' have been made out, and whether an order for security for the costs of the appeal should be made, it is appropriate to keep in mind the nature of the case and the public interest reasons which may lie behind the bringing of it."

– In applications for security for costs, impecuniosity is only a factor to be considered and not necessarily determinative. Regard has also been had to the public interest nature of cases, with the result that few applications for security have been successful.[8] This is a course which has also been applied by the New South Wales Court of Appeal in *Brown* v *Environmental Protection Authority*[9] and the aforementioned *Citizens Airport Environment Association* case. In *Brown*, the case was brought by a member of the public to test the lawfulness of a decision by the state Environmental Protection Authority (EPA), pursuant to a particular policy, to grant licences under the Pollution Control Act 1970 to a pulp

---

[6]For a full discussion of case law regarding costs in public interest litigation, see McElwain C, "The New Cost of Public Interest Litigation in New South Wales" (1993) 29 *Impact* 2-5 and Craig M, "Developments in Planning and Environmental Law and Practice" (1993) 34 *Environmental Law News*, 5-9.

[7](1994) 83 LGERA 107.

[8]See Kelly J, "Security for Costs and Public Interest Litigation" (1993) 34 *Environmental Law News* 13-18. For a discussion of security for costs and a general examination of other features and innovations of the court, see Cripps JS (former Chief Judge of the Court), "Chapter 2 – Administrative Law" in Bonyhady T, (ed), *Environmental Protection and Legal Change* Federation Press, Sydney, 1992 at 24–40 and Preston BJ, "Judicial Review in Australian Environmental Cases" (1992) 1:2 *Asia Pacific Law Review* 55-74.

[9](1993) unreported, NSW Court of Appeal, 1 April.

and paper mill on certain conditions. In refusing the application for security, Priestley JA had regard to a number of factors including:

" . . . that the provisions of the Environmental Offences and Penalties Act under which Mr Brown began his proceedings appear, as does related legislation, to be deliberately aimed at giving access to the Land and Environment Court, in matters of the present type, of a wider than ordinary kind . . . Another factor is that Mr Brown has a *right* of appeal to this Court."

– Importantly, undertakings as to damages for interim injunctions to restrain breaches of environmental law are not required as a matter of course. The absence of an undertaking is seen as only one factor to weigh in the balance of convenience. In *Ross v State Rail Authority of New South Wales*[10] the court, in granting an interlocutory injunction in the absence of an undertaking, referred to the open-standing provision (s 123), the wide discretion regarding the granting of relief under the EPAA 1979 (s 124) and to *F Hannan Pty Limited* v *Electricity Commission of New South Wales*[11] in which Street CJ stated that the task of the court was to administer social justice rather than simply justice between the parties.

– The court's discretion to make such orders as it sees fit (including refusing to grant relief) is a very wide one. Hence, relief can be moulded to fit the particular circumstances of a case and the social justice charter of the court.[12]

– Equitable defences such as laches, acquiescence and delay are unlikely to have the same impact in the enforcement of public law in the court as they may where the contest is one of a purely private, commercial nature.

– The court has been liberal in its orders for discovery and inspection of documents, as well as interrogatories, to the extent that most parties are prepared to produce their files and documents for inspection without order or argument. Further, claims of Crown privilege are now infrequent.

– Solicitor advocates, persons representing themselves and the use of *amicus curiae* (a friend of the court) are common. The flexible and relatively informal court process helps make this possible and endeavours to ensure that the court is a cost-effective jurisdiction which facilitates, rather than inhibits, public involvement.

---

[10](1987) 79 LGRA 91.
[11](1985) 66 LGRA 306 at 313.
[12]LECA 1979, ss 20(2) and 23 and s 124 of EPAA 1979.

VI. **Advantages of a specialist court**

There are a number of reasons why the advent of the Land and Environment Court has been an advantage in the environmental arena. The mixed personnel of the court and its specialist nature (and the substantial use of expert witnesses) have been successful in generating the expertise and precedents required to facilitate better, more consistent environmental decision-making. This has had positive flow-on effects to administrative decision-makers, business and industry. Mixed personnel allows for specialist appointments to match the diversity of the jurisdiction, either through the mix of judges and technical assessors or the matching of the expertise of assessors to particular cases. The creation of a specialist court has also elevated public and industry awareness of planning and environmental issues. This has been considerably aided by improved access for parties through open-standing provisions. By contrast, where jurisdiction remains fragmented the impact of environmental law on public consciousness is diminished.

The experience of almost 14 years of the court has demonstrated, in terms of costs, efficiency and justice, the following benefits of having an integrated, wide-ranging jurisdiction (a "one-stop shop"):

–   decreases multiple proceedings arising out of the same environmental dispute;
–   reduces costs and delays and may lead to cheaper project development and prices for consumers;
–   greater convenience, efficiency and effectiveness in development control decisions;
–   a greater degree of certainty in development projects;
–   a single combined jurisdiction is administratively cheaper than multiple separate tribunals;
–   litigation will often be reduced with consequent savings to the community.

VII. **Criticisms**

From time to time there have been criticisms of the court, as well as some misunderstandings. In this context it may be appropriate to use the UKELA Working Party Report (1993) as a basis for addressing some of these considerations.

A. **Appropriateness of an integrated, specialist jurisdiction**

There are a number of arguments made in this regard. First, it has been suggested that one should promote the integration of environmental law within existing systems, rather than create structures which would have the effect of segregating environmental matters. It has also been argued that there is nothing distinctive about environmental law to justify separate or specialist treatment, such as a specialist court. It is said that environmental law is, in fact, environmental issues arising under various existing areas of law, such as administrative, torts, criminal, nuisance and property/land law, and there is no reason why "toxic torts" or "environmental crime", for example, should be treated differently from other torts or crimes.

A number of responses may be made to this. To start with, environmental matters require specialist knowledge and have generated specialisation in various fields, including the law. The "segregation" of environmental law to a specialist court could be detrimental *if* this entailed a marginalisation of environmental considerations. The experience with the Land and Environment Court has been apposite. The creation of an integrated specialist jurisdiction has heightened government, industry and community perception of environmental issues and has facilitated a better integration of environmental considerations in decision-making processes. Concentrating jurisdiction over environmental matters in one court has similarly focused public attention.

While the skills a court brings to bear in judicial review, tortious or criminal matters may appear to be the same whether they are concerned with an environmental issue or any other case, there is still merit in the argument that judges experienced in environmental matters will be better able to understand and synthesise factual issues and expert evidence in the area. As discussed previously, a specialist jurisdiction has also proved to be more efficient and cost-effective, as well as enabling procedural reforms, such as costs in public interest litigation, to develop.

In Australia generally, environmental laws arise mainly under statute. Common law actions, such as nuisance, have generally proved inadequate to serve environmental ends and have been superseded largely by legislative initiatives.[13] Environmental law is now a readily identifiable body of law.

There are still, however, grey areas. For example, toxic torts are comparatively undeveloped in Australia. As far as I am aware no toxic tort suits (as such) have been brought.[13a] The question of whether toxic torts will become the subject of specific legislation or will be incorporated through a widening of existing boundaries of tort law, as in the United States, and whether they will come within the jurisdiction of the Land and Environment Court, lies in the future. However, no doubt similar arguments on the appropriateness of such jurisdiction as those made above can be anticipated.

---

[13]See for example *Bathurst City Council* v *Saban* (1985) 2 NSWLR 704 and *Baulkham Hills Shire Council* v *Domachuk* (1988) 66 LGRA 110.

[13a]See, however, *Alec Finlayson Pty Ltd* v *Armidale City Council & Anor*, Unrep Federal Court, Burchett J, 13 July 1994.

With regard to environmental crimes, a debate has already been taking place in Australia as to whether these are "real crimes" and the appropriate role of criminal law in the protection of the environment.[13b] However, no similar debate has arisen as to the suitability of the Land and Environment Court's criminal jurisdiction over environmental offences. No perception has arisen that prosecutions in the court are "technical infringements" requiring special treatment before a special court and not crimes. I would argue that the perception of environmental harm as a "crime", rather than a matter of relative insignificance, arises from the penalties imposed for such offences and the policies of the prosecuting agencies or, alternatively, the ability of the community to bring prosecutions, rather than the jurisdiction of a court. In New South Wales the penalties imposed are not insubstantial, being the most stringent in the country; the prosecution policy of the EPA has also been strong in recent years and the ability of members of the public (with the leave of the court) to bring prosecutions has recently been granted under legislation.

B. **Criminal enforcement**

It has been suggested that the need to deal with criminal as well as civil enforcement mechanisms has caused problems for the Land and Environment Court in its attempts to deformalise the judicial process. In practice, this has not occurred. The court observes the rules of evidence in this jurisdiction and has not attempted inappropriately to deformalise its procedures. The court is generally dealing with strict liability offences, with a maximum penalty of $125,000 for corporations and $60,000 for individuals, with no option to sentence an offender to a term of imprisonment. These offences are most commonly prosecuted and convictions are easier to secure. The substantial monetary penalties involved ensure that they are taken seriously by industry and the community. However, traditional criminal law doctrines may be inappropriate in the environmental arena with regard to strict liability offences. There may be a need to develop new approaches to such offences, which balance civil protections and the public interest.[14] The court has had to deal with relatively few *mens rea* offences (*i.e.* the "midnight dumper") and to date no prosecutor has sought a sentence of imprisonment. Nevertheless, the court has had no difficulty dealing with criminal prosecutions in accordance with the proper protections of the criminal law.

Having the majority of environmental offences prosecuted in the Land and Environment Court has probably better served the ends of justice by aiding the imposition of comparative and reasonably consistent penalties, since judges are able to build up experience in the area. By contrast, where criminal enforcement of environmental offences occurs in a fragmented jurisdiction

---

[13b]See, *e.g.*, Farrier, "In Search of Real Criminal Law", in Bonyhady (ed), *op cit* (n 8) at 79–124.
[14]See *Environmental Protection Authority* v *Capdate Pty Ltd & Phillips* (1993) 78 LGERA 349.

the public perception of their seriousness is likely to be diminished. Sentencing perceptions may also be affected by reason of the fact that they would form a small percentage of criminal work before a court.

C. Independence and inherent jurisdiction

Various commentators have voiced concern regarding the independence of the court as a result of it being a "creature of statute" and, therefore, vulnerable to the "whims of parliament". They have pointed to a lack of inherent jurisdiction.[14a] However, the court is in the same position as any other court in Australia, as all courts are created by statute – albeit by statutes of longer standing than the LECA 1979. In addition, the judges of the court, and in fact all state judges, were recently granted constitutional protection to ensure judicial independence.[15] *Inter alia*, these provisions ensure that no court can be abolished unless the judges of that court are appointed to a court of equivalent status.

With regard to these concerns a court has substantial advantages over a tribunal. These include judicial independence, which is pertinent in an area where government bodies are often parties to litigation, and a wider-ranging jurisdiction. Importantly, a superior court is able to secure obedience to its orders through contempt procedures, thus enhancing environmental protection.

D. Demarcation disputes *limits or boundary disputes*

While there have been a small number of such disputes, they are still a source of (sometimes strategic) inconvenience to litigants. Recent amendments have vested the court with express ancillary jurisdiction and this has improved the situation.[16] The breadth of this amendment is yet to be thoroughly tested, but it clearly has the potential to overcome most, if not all, demarcation problems. The possibility of cross-vesting legislation, in the event that the recent amendment is inadequate to resolve jurisdictional issues, is also under consideration. *conjer it to two or more bodies.*

E. Apportionment

It has been suggested that there are inefficiencies in the apportionment of hearings between assessors and judges. This has not been proven in fact and

---

[14a]In *Longwon Pty Ltd* v *Warringah Shire Council* (1993) 33 NSWLR 13, the NSW Court of Appeal confirmed that the Land and Environment Court possessed inherent jurisdiction.
[15]These 1992 amendments are to be found in Part 9 of the Constitution Act 1902 (NSW).
[16]LECA 1979, s 16(1A).

the combination of new rules of court introduced in July 1991 and references of questions of law to judges has ensured this. Legal issues before assessors are now rare, as are internal appeals from decisions of assessors on errors of law.[17]

F. **Multi-member boards**

Multi-member boards have been criticised as an inefficient use of resources and it is considered that the numbers sitting on any particular panel should be limited as far as possible. The court recognises that multi-member boards or panels can be inefficient; consequently these are utilised infrequently and only where appropriate to the circumstances of a particular case – for example, in Aboriginal land rights claims or where multiple expertise is required.

G. **"Mareva" injunctions**

"Mareva" injunctions were previously held to be unavailable. However, this has been rectified by amendments to the Environmental Offences and Penalties Act 1989.[18]

H. **Damages**

Lack of power to award damages and the issue of exemplary/aggravated damages is another criticism. My short answer to this is that it is a matter for law reform. Proposals have been made for the provision of civil damages, particularly as a means of moving away from criminal prosecutions, which some commentators consider inappropriate in certain environmental contexts. Civil enforcement is seen as better able to achieve environmental protection.[19] It is, therefore, possible that the court will acquire this jurisdiction in the future. At present the court has only limited power to award damages, although this has been extended recently by changes to local government law.[20]

I. **Appeals from magistrates**

As mentioned previously the court now has jurisdiction to hear appeals from magistrates on pollution charges, in lieu of the District Court. This is an

---

[17]LECA 1979, s 56A.
[18]Part 4 of the Act.
[19]See *Farrell* v *Dayban Pty Ltd* (1990) 69 LGRA 415 at 419.
[20]LECA 1979, s 20(2)(a) gives limited jurisdiction in damages; the court also has power to grant compensation under pollution statutes, *i.e.* for rehabilitation or clean-up costs, and under various provisions of the Local Government Act 1993.

improvement and part of the ongoing process of strengthening and consoli-
dating the court's jurisdiction where such matters have been overlooked in the
original formulation or as new environmental legislation is passed into law. It
has been argued that the court could have a still broader jurisdiction. I would
agree, so long as it extends only to matters properly considered part of
environmental law.

J. Centralised court

It has been suggested that a centralised court prejudices regions. While this
has not been the experience, this may, in part, be due to the geographic and
demographic characteristics of the state. Assessors of the court are regularly
on circuit and judges sit in country courts as often as is necessary and required.

K. Decisions by the court

It is said that there has been a temptation for governments to overrule or
exclude court decisions. Indeed, there was some history of this prior to 1988
which resulted in a public backlash. It may, however, be pointed out that most
legislative aberrations have followed rulings in the Court of Appeal, rather
than the Land and Environment Court. In fact, Parliament has acted rarely over
the past five years to seek to oust the court's jurisdiction or reverse a decision.
Political manoeuvrings can be expected to arise from time to time and have the
benefit of taking place in the public arena, where a final resolution is often
influenced by public lobbying.[21] However, the recent case of *Brown* v *EPA*[22] is
to be noted. Legislative amendments were made following the decision in the
court. These effectively thwarted a major portion of the appeal to the Court of
Appeal.[23] As a result, the appeal was withdrawn.

VIII. Other Australian jurisdictions

The issue of a preferred system of appeals and enforcement in the areas of
planning and environmental law has been the subject of scrutiny and debate

---

[21]The case of *Corkill* v *Forestry Commission of NSW (No 2)* (1991) 73 LGRA 126 regarding the Chaelundi forest is
an interesting illustration of this. The government sought to challenge this decision; however the appeal was
dismissed by the Court of Appeal – *Forestry Commission of NSW* v *Corkill* (1991) 73 LGRA 247. The government
then made regulations in an effort to curtail implications which it perceived the judgment may have with regard
to endangered fauna in all future developments. However, Parliament disallowed the regulation and, ultimately,
the Endangered Fauna (Interim Protection) Act 1991 was passed. The Act rationalised the requirements of the
law in this area and required a consideration of the impact on endangered fauna of any development. The Bill,
initiated by the opposition, was drafted with a one-year sunset clause, but has been extended from time to time
so that it remains in force today.
[22](1992–1993) 78 LGERA 119.
[23]Section 12A of the Protection of the Environment Administration Act 1991 was inserted.

around Australia over the past several years. A report commissioned for the federal government in 1990 recommended a single combined appellate and enforcement jurisdiction for development control in each state, necessarily providing a broad jurisdiction to resolve all planning and environmental issues.[24] The authors recommended a specialist court, including judges and commissioners and modelled substantially on the Land and Environment Court. The principal difference was that the specialist court would exist as a division of the Supreme Court of a State. The thrust of the report was adopted by all Australian planning ministers in late 1991 and a number of states are moving towards meeting the recommendation, notably Queensland, South Australia and Tasmania.

Queensland has recently built on the previously existing Local Government Court by renaming it the Planning and Environment Court and expanding its jurisdiction. The court is serviced by District Court Judges and remains an intermediate court. The jurisdiction of the court now includes the ability to make declarations and orders that were, under the old legislation, solely the province of the Supreme Court of Queensland. The court's jurisdiction does not, however, extend to prerogative writs, which remain with the Supreme Court. Under the Local Government (Planning and Environment) Act 1990 (Qld) (LGPEA 1990) the court has jurisdiction to hear and determine all matters which, by LGPEA 1990 or any other Act are required to be heard and determined, including every appeal and application for review which under LGPEA 1990 may be made to the court.[25] Other Acts granting jurisdiction to the court include the Nature Conservation Act, Contaminated Land Act and Heritage Act. Except for a right of appeal to the Queensland Court of Appeal, the jurisdiction of the court is exclusive and every determination of the court is final and conclusive.[26] The expansion of the statutory powers of the court were also accompanied by an open-standing provision substantially modelled on the wording of section 123 of the EPAA 1979 (NSW).[27] However, jurisdiction remains fragmented to the extent that criminal matters are still heard in magistrates' courts, where open standing has also been granted to any person to bring proceedings by way of complaint and summons for certain breaches of planning law.[28]

Another development in Queensland of some interest, is the government's proposal to pass a Bill of Rights.[29] Part 5 of the Bill includes a right to environmental protection and conservation and a right to ecologically

---

[24]Hayes B and Trenorden C, *Combined Jurisdiction for development appeals in the States and Territories*, Department of Industry, Technology and Commerce, Australian Government Publishing Service, Canberra, February 1990.
[25]LGPEA 1990, s 7.4(1).
[26]LGPEA 1990, s 7.4(3).
[27]LGPEA 1990, s 24.
[28]LGPEA 1990, s 2.23.
[29]Bill of Rights Bill 1993.

sustainable development, which include a "right to object . . . and to expect that government will accept and act on a reasonable objection" where the rights are not observed.[30] However, lest these be confused with open-standing provisions the Bill provides at the outset:

> "5.(1) A right stated in Part 4 (Economic and social rights) or Part 5 (Community and cultural rights) is not enforceable merely because of this Act.
>
> (2) Despite subsection (1), the Parliament –
>
> (a)   urges the Queensland community generally to observe the rights stated in Parts 4 and 5; and
>
> (b)   encourages persons to assert the rights in ways that do not involve the legal process or proceedings."

In South Australia a new court known as the Environment Resources and Development Court has recently been established by the Environment Resources and Development Act 1993 (S Aust). The court is a specialist court, established to deal exclusively with building, environmental and planning disputes and is separate from the existing Supreme, District and magistrates' courts. The court is to be comprised of legal and non-legal appointments, and will include District Court Judges, magistrates and Commissioners (who are equivalent to assessors in the Land and Environment Court). It will hear all merit appeals and criminal and civil enforcement proceedings. The court is not bound by the rules of evidence and is mandated to conduct itself with the minimum of formality and inform itself as it thinks fit, characteristics drawn from the Land and Environment Court. While the establishment of the court is a positive step and to be commended, there are major deficiencies. The court does not have jurisdiction over judicial review proceedings, which remain with the Supreme Court, and is a court of intermediate status. At this stage its jurisdiction over environmental issues is limited, although it is hoped to be expanded over time.

Tasmania is currently considering the establishment of a Resource Management and Planning Appeal Tribunal,[31] as part of a package of legislation to reform planning, development and environmental protection in the state.[32] The tribunal will utilise legal and non-legal members. Its jurisdiction will include merit or administrative appeals and civil enforcement. An attempt to relax the common law rules as to standing has been made for civil enforcement.[33] While the package contains some laudable and innovative changes in statutory powers, it has failed in its conception of a curial body. The

court?

---

[30]Clauses 44 and 45 of the Bill.

[31]Resource Management and Planning Appeal Tribunal Bill 1992.

[32]The package includes the Land Use Planning and Approvals Bill 1992; State Policies and Projects Bill 1992; Approvals (Deadline) Bill 1992; Land Use Planning and Approvals (Consequential and Miscellaneous Amendments) Bill 1992 and the Environmental Management and Pollution Control Bill 1993.

[33]Clause 45 of the Environmental Management and Pollution Control Bill 1993 grants standing to a person who, in the opinion of the tribunal, has a "proper interest".

outcome, I think, will be less efficient and effective than an integrated court of a superior status.

In the remainder of the Australian states and territories jurisdiction over environmental law continues to be fragmented. Most jurisdictions have planning and building appeals located within their administrative appeals tribunals. Usually, although not exclusively, judicial review or civil enforcement occurs within state or territory Supreme Courts. Criminal prosecutions are normally heard in the magistrates' courts. In the Commonwealth area jurisdiction is shared between the Administrative Appeals Tribunal and the Federal Court. However, judicial review of environmental law is restricted because of the requirement to establish common law standing[34] and the provisions of the Environment Protection (Impact of Proposals) Act 1974 (Cth) being drafted in such a way as to make it almost non-justiciable.

IX. **Standing**

Reading articles on European environmental law – particularly British – which bemoan the problems of establishing *locus standi* to seek to enforce breaches of environmental law, is like *déjà vu*.[35] "Any person" may bring proceedings in the Land and Environment Court to remedy or restrain a breach of environmental law.[36] No "special" interest in the subject-matter is required. An applicant for relief does not have to be a "person aggrieved". No leave of the court is required except in the case of civil or criminal enforcement of pollution legislation.[37] However, no "floodgates" of litigation have been opened. Most judicial review cases are concerned, not with vindicating some personal or property right, but to enforce breaches of environmental law in the public interest.

The success of the court is to be judged not only in terms of efficiency and effectiveness, but also in terms of access. Without statutory open standing the role of the court would be considerably reduced. The number of civil enforcement and judicial review applications by individuals, residents, conservation groups and other third parties (as distinct from consent or regulatory authorities) has shown modest but significant growth over the last decade. Importantly, a high proportion have succeeded in exposing and remedying breaches of the law, sometimes by state and local government agencies. In short, open standing has not been abused. The existence of "self-help" remedies to the public at large also acts as an incentive for regulators to

---

[34]*Australian Conservation Foundation* v *The Commonwealth of Australia* (1980) 146 CLR 493.
[35]See, *e.g.* Geddes A, *"Locus Standi* and EEC Environmental Measures" (1992) 4:1 JEL 29–39.
[36]EPAA 1979, s 123; Heritage Act 1977; s 153; National Parks and Wildlife Act 1974, s 176A; Wilderness Act 1987, s 27; Uranium Mining and Nuclear Facilities (Prohibitions) Act 1986, s 10; Environmentally Hazardous Chemicals Act 1985, s 57; and Local Government Act 1993, s 674 Fisheries Management Act 1994, s 282.
[37]Environmental Offences and Penalties Act 1989, ss 13(2A) and 25.

do their job. Additionally, civil enforcement of pollution breaches is slowly becoming more popular, leaving the more serious breaches to be dealt with under the criminal law.

One of the successes of the original legislative package has been Part 5 of the EPAA 1979 which controls the bulk of development activities by public authorities and draws on the National Environmental Policy Act 1970 in the United States. Part 5 compels the *anticipation* of environmental problems and requires them to be accounted for in the decision-making process. Section 111 of the EPAA 1979 is pivotal and imposes on a determining authority (usually a government agency) a duty to examine and take into account "to the fullest extent possible" all matters affecting or likely to affect the environment by reason of the proposed activity. In addition to this obligation, a duty to prepare and assess an environmental impact statement (EIS) will arise if the carrying out of the activity is "likely" to "significantly affect the environment".

The court may therefore be called upon to examine the lawfulness of an approval in the absence of consideration of an EIS, or the correctness of the decision, if any, by the determining authority, that an EIS was not required. Extensive case law has developed over the past decade to interpret these provisions and has acted as a guide to proponents and citizens alike.

The availability of legal aid in environmental cases is significant in challenges by resident and conservation groups. At the beginning of 1993 the State Legal Aid Commission terminated legal aid in the majority of civil cases including environmental law matters. This was as a result of the Commission's financial difficulties. The decision has serious implications for the enforcement of public interest environmental law and the New South Wales Environmental Defender's Office (EDO) through which most such actions are brought. The *Sydney Morning Herald* of 14 October 1993 reported that the Commission had decided to reintroduce legal aid in all civil areas except professional negligence suits and environmental matters. Without legal aid and an active EDO, public participation in the court will be deterred.[38]

X. Conclusion

Recently our Chief Justice, The Hon Murray Gleeson, emphasised four principal objectives of the legal system – effectiveness, efficiency, timeliness and, above all, justice. The Land and Environment Court has sought to achieve each of these objectives. The court has demonstrated the appropriateness of easy access to a superior court with an integrated, exclusive jurisdiction in planning and environmental law. Part of the court's success is, I believe, due to its mixed personnel – legal and technical. The opportunity of a judge to sit with

---

[38]For subsequent developments regarding the partial restoration of legal aid in public interest environmental matters, see Chapter 16, n 75 and accompanying text.

or to delegate matters to lay assessors ensures determination by persons with appropriate qualifications and experience. The wide discretion to make orders "as it thinks fit" and to punish for contempt those who disobey its orders, enhances its role as a specialist curial structure.

The wide-ranging jurisdiction of the court enables it to administer social justice in the legislative scheme of environmental laws, which travel far beyond justice *inter partes*. Its status as a superior court, with an integrated jurisdiction, means that it can, as far as is possible, resolve completely and finally all matters in controversy between the parties and avoid multiplicity of litigation. A by-product of the court's jurisdiction is the enhancement of the decision-making process and, hopefully, the avoidance of the need for further review. Having a specialist court has also served to elevate public, government and industry awareness of environmental issues.

Speaking from a position of acknowledged bias, I believe that the unique experiment has proved a success. It is time for others to grasp the nettle.

Contents of Chapter 15

Do We Need an Environmental Court in Britain?

Chapter 15

Do We Need an Environmental Court in Britain?

Glen McLeod

I. Introduction

In recent years there have been calls for the establishment of a specialist environmental court or tribunal. Dispute resolution[1] is, of course, only one aspect of the broader area of statutory and common law which we now call environmental law. In the United Kingdom this body of law is undergoing change in its content and how it is enforced. That process of change may, in itself, be a reason to reconsider our dispute resolution mechanisms.

However, before we focus too heavily on dispute resolution in isolation, let us not forget about the context in which disputes arise or even do not arise. That context includes the permitting processes, criminal offences, civil liability arising from public and private law and measures relating to nature conservation. These come within the relatively new notion of the body of environmental law in Great Britain. Each part has a peculiar history. Lawyers and others are now seeing the interconnectedness of the constituent parts, but together the parts are more a confederacy, which has "evolved through accretion rather than design",[2] than a properly integrated federation. It would indeed be a remarkable creation which could address adequately the dispute resolution requirements of all components of environmental law, particularly at present, when so much change is afoot, the end result of which is far from clear.

***Glen McLeod** was an environmental law partner of the London office of Denton Hall, solicitors, before recently returning to his native Western Australia to practise planning and environmental law with Mallesons Stephen Jacques, solicitors.
[1]This term includes alternative dispute-resolution methods, a useful summary of which is contained in Hayes BRM, and Trenorden CL, *Combined Jurisdiction for Development Appeals in the States and Territories*, Australian Government Publishing Service, Canberra, 1990 at 19-21.
[2]*Ibid* at 3.

II. **The call for a specialist environmental jurisdiction and some options for change**

The calls for a specialist environmental jurisdiction have come from some eminent lawyers. Professor P McAuslan suggested in 1991[3] that there is a strong case for the establishment of a court-like body with wide decision-making, advisory and regulatory making powers in the environmental field. Lord Woolf also made a call for a new kind of environmentally related jurisdiction in the 1991 Garner Lecture.[4] In 1992 Mr Robert Carnwath QC[5] called for the review of the structure of courts and agencies concerned with the supervision of environmental law. Before then he had drawn attention to difficulties in the system of planning enforcement[6] which, he argued, were brought about by the lack of a unified court jurisdiction for dealing with enforcement cases. More recently still, Professor Malcolm Grant has argued for an environmental court.[7] Mr John Bates, on the other hand, has, particularly in regard to criminal enforcement, argued for change within existing structures.[8]

Some suggested options for an alternative system have been canvassed by these authors. These need not be considered here in detail. Grant's three models provide a useful summary. They are as follows:

"*Model 1*
Division of High Court (or part of Administrative Division); applications for judicial review; statutory applications and appeals under Town and Country Planning Act 1990, Environmental Protection Act 1990 and other defined legislation; takes appeals and case stated from magistrates' and Crown Court.
No primary jurisdiction (except judicial review).
No "policy" jurisdiction.

Model 2
Multi-disciplinary, Environmental Court/Tribunal; High Court Judge as President; wide jurisdiction to determine its own procedure; independent counsel; ability to assign cases to inspectors; . . . to mixed panels.

Model 3
Two-tiered structure;

---

[3]McAuslan P, "The Role of Courts and other Judicial type bodies in Environmental Management" (1991) 3 *Journal of Environmental Law* 195.
[4](1992) 4 JEL 1.
[5][1992] *Journal of Planning and Environmental Law* 799.
[6]Carnwath R, *Enforcing Planning Control*, HMSO, May 1989.
[7]"Environmental Liability and Citizen Access: *Locus Standi*, US Citizen Suites and EC Common Interest Groups" in Grant M (ed), *Environmental Litigation: Towards an Environmental Court?*, United Kingdom Environmental Law Association, 1993 at 57.
[8]"Environmental Crime; the Criminal Justice Potential of an Environmental Tribunal", in Grant M (ed) *ibid* at 45.

1. Environmental inspectorate/commissioners bringing together the planning inspectorate and appellant decision officers in the Department of the Environment; hear and determine appeals and called-in cases under planning and environmental legislation; standing enforcement jurisdiction; criminal jurisdiction.
2. Environmental Court; appellant jurisdiction on questions of law from Inspectorate; primary jurisdiction in judicial review".[9]

There is clearly a rising tide of opinion in favour of change. Environmental law is now a recognised specialism, requiring of those who practice it an eclectic assemblage of skills. Clients[10] with problems of an environmental nature expect them to be dealt with by specialists. There is an increasing move away from the fragmentary approach of the past. Administratively, the interconnectedness of environmental issues was recognised as far back as 1970 when the Department of the Environment was created.[11] Recently, the need for an integrated approach to pollution control led to the introduction of the system of integrated pollution control (IPC) in Part I of the Environmental Protection Act 1990 (EPA 1990). Integration is a part of European Community (EC) environmental policy and the concept has recently been embodied in the draft Directive on Integrated Permitting and Pollution Control. Integrated enforcement is also moving closer with legislative and administrative changes under way to create a single environmental enforcement agency. The British Standards Institute's standard on environmental management[12] and the EC's "CEMAS"[13] Regulation on the same subject are also evidence of this trend. Against this background the call for an integrated approach to environmental dispute resolution does not seem extraordinary.

III. **"The law is life, not logic"**

It appears, therefore, that there are arguments in favour of change and assuming these arguments to be correct, the change required may logically include the establishment of some form of specialist environmental tribunal or court. However, it may also be worth bearing in mind Lord Simonds' observation that " . . . the law is life, not logic".[14] The relevance of this

---

[9]*Ibid* at 67.

[10]The author's clients, for example, in the waste, energy, property and other industries.

[11]Carnwath R cites a statement made in 1973 by the then Secretary of State for the Environment, Geoffrey Rippon QC, who said that the Department of the Environment was the first attempt by any country to "co-ordinate all environmental weapons under a single command", thereby providing "a total strategic approach to environmental management, protection and improvement" *op cit* at 801, citing Rippon [1973] *Journal of Planning and Environmental Law* 1.

[12]BS7750; 1992.

[13]Council Regulation (EEC) allowing voluntary participation by Companies in the Industrial Sector in a Community Eco-Management and Audit Scheme. OJ 1993 L168 at 1–18.

[14]*Gilmour* v *Coates* [1949] 1 All ER 848 at 856.

aphorism may be apparent when some of the parts of the body of environmental law are considered in more detail.

A. **Criminal law** *Wasted*

In regard to criminal law, Bates[15] has doubted the need for structural change. He is concerned that the forensic skills of the judiciary and legal profession may be dissipated by the options for an environmental court mentioned above (by analogy, there may be similar concerns about the common law, as to which, see below). He made reference to, among other things, the safeguards which have been built into the present criminal justice system. He referred, in particular, to trial by jury, some of the other complexities of criminal practice and procedure, including the admissibility of evidence and powers to imprison. He summarised his views as follows:

> " . . . the criminal aspect of the Environmental Court does not rest on the Court so much as on those actually trying the case. I would not see, for example, a special building being necessary. It would be much better if, in a Crown Court trial case the Judge was allocated from an Environmental List. It would be better, however, if he did have a different role from the Crown Court judge, so that he could deal with civil proceedings following on from criminal. In my view, this sort of consolidated process would make things quicker, would save costs and give both sides better access to justice."[16]

There is a precedent for a specialist environmental court having a criminal jurisdiction: the Land and Environment Court of New South Wales may impose heavy fines and prison sentences.[17] A former Chief Judge of that court, Mr Justice Cripps, has expressed the view that it was a mistake to mix up the civil and criminal enforcement mechanisms, making specific reference to the need to observe " . . . the whole panoply of criminal law, civil liberty doctrines . . . "[18] in a criminal jurisdiction.

Mr Justice Cripps' views are consistent with the doubts of Mr Bates. In regard to the jury trial, which was one of Mr Bates' particular concerns, there is no right of jury trial for offences heard by the New South Wales Land and Environment Court.

---

[15]*Op cit* at 51.
[16]*Ibid.*
[17]Mr Justice Cripps, "An Environmental Court in Practice: the Experience of the New South Wales Land and Environment Court", in Grant M (ed) *op cit* at 10. See also the paper by Mr Justice Hemmings MA, "The Utilisation of the Land and the Environment Court in Pollution Control", in Pollution Law Conference (17 September 1990) IRR Pty Ltd, Sydney. His Honor said: "Despite the wide ranging jurisdiction of the Court [referring to the NSW Land and Environment Court], the institution of proceedings by both individuals and public authorities concerning breaches of pollution laws has been sporadic and limited". In recent years, however, there has been a dramatic increase in the number of prosecutions.
[18]*Op cit.*

The criminal law has a life of its own. Whether that can be usefully adapted for a specialist environmental jurisdiction is, on the arguments of Bates, at least open to doubt.

B. **Tort**

Analogous considerations in relation to criminal law may apply to the law of tort, if it can be treated as part of environmental law. Due to its emphasis on private rights, with some exceptions, this has been doubted.[19] In practice, however, tortious actions, or the threat of them, can be a very important part of the environmental lawyers' armoury. Remedies open to private individuals can have a wider community benefit. One public authority has, in recent times, considered using the common law as an adjunct to or instead of its powers to prosecute. This was the National Rivers Authority (NRA), in connection with pollution of the rivers Doe, Dee and Rother in Yorkshire by Coalite Chemicals.[20] There have been large consolidated private nuisance actions,[21] and actions in the tort of public nuisance are very much in the public interest.

It is trite to say that if the criminal law has a life of its own, so does the law of tort. Whether tort can be usefully adapted to a specialist environmental court bears as much consideration as the similar question posed earlier in respect of the criminal law, albeit for different reasons.

Even the broad, New South Wales Land and Environment Court jurisdiction does not include the common law. Yet an environmental court which purports to fulfil even the more modest objectives of those who call for change, but does not include a common law jurisdiction for tortious actions, would, at least in Britain, be failing to integrate the component parts of environmental law.

The reality is that tort law is a very important part of the body of environmental law as currently constituted within Britain. Its importance is exemplified by the now famous *Cambridge Water* case.[22] The law in this case, and *obiter* statements relating to the rule in *Rylands* v *Fletcher*, coupled with provisions of the Water Resources Act 1991 (WRA 1991) were of most immediate concern to the financial sector and industry in Britain, because of the strictness of the liability which may attach to the consequences of industrial activity and, in the case of WRA 1991, possible lender liability. In the aftermath of the Court of Appeal decision (eventually overturned by the House of Lords), large clearing and merchant banks began to factor environmental liability

---

[19]See, *e.g.* the paper by Mr Justice Toohey of the High Court of Australia, "Environmental Law – Its place in the System", given at the Lawasia and National Environmental Law Association of Australia International Conference on Environmental Law (16 June 1989). See also Carnwath *op cit* at 801.

[20](October 1992) 213 *ENDS Report*, 5.

[21]For example, an action brought by residents of Poplar and Wapping against the London Docklands Development Corporation and Olympia and York in respect of noise and dust nuisance caused by the Canary Wharf Development which is currently before the court.

[22]*Cambridge Water Co* v *Eastern Counties Leather plc* [1994] 1 All ER 53.

considerations into the loan-risk assessment process. They began doing this out of concern for their securities and the possibility of more open-ended direct liability.[23]

Concern over developing a specialist jurisdiction to enhance environmental protection in the public interest may, therefore, be misdirected if that jurisdiction does not accommodate the laws which are likely to have the most effect upon first, those who provide the finance for industry to operate and, secondly, some parts of industry.

C. **Statutory civil liability**

Mention has been made of WRA 1991. As well as imposing criminal liability on polluting activity,[24] the Act empowers the NRA to carry out certain remedial works and, among other things, to recover the cost from the party who caused or knowingly permitted the relevant waters to be contaminated.[25] In any particular case, and this applies to all cases of which I have had experience, a party may, in addition, be liable for considerable clean-up expenses under the Act, be liable for a criminal offence and, at common law, for damages for nuisance or under the rule in *Rylands* v *Fletcher*. Quite often these matters come to a head when an application has been made for planning permission and the NRA is consulted by the planning authority. The NRA's views must be taken into account by the planning authority and could be instrumental in causing a public inquiry to be held into the application, either on appeal to the Secretary of State or by way of call-in (dealt with in more detail below).

Each of these potential disputes would be adjudicated in a different forum. There is a logical argument for having them heard under the same jurisdictional umbrella. However, in practice it does not work that way. I am not aware of any example of the NRA having taken a party to court to recover clean-up expenses under section 161. Section 161 of WRA 1991 is used frequently in negotiations, as an ultimate threat. The NRA has carried out works under the powers itself rarely and then only in an emergency.

In practice, therefore, there is usually little need for litigation under section 161. That does not vitiate against its importance. Criminal prosecutions under WRA 1991 usually do not go beyond magistrates' courts. There is little jurisdictional compatibility between that criminal jurisdiction, a dispute over planning permission and the common law jurisdiction in which the rights of private individuals are considered.

---

[23]The concern of the banking community was highlighted recently when the then Minister for the Environment Mr T Yeo indicated that banks will not be absolved from environmental lending (see (1993) *Financial Times*, 13 October and speech to the British Bankers' Association on the same date).
[24]Principally in s 85.
[25]Section 161.

In light of these practical considerations, some of the most important areas of environmental law in this country may not easily be brought within the jurisdiction of a single environmental court or tribunal.

IV. **Recent changes and uncertain future directions**

A. **Pollution control by permitting systems**

There are several important pollution control statutes, including the EPA 1990, WRA 1991 and the Radiation Protection Act 1993. These statutes all provide for the issue of permits to allow for certain polluting activities to be carried on. For present purposes it is convenient to consider one of these statutes in practice, that is EPA 1990.

One of the most important recent innovations in British environmental law was the embodiment into statute law of the concept of "best available techniques not entailing excessive cost" (BATNEEC) as part of the new IPC and local authority air pollution control (LAAPC) systems in Part I of EPA 1990. Among other things, this system replaced the statutory control of air pollution by a duty requiring the use of the "best practicable means" (BPM) to achieve certain ends. The details of these systems need not be of concern for present purposes. Importantly, the BATNEEC requirement is part of one objective which the regulatory authority must seek to achieve when formulating the conditions pursuant to which it grants an IPC or LAAPC authorisation for a process. In practice, this is done partly by specifying emission limits in authorisations, the details of which are recorded on a public register. Any member of the public can find out to what standards an authorised process should be operating. Subject to the practical difficulties of obtaining evidence, any person can either require the regulatory authority to enforce the conditions, ultimately by application for judicial review, or prosecute for a breach in the magistrates' court or Crown Court. In passing, it should be noted that the same pertains to discharge consents for aqueous effluent under WRA 1991, the relevant enforcement provision being section 85, which has been discussed above.

Returning to EPA 1990, it is interesting to contrast this new system with that which was previously in force. In the old system there are no authorisations, no comparable public register and no right to know whether the BPM was being employed. The BPM concept, which was effectively the counterpart of BATNEEC in the system of air pollution control replaced by Part I of EPA 1990, had been employed in British environmental legislation for well over 100 years without being defined in legislation or interpreted by a higher court. Instead, a tacit understanding between the regulator and the regulated grew up as to what it meant. This understanding was between engineers: those who worked for regulators and those who worked for industry. This was a very cosy arrangement for them, which the new, more objective, approach to Part I of EPA 1990 may overcome, but to what extent it is not clear.

The new systems have only been partly implemented. A number of applications for IPC and LAAPC have been made and some authorisations granted. Since 1991 there have been 56 appeals by way of written representations and one hearing.[26]

Whether BATNEEC will ultimately come to mean what Parliament intended, which in our system means what the courts think Parliament intended, or what engineers working on either side of the regulatory divide regard as workable or convenient (which is what happened under the old, more closed system) is unclear. There are obvious features of the new system which forever sweep away the full extent of the secretive cosiness of the old; the inherent objectivity of specified emission limits on a public register and no bar on standing to bring a prosecution, for example. However, in practice, the large and complicated IPC applications for major facilities are drawn up by engineers in industry and considered by engineers in Her Majesty's Inspectorate of Pollution (HMIP). There have been teething problems but, with the exceptions mentioned, these have not been resolved by appeal. Industry does not consider it expedient to become involved in formal disputes with HMIP, unless absolutely necessary. The number of appeals relating to applications for authorisations has been mentioned above. The procedure for appeals is under the same administrative umbrella as those for planning appeals. Unlike planning appeals, however, there is no appeal as of right on a point of law from a decision to the High Court. Aggrieved persons must use the less certain avenue of judicial review.

Although members of the public may have some input as to the necessity of BATNEEC when applications are advertised, they have no formal rights of standing in this system. There is a chance that the odd prosecution will go on appeal to a higher court where BATNEEC may be interpreted, but most prosecutions do not go beyond the magistrates' courts. With the exception of private prosecutions, most disputes are likely to be settled by notice procedures, under which an operator may be required to carry out works on the relevant process.[27]

B. **Waste licensing**

The system of waste regulation and licensing was also amended by EPA 1990. Some of the problems, referred to above, exhibited by the IPC and LAAPC systems, are also apparent in the new waste system, with the difference that, at

---

[26]Figures supplied by the Department of the Environment, October 1993. The figures include appeals under both IPC and LAAP. The single hearing was an IPC appeal. The figures also include several appeals relating to the public register of information and claims for confidentiality.
[27]Enforcement notices (EPA 1990, s 13); prohibition notices (EPA 1990, s 14).

least in respect of licensing, the new system relating to waste is not yet in operation. Authorities responsible for issuing licences are the waste regulation authorities (mostly county councils in England and Wales). This new system will replace the similar existing system, with some important amendments which are not relevant for present purposes. Not many applications for licences go on appeal. Since 1991 there have been only 53[28] appeals. I have been unable to ascertain how many of these were hearings but understand (and know from personal experience) that they are usually by a written representation procedure, rather than a hearing.

A feature which the waste licensing system has in common with the pollution control regimes in Part I of EPA 1990, is its appeal system. In particular, appeals are to the Secretary of State and there is no appeal as of right on a point of law. Private prosecutions are also possible but the practical likelihood of any kind of prosecution going on appeal to a higher court is not great.

C. The planning system

Unlike the pollution control and waste licensing systems, a detailed body jurisprudence relating to the permitting process and other aspects of the planning system, has developed. Most planning applications are made to and determined by metropolitan borough or district councils.[29]

Appeals are administered by a planning inspectorate and may be either by way of written representations or public inquiry. Since 1991 there have been 33,530 appeals by way of written representation and 3,313 public inquiries in England and Wales.[30] More will be said about the English planning system later, when comparing it to the Australian systems. Significantly, appeals on points of law from ministerial appeal decisions are possible, as of right. The decision-maker in the first instance is a local government authority. However, the central government has significant powers to "call-in" or determine planning applications on appeal.

D. Comment on the permitting systems

The permitting systems referred to above have procedural similarities. In terms of numbers and complexity of the law the planning appeal system is the most significant. In regard to the resolution of disputes, it may be too early to

---

[28]Information supplied by the Waste Management Information Bureau, Harwell, October 1993.
[29]The exceptions include waste disposal applications which are referred by district councils to county councils in England.
[30]Figures supplied by the Department of the Environment, October 1993.

determine the compatibility of the planning system with the new pollution control systems mentioned. Significantly, the systems are not compatible at present in regard to the supervisory jurisdiction of the higher courts.

E. **Judicial review and statutory appeals to the courts**

Judicial review can be a very effective weapon for the enforcement of environmental laws. How significant it is in Britain is not clear. There are no statistics on how many judicial review applications have been made in respect of environmental matters. Some well-known challenges have been brought by Greenpeace[31] to compel regulatory authorities to enforce the law and some planning decisions relating to environmental matters have been challenged under the procedure.[32]

In 1994, the Law Commission published a consultation paper entitled "Administrative Law: Judicial Review and Statutory Appeals",[33] which discussed various aspects of judicial review, including standing, discovery, procedural exclusivity, time-limits and the requirement to obtain leave to apply. The consultation period has closed but the Commission has yet to report on its findings. A number of anomalies in the present system were identified. The United Kingdom Environmental Law Association, in its submission to the Commission, drew attention to the lack of common procedure for legal challenge in environmental cases and the lack of a common approach to the problems discussed in the consultation paper. Different systems of challenge have developed for largely historical reasons. For example, to challenge an appeal decision of the Secretary of State for the Environment in a planning case an "aggrieved person" must make application to the court within a rigid six-week time-limit. The decision is immune from other forms of challenge. No leave of the court is required to make the application. However, in relation to an authorisation under Part I of EPA 1990, it is necessary to obtain leave and the time-limit is a more flexible three-month period. There is also no general immunity from other forms of challenge.[34]

---

[31]In 1992, Greenpeace challenged a decision of the NRA not to prosecute the chemical company Albright & Wilson, by an application for judicial review in the High Court. Leave to apply was granted but the application was not pursued. Earlier, the organisation had successfully prosecuted the company in respect of the same plant and discharges. In 1993, Greenpeace challenged a decision to grant British Nuclear Fuels a licence under the Radioactive Substances Act 1961. The challenge was unsuccessful, but the High Court expressly recognised Greenpeace's standing (see Chapter 16, n 16 for citations of recent Greenpeace cases).

[32]For example *R v Exeter City Council ex p JL Thomas & Co, Limited* [1990] 3 WLR 100.

[33]Consultation Paper No 126, HMSO, London.

[34]Submission of United Kingdom Environmental Law Association to Law Commission, on Consultation Paper No 126 (Administrative Law) Judicial Review and Statutory Appeals, 29 June 1993.

F. **Contaminated land**

Contaminated land was formerly very much a concern of the planning system. However, in recent years new statutory controls independent of the planning system have emerged. Possible legislative reform is under consideration both at national and EU levels. The extent to which the present law is under review may be gauged by the terms of reference of the interdepartmental inquiry into the subject, which read as follows:

> "To review the powers and duties of public authorities which relate to the identification, assessment and appropriate treatment or control of LAND that could cause POLLUTION of the environment or harm to human health, having regard to the need to minimise the costs which existing and new regulatory burdens place on the private sector; to consider the mechanisms for recovering authorities' costs in controlling or remedying POLLUTION of such LAND sufficient to ensure its safety for health and the environment, and its return to beneficial use where practicable; to consider the implications of these for the role of the Environment Agency; to report initially on any statutory changes needed in the short term and on the scope of any longer-term studies that should be put in hand; and to undertake and report on those studies."

From comments made by the Minister for the Environment, who is responsible for this Inquiry,[35] it would be surprising if this process led to substantial change in the law. Although it is understood that the minister has an open mind on the subject, it would require a very good case to persuade him to institute substantive change and there is no indication that such a case has been made out, even though this inquiry is well advanced.

As far as a body of jurisprudence relating to contaminated land is concerned, the statutory law is too new, or not even in force, for any reasonable guidance to have developed. The common law is in a state of flux. The government is reviewing the whole system, at a time when the future of relevant EC legislation is not clear. Just precisely what will emerge is difficult to predict.

G. **Enforcement**

The enforcement of environmental law is undergoing change. A new integrated enforcement agency is being developed, having responsibility for water, integrated pollution control and waste, but not planning, which will remain decentralised. A new more vigorous and objective culture of enforcement may also be emerging, particularly as a result of the separation of water and sewage services, from the regulation of water by the formation of the NRA and 10 regional water utility companies, under the Water Act 1989 (the

---

[35]Speech of Mr T Yeo made to the British Bankers' Association Conference, "Environmental Lender Liability and Risk", 13 October 1993.

relevant provisions have since been subsumed within the Water Industry Act 1991). The NRA has carried out its enforcement responsibilities in the manner distinguished by its vigour and detachment.

H. **Conclusions – change and uncertainty**

The following conclusions may be drawn from the foregoing discussion:

(i)   Environmental law is in a state of change. The precise nature and long-term effects of the changes are not clear.

(ii) There are inadequacies in at least some of the consenting procedures, brought about, in part, by the nature of the appeal systems, the inaccessibility of the courts, the closed nature of the system and, partly as a result of those factors, the lack of a relevant body of jurisprudence.

From these conclusions some important questions arise.

(i)   Should the component parts of the system be made more consistent?

(ii) When will we fully know the nature of the component parts, given the changes which are afoot?

(iii) Should the formulation of dispute resolution mechanisms await the answers to (i) and (ii) above?

(iv) What reforms are necessary to engender the development of a relevant body of environmental jurisprudence?

In answering these and no doubt other questions, the issue of whether there should be an integrated environmental jurisdiction may arise. However, that question is linked inextricably with some fundamental questions about the system. The question of whether there should be a separate environmental court or tribunal cannot, therefore, be considered in isolation and should not be a starting point as it would suffer from at least the following drawbacks:

(i)   attention would be deflected from deeper questions which need to be answered; and

(ii) being only part of a larger question, the answer by its nature would be inadequate and potentially dangerous because it may not take into account the effects which change may have on the broader system of administration and enforcement.

In short, before dispute-resolving mechanisms are examined, we need to identify the problems with which we are most concerned and address those problems; this may include changing the method of dispute resolution.

v. **The relevance of other jurisdictions**

A corollary to the above conclusions is that if the dispute-resolving mechanism of any other country is to be held out as a useful model, it should be considered in the context of the broader system of law and administration of that country. The Australian jurisdictions, particularly New South Wales, have often been mentioned, but there are important relevant differences between Australia and Britain. When looking to other models, it may also be instructive to consider the process by which those models were developed.

A. **Some comparisons between the British and Australian systems**

The circumstances in which disputes arise in Britain and Australia may not be entirely comparable. This certainly applies to the planning system. There is no Australian jurisdiction which has a planning system similar to that in this country, except in the broadest terms. The governing instruments of land-use allocation in Australia are legislative in nature, whereas in Britain, they are flexible statutory policies. My own experience from practising in Western Australia and in Britain is that disputes in the former jurisdiction tend to be more legalistic. It would appear that this may hold true when comparing New South Wales[36] and Britain. In the latter, in my experience, although there are often disputes about the meaning of the statutory policies, the arguments concentrate more on matters of principle, this being a result of case law. In Britain, breaches of planning permissions must be enforced initially by a non-criminal procedure, involving the issue of a notice to the offending party.[37] In Australia, however, breaches immediately give rise to an offence, although in practice informal notice of some kind usually precedes the taking of court action.

Appeals against the decisions of the planning authorities in Australia are made to courts or tribunals. In Western Australia there is also the option of appealing to a minister. In Britain, however, all appeals are to the Secretary of State for the Environment, although in practice most are delegated to an inspector.[38]

Although the planning appeal tribunals and courts in Australia do not have procedures which are as strict as those of other parts of the judicial system, they are more formal than the British system, at least in the state of which I have experience and I understand this to be so in other states, including New South Wales. For example, in Britain, failure to exchange witness statements within the requisite period before an inquiry, although theoretically in breach

---

[36]See Cripps *op cit* at 11.
[37]Under the Town and Country Planning Act 1990.
[38]Carnwath *op cit* at 805.

of the Inquiry Procedure Rules, could result in a cost order being made against the offending party. This happens rarely in practice. Comparable breaches of Australian procedural rules, however, may be viewed far more seriously and have greater consequences for the offending party.

The significance of these differences for present purposes is that the specialist *environmental* jurisdictions in Australia had and, to a large extent,[39] retain as their centre of gravity a planning appeal system. This should be borne in mind when considering the Australian systems as possible models for an environmental court or tribunal in this country, where planning not only differs but may also not feature in the same way within the broader body of environmental law.

The New South Wales' system was conceived in the late 1970s, at a time when the term "environmental law" was usually taken to be a synonym for planning law with, perhaps, a few pollution control laws appended. The forces which shape the needs of Britain in the 1990s, where environmental law has arrived as a separate area of practice, may not be the same as those which influenced the architects of the New South Wales' system in the 1970s.

B. **The process by which change takes place**

One approach to the process of arriving at a new system is that taken by New Zealand in the drafting of the Resource Management Act 1991. This Act affected over 50 statutes, repealing major portions of many of them, including legislation relating to planning, pollution control, mining and energy. In effect, the New Zealanders started again. Common procedures were established for obtaining consents and the planning tribunal was given an enhanced role.[40] South Australia has recently taken a less radical but still significant step by enacting the Development Act 1993. Among other things, the Act integrates the development and building appeals systems into a specialist court which has a supervisory and declaratory jurisdiction. It is understood that the court is regarded as somewhat embryonic in that other development and environmental-type jurisdictions such as heritage, pollution and native vegetation clearance may be added in the future.

It is interesting that the new bodies in New Zealand and South Australia came about with the enactment of substantial new-core legislation. The systems accommodate, or provision has being made for them to accommodate, the adjudication of a broad range of environmental disputes.

---

[39] With the possible exception of Western Australia which has a system not comparable to that in Gt Britain, for other reasons.
[40] See Randerson T, "The Resource Management Act 1991 – Empowering Framework rather than a blueprint" (1991) 356 *LawTalk* (2 September 1991), Wellington; McLean J, "New Zealand's Resource Management Act 1991: Process with Purpose?" (1992) 7:4 *Otago Law Review*.

If a comparable body is to be established in Britain, similar wide-ranging and significant legislative action in respect of the entire system may at least need to be considered.

VI. **Conclusion**

The scope of environmental law has been examined in this paper. Environmental law, in so far as it is practised in Britain, encompasses a broad range of (not necessarily) compatible subject areas.

There may be a *prima facie* case for some form of environmental court or tribunal, but there could be practical difficulties in devising a body which usefully covers the field of environmental law. A number of models for a court or tribunal may be appropriate, ranging from an administrative reorganisation of existing institutions to more radical and substantive change, involving the creation of a new, broad environmental jurisdiction. Given the current state of uncertainty of environmental law in Britain, it may be some time before we know, with some certainty, the full practicable extent of that jurisdiction.

The idea of an environmental court has logical appeal but there may be practical difficulties in devising a body which can properly cover the field of environmental law, as that law currently stands. It is to be queried whether the debate concerning the establishment of an environmental court should not be taking place within a broader discussion about the system of environmental law as a whole.

Section IV
Conclusion

Contents of Chapter 16

Public Interest Environmental Law – Commentary and Analysis

Chapter 16

Public Interest Environmental Law — Commentary and Analysis

David Robinson

In this final chapter the issues raised in previous chapters are set against a background of environmental legal activism around the world. I argue that public interest environmental law initiatives have greatest practical effect where certain preconditions exist. The chapter concludes by proposing a networking role for environmental lawyers.

First, however, an explanation is owed to Bowden's long-suffering, hypothetical industrial stakeholder[1] as to why, if participation is granted to citizens and interest groups in environmental management, this should extend to the right to litigate.

I. **The role of law**

Environmental law should perform three functions.[2] First, it should regulate, providing appropriation and management rules for the many conflicting interests claiming environmental goods. Second, it should act as an agent of change, providing processes and structuring institutions to enable the transition towards ecological sustainability.[3] Third, it should protect the public interest. One way in which it can achieve this last objective is through open decision-making in which the public can participate in drafting and enforcing the law. The hypothetical industrial stakeholder, however, argues that "soft participation" (the right to comment, but not to litigate), is sufficient to mould and secure broader support for the environmental initiatives of governments. To go further, however, and allow environmentalists to use court cases in campaigns is argued to be expensive and counter-productive.

---

*I thank my colleague John Dunkley for numerous suggestions on earlier drafts of this chapter.
[1] Chapter 8.
[2] Comino M and Mossop D, *Inland Rivers: Regulatory Strategies for Ecologically Sustainable Management*, Sydney, Environmental Defender's Office, 1994 at 12–13.
[3] See also n 93 *infra* and subsequent text.

The industrial stakeholder is sceptical of the international claims of the so-called "public interest environmental law movement". The movement, so the stakeholder argues, is driven, if not funded, from the United States, and reflects "social imperialism" in which activists in the United States evangelise their litigious values and approaches internationally. Just as the Bhopal disaster at the Union Carbide subsidiary in India was an American export, so too was the response of American lawyers who, as Anderson relates, arrived within one week of the explosion to chase ambulances and propose solutions to the tragedy in terms of pay-out figures for torts rendered.[4]

The industrialist points out that there are significant objections to North solutions for South environment and development priorities. These objections are implicit in the two-handed language of the Rio Declaration.[5]

There is ongoing debate about the role of law in global environmental protection, with some observers questioning whether the plethora of international treaties on the environment have been effective at all, let alone cost-effective.[6] They argue from the viewpoint of committed environmentalists, putting forward a broader, less sectoral perspective than that of the hypothetical industrialist. Non-compliance, non-implementation and non-enforcement with international environmental law, including both public international law treaties and domestic environmental laws in different countries is argued to be the rule, not the exception.

More integrated approaches are advocated than reliance on the law as a primary instrument for reversing degradation trends. Greater emphasis on social, economic, trade, historical, institutional and political conditions is necessary. Making foreign aid more dependent upon environmental safeguards, for example, is put forward as one way of achieving better results than international environmental treaties. The "North solution" has placed much emphasis on law, and with it, particularly in the United States, the right for citizens to enforce those laws in court where governments fail to act. Yet many countries do not have the civic, judicial and political traditions and institutions necessary for public interest litigation to play a worthwhile role. This view admits that environmental law has had some limited successes in world conservation, but believes that the conservation-by-legal-fiat, "literary conservation" and "paper parks" approach cannot be justified in cost-benefit terms. Legal responses to environmental problems are regarded as cosmetic surgery upon a patient with a vital illness. The cost of dedicating resources to legal systems is not just financial. Rather, extensive concentration on words in documents is argued as diverting political, media and public attention from designing and implementing conservation initiatives involving education, backed up by financial and other incentives, at a local level. For example, Latin

---

[4]See Chapter 7, especially section IV.
[5]See, *e.g.* principles 1, 2, 5, 6, 7, 8 and 12 of the Rio Declaration on Environment and Development, 1992.
[6]See, *e.g.* Latin HA, "The Mirage of International Environmental Law", forthcoming. Howard Latin is a Professor of Law at Rutgers Law School, 15 Washington St, Newark, NJ 07102, USA. Email:latin@andromeda.rutgers.edu.

suggests that environmental protection came to a standstill in many Third World countries for two years before the 1992 Rio Earth Summit while local politicians and agencies debated their positions.[7] Environmental law is viewed as being hostage to utopians, cynics and elitists. The assumption is that more treaties and laws adequately respond to biodiversity problems, whereas in reality they continue to divert attention from pragmatic, locally designed initiatives.

In response, it must be remembered that public interest environmental law places emphasis on participatory decision-making not just with regard to enforcement through court cases, but also regarding the formulation of policies and rules and their implementation. The public interest movement is concerned with global development and human rights issues and, as well as justice between litigants, greater consideration of the underlying environmental interests raised in litigation. In the field of development project funding, for example, the *Pergau Dam* case (see Chapter 10) illustrates the important role litigation can play in promoting public awareness of and political pressure for sustainability. However, while litigation is important, it is by no means the only or preferable strategy for public interest environmental law in developed countries, let alone in countries where financial, judicial, cultural, technical, institutional and other differences do not favour going to court. The "litigation is wasteful" argument has little merit, even in the United States, where litigation in fact plays a relatively small, "last resort", role in the activities of many public interest advocates.[8] The industrial stakeholder's objection to citizen suits is further outweighed by rule of law and practical law enforcement considerations. What matters is that environmental law is observed, and the possibility of citizen suits must surely increase the likelihood of such observance.

Defenders of the public interest environmental law movement[9] argue that the vindication of environmental rights in court is not peculiar to the United States, but forms part of a broader concept of justice which transcends particular jurisdictions, and which has had an independent evolution in a number of countries, most notably India.

On the other hand, it is clear that law has in the past been a fairly blunt tool for environmental protection. Many environmental problems are disproportionately caused by developed countries, as these exploit more resources per capita. Yet it is these countries, particularly the United States, which have the most evolved and interventionist environmental protection laws. One is led inescapably to the conclusion that law has failed to protect the environment. A major reason is that growth has higher priority than environmental protection in materialist societies, whether they be capitalist or socialist. Law has been

---

[7] *Ibid.*

[8] See Chapter 2 at n 76 and accompanying text.

[9] *e.g.* Bonine J, Professor of Law at Oregon University, and fellow members of the Environmental Law Alliance Worldwide (E-LAW). See Chapter 2 at n 59 and preceding text.

reactive, with environmental advocates seeking to claw back some measures for future environmental protection only after the ravages of resource exploitation have become apparent.[10]

For the present discussion on the role of law it is not necessary to take sides in the North-South' environment-development debate. The allegation that Americans export their litigious culture through the public interest environmental law movement is hyperbole which neglects the cooperative nature of relationships between activists around the world. These relationships involve education, law reform and implementation issues, not just court cases. The issue is ultimately one of fact and degree: faced with unprecedented environmental problems, many of them exacerbated by development pressures which the North faced earlier in its industrial evolution, many Southern countries wish to avail themselves of the basic protection which, to varying degrees, Northern countries have already incorporated into their legal systems. Albania is a case in point.

In Albania there are no specific environmental protection laws, let alone agencies to enforce them.[11] Since the fall of the Hoxha regime in 1990, the period of transition to free enterprise and democracy has been marked by lawlessness, chaotic emigration and economic and financial crises. In environmental terms, many formerly state-controlled forests and parks have been opportunistically clear-felled for fuel and foreign currency. Applications to construct toxic waste storage and processing facilities have been made by numerous foreign corporations seeking a nearby destination for waste exports from Western Europe. It is natural that Albania looks to the law, as well as economic and other means, to safeguard its environment. Thus the country is soon to sign and ratify the Basel Convention,[12] and is drafting an environmental impact assessment law using precedents including the European Community Directive[13] and the National Environmental Policy Act 1970 (USA). As a result of participating in the second conference of parties to the Basel Convention in Geneva, March 1994, for example, the Minister for the Environment of Germany agreed to repackage as an interim measure a shipment of pesticides banned in Germany which a German corporation had exported to Albania under the guise of foreign aid. Rather than such development of environmental protection law and participation in legal fora

---

[10]*e.g.* regarding the effect over two decades of the ambitious 1972 amendments to the Federal Water Pollution Control Act (US), which was supported by the vast bureaucracy of the Environment Protection Agency as well as enforced through citizen suits, one commentator has concluded: "Despite two decades of significant environmental law, the nation seems to have accomplished little more than an unstable holding action against even more rapid environmental deterioration."
Yeager, *The Limits of Law: The Public Regulation of Private Pollution*, Cambridge University Press, 1991.
[11]This paragraph is based on a discussion in May 1994 with Fatos Lulo, Lawyer, Committee of Environmental Preservation and Protection, "Zhan Dark" Boulevard, Ministry of Health and Environmental Protection, Tirana, Albania.
[12]Basel Convention on the Control of Transboundary Movements of Hazardous Wastes and their Disposal, 1989.
[13]EC Directive 85/337/EEC on the Assessment of the Effects of Certain Private and Public Projects on the Environment.

being regarded as the result of legal paternalism by the North, failure to develop the basic, protective legal standards associated with Northern investment and development would surely be the greater evil. Of course the subsequent issue of the adequacy of the legal response of the North then arises. To admit the insufficiency of law on its own, however, in no way diminishes the necessity for law, and highlights the desirability of improving the implementation and enforcement of environmental laws through public participation, including citizen suits.

II. **The emergence of public interest environmental law movements**

The scepticism as to the role of law in the above debate reflects an incomplete understanding of public interest environmental law. With this I commiserate. Public interest environmental law is a much vaunted but poorly defined field. I tackle the problem in the following section by describing the prerequisites or conditions under which public interest environmental law movements are emerging internationally.

The prerequisites for public interest environmental law may be evident in some countries more through law reform proposals than in existing rights. The work of activists in Britain illustrates the gap between environmental laws as they currently stand and what the public interest law movement would like them to be.

A. **Public interest environmental law and the UK**

The British approach to environmental regulation has long emphasised administrative discretion.[14] Legally binding planning instruments, quantitative emission standards for pollutants, a prosecution-supported enforcement policy and procedural rules enabling public interest litigation have been rejected in favour of a more flexible, qualitative, cooperative and private approach. Indeterminacy of mandate is the norm, not the exception for British regulatory agencies.[15] This approach envisages only a modest and reactive role for law in environmental protection. That role is to preserve procedural fairness and to provide a framework for environmental control by government

---

[14]"Administrative controls will for the foreseeable future remain at the heart of Britain's system of environmental control." UK Government, *This Common Inheritance*, London, HMSO, Cm 1200, 1990, Appendix A, cited in Rowan-Johnson J and Ross A, "Enforcement of Environmental Regulation in Britain: Strengthening the Link" [1994] *Journal of Planning and Environmental Law* 200. For a detailed comparative analysis from an American perspective, see Vogel D, *National Styles of Regulation: Environmental Policy in Great Britain and the United States*, Cornell University Press, 1986.
[15]Baldwin R and McCrudden C, *Regulation and Public Law*, Weidenfeld and Nicolson, 1987; cited in Rowan-Johnson J and Ross A, *op cit* (n 14).

agencies. Litigation to protect the environment is minimal because discretionary power is broad and largely non-justiciable, and the obstacles to citizens to take developers or polluters to court are substantial.

Recent British policy has focussed upon institutional reform and free market[16] and voluntary approaches to environmental protection. While regulation "will continue to play a vital role in protecting the environment",[17] the law has only a small role to play in the Government's policy on sustainable development.[18] The Government's law reform agenda is to integrate decision-making and control compliance costs, for example through amalgamating the various regulatory agencies. Where possible, deregulation is sought.[19] In short, the policy is to use law as a complementary, rather than a leading, catalytic or innovative tool for environmental protection.

Parliament's reluctance to impose binding, stringent and enforceable environmental protection duties through legislation has been mirrored in judicial reluctance to develop the common law for this purpose.[20]

British activists, however, are beginning to use the law in their campaigning. Greenpeace has taken a number of pollution and nuclear issue cases to court,[21] the Friends of the Earth have brought UK non-compliance with the

---

[16]"The market is the most effective mechanism for maintaining the momentum of development, sharing its benefits, and for shaping its course towards sustainability . . . " UK Government, *Sustainable Development: the UK Strategy*, London, HMSO, January 1994 at 16. The most notable example of the free market approach to environmental protection has been the privatisation of the water supply industry. For broader analysis of contemporary market approaches, see Ogus AI, *Regulation: Legal Form and Economic Theory*, Oxford, Clarendon Press, 1994.

[17]UK Government, *Sustainable Development: the UK Strategy*, op cit, at 213. Note the implication that, in the Government's view, environmental protection law to date has been adequate.

[18]Law is considered in only a few paragraphs of the 267 pages of *Sustainable Development: the UK Strategy* 1990. *Cf.* UK Government, *This Common Inheritance: The Third Year Report (Britain's Environmental Strategy)*, London, HMSO, May 1994, where approximately 100 of the 700 intended or recent environmental actions by the government relate to the drafting, ratification, implementation, enforcing and financing of legal initiatives, or initiatives ultimately expressed through international, European Community or national law.

[19]See the UK Government publications referred to in n 18.

[20]See the below discussion, in the text accompanying n 100, of *Cambridge Water Company v Eastern Counties Leather plc* [1994] 1 All ER 53.

[21]*British Nuclear Fuels v Greenpeace* [1992] 4 *Land Management and Environmental Law Report* (LMELR) 124 – demonstration and injunction; *Greenpeace v Albright & Wilson* [1991] 3 Issue 5 and [1992] 4 LMELR at 56 – private prosecution; *R v National Rivers Authority ex p Greenpeace* [1992] LMELR 4 at 56 – judicial review of enforcement agency; *R v Secretary of State for the Environment and British Nuclear Fuels ex p Greenpeace and Lancashire County Council* [1994] 6 *Environmental Law and Management* (ELM) at 44 and [1994] 6 ELM 82–83; (1994) *ENDS Report* 230 at 43 – High Court challenge of authorisation to allow start up of nuclear waste Thermal Oxide Reprocessing Plant (THORP) at Sellafield and the necessity of a public inquiry – Ministers erred in failing to apply EC law but, as a matter of discretion, judicial review declined – costs not awarded against Greenpeace; *R v HM Inspectorate of Pollution and Ministry of Agriculture, Fisheries and Food ex p Greenpeace* [1994] 1 WLR 570 – THORP, authorisations under the Radioactive Substances Act and *locus standi*; *Greenpeace International v EC Commission* 12 January 1994 *Environment Business* 4, [1994] 6 ELM 43 – aid granted prior to environmental assessment of oil fired power plant on Canary Islands – *locus standi* in the European Court of Justice – pending; *Greenpeace v ICI* 25 May 1993 *The Lawyer* and (1994) *ENDS Report* 234 – chemical discharges to sea – two private prosecutions – Greenpeace fails on technical and analytical grounds and is ordered to pay £29,000 costs – central issue of the legality of discharges of chemicals not specifically mentioned in discharge consents not addressed. (Case list compiled with the assistance of Rupert Bedford (rbedford@gn.apc.org), on electronic conference "e-law.public.int").

requirements of EC environmental law to the attention of the European Commission,[22] anglers' associations have taken court action to stop pollution to rivers from mismanagement of mining and farming operations,[23] and the Environmental Law Foundation, a network of lawyers and experts handling environmental cases for community groups is active.[24] The Law Centres Federation Environment Project has since 1991 conducted educational seminars, and a specialist environmental legal resource centre, EarthRights, has been established.

Thus in the United Kingdom, as well as many other countries, amongst the mass of discretionary, administrative approaches to environmental policy, the public interest environmental law banner can be found.

B. **Prerequisites for public interest environmental law**

Public interest environmental law movements are emerging in countries where the following conditions exist:[25]

1. communitarian ideals;
2. strong law;
3. alliances of reformist lawyers with legally informed activists;
4. broad rights of standing and participation in decision-making;
5. funding for public enforcement actions;
6. court practice and procedure receptive of diffuse interest litigation; and
7. activist judges and environmental institutions.

---

[22]*Commission* v *United Kingdom* [1993] *Water Law* 168 – bathing water and non-compliance with EC Directive; *Commission* v *United Kingdom* [1993] *Water Law* 59 and *R* v *Secretary of State for the Environment ex p Friends of the Earth* (1994) *ENDS Report* 231; 12 April 1994 *The Independent*; [1994] 6 ELM 88 – nitrates in drinking water and non-compliance with EC Directive –acceptance of undertakings by water supply companies to supply wholesome water not granted judicial review as a matter of discretion.

[23]*R* v *British Coal Corporation* (1993) 227 *ENDS Report* – Anglers Co-operative Association – water pollution from abandoned mines; *National Rivers Authority and Anglers Co-operative Association* v *Clarke* (1994) 232 *ENDS Report* 232 – farm slurry pollution – civil damages; *Anglers Co-operative Association* v *Welsh Water* (noted in (1993) 220 *ENDS Report* 38 – pending) – phosphate pollution – mandatory injunction sought.

[24]Approximately eight environmental cases a month are referred to members of the Environmental Law Foundation, a network of over 200 lawyers and environmental experts who provide initial assessment of environmental cases on a *pro-bono* basis, and charge at legal aid levels thereafter. Most cases in the first three years of its operation 1990–93 related to planning inquiries: building, landfill and quarry, noise and road developments. The 1993–94 Report of ELF reflects the non-litigious nature of decision-making in Britain. Planning inquiry advocacy aside, the successful half dozen ELF *court* cases reported have not involved final judgments. Rather, the successes have been achieved out of court, resulting from the mere grant of legal aid or leave to apply for judicial review proceedings, which has precipitated a change of attitude by local and other planning authorities.

[25]The following list of conditions is an amalgam, with some variations, of lists prepared by Preston BJ "Public Enforcement of Environmental Laws in Australia", 1991 (6) *Journal of Environmental Law and Litigation* 39–79 and Trubeck DM, Trubeck L and Becker J "Legal Services and the Administrative State: from Public Interest Law to Public Advocacy" in Blankenburg E ed, *Innovations in the Legal Services*, Cambridge Mass, Oelgeschlager Gunn & Hain, 1980, 131 at 134.

Different emphases on each of the above conditions account for great variation in public interest environmental law from country to country. For example, conditions 6 and 7 have been prominent in India. A combination of the other conditions has enabled public interest environmental law to develop in the United States in the form of advocacy, including litigation, for under-represented groups and interests. In some South American and South-East Asian countries, the growth of the public interest environmental law movement is due to a considerable degree to the existence of condition 3.[26] In Britain, however, public interest environmental law remains frustrated[27] because the prerequisites, particularly the second, are largely absent.

The following paragraphs discuss the prerequisites for the development of public interest environmental law movements in more detail.

1. *Communitarian ideals*

Underlying public interest environmental law is a communitarian (as opposed to Diceyan, individualist) attitude to constitutional law, politics and the rights and duties of citizens.[28]

The communitarian supports environmental law with "teeth" and public interest actions to test, extend and enforce it. The communitarian sees the function of citizen actions and the judiciary as checking and balancing the work of parliaments and bureaucrats.

The Diceyan liberal, on the other hand, believes in representative, not participatory democracy, and that the courts should only hear cases brought by individual citizens or interest groups if their private rights are at stake. The Diceyan liberal regards "public interest" cases as "campaigning by other means",[29] such activity being regarded as illegitimate because parliament alone is viewed as the forum for policy debate. As for pollution control, this is viewed as an issue for industry and regulators alone.[30]

The obstacle to the development of public interest environmental law which liberal, Diceyan attitudes pose is further considered below, in the context of activism and the judiciary.[31]

---

[26]See also Chapter 2 at n 59 and preceding text.

[27]The position in Britain with regard to environmental law is in contrast with other areas of public interest law, such as housing and immigration, which is well-developed. See Cooper J and Dhavan R (ed) *Public Interest Law*, Oxford, Blackwell, 1986.

[28]See Feldman D, "Public Interest Litigation and Constitutional Theory in Comparative Perspective" (1992) 55 *Modern Law Review* 44 and Robinson D, "Public Participation in Environmental Decision-Making" (1993) 10 *Environmental and Planning Law Journal* 320 at 320–321.

[29]See Chapter 8 at section III(A)(2) "Standards of Science".

[30]*Ibid*.

[31]See section II(B)(7) *infra*.

Of course communitarian and liberal attitudes are usually intertwined. For example, many liberals now advocate "soft"[32] or "low rung"[33] participation. If standing exists, the soft participationist favours broad, discretionary policies rather than strong laws capable of being used by activists in court.

I am careful not to draw party-political lines regarding the communitarian ethos. To do so would be to exclude the contribution of a significant sector of the community concerned about better environmental management. It would also fall back upon historic divisions which have ill-served us. The poor environmental management records of the former communist regimes of Eastern Europe, the laissez-faire capitalism of the early industrial revolution, and the "free market", self-interest, dutiless capitalism of the Thatcher years all point to the inadequacy of both right and left-wing materialist responses to environmental challenges.

The communitarian ideal develops differently from culture to culture. It extends to public environmental property the stewardship traditionally reserved for private property. It may well require new institutions[34] and notions of rights and obligations.[35] For example, one of the practical responsibilities of citizens is the maintenance of the rule of law.[36] In light of that responsibility, the denial of *locus standi* in environmental matters is properly characterised as an anomaly reflecting a passive, liberal notion of right, being the antithesis of the active, co-operative sense of civic right and *duty* which I advocate.

2. *Strong law*

By "strong" environmental law I mean "law to be applied", justiciable law, law with "teeth", or law setting ambitious, but achievable and equitable[37] environmental goals.

A fine line exists between strong law reflecting due environmental concern, and partisan law which fails to apportion fairly the full costs associated with conservation.

Strong legislation, in my view, should have explicit objectives. Rules and policy-making pursuant to it should proceed according to clear and accountable criteria, procedures and time-frames. The absence of these characteristics accounts to some degree for the immaturity of public interest environmental law in the United Kingdom. As described above, British environmental

---

[32]As referred to in section I *supra*, soft participation is the right to comment but not to litigate.

[33]Arnstein SR, "A Ladder of Citizen Participation" (1969) *Journal of the American Institute of Planners* 216.

[34]See, *e.g.* Ostrom E, *Governing the Commons: The Evolution of Institutions for Collective Action*, Cambridge University Press, 1991. See also the conclusion of du Bois in Chapter 6 of this book.

[35]A controversial and mixed exposition of the need for a "restored civic bond" and a "new social-ism" is Selbourne D, *The Principle of Duty*, London, Sinclair-Stevenson, 1994.

[36]Selbourne *op cit* at para 143.

[37]Du Bois reminds us of the concern for equitable sharing of costs in environmental protection. Chapter 6.

too discretionary

legislation facilitates ongoing, discretionary management by ministers and agencies. The legislation is silent as to the timing and manner of implementing its framework provisions.[38] Not for Westminster the American approach of explicit statutory objectives and mandatory action programmes, with citizen suit provisions to enforce them. Thus the Environmental Protection Act 1990, described by the Government as "providing the basic framework for much of our pollution control in Britain into the next century," and constituting the most important environmental legislation in 16 years, contains no statutory objective. Those searching for one find an indication – "An act to make provision for the improved control of pollution . . . " – at the beginning of the statute's prefatory words, however the miscellany of additional, limited and disparate purposes which follow in the prefatory words (to control shopping trolleys and dogs, for example) indicates a gradual and incremental approach. The absence of statutory objectives in British environmental legislation leaves those seeking to understand and implement the law with no unifying idea of its mission, let alone opportunities for activists to contest decisions inconsistent with those objectives.

Strong law is both substantive and procedural. An example of the latter is the criteria-specifying and deadline-forcing rights of action available in the United States.[39] Procedural rules should offer access to relevant information[40] and rights to participate in environmental rule and policy-making, as well as in their implementation.

Strong environmental law also extends beyond the discrete areas of planning, resource allocation, pollution control and natural area management law. Its principles should guide private and public decision-making generally, just as Treasury and budget considerations directly affect the work of all departments and businesses. Various ways of giving environmental law such cross-cutting effect exist. Environmental obligations and rights can be included in constitutions, as Fernandes has discussed regarding Brazil, or bills of rights.[41] Alternatively, legislation can require all government decision-making to include environmental impact assessment and to apply a

---

[38]*e.g.* the proposed system of establishing water quality classifications and objectives (Water Resources Act 1991 ss 82 to 84) and of setting standards, objectives, requirements or plans regarding emissions from prescribed processes (Environmental Protection Act 1990 s 3) is a matter for the Secretary of State to determine at his or her discretion, without any guiding principles as to when to act or as to the criteria to be used in making such arrangements. The requirements of EC Directives 75/440/EEC on surface water for drinking, 76/160/EEC on bathing waters, 76/464/EEC on dangerous substances in water and 88/609/EEC on emissions from large combustion plants account for the existing regulations and plans made in the UK pursuant to the legislation. How and when the further potential of the enabling sections will be acted upon remains discretionary. See also the discussion of s 143 of the Environmental Protection Act 1990 *infra* at n 104.

[39]See Chapter 2 at text accompanying n 17–18.

[40]Regarding access to information, see the text preceding n 19 *infra*.

[41]See, *e.g.* the Environmental Bill of Rights, Statutes of Ontario, 1993, Chapter 28, discussed in Walker S, "The Ontario Environmental Bill of Rights" (1994) 1 *Environmental Law Network International Newsletter* 10–12. The UK Labour Party has proposed a charter of environmental rights, including citizen rights to clean air and clean drinking water: *In Trust for Tomorrow*, London, Labour Party, 1994 at 49.

management of ·

precautionary approach and principles of intergenerational equity and sustainable development.[42] Strong environmental law must be supported by complementary administrative and political arrangements, but does not rest on these alone.[43]   *setting free*   *agriculture*

Winter has offered a provocative, theoretical account of strong environmental law.[44] He terms "emancipatory" the law associated with the agrarian and industrial revolutions, in which the creative, productive potential of humankind to exploit nature was liberated. Free trade law, limited liability concepts in tort and corporation law, and private rights in real and intellectual property law are examples of emancipatory law.

When irreversible, increasing problems of environmental degradation began to be appreciated, "interventionist law," beginning in Western countries in the 1970s, sought to curtail some aspects of emancipatory law. Germany's command-and-control pollution laws of the 1970s, based on deterministic notions of tolerance thresholds and technical feasibility, and supported by vast administrative agencies, are examples of interventionist law.

Winter argues that interventionist law has failed to a large degree. The scope for interventionist law to "denature" emancipatory law is limited. The state cannot artificially reverse the inherently exploitative, inventive, energy-releasing nature of emancipatory law. Consequently, emancipatory law must have environmental factors inscribed at the outset, so that economic and ecological goals "are immediately represented in it, and not always mediated *ex post facto* via controlling administrative programmes".[45] Winter challenges us to redefine emancipatory law, for example by adopting more sensitive tolerance limits, soft technology[46] and qualitative as well as quantitative

---

[42]*e.g.* s 6 of the Protection of the Environment Administration Act 1991 (NSW) requires the Environmental Protection Authority to have regard to the need to maintain ecologically sustainable development, through the implementation of the precautionary principle, the principle of inter-generational equity, conservation of biological diversity and ecological integrity, and improved valuation and pricing of environmental resources. Similarly, an explicit objective of the Fisheries Management Act 1994 (NSW) is to apply the principle of ecologically sustainable development in decision-making.

[43]An example of administrative and political arrangements unsupported by strong environmental laws is the Ministerial Committee on the Environment in the UK. "Green ministers" were nominated to consider the environmental implications of each department's activities. See UK Government, *This Common Inheritance: Britain's Environmental Strategy*, London, HMSO, September 1990 at para 18.4 and noted as "implemented" in UK Government, *This Common Inheritance: The Third Year Report (Britain's Environmental Strategy)*, London, HMSO, May 1994. "This amounts to the beginnings of a sensible structure, but is largely ignored. The green ministers have met together only a handful of times; in late 1993 one department was unable even to identify who the green minister was." Labour Party Policy Commission on the Environment, *In Trust for Tomorrow*, Labour Party, London, 1994 at 44.

[44]Winter G [translated by Blazek JR], "Perspectives for Environmental Law – Entering the Fourth Phase" (1989) 1 *Journal of Environmental Law*, Oxford University Press, 38–47.

[45]Winter *op cit* at 46.

[46]Soft technology "Enters into a productive exchange with nature and is not forced to use containment – a technology which strengthens the useful natural forces and substances, which is reversible when mistakes become apparent, which is tolerant of failure, which from the start takes the possibility of human error into account, which utilises useable substances and energy sparingly, and which recycles instead of allowing emissions to permanently escape" Winter *op cit* at 44.

benefits measurement. Environmental factors need to be better integrated in property, competition, tax depreciation, patent and standards law.

The implementation or application of strong law will inevitably, given its ambitious nature, be incomplete. The preceding chapters discuss many instances of incomplete application of the law. For example the control of toxic substance emissions under the Federal Water Pollution Control Act (USA) fell way behind schedule.[47] The impressive constitutional and legislative enshrinement of public interest environmental action in Brazil has not been backed up by judicial, financial and administrative reforms necessary to secure environmental rights in practice.[48] Worthy enabling provisions in UK environmental law have not been implemented.[49] Environmental problems continue despite a proliferation of international and national environmental laws.

Implementation is thus a critical issue, and one in which public interest advocates seek to complement the work of enforcement agencies. Whereas the agencies make greater use of criminal prosecutions, public interest environmental lawyers tend to utilise civil remedies, such as restraining orders, as these are easier to obtain and can have an immediate, preventive effect. In some cases, substantive breaches of development, pollution control or natural area conservation laws are involved. In other, judicial review cases, the issue is compliance with procedural requirements for environmental decision-making.

3. *Alliances of reformist lawyers with legally informed activists*

This condition for the evolution of public interest environmental law in any particular country presumes material well-being sufficient to satisfy basic human needs, civil liberty and dissatisfaction with existing policies on growth and development. Lawyers will often be allied with environmental activists, however the environment-development link demands broader alliances, for example with indigenous people's, women's and youth groups.

Public interest environmental lawyers are more interested in substantive outcomes than mere technical compliance with the letter of law. They reject the notion that law operates in an environmentally neutral or value-free way: the shocking inadequacy of environmental law is that it has served to license, rather than prevent, cumulative environmental degradation and loss of biodiversity.

Preventing illegality is of course a major concern, however raising the legal standards is just as important. This points to the broader role of lawyers in opinion-shaping and lobbying because laws can be improved and better

---

[47]See Chapter 2, text accompanying n 51 .
[48]See Chapter 5.
[49]See n 38 *supra* and n 5 at p 316 *infra*.

305

implemented only if constituencies demand action and are willing to pay for it.[50]

The remainder of this section on lawyer-activist alliances characterises interest representation, not just client representation, as a subject matter of public interest environmental law.

The ideological commitment of public interest lawyers can create problems not encountered in their more usual role of technical advisers. For example, the views of public interest lawyers may not always coincide with those of their clients. I have raised this issue in the American context.[51] Anderson explores the dialectic further in a fascinating analysis of legal and activist responses to the Bhopal disaster.[52] He argues for accurate representation of clients according to best professional practice. This is not the end of the matter, however. Best professional practice in terms of *client representation* may not comprehensively represent underlying environmental concerns which are often only raised indirectly in adversarial litigation. *Interest representation* constitutes an additional subject matter in public interest litigation.[53]

Varying responses to the challenge of interest representation can be seen in the United States, India, Brazil and the United Kingdom. In the United States, advocacy organisations with large memberships conduct much of the environmental litigation. These "membership organisations" contrast with smaller law firms who act for external clients in a traditional client-lawyer relationship. While in some cases *locus standi* is a problem, in others the membership organisations can deal with interests without the problem of having to represent an individual who may not, in all respects, express the broader environmental concerns. In the United States, as public interest law has gained recognition, the legal system has accommodated interest representation by developing standing, costs and procedural rules for public interest cases.[54] Indian public interest law also illustrates this evolution, thanks to the expansive interpretation of its Constitution taken by an activist judiciary,

---

[50]Krämer L, "The Open Society, its Lawyers and its Environment" (1989) 1 *Journal of Environmental Law* (OUP) 1–9. Anton makes a similar point in the international context. He argues that it is in the area of "supplying the necessary arguments and reasons that environmental protection measures are right and necessary that grassroots environmental groups provide a much needed contribution to enforcing international environmental law" Anton DK, "Defending the Environment Through International Law: Enforcing International Environmental Obligations", Australian Centre for Environmental Law – University of Adelaide, *"Defending the Environment" Public Interest Environmental Law Conference Papers*, 7–8 May 1994, 198 at 203–204.

[51]See Chapter 2 at section III(C) "Lawyer-Client Relationships'.

[52]See Chapter 7.

[53]Feldman *op cit* (n 28) at 45 (adapting Stewart RB, "The reformation of American administrative law" (1975) 88 *Harvard Law Review* 1667 at 1742–1744) has similarly distinguished "representative" activities of interest groups, in which they advance the interests of their members, from "surrogate" activities, characterised by advocacy for the material or ideological concerns of people unable or unwilling to represent themselves, for example future generations.

[54]See Chapters 1 and 2.

particularly in the acceptance of writ petitions, under which judges have conducted inquisitorial proceedings into pollution and other environmental problems.[55] In Brazil, certain non-governmental environmental organisations have statutory rights of standing which enable them to represent underlying, broader concerns or interests without the artifice and potential conflict of having to argue on behalf of a representative individual.[56] As for the legal system in the United Kingdom, Harding describes a number of features which make it inimical to public interest environmental law and then suggests potential avenues for using British law to better represent group interests.[57]

In class actions, issues involving both the representation of clients and of broader interests can emerge. They constitute an outer layer of the public interest onion.[58] Because class actions collectively represent clients with financial stakes, the need for best professional practice is clear, as Anderson highlights with regard to claims resulting from the Bhopal accident. However interest representation may also be desirable (for example, to restore the natural environment also damaged by a chemical escape). This may require more than lawyers diligently acting upon instructions from particular individuals whose primary concern may, quite understandably, be private compensation. The actual litigants may or may not reflect broader environmental concerns. Perhaps the inquisitorial, Indian board of inquiry approach is preferable, with a degree of independence for judges to instigate, set terms of reference and allocate resources for inquiry, and adversarial litigation inappropriate, in such instances of interest representation.

In conclusion, it is necessary but not sufficient for public interest law to provide best professional representation of individuals and groups. While there will always be an important role for public interest environmental advocacy by lawyers in small legal practices who act for external clients in the traditional relationship, interest representation is likely to become increasingly important. In interest representation, policy research and resources are required, and membership organisations can provide a constituency and filter for the views ultimately expressed by their lawyers.

Furthermore, increasing interest representation in environmental law points to the need for broad *locus standi* and flexible procedures, for example to accommodate many parties, and mix inquisitorial with adversarial features where appropriate, allowing judges to investigate public interest perspectives more adequately, where those are under-represented by the parties before them.

---

[55]See Chapters 6 and 7.
[56]See Chapter 5.
[57]See Chapter 12.
[58]See section C, *infra*. *Cf*. Feldman *op cit* (n 28) at 45, where interest group litigation (such as a class action) is not considered to be a part of public interest litigation.

4. Broad rights of standing

There are two aspects to the right to litigate in public interest cases.[59] First, should citizens have any power to bring public interest actions, or should this be exclusively the power of the state? Many of the chapters in this book argue against monopolistic state access to the courts, noting present anthropocentric and private law limitations of the law of standing.

Secondly, if citizens should have standing, should it be restricted in any way? Much contemporary debate concerns this issue. Robbins describes the "injury in fact" constitutional considerations and recent cases concerning the broad rights of standing in the United States.[60] Grosz, Reid and Harding comment upon the state of *locus standi* under the common law in Britain,[61] there being no statutory resolution of the matter, and the position of what constitutes "sufficient interest"[62] for an applicant to obtain judical review being "something of a legal minefield".[63] While the restrictive British approach to standing contrasts with the position in countries such as United States, Brazil and India, it is by no means on its own in the European context, as the survey of countries in Chapter 3 discloses, and as Berger describes in relation to Germany in particular.[64]

It is interesting to note that the proposed EC draft Access to Justice Directive would enable public interest actions by environmental organisations alone, although Member States would also be free to permit suits by individual citizens. While identifying the role of representative organisations as important for public interest advocacy, an inclusive, rather than an exclusive approach is still to be preferred.[65] Disaffected members of Greenpeace or the World Wide Fund for Nature (WWF), or any other citizen, should still have the right to approach the courts where they believe that the larger, non-government organisations have been "captured".[66]

The level of use of the open standing provision in the planning law of New South Wales, Australia, according to which "any person" can bring environmental enforcement proceedings,[67] has recently been analysed. Over the

---

[59]Feldman *op cit* (n 28) at n 9 therein.
[60]See Chapter 1.
[61]See Chapters 10, 11 and 12.
[62]Supreme Court Act 1981 s 31(3); Rules of the Supreme Court Ord 53 r 3(7).
[63]*R v Poole Borough Council ex p Beebee and others* [1991] JPL 643 per Schiemann J.
[64]See Chapter 4.
[65]In the terms of the proposed draft Directive, the "citizen suit" option (Art 9) should be retained or introduced by each Member State.
[66]*e.g.* in 1994 disaffected Greenpeace and WWF campaigners formed a splinter organisation, "Breach", opposed to the "deals and compromises" of the two major NGOs regarding the allocation of whaling quotas by the International Whaling Commission to Norway. "Capture" theory was formulated by Bernstein in 1955 to describe how government agencies bend to the interests supposedly being regulated (see Yaeger PC, *op cit* (n 10) at 38–39). It is possible that environmental organisations may also become captured, justifying the potential for "citizen" as well as group third-party enforcement cases.
[67]Section 123 of the Environmental Planning and Assessment Act 1979 (NSW).

period 1980-1993, some 125 applications seeking to restrain a breach of the law had gone to a full hearing pursuant to the provision. Of these, only 7% were general public interest cases, involving issues such as logging, mining and pollution licences. Most were brought by neighbours and others with private interests (55%), then resident action groups (25%), then applications by local councils and other statutory bodies. An influential commentator concluded:[68]

"At a time when public scrutiny of government is expanding, it is unthinkable that the right of review enshrined in section 123 should be repealed. The solution [to the problem of uncertainty and delay which is of concern to the business community], if one is required, lies in reform of the legislative and administrative processes of State and local government and not in removal of third party appeal rights."

The theoretical right to go to court, discussed in the preceding paragraphs, must be backed up with the means to do so and prompts a consideration of how public interest environmental litigation can be funded.

5. *Funding for public enforcement actions*

There is a socio-economic *caveat* on the potential role for legislative grants of standing to enable greater consideration of diffuse ecological concerns. Open-standing provisions can be empty vessels where access to justice is limited. Court cases can be the privilege of the middle-class, as du Bois has illustrated with regard to environmental cases brought in South Africa.[69]

Effective access to justice requires not only legislative rights to go to court, but also the resources, both institutional and financial, to do so. Fernandes makes this point in relation to Brazil, where broad rights of standing supported by legislative immunity of plaintiffs against adverse costs orders in civil public actions has resulted in little public interest litigation because conservationists lack funds to pay even their own lawyers, and because of problems in the judicial system inherited from the liberal and military regimes prior to 1988.[70]

While Anderson describes a degree of success of activists in relation to the Bhopal tragedy,[71] this success is more attributable to independent lobbying, informed by but not dependent on the court cases and the work of lawyers.

---

[68]Sturgess G, *Thirty Different Governments . . . Report of the Commission of Inquiry into Red Tape*, Sydney, 31 January 1994 at 124–129. Sturgess was formerly Director-General of the Cabinet Office of New South Wales under the conservative Liberal-National Party Government. The figures are those of the Land and Environment Court (Chief Justice Mahla Pearlman, "Public Participation in Planning Conflicts – 1980s Aberration or a 20th Century Inspiration?", address to the 28th Australian Legal Convention, 1993 at 12–14).
[69]See Chapter 6 text accompanying ns 26–28.
[70]Chapter 5.
[71]Chapter 7.

Public interest cases in India appear to be brought by a few activist lawyers in a largely *pro-bono* capacity and ultimately encouraged by a Supreme Court keenly aware, in a country of vast socio-economic inequality, of the need for special procedures to enable the investigation and resolution of public interest concerns.

The United States has sought to remove disincentives against public interest cases by encouraging public participation in environmental rule-making and enforcement and by developing special rules as to legal fees. Substantial grants from philanthropic organisations and contributions from hundreds of thousands of members have enabled the public interest law firms to go to court.[72] The great variety and number of resulting cases is evident in the comprehensive survey of Robbins.[73]

Alternative funding sources for public interest advocacy could be a tax on applications for planning or pollution approvals, or an additional court filing fee in environmental matters. In Alberta, Canada the cost of public participation in enquiries into development projects is paid for by the proponents.[74]

In New South Wales, legal aid for public interest environmental cases is available on a limited basis. Between 1984 and 1992 the criterion for eligibility was that a substantial public interest meriting assistance existed, taking into account both the environmental impact and the projected benefits of the project. Applications were considered by an independent committee comprising environmental, industry and legal representatives. The committee's recommendations were usually accepted by the Legal Aid Commission. While environmental grants constituted a minuscule proportion of the total legal aid budget, they became the most politically contentious aspect of legal aid, particularly when government agencies such as the Forestry Commission were successfully sued with legal aid funds. In 1992 the Legal Aid Commission availed itself of the opportunity presented by budget cuts to discontinue legal aid in environmental cases altogether. After strong opposition to the cuts, in 1994 legal aid for public interest environmental cases was restored, but with a smaller, fixed budget.[75]

The UK legal aid scheme is yet to provide the same degree of support for public interest litigation as in New South Wales. There are, however, moves afoot to decentralise the legal aid scheme and introduce what may prove to be a significant element of flexibility. Alongside the legal aid scheme there exist law centres and legal advice agencies funded variously by charitable trusts and

---

[72]Chapter 2.

[73]Chapter 1.

[74]Preston BJ, "Public Enforcement of Environmental Laws in Australia" (1991), 6 *Journal of Environmental Law and Litigation* 39 at 64–65.

[75]Total grants in 1994–95 will not exceed $100,000, and total annual grants thereafter will not exceed $50,000. Lump sum grants will indemnify recipients, pursuant to s 47 of the Legal Aid Commission Act, against adverse costs orders unless exceptional circumstances exist. Memorandum of Murphy T, for the Managing Director, to the Legal Aid Commissioners of New South Wales, 16 March 1994.

central and local government. In 1991 the Law Centres Federation turned its attention to environmental issues. Its educative initiative culminated in the setting up of "EarthRights: The Environmental Law and Resource Centre". In an experimental venture in 1994-95, the Legal Aid Board is funding EarthRights to work with a west London community in its campaign against the environmental impact of construction works and air pollution. Such funding permits a strategic dimension to be applied to public interest environmental legal work.

The often strident debate concerning legal aid funding for public interest environmental cases[76] appears to be at the crossroads of two distinct traditions. One is the liberal democratic British tradition of providing limited legal aid for impoverished individuals to bring private court actions. The other is the participatory democratic American tradition of keeping court doors open through broad *locus standi*, contingency fee rights and the "American rule" on costs, so long as plaintiffs can muster the resources to reach the court in the first place. The former is a closed system, with inherent disincentives to litigate. The latter is open, in which court cases are commonly used for policy debate as well as dispute resolution. While jurisdictions around the world must evolve their own approaches according to their traditions, institutions and needs, government funding in the form of case-specific grants of legal aid for non-government plaintiffs does not appear to represent a likely, significant source of funds for tomorrow's activists.[77] The welfare state, private law origins of legal aid are of a different nature to the participatory, political, public law origins of public interest litigation. As such, in those jurisdictions outside the United Kingdom where there is little tradition of legal aid in public interest cases, it may well be that the most likely funding avenue for legal activists proves to be through membership organisations, as exists in the United States.[78]

In conclusion, funding is likely to remain scarce to vindicate non-material, environmental interests. Few governments will be willing to finance environmental litigation because this will often be against their own resource management and regulatory agencies. Convincing governments and courts to remove the disincentives to litigation constituted by limited rights of standing

---

[76]*e.g.* the perspective of Bowden on legal aid in environmental cases in the United Kingdom stridently contrasts with those of Day and Grosz. See Chapters 8, 9 and 10. See also Cragg, "Legal Aid and Environmental Judicial Review" [1994] 1:1 *Environmental Judicial Review Bulletin* 3–5. Cragg concludes that the UK legal aid scheme should move towards one "that can recognise and find cost-effective strategic litigation in important public interest cases" (at 8).

[77]In countries with a legal aid tradition, general grants from legal aid, covering the overhead expenses of public interest community legal centres to give initial advice, undertake research, conduct education programmes and advocate law reform can fulfil the same function as grants from the philanthropic foundations in the United States. The Environmental Defender's Offices in Sydney and Brisbane, Australia, and the nascent EarthRights centre in London use general legal aid assistance for such purposes. Care is needed to distinguish such overhead expense assistance from case-specific legal aid grants for the purpose of financing specific court cases.

[78]See Chapter 2.

(section 4 above) and the loser-pays costs rule (section 6 below) appear to be more likely, though indirect ways to increase access to justice in public interest environmental disputes than lobbying government for funds to pay the legal bills of activists for instigating particular court cases.[79]

widely spread

6. *Court practice and procedure receptive of diffuse interest litigation*

This condition for public interest environmental law overlaps the first, namely that there exists a body of law to be applied.

Rules relating to undertakings for damages, security for costs and costs have been identified as requiring reform. The "loser pays" rule in a number of civil and common law jurisdictions[80] acts as a disincentive for public-minded citizens to litigate.[81] Innovations of the Land and Environment Court of New South Wales in this regard have been described.[82] These have been influenced by similar, and in many cases more extensive developments in the United States.[83] The proposed draft EC Access to Justice in Environmental Matters Directive would bring about such costs reform.[84] The UK Labour Party is also in favour.[85]

---

[79]This is, *e.g.* the policy of the Labour Opposition in the UK: "There will be no restriction to bring cases. Judges will have discretion to refuse cases they consider to be frivolous or vexatious. But the legislation establishing the [Environment Division of the High Court] will make it clear that environmental groups will have a legitimate role before the court . . .. To ensure that potential plaintiffs are not deterred by the possibility of heavy costs, as they are today, the Division will operate revised cost rules. Where the case is a public interest one (the judge will decide this), unsuccessful plaintiffs will not be made liable for the costs of the defendant . . .. It removes the threat of bankruptcy from plaintiffs taking cases that are of benefit to the community at large, but without increasing the cost to the public purse, and without encouraging unnecessary litigation . . .." – Labour Party Policy Commission on the Environment, *In Trust for Tomorrow*, London, Labour Party, July 1994 at 50.

[80]See the comparative survey of costs rules in Chapter 3.

[81]See also Derfner, "The True 'American Rule': Drafting Fee Legislation in the Public Interest" (1979) 2 *W New Eng L Rev* 251; Pfenningstorf, "The European Experience with Attorney Fee Shifting", (1984) 47 *Law & Contemp Probs* 37, 85–124.

[82]Chapter 14 at section V, particularly ns 6–9 and accompanying text; Chapter 6 at n 33. Contributions in 1994 to the debate on costs in public interest litigation in Australia include Bayne P, "Costs Orders on Review of Administrative Action", (1994) 68 *Australian Law Journal* 816 (advocating a "no order as to costs" (American rule) regime); *South Melbourne City Council* v *Hallam* (1994) 83 LGERA 307 (offering a conservative view on costs and public interest litigation); and Australian Law Reform Commission (ALRC), *Who Should Pay? A Review of the Litigation Costs Rules*, ALRC, Sydney, 1994 at 59–71 (issues paper).

[83]Chapters 1 and 2. See also Derfner, "The True 'American Rule': Drafting Fee Legislation in the Public Interest, (1979) 2 *W. New Eng L Rev* 251 an Krent, "Explaining One-Way Fee Shifting" (1993) 79 *Virginia L Rev* 2039.

[84]See Chapter 3, proposed Article 8.

[85]The Labour Party proposal is that prevailing defendants in public interest cases will not be able to recover costs. "This public interest approach is similar to existing rules for legally-aided cases. It also operates in the United States, Germany, Holland, Portugal, and Australia. It is also the approach adopted by the judge in the recent THORP decision." Labour Party Policy Commission on the Environment *op cit* (n 79). The THORP decision referred to is *R* v *Secretary of State for the Environment and Others ex p Greenpeace and Lancashire County Council* (1994) 6:2 *Environmental Law and Management* 44, (1994) *ENDS Report* 230, and the *Independent* 8 March 1994. In that case Potts J refused to order costs against Greenpeace as the case was of substantial public interest, leave had been granted and because Greenpeace had succeeded on one important argument, clarifying the law for the future.

In order to encourage plaintiffs to act through representative organisations, which may be best placed to advocate broader environmental interests, the fact that a significant environmental organisation with a substantial member-ship has lent its support to a public interest case, and the necessary filtering and appraisal implied by such support, may raise a presumption against application of the "loser pays" costs rule. No such presumption would apply to other plaintiffs, who would have to argue their public interest credentials. The proposed EC Directive for rights of standing for environmental organisations might provide one mechanism for determining when the presumption would apply. In many public interest cases, the ultimate questions for the court regarding costs include whether the plaintiff had a pecuniary interest in the outcome, whether the subject matter of the proceedings were of public interest, and whether arguable, significant legal issues were raised, sufficient to justify special circumstances to depart from the ordinary costs rule.[86]

Further issues relate to causation, the burden of proof (including the manner in which evidence is given and the application of the precautionary principle) and extended liability for environmental damage. For example, Day and Bowden consider, from the perspectives of plaintiffs and defendants, the vexed questions of whether governments and courts should reverse the onus of proof regarding causation, and extend strict liability to more types of environmental damage.[87]

7. Activist judges and environmental institutions

Another factor enabling the development of public interest environmental law is an activist judiciary. Activist judges are those having communitarian rather than liberal, individualistic constitutional values.[88]

The degree of radicalism of the judiciary is limited both by the system of appointment by the government of the day, and by the desire of judges to reflect the values of their particular jurisdiction. For example, communitarian values are widely held in response to India's socio-economic inequalities. They have Constitutional footing and have provided a springboard for judicial activism.[89] In the context of 1970s radicalism in the United States, activist judges interpreted provisions of the National Environmental Policy Act in order to require rigorous environmental assessment.[90] Some commentators argue that the law of standing in Britain has narrowed in recent years, in

---

[86]*Oshlak* v *Richmond River Council and Iron Gates Developments Pty Ltd* (1994) 82 LGERA 236 Land and Environment Court of New South Wales per Stein J; appeal to the Court of Appeal on the non-application of the usual "loser pays" costs rule pending.

[87]See Chapters 8 and 9.

[88]Terminology of Feldman *op cit* (n 28). See also section II(B)(I) *supra*.

[89]Feldman *op cit* (n 28) at 53–54; 64–57.

[90]See Chapter 2 at I(C).

conformity with the resurgence of liberal individualism during the Thatcher years.[91]

In contrast to the position of some activist judges in India and the United States, Harding argues that in Britain there is little constitutional basis upon which judges can intervene in social action cases. In Westminster-style *representative* democracy, participation has only a limited role. Governments are responsible for determining the public interest, and courts respect that responsibility by restricting the scope of public interest cases as these seek to develop principles which the government has chosen not to make.[92]

A recent case from the Philippines has discussed the basis upon which judges can make decisions to protect the environment.[93] Some children (represented by their parents) had initiated proceedings on behalf of themselves, others of their generation and of succeeding generations challenging the issuing of timber licensing agreements by a government minister. This petition was dismissed on the grounds of lack of cause of action and of being a political question "which properly pertains to the legislative or executive branches of government". The Supreme Court overturned the dismissal by the lower court, allowing the children to file the class suit on behalf of future generations. While one basis of its ruling was that the Philippines Constitution contains the right to a "balanced and healthful ecology",[94] the Court stated that rights associated with the right to self-preservation formed a category of rights which "predate all governments and constitutions . . . these basic rights need not even be written in the Constitution for they are assumed to exist from the inception of humankind . . . ".[95]

While statutory and constitutional provisions provide the stepping stones for judges, there is nevertheless a role for independent judicial activism.[96] Judges can play the crucial role of helping to *establish*, and not merely act upon

---

[91]Feldman *op cit* (n 28) at 52, comparing, amongst other cases, the broader attitude to standing in *IRC* v *National Federation of Self-Employed and Small Businesses Ltd* [1982] AC 617 with the rejection of standing claimed by a body incorporated to save a theatre in *R* v *Secretary of State for the Environment ex p Rose Theatre Trust* [1990] 1 All ER 754. *Cf.* Grosz (Chapter 10), who believes that the present law of standing does not present a problem for potential public interest litigants, provided the case has merit.

[92]Feldman *op cit* (n 28) at 49–50.

[93]*Juan Antonio, Anna Rosario and Jose Alfonso, all surnamed OPOSA, minors and represented by their parents Antonio and Rizalina Oposa, the Philippine Ecological Network, Incorporated, et al* v *Factoran (Secretary of the Department of Environment and Natural Resources) and Rosario (Justice at first instance)*. Republic of the Philippines Supreme Court, ruling 30 July 1993, GR No 101083 per Associate Justice Davide, with the concurrence of the Chief Justice and 15 other Associate Justices (Associate Justice Feliciano concurring in the result, but delivering a separate opinion); 5 (forthcoming) *South Asian Environmental Law Reporter* (Environmental Law Foundation, 3 Campbell Terrace, Colombo 10, Sri Lanka).

[94]Section 16, Constitution of the Republic of the Philippines.

[95]Transcript of judgment at 11.

[96]Kirby M, President, New South Wales Court of Appeal, "The Role of the Judge in Advancing Human Rights by Reference to International Rights Norms" (1988) 62 *Australian Law Journal* 514.

society's values with regard to the environment.[97] They can do this by giving legal cladding to environmental principles such as sustainability, intergenerational equity and, regarding a higher level of proof necessary to allow development, the precautionary principle.[98] Another way is, when faced with unclear law to apply in cases, to apply environmental principles.[99]

The leading judicial role is suggested in the alternative ground for the Philippines Supreme Court ruling, namely that the children could pursue their claim because environmental protection is a fundamental right, independent of whether the Constitution stated as much. The judgment indicates the Court's concerns for environmental protection and intergenerational equity, and of the willingness of the judges to develop the law in line with those concerns. Contrast this approach with the House of Lords' decision in the *Cambridge Water* case.[1]

Background to *Cambridge Water* is that long-established private rights under the common law of tort have been viewed as potential avenues for

---

[97]Tribe LH, "Technology assessment and the fourth discontinuity – the limits of instrumental rationality" (1972) 46 *Southern California Law Review* 617 at 640.

[98]*Leatch v National Parks and Wildlife Service & Another* (1993) 81 LGERA 270. The case concerned the proposal of a local council in New South Wales to site a new road in an area providing habitat to endangered fauna, including the Giant Burrowing Frog. The council submitted a Fauna Impact Statement to the National Parks and Wildlife Serve as required by the Endangered Fauna (Interim Protection) Act 1991 (NSW). The Service then issued a licence to "take or kill" the endangered species, enabling the council to proceed with the road. The applicant conservationist succeeded in having the licence declared invalid. Referring to the precautionary principle, according to which lack of scientific certainty of ensuing damage should not be used as reason to postpone measures to prevent environmental degradation, Stein J noted that there was almost no evidence of the population, habitat and behavioural patterns of the Giant Burrowing Frog, and that accordingly it could not be concluded with any certainty that a licence to "take or kill" should be granted. The precautionary principle has subsequently been considered in *Nicholls v Director of the National Parks and Wildlife Service, Forestry Commission of NSW and Minister for Planning*, Talbot J, unreported judgment 29 September 1994, and *Greenpeace Australia Ltd v Redbank Power Company PTy Ltd and Singleton Council*, Pealman J, unreported judgment 10 November 1994, Land and Environment Court (NSW). *Cf.* UK position – *R v SS for Trade and Industry*, High Court, judgment of 3 October, (1994) 237 ENDS 41. In judicial review proceedings held that art 130r EC Treaty did not have direct effect before national courts. SS not legally bound as to the manner of interpretation of his statutory powers.

[99]In *Environmental Protection Authority (EPA) v Caltex Refining Co Pty Ltd* (1993) 68 *Australian Law Journal Report* 127, for example, the EPA sought production of the records of the oil refiner in connection with alleged pollution offences. Caltex refused to supply the records, claiming the privilege against self-incrimination. The law in Australia was unclear as to whether the privilege protected corporations as well as individuals. It does so in the UK and New Zealand, but not in the USA. The first instance decision of Stein J in the Land and Environment Court of New South Wales upheld the EPA's argument that the privilege did not apply to corporations, but stated certain questions of law to the Court of Criminal Appeal. That court overturned the original decision, however this was ultimately reinstated by the High Court, because (per Mason CJ and Toohey J, Brennan and McHugh JJ concurring; Deane, Dawson and Gaudron JJ dissenting): "rationales for the availability of the privilege against self-incrimination to natural persons, both historical and modern, do not support the extension of the privilege to artificial legal entities such as corporations. The privilege in its modern form is in the nature of a human right, designed to protect individuals from oppressive methods of obtaining evidence of their guilt for use against them. In respect of natural person, a fair state-individual balance requires such protection; however, in respect of corporations, the privilege is not required to maintain an appropriate state-individual balance."
One might speculate that had the initial decision upheld the status quo view that corporations could claim the privilege, the EPA would have faced strong pressure not to appeal to the High Court, whose precedent, in the environmental context, ultimately vindicates the principle of access to information.

[1]*Cambridge Water Company v Eastern Counties Leather plc* [1994] 1 All ER 53.

environmental protection in the United Kingdom. When a case involving liability for environmental pollution came before the House of Lords, however, after noting that the protection and preservation of the environment is now perceived as being of crucial importance and that public bodies are taking significant steps to protect the environment and introduce polluter-pays legislation, the Lords concluded (at 76):

> "But it does not follow from these developments that a common law principle, such as the rule in *Rylands* v *Fletcher*, should be developed or rendered more strict to provide for liability in respect of such pollution. On the contrary, given that so much well-informed and carefully structured legislation is now being put in place for this purpose, there is less need for the courts to develop a common law principle to achieve the same end, and indeed it may well be undesirable that they should do so."

The particular facts and contexts of the Philippines and *Cambridge Water* cases are wildly different. However in the former the judges sought to contribute to the development of environmental protection law. The decision acknowledges that judges have a role to play in the broadened sense of environmental responsibility necessary from all sectors of society to achieve sustainable living.[2] Its approach is consistent with the sense of environmental urgency internationally expressed in the Rio Declaration on Environment and Development, 1992.

In the latter case, the Lords were unwilling to play a complementary role to legislation by developing a common law principle regarding liability for environmental pollution. The judgment reflects apparent satisfaction with the establishment, asserting but not substantiating the classical, liberal view that the development of environmental law can be left safely to the legislature alone.[3] On this very issue the Government had hardly impressed. In 1990 it signalled its intention to postpone consideration of the introduction of statutory liability.[4] In 1993 it withdrew its proposals to establish registers of

---

[2] A feature of environmental law in a number of countries is that "the obligations of government and citizenry are quickly enlarging": Lutz RE, "The Laws of Environmental Management: A Comparative Study" [1976] 24 *Am J of Comp Law* 447 at 463– 486.

[3] The dissenting judges in *Caltex* (n 99 at 154) expressed similar conservatism regarding to the judicial role with respect to parliament. They believed that the denial of the privilege against self-incrimination to corporations was a matter for parliament, not the courts.

[4] "The courts may be reluctant to exercise their jurisprudence in the context of environmental liability. But apparently Parliament is not going to help, not at any rate in the short term. Far from it. In its response to the Environment Select Committee report on Contaminated Land (1990) Cm 1161, the government has signalled its intention to await the outcome of extensive litigation on civil liability for contamination of land before considering the introduction of statutory liability": English R, "No fault liability: the *Cambridge Water* Case" [1993] *Journal of Planning and Environmental Law* 409 at 415.

contaminative uses, and instead set up a new review.[5] Later in 1993, though the Government was still undecided about what it would do to address the problem in the UK, the Government nevertheless argued against general action to remedy environmental damage at the European Community level.[6]

While the House of Lords judgment clarifies the common law, and contains environmentally benign indications that the "natural use" exception to liability under the rule in *Rylands* v *Fletcher*[7] should not be given an extended meaning, the absence of discussion as to the direction the law should take to ensure that historic pollution is cleaned up is disappointing. *Dicta* from the Lords could have acted as a catalyst for further consideration of options by the Government. Instead, the desire of the House of Lords and of the Government not to tread on each other's toes has sidestepped the problem.

The liberal, individualist view on the judicial role is that the need for judges to independently decide matters before them without fear or favour excludes any role in environmental protection:[8]

> "[The] premise that the Courts are or should be the promoters of environmental protection or a source of innovative approaches to that end must be rejected at the outset. We may be accused of such activism from time to time but that is not our role nor can it be our goal. Our Courts are reactive bodies – like spiders, we judges wait and watch to see what controversies may fly into our webs. Our methods of digesting the catch may be somewhat more diverse and varied than those of the spider but our universe of choice is limited. Our obligation is to resolve the dispute presented and on as narrow grounds as possible."

This view classifies environmental conservation[9] as a partisan cause. I disagree. Environmental conservation is a right and obligation of a basic

---

[5]The registers of land which had been subjected to contaminative uses were to be kept by local authorities pursuant to s 143 of the Environmental Protection Act 1990. On 24 March 1993 the Secretary of State for the Environment, Mr Howard withdrew the register proposals, and announced a new review of the problem of contaminated land, which resulted in a Department of the Environment consultation paper "Paying for our Past" in March 1994. See also Ball S and Bell S, *Environmental Law*, London, Blackstone Press, 2nd ed 1994 at 339 and 340.

[6]UK Government, "Response to the Communication from the Commission of the European Communities (COM (93) 47 final) – Green Paper on Remedying Environmental Damage" 8 October 1993 at para 1.2.

[7](1865) 3 H & C 774; LR 3 HL 330; [1866] LR 1 Ex. 265.

[8]Honourable Betty Binns Fletcher, of the United States Court of Appeals, 9th Circuit, in "The Judicial Approach to Environmental Litigation" in Proceedings of the International Conference on Environmental Law (NELA and Lawasia) Sydney, June 1989, 60. Cited with approval (in an address which otherwise reflects communitarian judicial attitudes) by Judge Christine Trenorden, Environment Resources and Development Court, South Australia; "Defending the Environment: the Role of the Courts", *"Defending the Environment" Public Interest Environmental Conference Papers* (see n 50) at 239 and 257.

[9]While it is possible that Judge Binns may have wished to distinguish environmental conservation from environmental protection, this is not evident from the thrust of her statement on the judicial role. I use the former, broader term in preference to the restrictive connotations of the latter. The International Commission on Monuments and Sites Athens Charter (1932) and Venice Charter (1964) (as adopted in Australia by the Burra Charter) uses the following definitions: " 'Conservation' means all the processes of looking after a place so as to retain its 'cultural significance'. It includes maintenance and may according to circumstance include 'preservation', 'restoration', 'reconstruction' and 'adaption' and will be commonly a combination of more than one of these.

nature,[10] of the type referred to in the Philippines Supreme Court decision above, and as illustrated by world-wide endorsement of the 1972 Stockholm Declaration[11] and the 1992 Rio Declaration. The issue is no longer "Should we conserve?" but "How do we conserve in a fair and sustainable manner?" Acceptance of the concept of sustainability has moved debate beyond the old question of "environment or development", in which the two were considered mutually exclusive, thus justifying judicial reluctance to take sides. Sufficient international and, in many countries, constitutional, public policy and legislative entrenchment of environmental conservation now exists for the concept to be regarded as non-contentious.[12] As it is unacceptable for litigants to argue against sustainability, it is surely time for judges to be comfortable with their role in promoting environmental conservation, even if initially only through the semantic, educative acceptance of that term, which is no more controversial than the notion of justice itself.

Similarly, the reactive, narrow judicial role suggested by the "spider web" model described above by Judge Binns appears increasingly inappropriate for public interest environmental issues. Alternative dispute resolution initiatives have been discussed.[13] Inquiries, pre-trial conferences and mediation may all play a role in environmental dispute resolution. Rather than seeing the judicial role as "to resolve the dispute presented and on as narrow grounds as possible", in some cases it may be appropriate to undertake a more expansive role, for example as illustrated by the inquisitorial approach in Indian Supreme Court inquiries in public interest cases. As Stein comments, the public interest may not always be represented by the parties before the Court,[14] and the court may wish to inform itself as it sees fit with the assistance

---

'Cultural significance' means aesthetic, historic, scientific or social value for past, present or future generations."
[10]Selbourne D *op cit* (n 35) at para 167: "Hence, all – those holding authority in the civic order and the state and the individual citizen alike – are under a general moral duty to respect and to safeguard the natural environment of such civic order as far as is possible and practical."
Selbourne continues [at para 168]: "There is also a general civic duty, applicable alike to individual citizens and to the civic order as a whole, of conservation (insofar as it is practicable) not only of natural resources but of the historic patrimony of the civil order, a civic duty which is related to that of respect for place."
[11]Du Bois cites Principle 1, relating to the universal environmental right and duty in the Introduction to Chapter 6.
[12]See, *e.g.* Brandl E and Bungert H, "Constitutional Entrenchment of Environmental Protection: A Comparative Analysis of Experiences Abroad" (1992) 16:1 *Harvard Environmental Law Review* 1. Seven German länder and Austria (1984), Switzerland (1983), Greece (1975), Spain (1978), Portugal (1982), Turkey (1982) and Brazil (1988) have constitutional environmental rights or statements of public policy for environmental protection or both. Many eastern European draft constitutions propose concurrent fundamental environmental rights and environmental statements of public policy "which may well serve as paradigms of environmental consciousness and explicit constitutions" for other countries.

To the above list can be added the Philippines (1987), South Africa (1993), Costa Rica (1994), and see UN Doc E/CN4/Sub 2/1992/7 *Human Rights and the Environment – Progress Report* prepared by Mrs Fatma Zohra Ksentini, Special Rapporteur regarding the incorporation of substantive environmental rights into the constitutions of other countries.
[13]See Chapters 14 and 15.
[14]See Chapter 14 at Section V.

of other experts. This broader role is all the more relevant where judicial-type bodies are created as "one-stop shops" for environmental dispute resolution,[15] and is consistent with the increasingly public nature of environmental regulation.[16]

India illustrates how a supreme court can play a more expansive role in countries where government agencies do not exist or are tardy and lax in observing the law. Du Bois notes that the expanded role raises questions of the separation of powers, as the Indian Supreme Court activism requires administrative implementation, while its political role can become that of a "parallel constituent body".[17] These roles have outgrown the private law origins of the court. Where courts conform to the "spider web" model, the parties select issues and present the evidence. However where broad discretion lies with judges as to which issues to investigate, how to gather the facts in subsequent inquiries, and how to supervise implementation of judicial orders on a continuing basis, more formal procedures are needed to prevent bias, allow all affected parties to be heard, and preserve a rule of law.

Du Bois has suggested that appropriate institutions for environmental dispute resolution would include courts, though not as the first port of call for relief, and so that litigation supports rather than dominates public interest environmental law. I add that such institutions must also address the issues of research, access to information, full cost accounting and consultation.

Decision-making must be informed by continuing, wide-ranging *research*. Complex issues require systematic treatment, such as that which the Resources Assessment Commission (RAC) of Australia briefly offered in commissioning, publishing and analysing research and presenting management options to government on forestry, coastal management and mining issues.[18]

Broad *access to information* can improve the accountability of regulatory and enforcement agencies, encourage regulatees to improve their performance, and enable the pressure of public concern to influence environmental policy and management. In some countries the second phase of the "right to know" debate exists. The first phase was winning a right to access the

---

[15]Lord Woolf, "Are the Judiciary Environmentally Myopic?" (1992) 4 *Journal of Environmental Law* 1; Justice Stein, Chapter 14 at Section VI.

[16]McAuslan P, "The Role of Courts and other Judicial-Type Bodies in Environmental Management" (1991) 3 *Journal of Environmental Law* 195 at 202.

[17]See Chapter 6 at text accompanying n 87.

[18]The Resource Assessment Commission Act 1989 (Commonwealth) established the RAC to inquire into the future use of Australia's natural resources, upon request from the government. See Galligan B and Lynch G, "Integrating Conservation and Development: Australia's Resource Assessment Commission and the Testing Case of Coronation Hill" (1992) 9 *Environmental and Planning Law Journal* 181. In December 1993 the RAC was "quietly dismantled" by starving it of funds while leaving the legislation intact: Elix J and Lambert J, "Public Participation in Federal Government Inquiries" in *"Defending the Environment" Public Interest Environmental Law Conference Papers* (see n 50), 149 at 151.

information. The second tries to make sense of the "data deluge" by improving the quality and intelligibility of the available information. This may entail, for example, standardisation of methods and measurements to enable time and place comparison of results and analysis of primary data by independent experts or auditors.[19] Ever-improving technology has the potential to make environmental information easier to find and analyse, as well as less expensive to disseminate. The Ministry of Environment and Energy in Ontario, for example, established in 1994 an electronic environmental registry pursuant to the Environmental Bill of Rights 1993. Information is accessible through any home, office or public library computer with a modem.

Full-cost accounting, which includes assessment of environmental and social impacts of products, projects and economies is used rarely by institutions and decision-makers. With units of measurement such as gross domestic product, which omit non-financial, environmental aspects of well-being, are inadequate. Courts and other environmental institutions can play a role in promoting the use and development of alternative economic indicators.[20]

Environmental institutions should *consult* broadly in rule-making and policy formulation. Consultation should not be limited to public inquiries regarding specific development projects. Participation procedures appropriate for a particular issue need not be at the expense of expert, efficient management, and can in fact improve the quality of management.[21] At minimum, a legal duty to take the results of consultations into account in final ministerial decision-making should exist.

The above outline of some of the qualities which environmental institutions should possess reinforces the viewpoint that courts should develop broader roles in environmental management, and have close links with research, fact-finding and consultative institutions. Such links would reflect the importance of education on environmental matters, and the need to develop specialist knowledge.[22] Stein[23] argues that specialist environmental courts can enable judges to develop that expertise. McLeod[24] suggests that in the United Kingdom such reform should only be considered in the context of a broader

---

[19]The Friends of the Earth (UK), for example, analyses water pollution monitoring data submitted to the National Rivers Authority by holders of authorisations with an elaborate geographic information system (GIS). It also publishes popular guides to understanding monitoring results (*Water Pollution: Finding the Facts* 1993; *River Pollution: A Sleuth's Guide* 1992).

[20]See, *e.g.* Anderson V, *Alternative Economic Indicators*, Routledge 1991; Adriaanse A, *Environmental Policy Performance Indicators [Holland]*, London, New Economics Foundation, 1993; Marks N and Jackson T, *Index of Sustainable Economic Welfare, a Pilot Index 1950–1990*, London, New Economics Foundation, 1994.

[21]See Chapter 2 at text accompanying n 70; Robinson *op cit* (n 28) at 332–335.

[22]Lord Woolf *op cit* (n 15 at p 319).

[23]Chapter 14.

[24]Chapter 15.

review of the regulatory framework for environmental management. While the UK Government has announced no intention of establishing a new, specialist court, the Labour Party has proposed a separate Environment Division of the High Court.[25]

C. Layers of the public interest environmental law onion

In the Introduction to this book a pluralist, inclusive approach to the subject matter was adopted. Public interest perspectives were characterised as putting forward causes other than those affecting the property or financial well-being of their advocates.

Yet even accepting the above characteristic, private and public interests will often be intertwined. For example, a neighbourhood or a sector of industry can lay some claim to representing a section of the public, and thus a public interest perspective. Oil companies in California have formed "public interest" advocacy organisations to lobby against closing national parks and wilderness areas to oil exploration.

In my view this is fair game. *The* public interest is more of a rhetorical expression than a clearly identifiable, single option in environmental decision-making. As participatory democracy places emphasis on a pluralistic approach to determining where the public interest lies, then odd bedfellows – oil companies alongside Greenpeace – will naturally vie for the public interest "centre stage".

Gradations of public interest exist in environmental law, like shells of an onion. The core is more strongly of public interest than the outer layers. For two reasons it is important that these gradations are appreciated. First, criticisms fairly laid only at the weakest, outer layer claimants of public interest need not tarnish the strongest, core claimants as well. The reverse could also apply: thinly veiled self-interest groups flying the public interest banner could

[25]"The obstacles to private enforcement can best be overcome by creating a separate Environment Division of the High Court, drawing on the successful experience in parts of Australia. This will speed up the judicial system in the environmental sphere, keep costs down, encourage responsible individuals and groups to take out public interest cases, and move some way to ensuring that the polluter really does pay . . . Specialist courts enable judges to build up the necessary expertise . . . Judges should sit in the Environment Division for two or three years, long enough to develop sufficient expertise but not so long that their division will become a judicial backwater or become vulnerable to any form of regulatory capture. As in Australia, the Environment Division will be made up of both lawyers and expert 'technical assessors' . . ." *Op cit* (n 79). The Environment Division would have both civil and criminal jurisdiction, and in other matters act as an investigative tribunal.

inappropriately attract procedural or funding benefits at the expense of plaintiffs concerned about wider environmental issues.[26]

Secondly, greater appreciation of the gradations of public and private interests in environmental issues is also relevant in the development of better judicial-type bodies for environmental dispute resolution. For example, McLeod argues that a new environmental court should be able to deal with tort claims, but that the difficulty in harmoniously conferring such jurisdiction weighs against a specialist court.[27] However an environmental court might logically focus on the public issues which distinguish environmental protection disputes from commercial and personal injury claims, and happily leave private tort claims to other courts.

At the core of the public interest environmental law onion lie issues of broad environmental and legal importance in which the plaintiff does not have a direct or indirect financial stake over and above any ordinary member of the public. Ironically, in many jurisdictions, this very quality may necessitate some legal acrobatics in order to obtain *locus standi*.

Perhaps the core tends to be occupied by membership organisations. These often have historical commitment to the relevant issue, the resources to comprehensively argue a public interest perspective, and many supporters who mould and give legitimacy to their platforms. In some countries, standing in environmental matters is limited to "accredited" environmental organisations who meet criteria relating to their objects, non-profit objectives, geographic scope and age.[28]

On the other hand, "capture" criticisms[29] can also be levelled at large membership organisations and a strong claim to allowing any person, not just "respectable" environmental organisations, to enforce environmental law in

---

[26]*e.g.* the issue of legal aid in class or single actions for damages resulting from alleged toxic torts, being a bone of contention in Day and Bowden's chapters, may be of a different nature to the question of aid for environmental protection cases seeking to confer no financial benefit on the plaintiff, in which a more liberal test could apply. In the former, the cost of litigation may be recoverable from injuries ultimately awarded, and the higher costs in running the initial, test case may be able to be shared amongst applicants of the same class. In the latter, a prevailing applicant will obtain equitable relief, such as a declaration or a restraining order, of an exclusively public interest nature, rather than an award of personal damages. On the other hand, the expense and risk associated with toxic tort test cases may prevent worthy cases from being brought unless legal aid *is* available. Further, the precedent and public interest effect of a successful toxic tort action can be considerable.

Similarly, criticisms that public interest environmental law panders to "Not In My Backyard" (NIMBY) objectors are properly directed only at that outer shell of the public interest onion comprised by neighbour or amenity groups (*e.g.* Mr Gummer, SS for the Environment, promised to sweep aside unreasonable objections to development. He criticised NIMBYISM as "an obsession with the bric-a-brac of the past and the substitution of preservation for conservation" (*Financial Times*, 12 October 1994). The NIMBY reaction may well be "a legitimate exercise of communal right" (Polden M, *Environmental Law Foundation Report 1993–94* London, at 1) and some local cases will raise objections to a proposed project which is coherent with an overall, alternative policy – cases of "thinking globally, acting locally". However other NIMBY cases may be no more than the acronym suggests – insular and unreceptive of broader, public interest considerations.

[27]See Chapter 15 at Section III. Ironically, defending NIMBYISM may serve to obscure, not clarify, the nature of public interest advocacy.

[28]See Chapter 3.

[29]See n 66 and accompanying text.

the courts is laid in jurisdictions where open standing exists, such as in the United States. As suggested, the difference may lie in that in the case of a relevant membership organisation, in questions as to undertakings as to damages, security for costs and liability for the prevailing party's costs, a public interest presumption may exist, whereas concerned citizen or purpose-created plaintiff associations may have to argue public interest as a preliminary issue for submission and summary determination in each case.[30] The key element in "core" public interest cases – whether brought by membership organisations or by concerned citizens – is the representation of *interests*.

The next layer of public interest claimants have amenity or indirect stakes. They may be resident action groups or government bodies concerned about decisions by other authorities.

Plaintiffs on the outside of the public interest onion have a particular interest in an environmental decision, for example neighbours to a development, industry associations, trade competitors or the individuals in a class action for damages. It is difficult to locate these latter claimants anywhere but in the outer layer. Given the unlikelihood that common law precedent will create new or more stringent duties of environmental protection,[31] public interest in toxic tort claims lies in the number of applicants or where injunctive relief, rather than damages is sought. A key element of cases in the outer ring of the onion is the representation of particular *clients*, rather than broader environmental interests.

III. **Future directions: lawyers as environmental network supporters**

The preceding chapters and the above sketch of common characteristics of public interest environmental law in a number of countries are but a random and incomplete introduction. The environmental conservation potential of public interest law in approaching North-South issues with equity for both place and person, in influencing policy and regulation, and in emphasising sustainability and publicising illegality and agency "capture" through court cases and consciousness-raising is vast.

Krämer has argued that environmental lawyers should be preventive, innovative and active.[32] I agree, and would add that many lawyers who

---

[30]See also the discussion preceding n 86.

[31]Further development of the common law to provide for liability for environmental pollution was rejected by the House of Lords in *Cambridge Water* (see n 1, p 315 and accompanying text). In *Burnie Port Authority* v *General Jones Pty Ltd* (unreported judgment of 24 March 1994) the High Court of Australia similarly rejected any extension of strict liability at common law, favouring instead the absorption of the rule in *Rylands* v *Fletcher* into the law of negligence, and highlighting "the deficiencies of the common law in responding to environmental degradation" (Iles A, "A Continuing Retreat form Strict Liability at Common Law: *Burnie Port Authority* v *General Jones Pty Ltd*" [1994] 2 *Australian Environmental Law News* 26 at 31).

[32]Krämer L, *op cit* (n 50) at 7–9.

presently do not regard themselves as practising environmental law can nevertheless contribute. Increasing public awareness, standards and liabilities suggest that environmental trends should be an integral part, for example, of the merger and acquisition or intellectual property lawyer's dialogue with clients.

One way for lawyers to adopt Krämer's approach is to assume the role of "network supporters". To gain access to electronic information networks such as the Internet, ongoing technical and resource assistance is provided to users by support organisations such as the Association for Peaceful Communications.[33] Network supporters enable personal computers to be linked using telephone lines, train people on how to use the network, help them to reach like-minded individuals and associations and inform them of relevant information sources and channels.[34] The functions of the environmental law network supporter would be similarly various, linking advisers from many disciplines with clients and interest groups, facilitating the sharing of environmental information, providing access to environmental justice and giving environmentally sound legal advice. Using analytical skills regarding information accessible from an ever-increasing array of disciplines and databases, the lawyer could act as coordinator, facilitator and introduction agent in addition to acting in the capacity of professional adviser.

The network support role emphasises broad involvement in civic affairs, with lawyers interacting with many groups, disciplines and sources of information. The network support lawyer would neither be dominated by commercial transactions about, but not in aid of the environment, nor would he or she vainly pursue absolute and utopian forms of environmental justice.[35] The emphasis in the practice of law would be for environmental principles to extend from the narrow band of transactions relating to planning, resource

---

[33]The Association for Peaceful Communications (APC) provides a computer network supporting peace, environment, human rights and development movements in approximately 90 countries. The membership of APC comprises non-profit, information technology organisations including GreenNet Ltd in the UK, IGC Networks (PeaceNet, EcoNet and ConflictNet) in the USA, GlasNet in Russia, NordNet in Sweden, Web in Canada, Alternex in Brazil, Chasque in Ecuador, Nicarao in Nicaragua, SangoNet in South Africa, Wamani in Argentina, ComLink in Russia and Pegasus in Australia. In addition to providing electronic mail and computer conferences or bulletin boards on specific subject matters, APC links with other networks such as GeoNet, Internet, HomeoNet, Janet, Bitnet and FIDO.

[34]The network support metaphor is inspired by the clear images used by the best environmental writers. Consider, for example, the strength of Hardin's metaphorical common, which individual cattle herders tragically, but rationally over-graze to the long-term detriment of the resource, the paradoxical word play in Stone's seminal article "Should Trees have Standing?", and Lovelock's Gaia hypothesis that the biosphere operates as a single organism, and one in which *homo sapiens* is but one, possibly expendable species. These simple images powerfully convey three of the most pervasive notions in environmental law, namely its public nature, its anthropocentric limitations and the need for a precautionary approach respectively. Hardin, "The Tragedy of the Commons" (1968) 162 *Science* 1243–1248; Stone C, "Do Trees have Standing", *University of Southern California Law Review*, Spring 1972; Lovelock JE, *Gaia: A New Look at Life on Earth*, Oxford University Press, 1979.

[35]Selbourne *op cit* (n 35) at para 137, in the context of legal justice generally.

management and pollution control to imbue all areas of law including property, standards, patent, corporate, taxation and competition law.[36]

In computer networks, support organisations provide individuals with means of accessing information contained in the network. In the environmental network, lawyers also have special access to information due to the fact that they play a hand in much decision-making regarding planning and pollution control. In addition, lawyers gain access to environmental information in connection with acquisitions and mergers, audits, impact assessment, expert evidence, regulatory drafting, public enquiries and enforcement cases. Industry, government and non-government sectors have recourse to lawyers who thus stand at the crossroads of environmental decision-making. As "network supporters", lawyers would utilise this position to help disseminate information and extend awareness of and responsibility for environmental problems.

The network supporter would play a critical and active role in developing environmental standards, practices and reporting adopted by professional and business associations. Environmental law professional associations can play an important part in promoting good practice and in influencing policy and law reform. More radically, the Environmental Law Alliance Worldwide (E-LAW) is beginning to play such a role, utilising electronic communication to extend the effectiveness and reach of environmental activism.[37] Broader alliances of environmental stakeholders, including industry, government, scientists and community organisations are also needed.

The "network support lawyer" could increase access to environmental justice. In addition to providing technical advice to commercial and government clients, the network supporter could assist non-commercial clients and interests in a *pro-bono* or reduced fee capacity. The role would increase access to environmental justice by helping clients gain access to relevant information, technical experts and the courts.

The network support lawyer would have an inter-disciplinary orientation. Given the failure of law alone to prevent environmental degradation, public support, financial commitment and information from other disciplines must be secured to ensure greater effectiveness. The network support lawyer would work with development, conservation, scientific, regulatory, economic and resource assessment organisations and interests. For example, environmental standards can assist in the choice of goods and services. In addition to advising on the legal status of standards with regard to environmental claims in product descriptions and advertising, the lawyer could encourage national and international networking amongst consumer groups, industry associations and standard-setting and enforcement agencies. In such networking, skills in communication, advocacy, diplomacy, comprehension, organisation and

---

[36]Winter *op cit* (n 44).
[37]See Chapter 2 at Section III(B).

presentation are called for. Lawyers could be catalysts and supporters of such networks.

The role of environmental network supporter would demand commitment to environmental principles over and above national and professional allegiances. The lawyer would seek to understand and learn from the experience of other jurisdictions. In so doing he or she would avoid the impasse to reform constituted by unexamined faith in the law, institutions and dispute resolution traditions of one's own country. The network supporter would, on the basis of environmental criteria, be open to preventive, co-operative and non-legal avenues of management, and would, for example, avoid knee-jerk reactions to systems containing elements of self-regulation.[38]

Finally, the lawyer would encourage the health of the environmental network by encouraging a broader sharing of environmental responsibility, by reviewing the network systematically, and by responding where legal or other environment protection arrangements are found lacking.

I hope that public interest environmental law and environmental law, indeed even law itself, become synonymous.[39] This would require an increasingly communitarian attitude to constitutional law, politics and the rights and duties of citizens. I do not take issue with the individualist, Diceyan legal paradigm[40] in the context of *private* law. The environment, however, is *public* property demanding management, and equitable sharing of costs, through truly "public" public law.

---

[38]Ayres I and Braithwaite J, *Responsive Regulation: Transcending the Deregulation Debate*, New York, Oxford University Press 1992; Ostrom *op cit* (n 34).
[39]Winter *op cit* (n 44) at 46–47.
[40]Discussed at ns 28–30 *supra* and accompanying text.

Index

ATTORNEY GENERAL,
  UK, 94
ATTORNEYS' FEES (US),
  CLF, 51
  EDF, 52
  exception to general principle, 25
  FWPCA campaign, and, 47–49
  general principles, 25, 46–47, 78–79
  NRDC, 58
  principle of payment in PIEL, 25
  SCLDF, 55
  statutory rights to, funding, as, 25–26
AUSTRALIA *See* LAND AND ENVIRONMENT
  COURT; SPECIALIST ENVIRONMENTAL
  COURTS

BHOPAL CASE,
  campaigns, 159–162, 163–164
  conclusion, 171
  costs, 156–158
  criminal law approach, 162, 168–171
  effect on PIEL in India, 171
  exclusion of citizens from process, 156–158
  forum change, 156
  fundamental rights approach, 162, 164–168
  history, 155–156
  human rights, 164–168
  interim relief, 160–161, 163
  justice, 171
  legislation, effect of, 157–158
  litigating strategies, 162–171
  NGOs, 156–157, 158–162
  political groups and litigation, 158–162,
    163–164
  result, 155–156, 161–162, 168–171
  settlement, 157–158, 159–162, 164
  tort approaches, 162, 163–164
  US court hearings, 156
BILL OF RIGHTS,
  Australia (Queensland), 269–270
  South Africa, proposed, 138
BRAZILIAN CONSTITUTION,
  civil public action, 121, 122, 124 *See also*
    CIVIL PUBLIC ACTION
  collective writ of mandamus, 122
  environmental protection generally, 118,
    121
  mandamus, collective writ of, 122
  Ministerio Publico, 124–125 *See also*
    MINISTERIO PUBLICO
  popular action, 120, 121 *See also* POPULAR
    ACTION
BURDEN OF PROOF,
  reversal of (UK), 181–182,191

CAMPAIGNS,
  India, Bhopal case *See also* BHOPAL CASE
  UK, pollution control, 238
  US,
    CLF, 50–51
    FWPCA, 47–49
    NRDC, 56–57
CANTONAL LAW (Switzerland), 80
CASES, PIEL *See* PIEL (cases)
CAUSATION *See* BURDEN OF PROOF
CITIZEN SUITS,
  appeals *See* APPEALS
  cases *See* PIEL (cases)
  complaints *See* COMPLAINTS
  criticism, 64–69
  defences *See* PIEL (defences)
  EC,
    Access to Justice Draft Directive, and,
      101, 106–107
    option for provisions, Access to Justice
      Draft Directive, 101, 106–107
  EPA *See* EPA
  Germany, 84–87
  litigation *See* LITIGATION
  Standing Doctrine *See* STANDING
    DOCTRINE
  UK *See* UK REFORM
  US,
    abstention, 24
    attorneys' fees *See* ATTORNEYS' FEES
      (US)
    cessation of illegal activity, 23
    choice of cases, 25
    creation of right of action, 77–78 *See also*
      FEDERAL LAW; STATE LAW
    effect of recent cases, 35, 79
    federal law,
      direct actions, 9–10
      judicial review *See* JUDICIAL REVIEW
    funding cases, 25–26 *See also* FUNDING
    injunctions, 9, 33–34
    legal basis *See* FEDERAL LAW; STATE LAW
    meaning, 77
    Michegan Studies, 79
    mootness, 23
    notice before filing, 22–23, 78
    number of, 79
    parallel federal or state enforcement,
      23–24, 34, 78
    relief,
      attorneys' fees, 10 *See also*
        ATTORNEYS' FEES
      civil penalties, 10, 32–33, 78
      declaratory, 10

FWPCA (US)—*cont.*
  cases, 32–33
  enactment, 40
  implementation, 42
  Lujan II case, 16
  participatory process, 43–44
  toxic pollutants, 57–58

GOVERNMENTAL ENVIRONMENTAL
  AGENCIES (US),
  discretionary duties, 5
  effect of ECO on, 64, 65–66
  EPA *See* EPA
  examples, 8
  litigation towards, 5
  mandatory duties, 5
  notification of, 6
  types of, 7
GREENPEACE 63, 178, 179, 222, 223, 299, 315
GROUP INTERESTS *See* COLLECTIVE
  INTERESTS

HER MAJESTY'S INSPECTORATE OF
  POLLUTION *See* HMIP
HIGH COURT,
  appeal of Planning Appeals Board decision,
    Ireland, 87
HMIP,
  enforcing agency (UK), 228, 249
  planning and pollution control, 235–237, 283
  public registers, 240
HUMAN RIGHTS,
  Bhopal case (India), 162, 164–168

IMPACT ASSESSMENT *See* EIA
INDIA *See* BHOPAL CASES
INDIAN CONSTITUTION,
  administrative implementation, 149–151
  criticisms, 149–150
  evolution of PIEL, 145–151
  interpretation of, 144, 148
  judicial role, 146–147, 149
  reform of, 150–151
  resolving problems in, 151–152
  standing, 145
  third party impact on PIEL, 147–149
INDUSTRY,
  Diceyan approach, 301–302
  sceptical arguments about PIEL, 295–298
  UK,
    explanation of role of law, 294–298
    interests and concerns of, 177–182, 281
    present legal situation, 184

INFORMATIONAL INJURIES (US) *See*
  INJURIES (informational)
INJUNCTIONS,
  Australia (New South Wales), mareva, 267
  Belgium, 83
  Brazil, 125
  Portugal, 92
  UK, interim, 95
  US,
    citizen suits, 9, 33–34, 66–67, 78
    violations of, 10
INJURIES,
  environmental (US), 17–20, 27, 30
  federal PIEL cases (US) *See* STANDING
    DOCTRINE
  informational (US),
    cases, 26–31
    failure to file EIS, 11
INSTITUTE FOR APPLIED ECOLOGY *See*
  ÖKO-INSTITUT E.V.
INTERGENERATIONAL EQUITY
  Philippines, 314–315
  Stockholm Declaration, 136
INTERIM RELIEF,
  Access to Justice Draft Proposed Directive
    (EC), 100–101, 105
  Belgium, 83
  Denmark, 84
  Germany, 85, 86
  India, Bhopal case, 160–161, 163
  Ireland, 88
  Italy, 89
  Netherlands, The, 91
  Spain, 93
  UK, 95
INTERNAL MARKET,
  EC, 95–96

JUDICIAL REVIEW,
  administrative acts and omissions, of,
    Access to Justice Draft Directive, 99–100, 104
  Australia,
    generally, 271
    New South Wales, 260
  Denmark, 84
  Germany, 84–85
  Ireland, 88
  Netherlands, The, 90–91
  Scotland, standing, 213–214
  South Africa, 137–138
  sub-statutory rules, of, 100, 104
  UK,
    amount of, 178, 224
    costs, 187